THE LANGUAGE OF LITERATURE

THE *InterActive* READER™ PLUS

for English Learners

McDougal Littell
A HOUGHTON MIFFLIN COMPANY
Evanston, Illinois • Boston • Dallas

Reading Consultants, *The InterActive Reader™ Plus*

Sharon Sicinski-Skeans, Ph.D. Assistant Professor of Reading, University of Houston-Clear Lake; former K–12 Language Arts Program Director, Spring Independent School District, Houston, Texas.
Olga Bautista Reading Coordinator, Will C. Wood Middle School, Sacramento, California.

Senior Consultants, *The Language of Literature*

Arthur N. Applebee Professor of Education, State University of New York at Albany; Director, National Research Center on English Learning and Achievements; Senior Fellow, Center for Writing and Literacy.
Andrea B. Bermúdez Professor of Studies in Language and Culture; Director, Research Center for Language and Culture; Chair, Foundations and Professional Studies, University of Houston-Clear Lake.
Sheridan Blau Senior Lecturer in English and Education and former Director of Composition, University of California at Santa Barbara; Director, South Coast Writing Project; Director, Literature Institute for Teachers; Past President, National Council of Teachers of English.
Rebekah Caplan Coordinator, English Language Arts K–12, Oakland Unified School District, Oakland, California; Teacher-Consultant, Bay Area Writing Project, University of California at Berkeley; served on the California State English Assessment Development Team for Language Arts.
Peter Elbow Professor of English, University of Massachusetts at Amherst; Fellow, Bard Center for Writing and Thinking.
Susan Hynds Professor and Director of English Education, Syracuse University, Syracuse, New York.
Judith A. Langer Professor of Education, State University of New York at Albany; Director, National Research Center on English Learning and Achievements; Director, Albany Institute for Research on Education.
James Marshall Professor of English and English Education, University of Iowa, Iowa City.

Acknowledgments

Atheneum Books for Young Readers: Excerpt from "Eleanor Roosevelt," from *Great Lives: Human Rights* by William Jay Jacobs. Copyright © 1990 by William Jay Jacobs. Reprinted with the permission of Atheneum Books for Young Readers, an imprint of Simon & Schuster Children's Publishing Division.

Susan Bergholz Literary Services: "Names/Nombres" by Julia Alvarez. Copyright © 1985 by Julia Alvarez. First published in *Nuestro,* March 1985. Copyright © 1985 by Julia Alvarez. Reprinted by permission of Susan Bergholz Literary Services, New York. All rights reserved.

Continued on page 433.

ISBN-13: 978-0-618-31018-0   ISBN-10: 0-618-31018-5

11 12 13 14 15–DWI–08 07 06

Table of Contents

Introducing *The InterActive Reader™ Plus*

The InterActive Reader™ Plus is a new kind of literature book. As you will see, this book helps you become an active reader. It is a book to mark on, to write in, and to make your own. You can use it in class *and* take it home.

An Easy-to-Carry Literature Text

This book won't weigh you down—it can fit as comfortably in your hand as it can in your backpack. Yet it contains works by such important authors as . . .

Julia Alvarez, whose personal essay "Names/Nombres" tells the story of a young girl trying to fit in.

Ray Bradbury, whose story "Dark They Were, and Golden-Eyed" recounts how colonists on Mars adapt to their new home.

Virginia Hamilton, whose research and storytelling combine in *Anthony Burns: The Defeat and Triumph of a Fugitive Slave.*

You will read these selections and other great literature—plays, poems, stories, and nonfiction. In addition, you will learn how to understand the texts you use in classes, on tests, and in the real world, and you will study and practice specific strategies for taking standardized tests.

Help for Reading

The InterActive Reader™ Plus helps you understand many challenging works of literature. Here's how.

Before-You-Read Activities A prereading page helps you make connections to your everyday life and gives you a key to understanding the selection.

Preview A preview of every selection tells you what to expect.

Reading Tips Reading tips give useful help throughout.

Focus Each longer piece is broken into smaller "bites" or sections. A focus at the beginning of each section tells you what to look for.

Pause and Reflect At the end of each section, a quick question or two helps you check your understanding.

Read Aloud Specific passages are marked for you to read aloud. You will use your voice and ears to interpret literature.

Reread This feature directs you to passages where a lot of action, change, or meaning is packed in a few lines.

Mark It Up This feature invites you to mark your own notes and questions right on the page.

Vocabulary Support

Words to Know Important new words are underlined. Their definitions appear in a Words to Know section at the bottom of any page where they occur in the selection. You will work with these words in the Words to Know SkillBuilder pages.

Personal Word List As you read, you will want to add some words from the selections to your own vocabulary. Write these words in your Personal Word List on page 420.

SkillBuilder Pages

After each literary selection, you will find these SkillBuilder pages:

- Active Reading SkillBuilder
- Literary Analysis SkillBuilder
- Words to Know SkillBuilder (for most selections)

These pages will help you practice and apply important skills.

The InterActive Reader™ Plus for English Learners

The InterActive Reader™ Plus for English Learners provides all of the literature selections and all of the features from the *InterActive Reader™ Plus*. Special additional features include:

Section summaries A brief summary helps get you started with each section or chunk of the text.

More About . . . These notes provide key background information about specific elements of the text such as historical events, scientific concepts, or political situations needed for understanding the selection.

What Does It Mean? These brief notes clearly explain any confusing words, phrases, references, or other constructions.

English Learner Support Here you will find special help with vocabulary, language, and culture issues that may interfere with understanding the selection.

Reading Check These questions at key points in the text help you clarify what is happening in the selection.

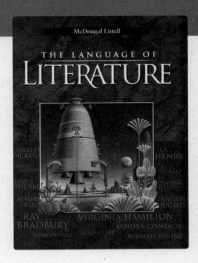

Links to *The Language of Literature*

If you are using McDougal Littell's *The Language of Literature*, you will find *The InterActive Reader™ Plus* to be a perfect companion. The literary selections in the reader can all be found in that book. *The InterActive Reader™ Plus* lets you read certain core selections from *The Language of Literature* more slowly and in greater depth.

Read on to learn more!

Academic and Informational Reading

Here is a special collection of real world examples to help you read every kind of informational material, from textbooks to technical directions. The strategies you learn will help you on tests, in other classes, and in the world outside of school. You will find strategies for the following:

Analyzing Text Features This section will help you read many different types of magazine articles and textbooks. You will learn how titles, subtitles, lists, graphics, many different kinds of visuals, and other special features work in magazines and textbooks. After studying this section you will be ready to read even the most complex material.

Understanding Visuals Tables, charts, graphs, maps, and diagrams all require special reading skills. As you learn the common elements of various visual texts, you will learn to read these materials with accuracy and skill.

Recognizing Text Structures Informational texts can be organized in many different ways. In this section you will study the following structures and learn about special key words that will help you identify the organizational patterns:

- Main Idea and Supporting Details
- Problem and Solution
- Sequence
- Cause and Effect
- Comparison and Contrast
- Argument

Reading in the Content Areas You will learn special strategies for reading social studies, science, and mathematics texts.

Reading Beyond the Classroom In this section you will encounter applications, schedules, technical directions, product information, Web pages, and other readings. Learning to analyze these texts will help you in your everyday life and on some standardized tests.

Test Preparation Strategies

In this section, you will find strategies and practice to help you succeed on many different kinds of standardized tests. After closely studying a variety of test formats through annotated examples, you will have an opportunity to practice each format on your own. Additional support will help you think through your answers. You will find strategies for the following:

Successful Test Taking This section provides many suggestions for preparing for and taking tests. The information ranges from analyzing test questions to tips for answering multiple-choice and open-ended questions.

Reading Tests: Long Selections You will learn how to analyze the structure of a lengthy reading and prepare to answer the comprehension questions that follow it.

Reading Tests: Short Selections These selections may be a paragraph of text, a poem, a chart or graph, or some other item. You will practice the special range of comprehension skills required for these pieces.

Functional Reading Tests These real-world texts present special challenges. You will learn about the various test formats that use applications, product labels, technical directions, Web pages, and more.

Revising-and-Editing Tests These materials test your understanding of English grammar and usage. You may encounter capitalization and punctuation questions. Sometimes the focus is on usage questions such as verb tenses or pronoun agreement issues. You will become familiar with these formats through the guided practice in this section.

Writing Tests Writing prompts and sample student essays will help you understand how to analyze a prompt and what elements make a successful written response. Scoring rubrics and a prompt for practice will prepare you for the writing tests you will take.

User's Guide

The InterActive Reader™ Plus for English Learners has an easy-to-follow organization, as shown by these sample pages from "Eleanor Roosevelt."

Connect to Your Life

These activities help you see connections between your own life and what happens in the selection.

Key to the Selection

This section provides a "key" to help you unlock the selection so that you can understand and enjoy it. One of these four kinds of keys will appear:

- **What You Need to Know**—important background information.
- **What's the Big Idea?**—an introduction to key words or concepts in the selection.
- **What Do You Think?**—a preview of an important quotation from the selection.
- **What to Listen For**—a chance to examine the sound and rhythm of a piece.

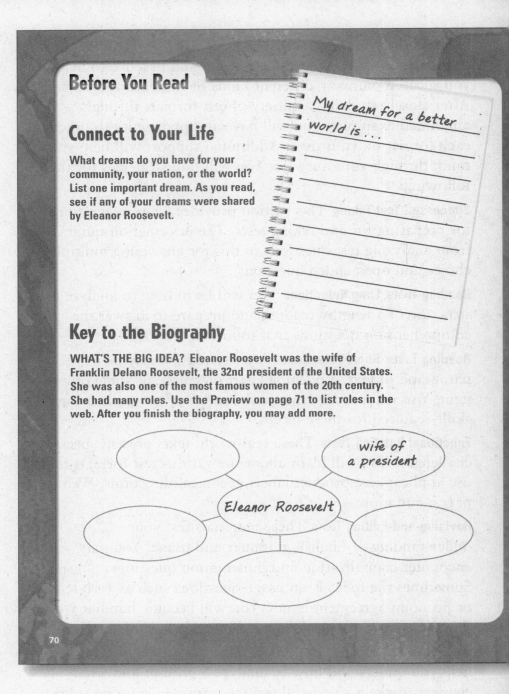

Before You Read

Connect to Your Life

What dreams do you have for your community, your nation, or the world? List one important dream. As you read, see if any of your dreams were shared by Eleanor Roosevelt.

My dream for a better world is . . .

Key to the Biography

WHAT'S THE BIG IDEA? Eleanor Roosevelt was the wife of Franklin Delano Roosevelt, the 32nd president of the United States. She was also one of the most famous women of the 20th century. She had many roles. Use the Preview on page 71 to list roles in the web. After you finish the biography, you may add more.

wife of a president

Eleanor Roosevelt

70

Eleanor Roosevelt

by William Jay Jacobs

PREVIEW Eleanor Roosevelt was much more than the wife of a president. Her life spanned a period of dramatic changes in the United States and the world. As First Lady, Eleanor Roosevelt struggled to end poverty and racism in the United States. As first American Ambassador to the United Nations, she had a central role in writing the Declaration of Human Rights.

71

PREVIEW

This feature tells you what the selection is about. It may also raise a question that helps you set a purpose for reading.

And there's more!

User's Guide *continued*

1 FOCUS

Every selection is broken down into parts. A Focus introduces each part and tells you what to look for as you read.

2 MARK IT UP

This feature may appear in the Focus or in the side column next to a boxed passage. It asks you to underline or circle key details in the text.

3 As the biography begins . . .

Each part of the selection begins with a brief summary. The bulleted sentences tell you what to expect in the part you will read next.

4 English Learner Support

This feature helps you understand difficult words and phrases in the English language. Some notes explain ideas from American culture. When you see words in blue type, look for this feature in the side column.

---

3 As the biography begins . . .

- The narrator tells about Eleanor's childhood and family background.
- Eleanor has many fears.

4 English Learner Support
Culture

Fairy Tale The term *ugly duckling* refers to a plain or unattractive child. It comes from a famous fairy tale written by the Danish author Hans Christian Anderson. In this tale, a family of ducks includes one duckling that is different from the others. The young bird surprises everyone by growing up to be a beautiful swan.

5 MARK IT UP KEEP TRACK
Remember to use these marks to keep track of your reading:

- ✱ This is important.
- ? I have a question about this.
- ! This is a surprise.

The InterActive Reader PLUS
72 For English Learners

---

1 FOCUS
In this part you will read about Eleanor Roosevelt as a child.

2 MARK IT UP As you read, circle details that tell she was unhappy. An example is highlighted.

Eleanor Roosevelt was the wife of President Franklin Delano Roosevelt. But Eleanor was much more than just a president's wife, an echo of her husband's career.

Sad and lonely as a child, Eleanor was called "Granny" by her mother because of her seriousness. People teased her about her looks and called her the "ugly duckling." . . .

Yet despite all of the disappointments, the bitterness, the misery she experienced, Eleanor Roosevelt refused to give up. Instead she turned her unhappiness and pain to strength. She devoted her life to helping others. Today she is remembered as one of America's greatest women.

Eleanor was born in a fine townhouse in Manhattan. Her family also owned an elegant mansion along the Hudson River, where they spent weekends and summers. As a child Eleanor went to fashionable parties. A servant took care of her and taught her to speak French. Her mother, the beautiful Anna Hall Roosevelt, wore magnificent jewels and fine clothing. Her father, Elliott Roosevelt, had his own hunting lodge and liked to sail and to play tennis and polo. Elliott, who loved Eleanor dearly, was the younger brother of Theodore Roosevelt, who in 1901 became president of the United States. The Roosevelt family, one of America's oldest, wealthiest families, was respected and admired.

To the outside world it might have seemed that Eleanor had everything that any child could want—everything that could make her happy. But she was not happy. Instead her childhood was very sad.

5 MARK IT UP KEEP TRACK

This easy-to-use marking system helps you track your understanding. Turn to page xiv to see a model of how the system can be used.

Almost from the day of her birth, October 11, 1884, people noticed that she was an unattractive child. As she grew older, she could not help but notice her mother's extraordinary beauty, as well as the beauty of
40 her aunts and cousins. Eleanor was plain looking, ordinary, even, as some called her, homely. For a time she had to wear a bulky brace on her back to straighten her crooked spine.

When Eleanor was born, her parents had wanted a boy. They were scarcely able to hide their disappointment. Later, with the arrival of two boys, Elliott and Hall, Eleanor watched her mother hold the boys on her lap and lovingly stroke their hair, while for Eleanor there seemed only coolness, distance.
50 Feeling unwanted, Eleanor became shy and withdrawn.[1] She also developed many fears. She was afraid of the dark, afraid of animals, afraid of other children, afraid of being scolded, afraid of strangers, afraid that people would not like her. She was a frightened, lonely little girl.

6 Pause & Reflect

FOCUS
Eleanor Roosevelt's parents died while she was young. Read to find out what happened to her after their deaths.

MARK IT UP As you read, circle **details** that help you understand what Roosevelt's life with her grandmother was like.

The one joy in the early years of her life was her father, who always seemed to care for her, love her. He used
60 to dance with her, to pick her up and throw her into the air while she laughed and laughed. He called her "little golden hair" or "darling little Nell."

---

1. **withdrawn:** detached from others, solitary, isolated.

Pause & Reflect

1. Circle the words below that describe Eleanor Roosevelt. **(Clarify)**

outgoing	lonely
cheerful	playful
serious	afraid

2. What kind of family did Eleanor Roosevelt come from? Write three words or phrases that describe her family. **(Clarify)**

As the biography continues . . .

- As a child, Eleanor experiences great loss.
- She is sent to live with her grandmother.
- Eleanor is often neglected.

Eleanor Roosevelt 73

6 Pause & Reflect

Whenever you see these words in the selection, stop reading. Go to the side column and answer the questions. Then move ahead to the next Focus and continue your reading.

These questions at the end of every section follow up the Focus activity at the beginning of each section. They give you a quick check of your understanding.

And there's more!

Student Model

These pages show how one student used *The InterActive Reader™ Plus for English Learners* for the selection "Eleanor Roosevelt."

Note how this student used the following symbols:

* marks a place where something is important—a main idea, topic sentence, or important detail.

? marks a place where something is unclear or confusing.

! marks a surprising or critical fact, or a turning point in the action—not just a main idea, but a major event or theme.

WORDS TO KNOW
Important **Words to Know** are underlined in each section. Definitions are given at the bottom of the page.

As the biography continues . . .

- Franklin becomes more involved in politics.
- Eleanor works to support her country during World War I.
- Eleanor supports Franklin after he suffers a serious illness.

Why did the U.S. enter the war?

READING TIP The years between 1905 and 1921 were busy ones for the Roosevelts. Make a time line like the one below to record the major events that took place during those years.

Franklin and Eleanor marry.

```
1905   1910   1915   1920   1925
```

MORE ABOUT . . .

(POLIO) Polio is caused by a viral infection. It can cause paralysis, or the inability to move part of one's body. Polio was widespread in the first half of the 20th century. By 1955, a strong vaccine was developed that eliminated the disease almost completely.

The InterActive Reader PLUS
80 For English Learners

FOCUS
A disaster threatens Franklin's political career.

MARK IT UP > Circle details that tell you about the disaster and Eleanor's response to it.

Meanwhile Franklin's career in politics advanced rapidly. In 1910 he was elected to the New York State Senate. In 1913 President Wilson appointed him Assistant Secretary of the Navy—a powerful position in the national government, which required the Roosevelts to move to Washington, D.C.

? In 1917 the United States entered World War I as an active combatant. Like many socially prominent women, Eleanor threw herself into the war effort. Sometimes she worked fifteen and sixteen hours a day. She made sandwiches for soldiers passing through the nation's capital. She knitted sweaters. She used Franklin's influence to get the Red Cross to build a recreation room for soldiers who had been shell-shocked in combat. . . .

In 1920 the Democratic Party chose Franklin as its candidate for vice president of the United States. Even though the Republicans won the election, Roosevelt became a well-known figure in national politics. All the time, Eleanor stood by his side, smiling, doing what was expected of her as a candidate's wife.

She did what was expected—and much more—in the summer of 1921 when disaster struck the Roosevelt family. While on vacation Franklin suddenly fell ill with infantile paralysis—polio—the horrible disease that each year used to kill or cripple thousands of children, and many adults as well. When Franklin became a victim of polio, nobody knew what caused the disease or how to cure it.

WORDS TO KNOW
combatant (kəm-băt'nt) *n.* fighter
prominent (prŏm'ə-nənt) *adj.* well-known; widely recognized

Franklin lived, but the lower part of his body remained paralyzed. For the rest of his life he never again had the use of his legs. He had to be lifted and carried from place to place. He had to wear heavy steel braces from his waist to the heels of his shoes.

His mother, as well as many of his advisers, urged him to give up politics, to live the life of a country gentleman on the Roosevelt estate at Hyde Park, New 300 York. This time, Eleanor, calm and strong, stood up for her ideas. She argued that he should not be treated like a sick person, tucked away in the country, inactive, just waiting for death to come.

Franklin agreed. Slowly he recovered his health. His energy returned. In 1928 he was elected governor of New York. Then, just four years later, he was elected president of the United States.

Pause & Reflect

FOCUS
Eleanor fought strongly for various causes.

MARK IT UP Put a star in the margin beside Eleanor's causes.

Meanwhile Eleanor had changed. To keep Franklin in 310 the public eye while he was recovering, she had gotten involved in politics herself. It was, she thought, her "duty." From childhood she had been taught "to do the thing that has to be done, the way it has to be done, when it has to be done."

With the help of Franklin's adviser Louis Howe, she made fund-raising speeches for the Democratic Party ✱ all around New York State. She helped in the work of 320 the League of Women Voters,[6] the Consumer's League, ✱
✱

---

6. **League . . .** : organizations devoted to national improvement through political education or improvement of working conditions.

Pause & Reflect

1. How did Eleanor Roosevelt help her husband cope with polio? **(Summarize)**

She encouraged him to continue with politics.

2. Review the details you circled. Why might Eleanor have become stronger after Franklin became ill with polio? **(Draw Conclusions)**

He might depend on her now, and she would have to be strong.

As the biography continues . . .

- Eleanor becomes more involved in politics.
- She fights for causes she believes in.
- She talks with Franklin, now President of the United States, about social change.

Eleanor Roosevelt **81**

Before You Read

Connect to Your Life

What do you or your friends do to make others notice and admire you? Think back over the past two days. Make some notes about something you did or something you saw someone do to get attention.

Day One	In the cafeteria, my friend tried to juggle some apples left over from dessert.
Day Two	

Key to the Story

WHAT DO YOU THINK of someone in French class who does what is described in the sentence below?

He tried to bluff his way out by making noises that sounded French.

Bluff is a word that means "to pretend to have more or know more than you really do."

What would you say to the boy in the story who tries to bluff? Write your response in the balloon.

Seventh Grade

by Gary Soto

PREVIEW On the first day of seventh grade, Victor signs up for French class so he can be near Teresa, a girl he likes. How can Victor get Teresa to notice him?

As the story begins . . .

- It is Victor Rodriguez's first day in seventh grade.
- Victor is happy that Teresa, a girl he likes, will be in his French class.

MORE ABOUT . . .

FRESNO, CALIFORNIA Victor lives in Fresno, a city south of San Francisco, in a beautiful valley surrounded by mountains. It is the eighth largest city in California and the largest food producer in the United States.

READING TIP In this story you will find some Spanish and French words and expressions. Be sure to check the footnotes if you need help understanding these terms.

MARK IT UP Underline the phrases that Victor is saying to himself.

FOCUS

As the story opens, you meet Victor on his first day in seventh grade. Read to find out what he is like.

MARK IT UP As you read, circle details that tell you what Victor thinks about. An example is highlighted.

On the first day of school, Victor stood in line half an hour before he came to a wobbly card table. He was handed a packet of papers and a computer card on which he listed his one <u>elective</u>, French. He already spoke Spanish and English, but he thought some
10 day he might travel to France, where it was cool; not like Fresno, where summer days reached 110 degrees in the shade. There were rivers in France, and huge churches, and fair-skinned people everywhere, the way there were brown people all around Victor.

Besides, Teresa, a girl he had liked since they were in catechism classes[1] at Saint Theresa's, was taking French, too. With any luck they would be in the same class. Teresa is going to be my girl this year, he
20 promised himself as he left the gym full of students in their new fall clothes. She was cute. And good in math, too, Victor thought as he walked down the hall to his homeroom. He ran into his friend, Michael Torres, by the water fountain that never turned off.

They shook hands, *raza*-style,[2] and jerked their heads at one another in a *saludo de vato*.[3] "How come you're making a face?" asked Victor.

"I ain't making a face, *ese*.[4] This *is* my face." Michael said his face had changed during the summer.

---

1. catechism classes (kăt′ĭ-kĭz′əm): formal classes in religious instruction.
2. *raza*-style (rä′sä) *Spanish:* in the familiar manner that local Chicanos greet each other.
3. *saludo de vato* (sä-lōō′dō dĕ bä′tō) *Spanish:* greeting between Chicano buddies.
4. ese (ĕ′sĕ) *Spanish:* a slang term used when addressing someone, as in "Hey, man."

WORDS TO KNOW
elective (ĭ-lĕk′tĭv) *n.* an optional academic course or subject

30 He had read a *GQ* magazine[5] that his older brother had borrowed from the Book Mobile[6] and noticed that the male models all had the same look on their faces. They would stand, one arm around a beautiful woman, and *scowl*. They would sit at a pool, their rippled stomachs dark with shadow, and *scowl*. They would sit at dinner tables, cool drinks in their hands, and *scowl*.

"I think it works," Michael said. He scowled and let his upper lip <u>quiver</u>. His teeth showed along with the
40 <u>ferocity</u> of his soul. "Belinda Reyes walked by a while ago and looked at me," he said.

Victor didn't say anything, though he thought his friend looked pretty strange. They talked about recent movies, baseball, their parents, and the horrors of picking grapes in order to buy their fall clothes. Picking grapes was like living in Siberia, except hot and more boring.

"What classes are you taking?" Michael said, scowling.

50 "French. How 'bout you?"

"Spanish. I ain't so good at it, even if I'm Mexican."

"I'm not either, but I'm better at it than math, that's for sure."

A tinny, three-beat bell propelled students to their homerooms. The two friends socked each other in the arm and went their ways, Victor thinking, man, that's weird. Michael thinks making a face makes him handsome.

---

5. **GQ magazine:** *Gentleman's Quarterly* magazine, a fashion magazine for men.

6. **Book Mobile:** a library van that brings books and magazines for people to borrow.

WORDS TO KNOW
scowl (skoul) *v.* to look angry by drawing the eyebrows together and frowning
quiver (kwĭv′ər) *v.* to shake with a slight, rapid movement
ferocity (fə-rŏs′ĭ-tē) *n.* extreme fierceness; intensity

READING CHECK Why is Michael scowling? How does he think it will make him look? Try scowling. How does it make you feel?

MORE ABOUT . . .

SIBERIA Siberia is a region in northern Russia known for its cold temperatures and harsh living conditions. In the past, Russian prisoners were sent to Siberia to work in labor camps.

English Learner Support
Language
Dialect The words in blue are in dialect, the way a certain group of people speaks. *How 'bout you?* means "How about you?" and *ain't* means "am not."

Pause & Reflect

Review the details you circled. What does Victor think about? Cross out the phrase that does not apply. **(Clarify)**

visiting France

trying out for basketball

how cute Teresa is

how strange Michael looks

As the story continues ...

• Victor speaks to Teresa as they both leave homeroom.

• At lunch, Victor looks for Teresa.

English Learner Support

Language

Fragment *And, of course, French* is not a complete sentence. It is a fragment because there is no action word, such as *sit, speak,* or *think.* Here, the writer tells us that Victor is excited about his French class.

On the way to his homeroom, Victor tried a scowl.
60 He felt foolish, until out of the corner of his eye he saw a girl looking at him. Umm, he thought, maybe it does work. He scowled with greater <u>conviction</u>.

Pause & Reflect

FOCUS

Victor wants Teresa to be his girl. He tries to show her that he likes her.

MARK IT UP As you read, circle details that tell you what Victor does to show Teresa he likes her.

In homeroom, roll was taken, emergency cards were passed out, and they were given a bulletin to take home to their parents. The principal, Mr. Belton, spoke over the crackling
70 loudspeaker, welcoming the students to a new year, new experiences, and new friendships. The students squirmed in their chairs and ignored him. They were anxious to go to first period. Victor sat calmly, thinking of Teresa, who sat two rows away, reading a paperback novel. This would be his lucky year. She was in his homeroom, and would probably be in his English and math classes. And, of course, French.

The bell rang for first period, and the students
80 herded noisily through the door. Only Teresa <u>lingered</u>, talking with the homeroom teacher.

"So you think I should talk to Mrs. Gaines?" she asked the teacher. "She would know about ballet?"

"She would be a good bet," the teacher said. Then added, "Or the gym teacher, Mrs. Garza."

WORDS TO KNOW
conviction (kən-vĭk'shən) *n.* a strong belief; assuredness
linger (lĭng'gər) *v.* to continue to stay; delay leaving

Victor lingered, keeping his head down and staring at his desk. He wanted to leave when she did so he could bump into her and say something clever.

He watched her on the sly. As she turned to leave, he stood up and hurried to the door, where he managed to catch her eye. She smiled and said, "Hi, Victor."

He smiled back and said, "Yeah, that's me." His brown face blushed. Why hadn't he said, "Hi, Teresa," or "How was your summer?" or something nice?

As Teresa walked down the hall, Victor walked the other way, looking back, admiring how gracefully she walked, one foot in front of the other. So much for being in the same class, he thought. As he trudged to English, he practiced scowling.

In English they reviewed the parts of speech. Mr. Lucas, a portly man, waddled down the aisle, asking, "What is a noun?"

"A person, place, or thing," said the class in unison.

"Yes, now somebody give me an example of a person—you, Victor Rodriguez."

"Teresa," Victor said automatically. Some of the girls giggled. They knew he had a crush on Teresa. He felt himself blushing again.

"Correct," Mr. Lucas said. "Now provide me with a place."

Mr. Lucas called on a freckled kid who answered, "Teresa's house with a kitchen full of big brothers."

After English, Victor had math, his weakest subject. He sat in the back by the window, hoping he would not be called on. Victor understood most of the

90

100

110

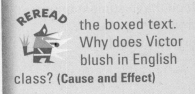
WORDS TO KNOW
trudge (trŭj) *v.* to walk heavily; plod
portly (pôrt'lē) *adj.* stout or overweight

problems, but some of the stuff looked like the teacher made it up as she went along. It was confusing, like the inside of a watch.

120 After math he had a fifteen-minute break, then social studies, and, finally, lunch. He bought a tuna casserole with buttered rolls, some fruit cocktail, and milk. He sat with Michael, who practiced scowling between bites.

Girls walked by and looked at him.

"See what I mean, Vic?" Michael scowled. "They love it."

"Yeah, I guess so."

They ate slowly, Victor scanning the horizon for a 130 glimpse of Teresa. He didn't see her. She must have brought lunch, he thought, and is eating outside. Victor scraped his plate and left Michael, who was busy scowling at a girl two tables away.

The small, triangle-shaped campus bustled with students talking about their new classes. Everyone was in a sunny mood. Victor hurried to the bag lunch area, where he sat down and opened his math book. He moved his lips as if he were reading, but his mind was somewhere else. He raised his eyes slowly and looked 140 around. No Teresa.

He lowered his eyes, pretending to study, then looked slowly to the left. No Teresa. He turned a page in the book and stared at some math problems that scared him because he knew he would have to do them eventually. He looked to the right. Still no sign of her. He stretched out lazily in an attempt to disguise his snooping.

Then he saw her. She was sitting with a girlfriend under a plum tree. Victor moved to a table near her 150 and daydreamed about taking her to a movie. When

the bell sounded, Teresa looked up, and their eyes met. She smiled sweetly and gathered her books. Her next class was French, same as Victor's.

Pause & Reflect

FOCUS

In French class, Victor pretends to know French to impress Teresa. Read to find out what happens.

They were among the last students to arrive in class, so all the good desks in the back had already been taken. Victor was forced to sit near the front, a few desks away

160 from Teresa, while Mr. Bueller wrote French words on the chalkboard. The bell rang, and Mr. Bueller wiped his hands, turned to the class, and said, *"Bonjour."*[7]

"*Bonjour,*" braved a few students.

"*Bonjour,*" Victor whispered. He wondered if Teresa heard him.

Mr. Bueller said that if the students studied hard, at the end of the year they could go to France and be understood by the populace.

One kid raised his hand and asked, "What's

170 'populace'?"

"The people, the people of France."

Mr. Bueller asked if anyone knew French. Victor raised his hand, wanting to impress Teresa. The teacher beamed and said, *"Très bien. Parlez-vous français?"*[8]

Pause & Reflect

How does Victor show that he likes Teresa? Circle three phrases below. (Clarify)

waits for her after homeroom

says her name in English class

introduces her to his friends

looks for her during lunch

As the story ends . . .

• During French class Victor tries to impress Teresa by pretending to know French.

• When French class is over, Victor finally speaks with Teresa.

READING CHECK Why does Victor pretend that he can speak French?

---

7. *Bonjour* (bôn′zhōor) *French*: Good day.

8. *Très bien. Parlez-vous français?* (trĕ byăn pär′lā vōō frän′sĕ) *French*: Very good. Do you speak French?

Victor didn't know what to say. The teacher wet his lips and asked something else in French. The room grew silent. Victor felt all eyes staring at him. He tried to <u>bluff</u> his way out by making noises that sounded
180 French.

"La me vave me con le grandma," he said uncertainly.

Mr. Bueller, wrinkling his face in curiosity, asked him to speak up.

> Great rosebushes of red bloomed on Victor's cheeks. A river of nervous sweat ran down his palms. He felt awful. Teresa sat a few desks away, no doubt thinking he was a fool. Without looking at Mr. Bueller, Victor mumbled, "Frenchie oh wewe gee in September."

190 Mr. Bueller asked Victor to repeat what he said.

"Frenchie oh wewe gee in September," Victor repeated.

Mr. Bueller understood that the boy didn't know French and turned away. He walked to the blackboard and pointed to the words on the board with his steel-edged ruler.

"*Le bateau,*" he sang.

"*Le bateau,*" the students repeated.
200 "*Le bateau est sur l'eau,*"[9] he sang.

"*Le bateau est sur l'eau.*"

Victor was too weak from failure to join the class. He stared at the board and wished he had taken Spanish, not French. Better yet, he wished he could start his life over. He had never been so embarrassed. He bit his thumb until he tore off a sliver of skin.

---

9. *Le bateau est sur l'eau.* (lə bä′tō ĕ sür lō) *French:* The boat is on the water.

WORDS TO KNOW
bluff (blŭf) *v.* to mislead or deceive; to fake

READ ALOUD the boxed paragraph. How does Victor feel when Mr. Bueller asks him questions in French? Check one word below. **(Infer)**

❏ angry
❏ proud
❏ embarrassed
❏ happy

The bell sounded for fifth period, and Victor shot out of the room, avoiding the stares of the other kids, but had to return for his math book. He looked
210 sheepishly at the teacher, who was erasing the board, then widened his eyes in terror at Teresa who stood in front of him. "I didn't know you knew French," she said. "That was good."

Mr. Bueller looked at Victor, and Victor looked back. Oh please, don't say anything, Victor pleaded with his eyes. I'll wash your car, mow your lawn, walk your dog—anything! I'll be your best student, and I'll clean your erasers after school.

Mr. Bueller shuffled through the papers on his desk.
220 He smiled and hummed as he sat down to work. He remembered his college years when he dated a girlfriend in borrowed cars. She thought he was rich because each time he picked her up he had a different car. It was fun until he had spent all his money on her and had to write home to his parents because he was broke.

Victor couldn't stand to look at Teresa. He was sweaty with shame. "Yeah, well, I picked up a few things from movies and books and stuff like that."
230 They left the class together. Teresa asked him if he would help her with her French.

"Sure, anytime," Victor said.

"I won't be bothering you, will I?"

"Oh no, I like being bothered."

"*Bonjour*," Teresa said, leaving him outside her next class. She smiled and pushed wisps of hair from her face.

WHAT DOES IT MEAN?
Avoiding means "keeping away from."

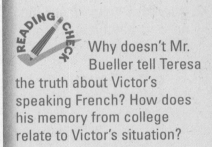

READING CHECK

Why doesn't Mr. Bueller tell Teresa the truth about Victor's speaking French? How does his memory from college relate to Victor's situation?

WORDS TO KNOW
sheepishly (shē′pish-lē) *adv.* with a bashful or embarrassed look

Pause & Reflect

1. How does Teresa react to Victor's performance in French class? Check three phrases below. **(Summarize)**

   ❑ laughs at him

   ❑ praises him

   ❑ smiles at him

   ❑ asks him to help her study

2. Why does Victor check out not one, but three, French textbooks? **(Infer)**

   _____

   _____

   _____

   _____

3. What was your reaction to Victor's lie about speaking French? **(Connect)**

   _____

   _____

   _____

   _____

   _____

What do you think Teresa's attitude toward school and learning is? Mark details in the story to support your views. **(Infer)**

"Yeah, right, *bonjour*," Victor said. He turned and headed to his class. The rosebushes of shame on his 240 face became bouquets of love. Teresa is a great girl, he thought. And Mr. Bueller is a good guy.

He raced to metal shop. After metal shop there was biology, and after biology a long sprint to the public library, where he checked out three French textbooks.

He was going to like seventh grade. ❖

Pause & Reflect

Active Reading SkillBuilder

Connecting

As you read the story "Seventh Grade," try to think of similar experiences you have had in your own life. Use the chart to **connect** the setting, the story events, and what Victor says and does to your experiences.

What Victor and I Have in Common	How Victor and I Are Different
We both have trouble with math.	

Follow Up: Try comparing yourself with a minor character in the story, such as Victor's friend Michael. List similarities and differences.

Literary Analysis SkillBuilder

Setting

The **setting** of a story is the time when and the place where the events of the story occur. Setting is important to why events happen in a story. Read through "Seventh Grade" to find examples of setting and think about details that the author uses to help you picture Victor's school. Then think about the feelings of the characters in that setting. Write your findings on the chart. A sample is provided.

Setting	Details	Character's
Fresno, California, in late summer	110 degrees in the shade	Victor doesn't like the heat.

Words to Know SkillBuilder

Words to Know

bluff	elective	linger	quiver	sheepishly
conviction	ferocity	portly	scowl	trudge

A. Replace the underlined word(s) in each sentence with a form of a Word to Know. Write the word on the line.

_____ 1. Mr. Lucas was a large, <u>stout</u> man.

_____ 2. Victor tried to <u>fool</u> his classmates by saying he knew how to speak French.

_____ 3. Knowing Teresa was nearby, Victor would <u>stand around waiting</u> in the hallway.

_____ 4. Michael <u>frowned</u> to impress the girls.

_____ 5. Spanish was an <u>optional</u> class for students.

_____ 6. When he realized Teresa was not in his English class, Victor began to <u>plod</u> down the hall.

_____ 7. Victor tells himself with <u>confidence</u> that Teresa will be his girl this year.

_____ 8. When Michael scowled, his upper lip <u>trembled</u> slightly.

_____ 9. When he could not speak French, Victor looked at Mr. Bueller <u>with embarrassment</u>.

_____ 10. Michael's expression was so full of <u>intensity</u> that Belinda stopped and looked at him.

B. The following words have more than one meaning: *bluff* and *quiver*. On a separate sheet of paper write a sentence for each of these words, using meanings different from the ones in "Seventh Grade."

Before You Read

Connect to Your Life

An African proverb says, "It takes two parents to produce a child, but it takes an entire village to raise a child." What values do you associate with community spirit?

Key to the Story

WHAT'S THE BIG IDEA? Not all teachers are found in school. The boy in this story learns from an elderly woman. Who are the important teachers in your life? In the boxes below, name two. Describe how each person has been a teacher in your life. An example has been done.

Grandmother		
She told me stories about when she was a girl. She also taught me songs she knew.		

Thank You, M'am

by Langston Hughes

PREVIEW Langston Hughes was an African-American author and poet. He set this story in Harlem in the late 1950s. The main characters are two strangers—a troubled youth and an older woman. Late one night, they meet in an unusual way.

As the story begins . . .

- A woman is walking alone late at night in the city.
- A boy runs up behind her.
- The woman's actions surprise the boy.

READING TIP In this story, certain words and phrases may be confusing. The writer uses **dialect** and **slang**—the speech patterns of a certain group of people—to make the characters come alive. Don't worry if you can't figure out all of the words. Try reading aloud the **dialogue**, or words spoken by the characters, to understand what they are saying.

FOCUS

A woman is walking alone at night. Suddenly, a boy runs up behind her. Read to find out what he does and how she reacts.

MARK IT UP ❯ Underline details that show the woman's reaction. An example is highlighted.

She was a large woman with a large purse that had everything in it but hammer and nails. It had a long strap, and she carried it slung across her shoulder. It was about eleven o'clock at night, and she was walking alone, when a boy ran up behind her and 10 tried to snatch her purse. The strap broke with the single tug the boy gave it from behind. But the boy's weight and the weight of the purse combined caused him to lose his balance so, instead of taking off full blast as he had hoped, the boy fell on his back on the sidewalk, and his legs flew up. The large woman simply turned around and kicked him right square in his blue-jeaned sitter. Then she reached down, picked the boy up by his shirt front, and shook him until his teeth rattled.

20 After that the woman said, "Pick up my pocketbook, boy, and give it here."

She still held him. But she bent down enough to permit him to stoop and pick up her purse. Then she said, "Now ain't you ashamed of yourself?"

Firmly gripped by his shirt front, the boy said, "Yes'm."

The woman said, "What did you want to do it for?"

The boy said, "I didn't aim to."

She said, "You a lie!"

30 By that time two or three people passed, stopped, turned to look, and some stood watching.

"If I turn you loose, will you run?" asked the woman.

"Yes'm," said the boy.

"Then I won't turn you loose," said the woman. She did not release him.

"I'm very sorry, lady, I'm sorry," whispered the boy.

"Um-hum! And your face is dirty. I got a great mind to wash your face for you. Ain't you got nobody home to tell you to wash your face?"

40 "No'm," said the boy.

"Then it will get washed this evening," said the large woman starting up the street, dragging the frightened boy behind her.

He looked as if he were fourteen or fifteen, <u>frail</u> and willow-wild, in tennis shoes and blue jeans.

The woman said, "You ought to be my son. I would teach you right from wrong. Least I can do right now is to wash your face. Are you hungry?"

"No'm," said the being-dragged boy. "I just want
50 you to turn me loose."

"Was I bothering *you* when I turned that corner?" asked the woman.

"No'm."

"But you put yourself in contact with *me*," said the woman. "If you think that that contact is not going to last awhile, you got another thought coming. When I get through with you, sir, you are going to remember Mrs. Luella Bates Washington Jones."

Pause & Reflect

FOCUS

Read to find out what happens when Mrs. Jones takes the boy home with her.

MARK IT UP Underline details that show you how Mrs. Jones treats him.

Sweat popped out on the
60 boy's face and he began to struggle. Mrs. Jones stopped, jerked him around in front of her, put a half nelson[1] about his neck, and continued to drag him up the street. When

---

1. **half nelson:** a wrestling hold with one arm under the opponent's arm from behind to the back of the neck.

WORDS TO KNOW
frail (frāl) *adj.* delicate; weak and fragile

Pause & Reflect

1. What does the woman do to the boy after he tries to steal her purse? Check three phrases below. **(Summarize)**

   ❑ picks the boy up by his shirt front

   ❑ asks him why he wanted to steal her purse

   ❑ calls for the police

   ❑ asks about his life at home

2. What do you think Mrs. Jones is going to do to the boy? **(Predict)**

   _____

   _____

   _____

As the story continues...

• Mrs. Jones drags the boy home with her.

• The boy explains why he tried to steal her purse.

she got to her door, she dragged the boy inside, down a hall, and into a large kitchenette-furnished room at the rear of the house. She switched on the light and left the door open. The boy could hear other roomers laughing and talking in the large house. Some of their doors were open, too, so he knew he and the woman were not alone. The woman still had him by the neck in the middle of her room.

She said, "What is your name?"

"Roger," answered the boy.

"Then, Roger, you go to that sink and wash your face," said the woman, whereupon she turned him loose—at last. Roger looked at the door—looked at the woman—looked at the door—*and went to the sink*.

"Let the water run until it gets warm," she said. "Here's a clean towel."

"You gonna take me to jail?" asked the boy, bending over the sink.

"Not with that face, I would not take you nowhere," said the woman. "Here I am trying to get home to cook me a bite to eat and you snatch my pocketbook! Maybe you ain't been to your supper either, late as it be. Have you?"

"There's nobody home at my house," said the boy.

"Then we'll eat," said the woman. "I believe you're hungry—or been hungry—to try to snatch my pocketbook."

"I wanted a pair of blue suede shoes," said the boy.

"Well, you didn't have to snatch my pocketbook to get some suede shoes," said Mrs. Luella Bates Washington Jones. "You could of asked me."

"M'am?"

The water dripping from his face, the boy looked at her. There was a long pause. A very long pause. After he had dried his face and not knowing what else to do

WORDS TO KNOW
suede (swād) *n.* leather with a soft, fuzzy surface

dried it again, the boy turned around, wondering what next. The door was open. He could make a dash for it down the hall. He could run, run, run, run, *run!*

Pause & Reflect

FOCUS

Read to find out what happens when Roger and Mrs. Jones say good-bye.

The woman was sitting on the day-bed. After a while she said, "I were young once and I wanted things I could not get."

There was another long

110 pause. The boy's mouth opened. Then he frowned, but not knowing he frowned.

The woman said, "Um-hum! You thought I was going to say *but,* didn't you? You thought I was going to say, *but I didn't snatch people's pocketbooks.* Well, I wasn't going to say that." Pause. Silence. "I have done things, too, which I would not tell you, son—neither tell God, if he didn't already know. So you set down while I fix us something to eat. You might run that comb through your hair so you will look <u>presentable</u>."

In another corner of the room behind a screen was a
120 gas plate and an icebox. Mrs. Jones got up and went behind the screen. The woman did not watch the boy to see if he was going to run now, nor did she watch her purse which she left behind her on the day-bed. But the boy took care to sit on the far side of the room where he thought she could easily see him out of the corner of her eye, if she wanted to. He did not trust the woman *not* to trust him. And he did not want to be <u>mistrusted</u> now.

WORDS TO KNOW
presentable (prĭ-zĕnʹtə-bəl) *adj.* fit to be seen by people
mistrust (mĭs-trŭstʹ) *v.* to have no confidence in

Pause & Reflect

Why doesn't Roger just run out of the room? **(Cause and Effect)**

As the story ends . . .

• Mrs. Jones cooks supper and they eat together.
• She gives Roger some advice and says goodnight.

English Learner Support
Vocabulary
Day-bed A *day-bed* is a couch without a back that can be used as a bed.

English Learner Support
Vocabulary
Kitchen Words A *gas plate* is a small gas-powered cooking surface that sits on a tabletop. An *icebox* is a refrigerator.

Dialect The words in blue mean that Roger would feel guilty wearing the shoes because he had stolen money to buy them. The expression *come by devilish* is dialect that means "gotten in a dishonest way."

Pause & Reflect

Why do you think Mrs. Jones told Roger about the things she wanted but "could not get?" **(Cause and Effect)**

Roger never states his opinion of Mrs. Jones. What do you believe he thinks of her? Mark passages in the story that support your views. **(Infer)**

"Do you need somebody to go to the store," asked the boy, "maybe to get some milk or something?"

"Don't believe I do," said the woman, "unless you just want sweet milk yourself. I was going to make cocoa out of this canned milk I got here."

"That will be fine," said the boy.

She heated some lima beans and ham she had in the icebox, made the cocoa, and set the table. The woman did not ask the boy anything about where he lived, or his folks, or anything else that would embarrass him. Instead, as they ate, she told him about her job in a hotel beauty-shop that stayed open late, what the work was like, and how all kinds of women came in and out, blondes, red-heads, and Spanish. Then she cut him a half of her ten-cent cake.

"Eat some more, son," she said.

When they were finished eating she got up and said, "Now, here, take this ten dollars and buy yourself some blue suede shoes. And next time, do not make the mistake of latching onto *my* pocketbook *nor nobody else's*—because shoes come by devilish like that will burn your feet. I got to get my rest now. But I wish you would behave yourself, son, from here on in."

She led him down the hall to the front door and opened it. "Goodnight! Behave yourself, boy!" she said, looking out into the street.

The boy wanted to say something else other than "Thank you, m'am" to Mrs. Luella Bates Washington Jones, but he couldn't do so as he turned at the <u>barren</u> stoop and looked back at the large woman in the door. He barely managed to say "Thank you" before she shut the door. And he never saw her again. ❖

Pause & Reflect

WORDS TO KNOW
barren (băr′ən) *adj.* empty; deserted

Active Reading SkillBuilder

Cause and Effect

Often, the events in a story are related by **cause and effect.** A cause is an event that occurs first and brings about a second event, called an effect. Use the chart below to help you connect causes and effects. For each event in the left column, write down the effect it produces. One example has been done for you.

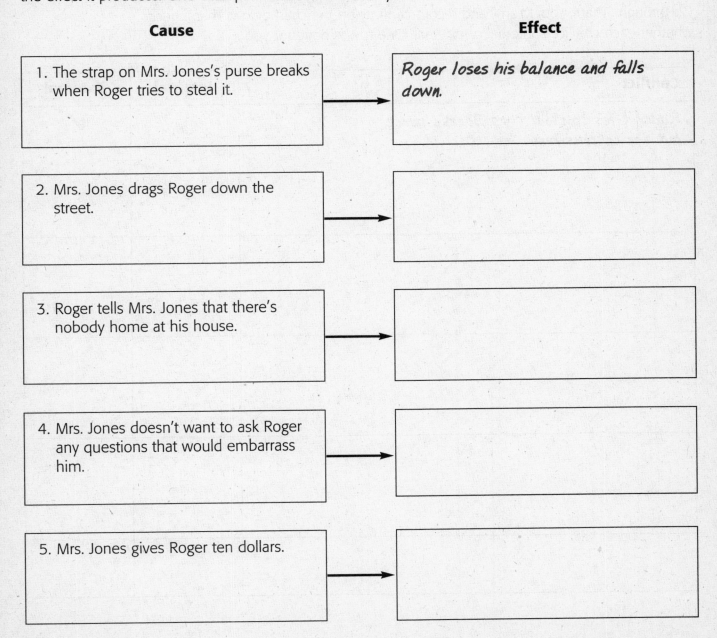

Cause   **Effect**

1. The strap on Mrs. Jones's purse breaks when Roger tries to steal it. → *Roger loses his balance and falls down.*

2. Mrs. Jones drags Roger down the street. →

3. Roger tells Mrs. Jones that there's nobody home at his house. →

4. Mrs. Jones doesn't want to ask Roger any questions that would embarrass him. →

5. Mrs. Jones gives Roger ten dollars. →

Active Reading SkillBuilder

Conflict

A plot is usually centered around a **conflict.** Conflict occurs when a character encounters an opposing force. The force can be outside the character—in the form of another character, a physical obstacle, nature, or society. This is called an **external conflict.** An **internal conflict** involves a character's struggle within himself or herself. Go through "Thank You, M'am" and record conflicts on the chart below. Then check whether each conflict is internal or external. One row is done for you.

Conflict	Internal	External
Roger tries to steal Mrs. Jones's purse, but she catches him.		✔

Words to Know SkillBuilder

Words to Know

| barren | frail | mistrust | presentable | suede |

A. Use the correct Words to Know to fill in the blanks in the sentences below.

1. Mrs. Jones made Roger wash his face and hands so that he would look _____.

2. Despite the fact that Mrs. Jones was kind to him, Roger still felt a lot of _____ about her.

3. When she finally got a good look at him, Mrs. Jones thought that Roger looked thin and _____.

4. To get to her house, Mrs. Jones led Roger down a street that was empty and _____.

5. Roger told Mrs. Jones that he wanted to steal her pocketbook so that he would have money to buy blue _____ shoes.

B. On each blank line, write the word from the word list that the rhyme describes.

If they order coffee, and I bring them tea,
The people who ordered might feel this about me.

_____
(1)

If I comb my hair and wash my face,
I would look this just about any place.

_____
(2)

You would call a room this if you went in the door,
And saw it was empty from ceiling to floor.

_____
(3)

You might use this for shoes and vests and such
To make them warm to wear and soft to touch.

_____
(4)

C. On a separate sheet of paper, describe what Roger looks like and feels like as he leaves Mrs. Jones's house. Use at least **two** of the Words to Know.

Before You Read

Connect to Your Life

Think about a time when someone new joined your class. If you were the newcomer, how might you try to fit in? Use drawings and captions to show two ways.

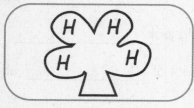

Join a club.

Key to the Essay

WHAT'S THE BIG IDEA? What's in a name? Think about your family name, your given name, or your nickname. Fill in the organizer below to explore how you feel about your name.

My name: _____

What's interesting about this name?

_____

_____

_____

I would prefer to have

❑ my name

another name: _____

Has it ever caused a problem?

❑ yes   ❑ no

NAMES

Nombres

by Julia Alvarez

PREVIEW Julia Alvarez's family came to the United States from the Dominican Republic. In this essay she describes the wrong pronunciations of her name and those of other members of her family. Her feelings about those mispronunciations and about her nicknames changed as she grew up.

~

NAMES

As the essay begins . . .

• The Alvarez family is moving to New York City from the Dominican Republic.

MORE ABOUT . . .

(IMMIGRATION) As part of the immigration process— coming to live in the United States from a foreign country—the Alvarez family had to go through customs. They had to prove that they were not carrying anything illegal into the country.

English Learner Support
Vocabulary

Spanish Words This essay contains some Spanish names and words.

• If you have a Spanish-speaking friend, ask him or her how to say the words.

• If you speak Spanish, help students who do not to say the words correctly.

• The footnotes can also help you.

FOCUS

In this part the author tells about the new names she and her family received in New York City.

||||| **MARK IT UP** > As you read, circle each of these new names.

When we arrived in New York City, our names changed almost immediately. At (Immigration,) the officer asked my father, *Mister Elbures,* if he had anything to declare. My father shook his head no, and we were waved through. I was too afraid we wouldn't be let in if I
10 corrected the man's pronunciation, but I said our name to myself, opening my mouth wide for the organ blast of the *a,* trilling my tongue[1] for the drumroll of the *r, All-vah-rrr-es!* How could anyone get *Elbures* out of that orchestra of sound?

At the hotel my mother was *Missus Alburest,* and I was *little girl,* as in, "Hey, little girl, stop riding the elevator up and down. It's *not* a toy."

When we moved into our new apartment building, the super[2] called my father *Mister Alberase,* and the
20 neighbors who became mother's friends pronounced her name *Jew-lee-ah* instead of *Hoo-lee-ah.* I, her namesake, was known as *Hoo-lee-tah* at home. But at school I was *Judy* or *Judith,* and once an English teacher mistook me for *Juliet.*

It took a while to get used to my new names. I wondered if I shouldn't correct my teachers and new friends. But my mother argued that it didn't matter. "You know what your friend Shakespeare said, 'A rose by any other name would smell as sweet.'" My
30 family had gotten into the habit of calling any literary figure "my friend" because I had begun to write poems and stories in English class.

---

1. **trilling my tongue:** rapid vibration of the tongue against the roof of the mouth, as in pronouncing a Spanish *r.*

2. **super:** superintendent of an apartment building.

By the time I was in high school, I was a popular kid, and it showed in my name. Friends called me *Jules* or *Hey Jude,* and once a group of troublemaking friends my mother forbade me to hang out with called me *Alcatraz.*[3] I was *Hoo-lee-tah* only to Mami and Papi and uncles and aunts who came over to eat *sancocho*[4] on Sunday afternoons—old world folk
40 whom I would just as soon go back to where they came from and leave me to pursue whatever mischief I wanted to in America. JUDY ALCATRAZ: the name on the wanted poster would read. Who would ever trace her to me?

Pause & Reflect

FOCUS

Alvarez's sisters also were called by new names. Read to find out about these names.

My older sister had the hardest time getting an American name for herself because *Mauricia* did not translate into English.

50 <u>Ironically</u>, although she had the most foreign-sounding name, she and I were the Americans in the family. We had been born in New York City when our parents had first tried immigration and then gone back "home," too homesick to stay. My mother often told

---

3. **Alcatraz:** former federal prison on an island in San Francisco Bay, known also as "the Rock."

4. *sancocho* (säng-kō'chō) *Spanish:* traditional Caribbean stew of meat and vegetables.

WORDS TO KNOW
ironically (ī-rŏn'ĭk-əl-lē) *adv.* in a way that is contrary to what is expected or intended

---

Pause & Reflect

1. Cross out the word below that does *not* describe Alvarez's attitude toward the "new names."**(Infer)**

   amused   angry

   surprised   annoyed

2. Do you agree with Alvarez's mother that it doesn't matter what name friends and teachers call you? **(Evaluate)**

   AGREE / DISAGREE, because

_____

_____

_____

As the essay continues . . .

• Alvarez's mother explains the origin of her sister's name.

English Learner Support

Language

Verb Endings To *coo* is to make a soft cry, like the sound of a dove, to show delight and affection. This verb appears with two different verb endings on this page: *cooing* and *cooed.*

coo + ing = cooing

coo + ed = cooed

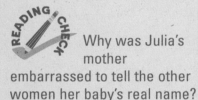

READING CHECK Why was Julia's mother embarrassed to tell the other women her baby's real name?

WHAT DOES IT MEAN? *Pitied* means "felt sorry for."

the story of how she had almost changed my sister's name in the hospital.

After the delivery, Mami and some other new mothers were cooing over their new baby sons and daughters and exchanging names and weights and
60 delivery stories. My mother was embarrassed among the Sallys and Janes and Georges and Johns to reveal the rich, noisy name of *Mauricia,* so when her turn came to brag, she gave her baby's name as *Maureen.*

"Why'd ya give her an Irish name with so many pretty Spanish names to choose from?" one of the women asked her.

My mother blushed and admitted her baby's real name to the group. Her mother-in-law had recently died, she apologized, and her husband had insisted
70 that the first daughter be named after his mother, *Mauran.* My mother thought it the ugliest name she had ever heard, and she talked my father into what she believed was an improvement, a combination of *Mauran* and her own mother's name, *Felicia.*

"Her name is Mao-ree-shee-ah," my mother said to the group.

"Why, that's a beautiful name," the new mothers cried. *"Moor-ee-sha, Moor-ee-sha,"* they cooed into the pink blanket. *Moor-ee-sha* it was when we
80 returned to the States eleven years later. Sometimes, American tongues found even that mispronunciation tough to say and called her *Maria* or *Marsha* or *Maudy* from her nickname *Maury.* I pitied her. What an awful name to have to transport across borders!

My little sister, Ana, had the easiest time of all. She was plain *Anne*—that is, only her name was plain, for she turned out to be the pale, blond "American beauty" in the family. The only Hispanic-seeming

thing about her was the affectionate nicknames her
90 boyfriends sometimes gave her. *Anita,* or as one goofy
guy used to sing to her to the tune of the banana
advertisement, *Anita Banana.*

Later, during her college years in the late 60's, there
was a push to pronounce Third World⁵ names
correctly. I remember calling her long distance at her
group house and a roommate answering.

"Can I speak to Ana?" I asked, pronouncing her
name the American way.

"Ana?" The man's voice hesitated. "Oh! You must
100 mean *Ah-nah!*"

Pause & Reflect

FOCUS

In high school Alvarez
wanted just to fit in. Read
to find out how she felt
when she was seen as
being different.

▥ MARK IT UP ⟩ As you
read, circle **details** that
help you understand
Alvarez's feelings.

Our first few years in the
States, though, <u>ethnicity</u> was
not yet "in." Those were the
blond, blue-eyed, bobby-sock
years of junior high and high
school before the 60's <u>ushered</u>
in peasant blouses, hoop
earrings, *sarapes.*⁶ My <u>initial</u>
desire to be known by my
110 correct Dominican name faded. I just wanted to be
Judy and <u>merge</u> with the Sallys and Janes in my class.
But, <u>inevitably</u>, my accent and coloring gave me away.
"So where are you from, Judy?"

---

5. **Third World:** the developing nations of Latin America, Africa, and Asia.
6. *sarapes* (sä-rä′pěs) *Spanish:* long, blanket-like shawls.

WORDS TO KNOW
  ethnicity (ĕth-nĭs′ĭ-tē) *n.* a racial, national, or cultural heritage
  usher (ŭsh′ər) *v.* to make known the presence or arrival of; to introduce
  initial (ĭ-nĭsh′əl) *adj.* first
  merge (mûrj) *v.* to blend together
  inevitably (ĭn-ĕv′ĭ-tə-blē) *adv.* impossible to avoid or prevent

English Learner Support
Vocabulary

Idiom *There was a push*
means that people thought
it was important to do
something.

Pause & Reflect

▥ MARK IT UP ⟩ Reread the
boxed text on page 30. Star
details that explain where the
name *Mauricia* comes from.
(Clarify)

📄 As the essay continues . . .

• Alvarez likes living in
  America and wants to fit in.

• Her friends are curious
  about her background.

MORE ABOUT . . .

THE DOMINICAN REPUBLIC

The small country of the **Dominican Republic** is on the same island in the West Indies as Haiti. The population of the entire country is only slightly larger than that of New York City. Find the Dominican Republic on a map.

Pause & Reflect

What was Alvarez feeling when she answered the question "Where are you from, Judy?" **(Generalize)**

"New York," I told my classmates. After all, I had been born blocks away at Columbia Presbyterian Hospital.

"I mean, *originally.*"

"From the Caribbean," I answered vaguely, for if I <u>specified</u>, no one was quite sure what continent our
120 island was located on.

"Really? I've been to Bermuda. We went last April for spring vacation. I got the worst sunburn! So, are you from Portoriko?"

"No," I shook my head. "From the Dominican Republic."

"Where's that?"

"South of Bermuda."

They were just being curious, I knew, but I burned with shame whenever they singled me out as a
130 "foreigner," a rare, <u>exotic</u> friend.

"Say your name in Spanish, oh, please say it!" I had made mouths drop one day by rattling off my full name, which, according to Dominican custom, included my middle names, Mother's and Father's surnames for four generations back.

"Julia Altagracia María Teresa Álvarez Tavares Perello Espaillat Julia Pérez Rochet González." I pronounced it slowly, a name as <u>chaotic</u> with sounds as a Middle Eastern bazaar or market day in a South
140 American village.

Pause & Reflect

WORDS TO KNOW
  specify (spĕs′ə-fī) *v.* to make known or identify
  exotic (ĭg-zŏt′ĭk) *adj.* unusual or different
  chaotic (kā-ŏt′ĭk) *adj.* confused; disordered

FOCUS

In this part Alvarez describes her extended family. You will meet some of her aunts and uncles.

MARK IT UP As you read, circle **details** that help you understand Alvarez's feelings toward her family.

I suffered most whenever my extended family attended school occasions. For my graduation, they all came, the whole noisy, foreign-looking lot of fat aunts in their dark mourning dresses[7] and hair nets, uncles with full, droopy mustaches and baby-blue or 150 salmon-colored suits and white pointy shoes and fedora hats,[8] the many little cousins who snuck in without tickets. They sat in the first row in order to better understand the Americans' fast-spoken English. But how could they listen when they were constantly speaking among themselves in florid-sounding[9] phrases, rococo[10] consonants, rich, rhyming vowels? Their loud voices carried.

Introducing them to my friends was a further trial to me. These relatives had such complicated names and 160 there were so many of them, and their relationships to myself were so <u>convoluted</u>. There was my Tía[11] Josefina, who was not really an aunt but a much older cousin. And her daughter, Aída Margarita, who was adopted, *una hija de crianza*.[12] My uncle of affection, Tío José, brought my *madrina*[13] Tía Amelia and her *comadre*[14] Tía Pilar. My friends rarely had more than

As the essay ends . . .

• Julia describes her large extended family.

• At her high school graduation, she compares her family to her friends' families.

MARK IT UP Reread the boxed passage. Underline details that help you picture the author's extended family. (Visualize)

WHAT DOES IT MEAN?
A *further trial* means "another difficult experience."

---

7. **mourning dresses:** dark-colored clothing worn to remember the dead.

8. **fedora hats** (fĭ-dôr′ə): soft felt hats with low crowns.

9. **florid-sounding:** flowery; very ornate.

10. **rococo** (rə-kō′kō): elaborate; flamboyant.

11. *Tía/Tío* (tē′ä, tē′ō) *Spanish:* Aunt/Uncle.

12. *una hija de crianza* (ōō′nä ē′hä dě kryän′sä) *Spanish:* a child raised as if one's own daughter.

13. *madrina* (mä-drē′nä) *Spanish:* godmother.

14. *comadre* (kō-mä′drě) *Spanish:* close friend.

WORDS TO KNOW
convoluted (kŏn′və-lōō′tĭd) *adj.* difficult to understand; complicated

Pause & Reflect

What **purpose** do you think the author had in writing "Names/Nombres"? Check the ones that apply and provide reasons for your answers.

❏ to entertain

❏ to inform

❏ to express an opinion

❏ to persuade

_____

_____

_____

_____

CHALLENGE

What are the advantages of having two cultures and knowing two languages? What might the disadvantages be? (Evaluate)

Pros

1. _____

2. _____

3. _____

Cons

1. _____

2. _____

3. _____

their nuclear family[15] to introduce, youthful, glamorous-looking couples ("Mom and Dad") who skied and played tennis and took their kids for spring

170 vacations to Bermuda.

After the commencement ceremony, my family waited outside in the parking lot while my friends and I signed yearbooks with nicknames which recalled our high school good times: "Beans" and "Pepperoni" and "Alcatraz." We hugged and cried and promised to keep in touch.

Sometimes if our goodbyes went on too long, I heard my father's voice calling out across the parking lot. *"Hoo-lee-tah! Vámonos!"*[16]

180 Back home, my *tíos* and *tías* and *primas*,[17] Mami and Papi, and *mis hermanas*[18] had a party for me with *sancocho* and a store-bought *pudín*,[19] inscribed with *Happy Graduation, Julie.* There were many gifts—that was a plus to a large family! I got several wallets and a suitcase with my initials and a graduation charm from my godmother and money from my uncles. The biggest gift was a portable typewriter from my parents for writing my stories and poems.

Someday, the family predicted, my name would be

190 well-known throughout the United States. I laughed to myself, wondering which one I would go by. ❖

Pause & Reflect

---

15. **nuclear family:** a family unit consisting of a mother and father and their children.

16. *Vámonos* (bä′mō-nōs) *Spanish:* Let's go.

17. *primas* (prē′mäs) *Spanish:* cousins.

18. *mis hermanas* (mēs ĕr-mä′näs) *Spanish:* my sisters.

19. *pudín* (pōō-thēn′) *Spanish:* pudding.

Active Reading SkillBuilder

Identifying Author's Purpose

An author may have four main **purposes** for writing: to entertain, to inform, to express an opinion, to persuade. In a single piece of writing, an author may have more than one purpose in mind. Use the following chart to help you identify Julia Alvarez's purpose(s) for writing "Names/Nombres." Identify text that supports your ideas.

Purpose	Supporting Text
to inform	"When we arrived in New York City, our names changed almost immediately."

Literary Analysis SkillBuilder

Personal Essay

When authors want to explore events or issues in their own lives, they often write a **personal essay,** a nonfiction piece that deals with a single subject. Because both the content and the tone of a personal essay express the author's thoughts, feelings, and opinions, the reader gets a good picture of what the author is like. Use the web below to show some of the things you learned about Julia Alvarez from reading "Names/Nombres."

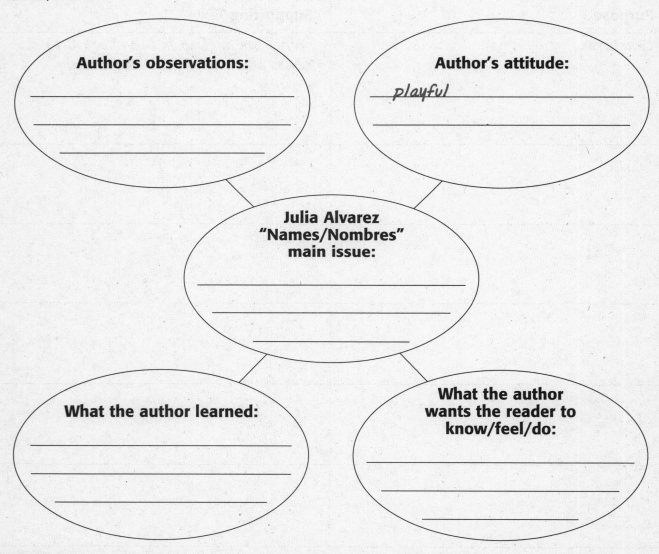

Author's observations:
_____
_____
_____

Author's attitude:
_____ *playful* _____
_____

Julia Alvarez
"Names/Nombres"
main issue:
_____
_____
_____

What the author learned:
_____
_____
_____

What the author
wants the reader to
know/feel/do:
_____
_____
_____

Follow Up: Working with a partner, use what you have learned about Julia Alvarez to write a dialogue between the author and a reporter. Present your dialogue to the class.

Words to Know SkillBuilder

Words to Know

chaotic	ethnicity	inevitably	ironically	specify
convoluted	exotic	initial	merge	usher

A. Write the Word to Know that best describes or defines each sentence or phrase below.

1. A person who is unusual in an interesting way might be called this. _____

2. An auditorium filled with a lot of unruly movement and noise _____

3. Another word for *complicated* _____

4. Where your ancestors come from determines this. _____

5. A shorter way of saying, "It was bound to happen." _____

6. Oddly enough _____

7. First or immediate response _____

8. When two roads or two paths come together, they do this. _____

9. When you want something done in an exact way, it is good to do this. _____

10. To lead into a theater _____

B. Write about what it might be like for Julia Alvarez to come into the United States as an immigrant from the Dominican Republic at the beginning of the 21st century. Use at least **five** Words to Know in your writing.

_____

_____

_____

_____

Before You Read

Connect to Your Life

How important is our imagination? Think of the many ways in which people use their imaginations to create things. Use the concept web below to write some things that you create from your imagination.

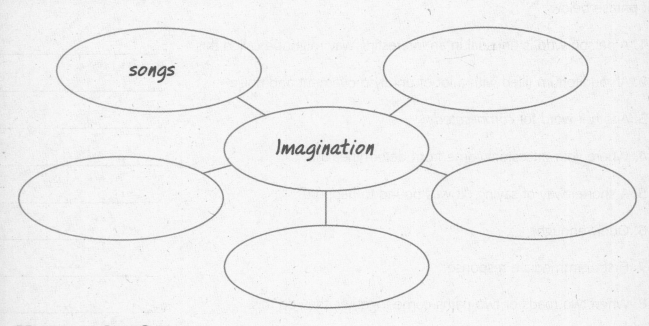

songs

Imagination

Key to the Story

WHAT YOU NEED TO KNOW A memorial is a place, event, or object that is meant to honor the memory of the past. The Vietnam Veterans Memorial in Washington, D.C., sometimes known as "The Wall," is a long marble wall on which are carved the names of the more than 58,000 American men and women who died in the Vietnam war between 1962 and 1973. A memorial can be anything from a holiday to a poem. Name a memorial that you know about.

Memorial: _____

ZEBRA

by Chaim Potok

PREVIEW A boy named Adam Zebrin, whom everybody calls Zebra, notices a tall stranger collecting bits of junk out of trash cans near his school. When the stranger asks Zebra whether his school needs an art class, the two begin a deep and important friendship.

As the story begins . . .

- The main character is a boy everyone calls Zebra.
- Zebra loves to run and feel the wind on his face.
- One day something happens to him that stops him from running.

English Learner Support

Language

Exposition Some stories contain exposition—sections that tell what happened in the past, before the start of the story. Pages 40–41 of this story are exposition. These pages describe what happened to Zebra before the main story begins.

MARK IT UP ⟩ KEEP TRACK
Remember to use these marks to keep track of your reading:

✱ This is important.

? I have a question about this.

! This is a surprise.

FOCUS

Meet a boy called Zebra. Read to find out how he feels about running and how he gets hurt.

MARK IT UP ⟩ As you read, underline details that help you understand how Zebra feels about running. An example is highlighted.

His name was Adam Martin Zebrin, but everyone in his neighborhood called him Zebra. He couldn't remember when he began to be called by that name. Perhaps they started to call him Zebra when he first began running. Or maybe he began running when they
10   started to call him Zebra.

He loved the name and he loved to run.

When he was very young, his parents took him to a zoo, where he saw zebras for the first time. They were odd-looking creatures, like stubby horses, short-legged, thick-necked, with dark and white stripes.

Then one day he went with his parents to a movie about Africa, and he saw zebras, hundreds of them, thundering across a grassy plain, dust rising in boiling brown clouds.

20   Was he already running before he saw that movie, or did he begin to run afterward? No one seemed able to remember.

He would go running through the neighborhood for the sheer joy of feeling the wind on his face. People said that when he ran he arched his head up and back, and his face kind of flattened out. One of his teachers told him it was clever to run that way, his balance was better. But the truth was he ran that way, his head thrown back, because he loved to feel the wind
30   rushing across his neck.

Each time, after only a few minutes of running, his legs would begin to feel wondrously light. He would run past the school and the homes on the street beyond the church. All the neighbors knew him and would wave and call out, "Go, Zebra!" And sometimes one or two of their dogs would run with him awhile, barking.

He would imagine himself a zebra on the African plain. Running.

40 There was a hill on Franklin Avenue, a steep hill. By the time he reached that hill, he would feel his legs so light it was as if he had no legs at all and was flying. He would begin to descend the hill, certain as he ran that he needed only to give himself the slightest push and off he would go, and instead of a zebra he would become the bird he had once seen in a movie about Alaska, he would swiftly change into an eagle, soaring higher and higher, as light as the gentlest breeze, the cool wind caressing his arms and legs and neck.

50 Then, a year ago, racing down Franklin Avenue, he had given himself that push and had begun to turn into an eagle, when a huge rushing shadow appeared in his line of vision and crashed into him and plunged him into a darkness from which he emerged very, very slowly. . . .

"Never, never, *never* run down that hill so fast that you can't stop at the corner," his mother had warned him again and again.

60 His schoolmates and friends kept calling him Zebra even after they all knew that the doctors had told him he would never be able to run like that again.

His leg would heal in time, the doctors said, and perhaps in a year or so the brace would come off. But they were not at all certain about his hand. From time to time his injured hand, which he still wore in a sling, would begin to hurt. The doctors said they could find no cause for the pain.

 Pause & Reflect

Pause & Reflect

1. Circle the phrase below that does *not* describe what Zebra liked about running. (**Summarize**)
   keeping his head up
   feeling the wind
   stirring up dust as he runs
   feeling he can almost fly

2. How does Zebra get hurt? (**Infer**)

   _____

   _____

   _____

3. |||**MARK IT UP** ⇗ After his accident, the doctors tell Zebra that his leg will heal in time. What are they uncertain about? Circle the sentence in the story that tells the answer. (**Clarify**)

As the story continues . . .

- Zebra's hand hurts so badly that it's hard for him to act normally.
- He watches a man looking through a trash can.
- Zebra notices something unusual about the man.

English Learner Support

Culture

Fashion Writers sometimes show what a character is like by describing how the character dresses. Mr. Morgan, Zebra's teacher, wears a *smart suit,* or clothing that is tasteful and fashionable. He also wears a *bow tie,* a butterfly-shaped necktie that is knotted and worn close to the throat.

English Learner Support

Vocabulary

Chain-Link Fence This is a kind of fence made of thick steel wire in a diamond-shaped pattern.

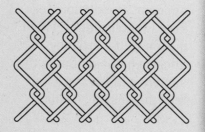

FOCUS

Read to find out about a mysterious man whom Zebra notices outside his school.

MARK IT UP As you read, circle details that help you picture the man.

One morning, during Mr. Morgan's geography class, Zebra's hand began to hurt badly. He sat staring out the window at the sky. Mr. Morgan, a stiff-mannered person in his early fifties, given to smart suits and dapper[1] bow ties, called on him to respond to a question. Zebra stumbled about in vain for the answer. Mr. Morgan told him to pay attention to the geography inside the classroom and not to the geography outside.

"In this class, young man, you will concentrate your attention upon the earth, not upon the sky," Mr. Morgan said.

Later, in the schoolyard during the midmorning recess, Zebra stood near the tall fence, looking out at the street and listening to the noises behind him.

His schoolmates were racing about, playing exuberantly, shouting and laughing with full voices. Their joyous sounds went ringing through the quiet street.

Most times Zebra would stand alongside the basketball court or behind the wire screen at home plate and watch the games. That day, because his hand hurt so badly, he stood alone behind the chain-link fence of the schoolyard.

That's how he happened to see the man. And that's how the man happened to see him.

One minute the side street on which the school stood was strangely empty, without people or traffic, without even any of the dogs that often roamed about

---
1. **dapper:** neatly dressed; stylish.

WORDS TO KNOW
exuberantly (ĭg-zoo′bər-ənt-lē) *adv.* full of enthusiasm or joy

the neighborhood—vacant and silent, as if it were already in the full heat of summer. The red-brick ranch house that belonged to Mr. Morgan, and the white clapboard two-story house in which Mrs. English lived, and the other homes on the street, with their columned front porches and their back patios, and the tall oaks—all stood curiously still in the warm golden light of the mid-morning sun.

Then a man emerged from wide and busy Franklin
110 Avenue at the far end of the street.

Zebra saw the man stop at the corner and stand looking at a public trash can. He watched as the man poked his hand into the can and fished about but seemed to find nothing he wanted. He withdrew the hand and, raising it to shield his eyes from the sunlight, glanced at the street sign on the lamppost.

He started to walk up the street in the direction of the school.

He was tall and wiry, and looked to be about forty
120 years old. In his right hand he carried a bulging brown plastic bag. He wore a khaki army jacket, a blue denim shirt, blue jeans, and brown cowboy boots. His <u>gaunt</u> face and muscular neck were reddened by exposure to the sun. Long brown hair spilled out below his dark-blue farmer's cap. On the front of the cap, in large orange letters, were the words LAND ROVER.[2]

He walked with his eyes on the sidewalk and the curb, as if looking for something, and he went right past Zebra without noticing him.
130 Zebra's hand hurt very much. He was about to turn away when he saw the man stop and look around and peer up at the red-brick wall of the school. The man set down the bag and took off his cap and stuffed it

WHAT DOES IT MEAN? *Vacant* means "empty."

READING TIP Look for the details that help you **visualize,** or form a mental picture of, the man. Try to imagine how he would look if he was standing in front of you.

---

2. **Land Rover:** a type of sport utility vehicle.

WORDS TO KNOW
gaunt (gônt) *adj.* thin and bony

Zebra **43**

Pause & Reflect

READ ALOUD the boxed passage. What can you **conclude** about the man?

_____

_____

As the story continues . . .

- The man questions Zebra about school and his plans for the summer.

- He tells Zebra his name is John Wilson.

- Zebra suggests that Mr. Wilson talk to the assistant principal.

English Learner Support

Language

Dialect _You-all_ is a form of the plural pronoun _you._ It is used by some people in southern parts of the United States.

into a pocket of his jacket. From one of his jeans pockets he removed a handkerchief, with which he then wiped his face. He shoved the handkerchief back into the pocket and put the cap back on his head.

Then he turned and saw Zebra.

He picked up the bag and started down the street to
140 where Zebra was standing. When the man was about ten feet away, Zebra noticed that the left sleeve of his jacket was empty.

Pause & Reflect

FOCUS

The stranger asks Zebra questions about his school. Read to find out how Zebra reacts to the stranger.

The man came up to Zebra and said in a low, friendly, shy voice, "Hello."

Zebra answered with a cautious "Hello," trying not to look at the empty sleeve, which had been tucked into the man's jacket pocket.

150 The man asked, with a distinct Southern accent, "What's your name, son?"

Zebra said, "Adam."

"What kind of school is this here school, Adam?"

"It's a good school," Zebra answered.

"How long before you-all begin your summer vacation?"

"Three days," Zebra said.

"Anything special happen here during the summer?"

"During the summer? Nothing goes on here. There
160 are no classes."

"What do you-all do during the summer?"

"Some of us go to camp. Some of us hang around. We find things to do."

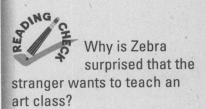

Zebra's hand had begun to tingle and throb. Why was the man asking all those questions? Zebra thought maybe he shouldn't be talking to him at all. He seemed vaguely <u>menacing</u> in that army jacket, the dark-blue cap with the words LAND ROVER on it in orange letters, and the empty sleeve. Yet there was
170 kindness in his gray eyes and ruddy³ features.

The man gazed past Zebra at the students playing in the yard. "Adam, do you think your school would be interested in having someone teach an art class during the summer?"

That took Zebra by surprise. "An *art* class?"

"Drawing, sculpting, things like that."

Zebra was trying *very hard* not to look at the man's empty sleeve. "I don't know. . . ."

"Where's the school office, Adam?"
180 "On Washington Avenue. Go to the end of the street and turn right."

"Thanks," the man said. He hesitated a moment. Then he asked, in a quiet voice, "What happened to you, Adam?"

"A car hit me," Zebra said. "It was my fault."

The man seemed to <u>wince</u>.

> For a flash of a second, Zebra thought to ask the man what had happened to *him*. The words were on his tongue. But he kept himself from saying anything.

The man started back up the street, carrying the
190 brown plastic bag.

Zebra suddenly called, "Hey, mister."

The man stopped and turned. "My name is John Wilson," he said softly.

"Mr. Wilson, when you go into the school office, you'll see signs on two doors. One says 'Dr. Winter,' and the other says 'Mrs. English.' Ask for Mrs. English."

---

3. **ruddy:** reddish.

WORDS TO KNOW
 menacing (mĕn′ĭs-ĭng) *adj.* threatening
 wince (wĭns) *v.* to shrink as in pain or distress

 READING CHECK Why is Zebra surprised that the stranger wants to teach an art class?

REREAD the boxed passage. If you were Zebra, would you have asked the man what happened to him? **(Connect)**
YES / NO, because

_____

_____

_____

Zebra **45**

Pause & Reflect

1. The stranger asks Zebra some questions about his school. What does he want to know? Check two phrases below. (**Summarize**)
   - ❏ when vacation begins
   - ❏ what sports teams the school has
   - ❏ whether students might like an art class
   - ❏ how many students are in the school

2. Why does Zebra visit the school nurse? (**Cause and Effect**)

Dr. Winter, the principal, was a <u>disciplinarian</u> and a grump. Mrs. English, the assistant principal, was generous and kind. Dr. Winter would probably tell the
200 man to call his secretary for an appointment. Mrs. English might invite him into her office and offer him a cup of coffee and listen to what he had to say.

The man hesitated, looking at Zebra.

"Appreciate the advice," he said.

Zebra watched him walk to the corner.

Under the lamppost was a trash can. Zebra saw the man set down the plastic bag and stick his hand into the can and haul out a battered umbrella.

The man tried to open the umbrella, but its metal
210 ribs were broken. The black fabric dangled flat and limp from the pole. He put the umbrella into the plastic bag and headed for the entrance to the school.

A moment later, Zebra heard the whistle that signaled the end of recess. He followed his classmates at a distance, careful to avoid anyone's bumping against his hand.

He sat through his algebra class, copying the problems on the blackboard while holding down his notebook with his left elbow. The sling chafed[4] his neck
220 and felt warm and clumsy on his bare arm. There were sharp pains now in the two curled fingers of his hand.

Right after the class he went downstairs to the office of Mrs. Walsh, a cheerful, gray-haired woman in a white nurse's uniform.

She said, "I'm sorry I can't do very much for you, Adam, except give you two Tylenols."

He swallowed the Tylenols down with water.

Pause & Reflect

---

4. **chafed** (chāft): irritated by rubbing.

WORDS TO KNOW
disciplinarian (dĭs′ə-plə-nâr′ē-ən) *n.* someone who enforces strict discipline

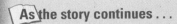

FOCUS

Zebra returns to school for his classes. In one of his classes students tell stories.

MARK IT UP > As you read, circle details that describe the stories the students tell.

On his way back up to the second floor, he saw the man
230 with the dark-blue cap emerge from the school office with Mrs. English. He stopped on the stairs and watched as the man and Mrs. English stood talking together. Mrs. English nodded and smiled and shook the man's hand.

The man walked down the corridor, carrying the plastic bag, and left the school building.

240 Zebra went slowly to his next class.

The class was taught by Mrs. English, who came hurrying into the room some minutes after the bell had rung.

"I apologize for being late," she said, sounding a little out of breath. "There was an important matter I had to attend to."

Mrs. English was a tall, gracious woman in her forties. It was common knowledge that early in her life she had been a journalist on a Chicago newspaper and
250 had written short stories, which she could not get published. Soon after her marriage to a doctor, she had become a teacher.

This was the only class Mrs. English taught.

Ten students from the upper school—seventh and eighth grades—were chosen every year for this class. They met for an hour three times a week and told one another stories. Each story would be discussed and analyzed by Mrs. English and the class.

Mrs. English called it a class in the *imagination*.
260 Zebra was grateful he did not have to take notes in this class. He had only to listen to the stories.

That day, Andrea, the freckle-faced, redheaded girl with very thick glasses who sat next to Zebra, told

As the story continues . . .

• Zebra watches John Wilson speak with Mrs. English.

• Zebra tells a sad story in his storytelling class.

English Learner Support
Vocabulary

Common Knowledge The phrase *it was common knowledge* means "everyone knew."

WHAT DOES IT MEAN?
Analyzed means that the class looked carefully at the meaning of each part of a story.

READING TIP Make note of each time Zebra speaks with Andrea. Think about how they treat each other and what they think of each other.

about a woman scientist who discovered a method of healing trees that had been blasted apart by lightning.

Mark, who had something wrong with his upper lip, told in his quavery[5] voice about a selfish space cadet who stepped into a time machine and met his future self, who turned out to be a hateful person, and how the cadet then returned to the present and changed himself.

Kevin talked in blurred, high-pitched tones and often related parts of his stories with his hands. Mrs. English would quietly repeat many of his sentences. Today he told about an explorer who set out on a journey through a valley filled with yellow stones and surrounded by red mountains, where he encountered[6] an army of green shadows that had been at war for hundreds of years with an army of purple shadows. The explorer showed them how to make peace.

> When it was Zebra's turn, he told a story about a bird that one day crashed against a closed windowpane and broke a wing. A boy tried to heal the wing but couldn't. The bird died, and the boy buried it under a tree on his lawn.

When he had finished, there was silence. Everyone in the class was looking at him.

"You always tell such sad stories," Andrea said.

The bell rang. Mrs. English dismissed the class.

In the hallway, Andrea said to Zebra, "You know, you are a very gloomy life form."

"Andrea, get off my case," Zebra said.

English Learner Support
Vocabulary
Idiom *Get off my case* means "stop bothering me."

Pause & Reflect

READ ALOUD the boxed passage. What does Zebra's story tell you about his feelings? **(Infer)**

Pause & Reflect

---

5. **quavery** (kwā′vər-ē): quivering or trembling.

6. **encountered**: met unexpectedly.

FOCUS

Zebra meets John Wilson again. Read to find out what happens at their second meeting.

He went out to the schoolyard for the midafternoon recess. On the other side of the chain-link fence was the man in the dark-blue cap.

Zebra went over to him.

300 "Hello again, Adam," the man said. "I've been waiting for you."

"Hello," said Zebra.

"Thanks much for suggesting I talk to Mrs. English."

"You're welcome."

"Adam, you at all interested in art?"

"No."

"You ever try your hand at it?"

"I've made drawings for class. I don't like it."

"Well, just in case you change your mind, I'm giving

310 an art class in your school during the summer."

"I'm going to camp in August," Zebra said.

"There's the big long month of July."

"I don't think so," Zebra said.

"Well, okay, suit yourself. I'd like to give you something, a little thank-you gift."

He reached into an inside pocket and drew out a small pad and a pen. He placed the pad against the fence.

"Adam, you want to help me out a little bit here? Put your fingers through the fence and grab hold of

320 the pad."

Extending the fingers of his right hand, Zebra held the pad to the fence and watched as the man began to work with the pen. He felt the pad move slightly.

"I need you to hold it real still," the man said.

As the story continues . . .

- John Wilson waits for Zebra at recess.
- He asks Zebra if he likes art.
- Mr. Wilson draws something while Zebra holds the pad for him.

English Learner Support

Vocabulary

Idioms To *try your hand* at something is to try to do something you haven't done before. When John Wilson says *suit yourself,* he means that Zebra should do whatever Zebra wants to do. *Help me out* means the same as "help me."

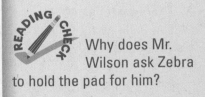

Why does Mr. Wilson ask Zebra to hold the pad for him?

Pause & Reflect

1. **▌MARK IT UP ▷** Reread the boxed passage. Circle the words or phrases that especially help you to imagine John Wilson as he is drawing. **(Visualize)**

2. Zebra is curious about John Wilson. Write one **question** you think Zebra might want to ask Mr. Wilson.

I want to know

_____

_____

_____

_____

_____

▷ **As the story continues . . .**

• John Wilson gives Zebra a special gift.

• Zebra tells Mr. Wilson about his nickname.

• As Zebra watches Mr. Wilson walk away, he has a strange feeling.

He was standing bent over, very close to Zebra. The words LAND ROVER on his cap shone in the afternoon sunlight. As he worked, he glanced often at Zebra. His tongue kept pushing up against the insides of his cheeks, making tiny hills rise and fall on his face.
330 Wrinkles formed <u>intricate</u> spidery webs in the skin below his gray eyes. On his smooth forehead, in the blue and purple shadows beneath the peak of his cap, lay glistening beads of sweat. And his hand—how dirty it was, the fingers and palm smudged with black ink and <u>encrusted</u> with colors.

Then Zebra glanced down and noticed the plastic bag near the man's feet. It lay partly open. Zebra was able to see a large pink armless doll, a dull metallic object that looked like a dented frying pan, old
340 newspapers, strings of cord, crumpled pieces of red and blue cloth, and the broken umbrella.

"One more minute is all I need," the man said.

Pause & Reflect

FOCUS

Read to find out about John Wilson's gift and how Zebra reacts to it.

▌MARK IT UP ▷ As you read, underline details that help you to understand Zebra's reaction.

He stepped back, looked at the pad, and nodded slowly. He put the pen back into his pocket and tore the top page from the pad. He rolled up the page and pushed it through the fence. Then he
350 took the pad from Zebra.

"See you around, Adam," the man said, picking up the plastic bag.

WORDS TO KNOW
intricate (ĭn'trĭ-kĭt) *adj.* arranged in a complex way
encrusted (ĕn-krŭst'əd) *adj.* covered with crusts

Zebra unrolled the sheet of paper and saw a line drawing, a perfect image of his face.

He was looking at himself as if in a mirror. His long straight nose and thin lips and sad eyes and gaunt face; his dark hair and smallish ears and the scar on his forehead where he had hurt himself years before while roller skating.

360 In the lower right-hand corner of the page the man had written: "To Adam, with thanks. John Wilson."

Zebra raised his eyes from the drawing. The man was walking away.

Zebra called out, "Mr. Wilson, all my friends call me Zebra."

The man turned, looking surprised.

"From my last name," Adam said. "Zebrin. Adam Martin Zebrin. They call me Zebra."

"Is that right?" the man said, starting back toward 370 the fence. "Well, in that case you want to give me back that piece of paper."

He took the pad and pen from his pocket, placed the page on the pad, and, with Zebra holding the pad to the fence, did something to the page and then handed it back.

"You take real good care of yourself, Zebra," the man said.

He went off toward Franklin Avenue.

Zebra looked at the drawing. The man had crossed 380 out Adam and over it had drawn an animal with a stubby neck and short legs and a striped body.

A zebra!

Its legs were in full gallop. It seemed as if it would gallop right off the page.

A strong breeze rippled across the drawing, causing it to flutter like a flag in Zebra's hand. He looked out at the street.

READ ALOUD the boxed passage. What do you think Zebra is feeling when he sees Mr. Wilson's drawing? (Infer)

READING CHECK Why was it important for Zebra to tell John Wilson about his nickname? How did Mr. Wilson respond?

Pause & Reflect

What does John Wilson add to his gift that makes it so special to Zebra? (Clarify)

As the story continues . . .

- The zebra in the drawing seems to move and change.
- At school Zebra sees a notice for Mr. Wilson's art class.
- Zebra learns where Mr. Wilson is from and how he was injured.

The man was walking slowly in the shadows of the tall oaks. Zebra had the odd sensation that all the
390 houses on the street had turned toward the man and were watching him as he walked along. How strange that was: the windows and porches and columns and front doors following intently the slow walk of that tall, one-armed man—until he turned into Franklin Avenue and was gone.

The whistle blew, and Zebra went inside. Seated at his desk, he slipped the drawing carefully into one of his notebooks.

From time to time he glanced at it.
400 Just before the bell signaled the end of the school day, he looked at it again.

Now *that* was strange!

He thought he remembered that the zebra had been drawn directly over his name: the head over the A and the tail over the M. Didn't it seem now to have moved a little beyond the A?

Probably he was running a fever again. He would run mysterious fevers off and on for about three weeks after each operation on his hand. Fevers sometimes did
410 that to him: excited his imagination.

Pause & Reflect

FOCUS

Zebra is stirred by John Wilson's drawing. Later, in school, he learns more about John Wilson.

MARK IT UP Underline questions Zebra asks and key words in the answers he receives.

He lived four blocks from the school. The school bus dropped him off at his corner. In his schoolbag he carried his books and the notebook with the drawing.

His mother offered him a snack, but he said he wasn't

hungry. Up in his room, he looked again at the
420 drawing and was astonished to discover that the zebra
had reached the edge of his name and appeared <u>poised</u>
to leap off.

It *had* to be a fever that was causing him to see the
zebra that way. And sure enough, when his mother
took his temperature, the thermometer registered
102.6 degrees.

She gave him his medicine, but it didn't seem to
have much effect, because when he woke at night and
switched on his desk light and peered at the drawing,
430 he saw the little zebra galloping across the page, along
the contours of his face, over the hills and valleys of
his eyes and nose and mouth, and he heard the tiny
clickings of its hooves as cloudlets of dust rose in its
wake.

He knew he was asleep. He knew it was the fever
working upon his imagination.

But it was so real.

The little zebra running . . .

When he woke in the morning the fever was gone,
440 and the zebra was quietly in its place over ADAM.

Later, as he entered the school, he noticed a large
sign on the bulletin board in the hallway:

SUMMER ART CLASS

The well-known American artist Mr. John Wilson
will conduct an art class during the summer for
students in 7th and 8th grades. For details, speak to
Mrs. English. There will be no tuition fee for this class.

During the morning, between classes, Zebra ran into
Mrs. English in the second-floor hallway.
450 "Mrs. English, about the summer art class . . . is it
okay to ask where—um—where Mr. Wilson is from?"

WORDS TO KNOW
poised (poizd) *adj.* balanced or held in suspension

 How does Zebra
know he still has
a fever in the middle of the
night? How does the fever
affect his imagination?

READING TIP Write down the
questions *who,
what, where,
when,* and *why.* Then answer
these questions with details
about the summer art class.

"He is from a small town in Virginia. Are you thinking of signing up for his class?"

"I can't draw," Zebra said.

"Drawing is something you can learn."

"Mrs. English, is it okay to ask how did Mr. Wilson—um—get hurt?"

The school corridors were always crowded between classes. Zebra and Mrs. English formed a little island in the bustling, student-jammed hallway.

"Mr. Wilson was wounded in the war in (Vietnam)," Mrs. English said. "I would urge you to join his class. You will get to use your imagination."

For the next hour, Zebra sat impatiently through Mr. Morgan's geography class, and afterward he went up to the teacher.

"Mr. Morgan, could I—um—ask where is Vietnam?"

Mr. Morgan smoothed down the jacket of his beige summer suit, touched his bow tie, rolled down a wall map, picked up his pointer, and cleared his throat.

"Vietnam is this long, narrow country in southeast Asia, bordered by China, Laos, and Cambodia. It is a land of valleys in the north, coastal plains in the center, and marshes in the south. There are barren mountains and tropical rain forests. Its chief crops are rice, rubber, fruits, and vegetables. The population numbers close to seventy million people. Between 1962 and 1973, America fought a terrible war there to prevent the south from falling into the hands of the communist north. We lost the war."

"Thank you."

"I am impressed by your suddenly awakened interest in geography, young man, though I must remind you that your class is studying the Mediterranean," said Mr. Morgan.

MORE ABOUT . . .

VIETNAM John Wilson is a war veteran, which means he served as a soldier during the Vietnam War. After they returned home, many veterans suffered from physical and emotional wounds.

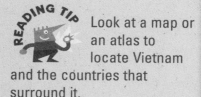

READING TIP Look at a map or an atlas to locate Vietnam and the countries that surround it.

During the afternoon recess, Zebra was watching a heated basketball game, when he looked across the yard and saw John Wilson walk by, carrying a laden[7] plastic bag. Some while later, he came back along the 490 street, empty-handed.

Pause & Reflect

FOCUS

Zebra learns more about John Wilson and signs up for the art class. Find out about his first day.

MARK IT UP Circle details that show how John Wilson teaches.

Over supper that evening, Zebra told his parents he was thinking of taking a summer art class offered by the school.

His father said, "Well, I think that's a fine idea."

"Wait a minute. I'm not so sure," his mother said.

"It'll get him off the streets," his father said. "He'll 500 become a Matisse[8] instead of a lawyer like his dad. Right, Adam?"

"Just you be very careful," his mother said to Adam. "Don't do anything that might injure your hand."

"How can drawing hurt his left hand, for heaven's sake?" said his father.

That night, Zebra lay in bed looking at his hand. It was a dread and a mystery to him, his own hand. The fingers were all there, but like dead leaves that never fell, the ring and little fingers were rigid and curled, 510 the others barely moved. The doctors said it would take time to bring them back to life. So many broken bones. So many torn muscles and tendons. So many injured nerves. The dark shadow had sprung upon him so suddenly. How stupid, stupid, *stupid* he had been!

---

7. **laden** (lād'n): heavy, hard to carry.

8. **Matisse** (mə-tēs') (1869–1954): a French painter who was one of the most well-known artists of the 20th century.

Pause & Reflect

How did John Wilson get hurt? (Clarify)

_____

_____

_____

As the story continues...

• Zebra signs up for Mr. Wilson's art class.

• Zebra learns from Mrs. English what Mr. Wilson did during the Vietnam War.

English Learner Support
Language

Simile The blue text is a *simile*—it compares two things using the word *like* or *as.* Zebra's fingers are compared to dead leaves that remain on a tree branch.

He couldn't sleep. He went over to his desk and looked at John Wilson's drawing. The galloping little zebra stood very still over ADAM.

Early the following afternoon, on the last day of school, Zebra went to Mrs. English's office and signed 520 up for John Wilson's summer art class.

"The class will meet every weekday from ten in the morning until one," said Mrs. English. "Starting Monday."

Zebra noticed the three plastic bags in a corner of the office.

"Mrs. English, is it okay to ask what Mr. Wilson—um—did in Vietnam?"

"He told me he was a helicopter pilot," Mrs. English said. "Oh, I neglected to mention that you are 530 to bring an unlined notebook and a pencil to the class."

"That's all? A notebook and a pencil?"

Mrs. English smiled. "And your imagination."

When Zebra entered the art class the next Monday morning, he found about fifteen students there—including Andrea from his class with Mrs. English.

The walls of the room were bare. Everything had been removed for the summer. Zebra noticed two plastic bags on the floor beneath the blackboard.

He sat down at the desk next to Andrea's.

540 She wore blue jeans and a yellow summer blouse with blue stripes. Her long red hair was tied behind her head with a dark-blue ribbon. She gazed at Zebra through her thick glasses, leaned over, and said, "Are you going to make gloomy drawings, too?"

Just then John Wilson walked in, carrying a plastic bag, which he put down on the floor next to the two others.

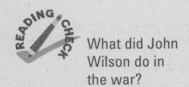

What did John Wilson do in the war?

He stood alongside the front desk, wearing a light-blue long-sleeved shirt and jeans. The left shirtsleeve
550 had been folded back and pinned to the shirt. The dark-blue cap with the words LAND ROVER sat <u>jauntily</u> on his head.

"Good morning to you-all," he said, with a shy smile. "Mighty glad you're here. We're going to do two things this summer. We're going to make paper into faces and garbage into people. I can see by your expressions that you don't know what I'm talking about, right? Well, I'm about to show you."

He asked everyone to draw the face of someone
560 sitting nearby.

Zebra hesitated, looked around, then made a drawing of Andrea. Andrea carefully drew Zebra.

He showed Andrea his drawing.

"It's awful." She grimaced. "I look like a mouse."

Her drawing of him was good. But was his face really so sad?

John Wilson went from desk to desk, peering intently at the drawings. He paused a long moment over Zebra's drawing. Then he spent more than an
570 hour demonstrating with chalk on the blackboard how they should not be thinking *eyes* or *lips* or *hands* while drawing, but should think only *lines* and *curves* and *shapes;* how they should be looking at where everything was situated in relation to the edge of the paper; and how they should not be looking *directly* at the edges of what they were drawing but at the space *outside* the edges.

Zebra stared in wonder at how fast John Wilson's hand raced across the blackboard, and at the empty
580 sleeve rising and falling lightly against the shirt.

WORDS TO KNOW
jauntily (jôn'tĭ-lē) *adv.* in a light and carefree way

READ ALOUD the boxed passage. What do you think John Wilson means? **(Infer)**

_____

_____

_____

As the story continues . . .

- John Wilson shows the students how to use garbage to create sculpture.

- Something exciting happens while Zebra works on an art project at home.

READING CHECK What does Mr. Wilson collect in his plastic bags? Why does he collect these things?

English Learner Support
Vocabulary

Idiom _Applause_ is when a group of people clap their hands to indicate approval or excitement. When Zebra's class "bursts into applause," they begin clapping to show that they like John Wilson's sculpture.

"You-all are going to learn how to _see_ in a new way," John Wilson said.

They made another drawing of the same face.

"Now I look like a horse," Andrea said. "Are you going to add stripes?"

"You are one big pain, Andrea," Zebra said.

Pause & Reflect

FOCUS

Read to find out about the art projects Zebra does.

MARK IT UP > Circle the details that tell you about these projects.

Shortly before noon, John Wilson laid out on his desk the contents of the plastic bags: a clutter of junked broken objects, including the doll and the umbrella.

Using strips of cloth, some lengths of string, crumpled newspaper, his pen, and his one hand, he swiftly transformed the battered doll into a red-nosed, umbrella-carrying clown, with baggy pants, a tattered coat, a derby hat, and a somber smile. Turning over the battered frying pan, he made it into a pedestal, on which he placed the clown.

"That's a sculpture," John Wilson said, with his shy smile. "Garbage into people."

The class burst into applause. The clown on the frying pan looked as if it might take a bow.

"You-all will be doing that, too, before we're done," John Wilson said. "Now I would like you to sign and date your drawings and give them to me."

When they returned the next morning the drawings were on a wall.

Gradually, in the days that followed, the walls began
610 to fill with drawings. Sculptures made by the students
were looked at with care, discussed by John Wilson
and the class, and then placed on shelves along the
walls: a miniature bicycle made of wire; a parrot made
of an old sofa cushion; a cowboy made of rope and
string; a fat lady made of a dented metal pitcher; a
zebra made of glued-together scraps of cardboard.

"I like your zebra," Andrea said.

"Thanks," Zebra said. "I like your parrot."

One morning John Wilson asked the class members to
620 make a contour drawing of their right or left hand.
Zebra felt himself sweating and trembling as he worked.

"That's real nice," John Wilson said, when he saw
Andrea's drawing.

He gazed at the drawing made by Zebra.

"You-all were looking at your hand," he said. "You
ought to have been looking at the edge of your hand
and at the space outside."

Zebra drew his hand again. Strange and ugly, the
two fingers lay rigid and curled. But astonishingly, it
630 looked like a hand this time.

One day, a few minutes before the end of class, John
Wilson gave everyone an assignment: draw or make
something at home, something very special that each
person *felt deeply* about. And bring it to class.

Zebra remembered seeing a book titled *Incredible
Cross-Sections* on a shelf in the family room at home.
He found the book and took it into his room.

There was a color drawing of a rescue helicopter on
one of the Contents pages. On pages 30 and 31, the
640 helicopter was shown in pieces, its complicated insides
displayed in detailed drawings. Rotor blades, control
rods, electronics equipment, radar scanner, tail rotor,
engine, lifeline, winch—all its many parts.

REREAD the boxed
passage. How is
Zebra learning to
see in a new way? **(Infer)**

WHAT DOES IT MEAN?
Astonishingly means "in a
way that makes people feel
amazed or very surprised."

Zebra sat at his desk, gazing intently at the space outside the edges of the helicopter on the Contents page.

He made an outline drawing and brought it to class the next morning.

John Wilson looked at it. Was there a stiffening of
650 his muscular neck, a sudden <u>tensing</u> of the hand that held the drawing?

He took the drawing and tacked it to the wall.

The next day he gave them all the same home assignment: draw or make something they *felt very deeply* about.

That afternoon, Zebra went rummaging through the trash bin in his kitchen and the garbage cans that stood near the back door of his home. He found some sardine cans, a broken eggbeater, pieces of cardboard, chipped
660 buttons, bent bobby pins, and other odds and ends.

With the help of epoxy glue, he began to make of those bits of garbage a kind of helicopter. For support, he used his desktop, the floor, his knees, the elbow of his left arm, at one point even his chin. Struggling with the last piece—a button he wanted to position as a wheel—he realized that without thinking he had been using his left hand, and the two curled fingers had straightened slightly to his needs.

His heart beat thunderously. There had been so
670 many hope-filled moments before, all of them ending in bitter disappointment. He would say nothing. Let the therapist or the doctors tell him. . . .

The following morning, he brought the helicopter to the class.

"Eeewwww, what is *that*?" Andrea grimaced.

"Something to eat you with," Zebra said.

WORDS TO KNOW
tensing (těns'ĭng) *n.* a tightening or becoming taut **tense** *v.*

"Get human, Zebra. Mr. Wilson will have a laughing fit over that."

But John Wilson didn't laugh. He held the helicopter
680 in his hand a long moment, turning it this way and that, nodded at Zebra, and placed it on a windowsill, where it shimmered in the summer sunlight.

Pause & Reflect

Pause & Reflect

Why do you think Zebra makes a helicopter? (Infer)

FOCUS

Zebra gives his teacher something to remember him by. Read to find out what it is.

The next day, John Wilson informed everyone that three students would be leaving the class at the end of July. He asked each of those students to make a drawing for him that he would get to keep. Something to remember them by. All their other
690 drawings and sculptures they could take home.

Zebra lay awake a long time that night, staring into the darkness of his room. He could think of nothing to draw for John Wilson.

In the morning, he sat gazing out the classroom window at the sky and at the helicopter on the sill.

"What are you going to draw for him?" Andrea asked.
Zebra shrugged and said he didn't know.
"Use your imagination," she said. Then she said, "Wait, what am I seeing here? Are you able to move
700 those fingers?"
"I think so."
"You *think* so?"
"The doctors said there was some improvement."
Her eyes glistened behind the thick lenses. She seemed genuinely happy.

As the story continues . . .

• The art class will be ending soon for Zebra.

• Mr. Wilson asks Zebra to make him a special drawing.

 READ ALOUD the boxed passage. How has Zebra's relationship with Andrea changed during the art class? (Compare and Contrast)

He sat looking out the window. Dark birds wheeled and soared. There was the sound of traffic. The helicopter sat on the windowsill, its eggbeater rotor blades ready to move to full throttle.

710   Later that day, Zebra sat at his desk at home, working on a drawing. He held the large sheet of paper in place by pressing down on it with the palm and fingers of his left hand. He drew a landscape: hills and valleys, forests and flatlands, rivers and plateaus. Oddly, it all seemed to resemble a face.

Racing together over that landscape were a helicopter and a zebra.

It was all he could think to draw. It was not a very good drawing. He signed it: "To JOHN WILSON, with
720 thanks. Zebra."

The next morning, John Wilson looked at the drawing and asked Zebra to write on top of the name "John Wilson" the name "Leon."

"He was an old buddy of mine, an artist. We were in Vietnam together. Would've been a much better artist than I'll ever be."

Zebra wrote in the new name.

"Thank you kindly," John Wilson said, taking the drawing. "Zebra, you have yourself a good time in
730 camp and a good life. It was real nice knowing you."

He shook Zebra's hand. How strong his fingers felt!

"I think I'm going to miss you a little," Andrea said to Zebra after the class.

"I'll only be away a month."

"Can I help you carry some of those drawings?"

"Sure. I'll carry the helicopter."

Pause & Reflect

1. [MARK IT UP] Underline the significant details of the drawing that Zebra gives to John Wilson. Why do you think Zebra draws a helicopter and a zebra racing together? (Infer)

2. John Wilson tells Zebra to write the name "Leon" on his drawing. Why is this name important to John Wilson? (Infer)

FOCUS

Zebra goes to camp and then begins school again. One day, John Wilson sends him a package.

⫼ MARK IT UP ❯ As you read, underline details that tell you about John Wilson's gift and Zebra's reaction.

Zebra went off to a camp in the Adirondack Mountains. He hiked and read and 740 watched others playing ball. In the arts and crafts program he made some good drawings and even got to learn a little bit about watercolors. He put together clowns and airplanes and helicopters out of discarded cardboard and wood and clothing. From time to time his hand hurt, but the fingers seemed slowly to be coming back to life.

750 "Patience, young man," the doctors told him when he returned to the city. "You're getting there."

One or two additional operations were still necessary. But there was no urgency. And he no longer needed the leg brace.

On the first day of school, one of the secretaries found him in the hallway and told him to report to Mrs. English.

"Did you have a good summer?" Mrs. English asked.

760 "It was okay," Zebra said.

"This came for you in the mail."

She handed him a large brown envelope. It was addressed to Adam Zebrin, Eighth Grade, at the school. The sender was John Wilson, with a return address in Virginia.

"Adam, I admit I'm very curious to see what's inside," Mrs. English said.

She helped Zebra open the envelope.

🗎 As the story ends . . .

• Zebra's hand and body start to heal.

• When school starts again, Zebra receives a package from John Wilson.

• Zebra thinks about Mr. Wilson and about how his life has changed because of him.

English Learner Support

Culture

Camp Many young people spend their summer vacations at camp. Zebra's camp is away from the city, where he can hike and do other outdoor activities.

READING TIP Continue to use a map or an atlas to locate places mentioned in the story. For example, find the Adirondack Mountains and Virginia.

Between two pieces of cardboard were a letter and a large color photograph.

The photograph showed John Wilson down on his right knee before a glistening dark wall. He wore his army jacket and blue jeans and boots, and the cap with the words LAND ROVER. Leaning against the wall to his right was Zebra's drawing of the helicopter and the zebra racing together across a facelike landscape. The drawing was enclosed in a narrow frame.

The wall behind John Wilson seemed to glitter with a strange black light.

Zebra read the letter and showed it to Mrs. English.

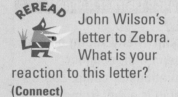

Dear Zebra,

One of the people whose names are on this wall was among my very closest friends. He was an artist named Leon Kellner. Each year I visit him and leave a gift—something very special that someone creates and gives me. I leave it near his name for a few hours, and then I take it to my studio in Virginia, where I keep a collection of those gifts. All year long I work in my studio, but come summer I go looking for another gift to give him.

Thank you for your gift.

Your friend,

John Wilson

P.S. I hope your hand is healing.

Mrs. English stood staring awhile at the letter. She turned away and touched her eyes. Then she went to a shelf on the wall behind her, took down a large book, leafed through it quickly, found what she was searching for, and held it out for Zebra to see.

800   Zebra found himself looking at the glistening black wall of the (Vietnam Memorial) in Washington, D.C. And at the names on it, the thousands of names. . . .

> Later, in the schoolyard during recess, Zebra stood alone at the chain-link fence and gazed down the street toward Franklin Avenue. He thought how strange it was that all the houses on this street had seemed to turn toward John Wilson that day, the windows and porches and columns and doors, as if saluting him.
>
> Had that been only his imagination?

810   Maybe, Zebra thought, just maybe he could go for a walk to Franklin Avenue on Saturday or Sunday. He had not walked along Franklin Avenue since the accident; had not gone down that steep hill. Yes, he would walk carefully down that hill to the corner and walk back up and past the school and then the four blocks home.

Andrea came over to him.

"We didn't get picked for the story class with Mrs. English," she said. "I won't have to listen to any more of your gloomy stories."

820   Zebra said nothing.

"You know, I think I'll walk home today instead of taking the school bus," Andrea said.

"Actually, I think I'll walk, too," Zebra said. "I was thinking maybe I could pick up some really neat stuff in the street."

"You are becoming a pleasant life form," Andrea said. ❖

Pause & Reflect

MORE ABOUT . . .

(VIETNAM MEMORIAL) A war memorial was built in Washington, D.C., to honor the soldiers who served in the Vietnam War. The wall is made of shiny, black granite and is shaped like a *V*. It is carved with the names of the 58,000 American soldiers killed or missing in action during the war. Many people visit the wall to pay their respects and to remember their friends and loved ones.

Pause & Reflect

 READ ALOUD the boxed passage. What does it tell you about how Zebra feels about his friend? (Infer)

 CHALLENGE John Wilson tells his students, "You-all are going to learn how to see in a new way." By the end of the story, what does Zebra see in a new way? Mark passages in the story that support your ideas. (Analyze)

NOTES

MARK IT UP If you were a student in John Wilson's class, how would you respond to his assignment about making something that you "felt deeply" about? Sketch a drawing, painting, or sculpture you would bring to class. **(Connect)**

Active Reading SkillBuilder

Making Inferences

Making an **inference** is reading between the lines or making a logical conclusion based on information and common sense. You make inferences all the time, not just in reading. When reading, you usually infer by combining the details from the text with what you know from your experiences. You can make inferences about plots, settings, and characters. Use the graphic organizer below to help you make inferences about the events and characters in "Zebra."

Character or Event:	
Zebra's accident	

Details from Story:	**My Experiences:**
When he was running, Zebra saw a "huge rushing shadow" crashing into him.	"Huge rushing shadows" are usually made by oncoming cars.

What I can infer:
Zebra was hit by a car.

Character or Event:	

Details from Story:	**My Experiences:**

What I can infer:

Literary Analysis SkillBuilder

Character

People, animals, and imaginary creatures that take part in the action of a story are called **characters.** Short stories usually focus on one or two main characters. They act in such a way that readers can understand their traits and motives. **Traits** are qualities of a character's personality, like cheerfulness or bravery. **Motives** are the emotions, wants, or needs that cause a character to act or react in a certain way. Use the graphic organizer below to describe one of the main characters from the story.

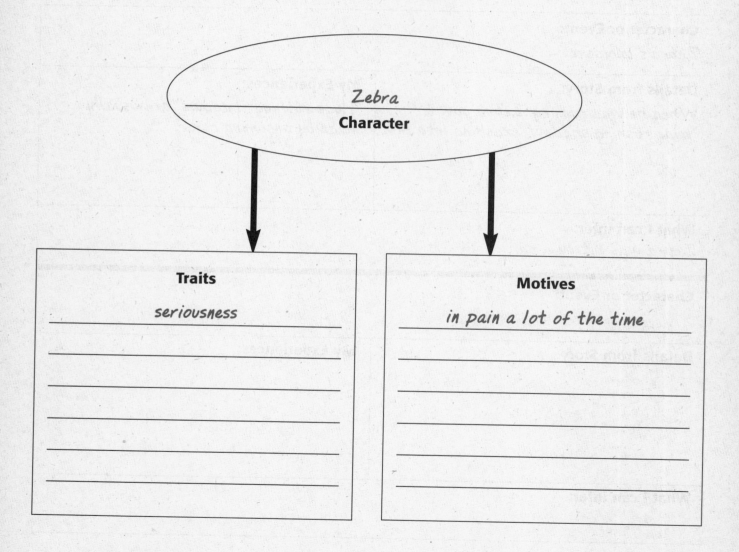

Zebra

Character

Traits

seriousness

Motives

in pain a lot of the time

Words to Know SkillBuilder

Words to Know

disciplinarian	exuberantly	intricate	menacing	tensing
encrusted	gaunt	jauntily	poised	wince

A. Fill in the blanks below with the Word to Know that best completes the sentence.

1. With a great burst of energy, Zebra loved to run _____ around his neighborhood.

2. After his accident, when his hand and leg were hurting him, Zebra would _____ with pain.

3. When John Wilson made a drawing of him, Zebra saw that his face looked thin and _____.

4. Doctor Winter, Zebra's principal, was a strict _____.

5. As John Wilson drew, Zebra watched the wrinkles in his face form _____ designs like long spider webs.

B. Fill in each set of blanks with a word from the list.

1. If you like to sculpt with clay, your hands might be in this condition. — — — — — — — — —

2. This is the way you might walk when you are feeling casual and carefree about life. — — — — — — — —

3. This word describes a person who looks scary. — — — — — — — —

4. You are ready at the starting line, but the race has not yet begun. — — — — — —

5. When you exercise, you go back and forth between relaxing your muscles and doing this to them. — — — — — — —

Before You Read

Connect to Your Life

What dreams do you have for your community, your nation, or the world? List one important dream. As you read, see if any of your dreams were shared by Eleanor Roosevelt.

My dream for a better world is . . .

Key to the Biography

WHAT'S THE BIG IDEA? Eleanor Roosevelt was the wife of Franklin Delano Roosevelt, the 32nd president of the United States. She was also one of the most famous women of the 20th century. She had many roles. Use the Preview on page 71 to list roles in the web. After you finish the biography, you may add more.

Eleanor Roosevelt

wife of a president

Eleanor Roosevelt

by William Jay Jacobs

PREVIEW Eleanor Roosevelt was much more than the wife of a president. Her life spanned a period of dramatic changes in the United States and the world. As First Lady, Eleanor Roosevelt struggled to end poverty and racism in the United States. As first American Ambassador to the United Nations, she had a central role in writing the Declaration of Human Rights.

- The narrator tells about Eleanor's childhood and family background.
- Eleanor has many fears.

English Learner Support
Culture

Fairy Tale The term *ugly duckling* refers to a plain or unattractive child. It comes from a famous fairy tale written by the Danish author Hans Christian Anderson. In this tale, a family of ducks includes one duckling that is different from the others. The young bird surprises everyone by growing up to be a beautiful swan.

MARK IT UP > **KEEP TRACK**
Remember to use these marks to keep track of your reading:

- ✱ This is important.
- ? I have a question about this.
- ! This is a surprise.

FOCUS

In this part you will read about Eleanor Roosevelt as a child.

MARK IT UP > As you read, circle details that tell she was unhappy. An example is highlighted.

Eleanor Roosevelt was the wife of President Franklin Delano Roosevelt. But Eleanor was much more than just a president's wife, an echo of her husband's career. Sad and lonely as a child, Eleanor was called "Granny" by her mother because of her seriousness. People
10 teased her about her looks and called her the "ugly duckling.". . .

Yet despite all of the disappointments, the bitterness, the misery she experienced, Eleanor Roosevelt refused to give up. Instead she turned her unhappiness and pain to strength. She devoted her life to helping others. Today she is remembered as one of America's greatest women.

Eleanor was born in a fine townhouse in Manhattan. Her family also owned an elegant mansion
20 along the Hudson River, where they spent weekends and summers. As a child Eleanor went to fashionable parties. A servant took care of her and taught her to speak French. Her mother, the beautiful Anna Hall Roosevelt, wore magnificent jewels and fine clothing. Her father, Elliott Roosevelt, had his own hunting lodge and liked to sail and to play tennis and polo. Elliott, who loved Eleanor dearly, was the younger brother of Theodore Roosevelt, who in 1901 became president of the United States. The Roosevelt family,
30 one of America's oldest, wealthiest families, was respected and admired.

To the outside world it might have seemed that Eleanor had everything that any child could want— everything that could make her happy. But she was not happy. Instead her childhood was very sad.

Almost from the day of her birth, October 11, 1884, people noticed that she was an unattractive child. As she grew older, she could not help but notice her mother's extraordinary beauty, as well as the beauty of her aunts and cousins. Eleanor was plain looking, ordinary, even, as some called her, homely. For a time she had to wear a bulky brace on her back to straighten her crooked spine.

When Eleanor was born, her parents had wanted a boy. They were scarcely able to hide their disappointment. Later, with the arrival of two boys, Elliott and Hall, Eleanor watched her mother hold the boys on her lap and lovingly stroke their hair, while for Eleanor there seemed only coolness, distance.

Feeling unwanted, Eleanor became shy and withdrawn.[1] She also developed many fears. She was afraid of the dark, afraid of animals, afraid of other children, afraid of being scolded, afraid of strangers, afraid that people would not like her. She was a frightened, lonely little girl.

Pause & Reflect

FOCUS

Eleanor Roosevelt's parents died while she was young. Read to find out what happened to her after their deaths.

MARK IT UP As you read, circle **details** that help you understand what Roosevelt's life with her grandmother was like.

The one joy in the early years of her life was her father, who always seemed to care for her, love her. He used to dance with her, to pick her up and throw her into the air while she laughed and laughed. He called her "little golden hair" or "darling little Nell."

---

1. **withdrawn:** detached from others, solitary, isolated.

Pause & Reflect

1. Circle the words below that describe Eleanor Roosevelt. **(Clarify)**

   outgoing   lonely
   cheerful   playful
   serious   afraid

2. What kind of family did Eleanor Roosevelt come from? Write three words or phrases that describe her family. **(Clarify)**

As the biography continues . . .

• As a child, Eleanor experiences great loss.

• She is sent to live with her grandmother.

• Eleanor is often neglected.

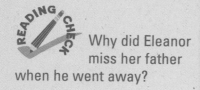
READING TIP This biography is written in chronological order, the order in which events happen. Words such as *before, during, after, first, next, while,* and *later* show the order of events. As you read, create a chart like the one below to keep track of the chronological order of key events in Eleanor Roosevelt's life.

Event 1
Event 2
Event 3
Event 4
Event 5
Event 6

Then, when she was six, her father left. An alcoholic, he went to live in a sanitarium[2] in Virginia in an attempt to deal with his drinking problem. Eleanor missed him greatly.

70 Next her mother became ill with painful headaches. Sometimes for hours at a time Eleanor would sit holding her mother's head in her lap and stroking her forehead. Nothing else seemed to relieve the pain. At those times Eleanor often remembered how her mother had teased her about her looks and called her "Granny." But even at the age of seven Eleanor was glad to be helping someone, glad to be needed—and noticed.

The next year, when Eleanor was eight, her mother, 80 the beautiful Anna, died. Afterward her brother Elliott suddenly caught diphtheria[3] and he, too, died. Eleanor and her baby brother, Hall, were taken to live with their grandmother in Manhattan.

A few months later another tragedy struck. Elliott Roosevelt, Eleanor's father, also died. Within eighteen months Eleanor had lost her mother, a brother, and her dear father.

For the rest of her life Eleanor carried with her the letters that her father had written to her from the 90 sanitarium. In them he had told her to be brave, to become well educated, and to grow up into a woman he could be proud of, a woman who helped people who were suffering.

Only ten years old when her father died, Eleanor decided even then to live the kind of life he had described—a life that would have made him proud of her.

Few things in life came easily for Eleanor, but the first few years after her father's death proved

---

2. **sanitarium** (săn′ĭ-târ′ē-əm): an institution for the care of people with a specific disease or other health problem.

3. **diphtheria** (dĭf-thîr′ē-ə): a serious infectious disease.

100 exceptionally hard. Grandmother Hall's dark and gloomy townhouse had no place for children to play. The family ate meals in silence. Every morning Eleanor and Hall were expected to take cold baths for their health. Eleanor had to work at better posture by walking with her arms behind her back, clamped over a walking stick.

Instead of making new friends, Eleanor often sat alone in her room and read. For many months after her father's death she pretended that he was still alive.
110 She made him the hero of stories she wrote for school. Sometimes, alone and unhappy, she just cried.

Some of her few moments of happiness came from visiting her uncle, Theodore Roosevelt, in Oyster Bay, Long Island. A visit with Uncle Ted meant playing games and romping outdoors with the many Roosevelt children.

Once Uncle Ted threw her into the water to teach her how to swim, but when she started to sink, he had to rescue her. Often he would read to the children old
120 Norse tales and poetry. It was at Sagamore Hill, Uncle Ted's home, that Eleanor first learned how much fun it could be to read books aloud.

For most of the time Eleanor's life was grim. Although her parents had left plenty of money for her upbringing, she had only two dresses to wear to school. Once she spilled ink on one of them, and since the other was in the wash, she had to wear the dress with large ink stains on it to school the next day. It was not that Grandmother Hall was stingy. Rather,
130 she was old and often confused. Nor did she show much warmth or love for Eleanor and her brother. Usually she just neglected them.

Pause & Reflect

REREAD the boxed passage. Why was Grandmother Hall's house such a difficult place for a child to live? (Summarize)

Pause & Reflect

1. MARK IT UP Star details on this page about Eleanor's grandmother. What kind of person was she? (Evaluate)

2. **REREAD** the boxed text on page 74. What three things did Eleanor's father ask her to do in life? (Clarify)

- Eleanor goes away to boarding school.
- At school, she develops healthy and athletic habits and makes new friends.
- She returns to her grandmother's home.

MORE ABOUT . . .

BOARDING SCHOOL Children who go to boarding school live at the school while they attend classes. Some students return home for weekends, but most live for months away from home.

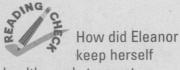

READING CHECK How did Eleanor keep herself healthy and strong at Allenswood?

English Learner Support

Vocabulary

Mademoiselle In the French language, this is a way to address an unmarried woman.

French ➞ Mademoiselle

English ➞ Ms. or Miss

FOCUS

After her fifteenth birthday, Roosevelt's life changed again. Read to find out how.

MARK IT UP > As you read, circle details that help you understand how Eleanor changes.

Just before Eleanor turned fifteen, Grandmother Hall decided to send her to boarding school in England. The school she chose was Allenswood, a private academy for girls located on 140 the outskirts of London.

It was at Allenswood that Eleanor, still thinking of herself as an "ugly duckling," first dared to believe that one day she might be able to become a swan.

At Allenswood she worked to toughen herself physically. Every day she did exercises in the morning and took a cold shower. Although she did not like competitive team sports, as a matter of self-discipline she tried out for field hockey. Not only did she make 150 the team but, because she played so hard, also won the respect of her teammates.

They called her by her family nickname, "Totty," and showed their affection for her by putting books and flowers in her room, as was the custom at Allenswood. Never before had she experienced the pleasure of having schoolmates actually admire her rather than tease her.

At Allenswood, too, she began to look after her health. She finally broke the habit of chewing her 160 fingernails. She learned to eat nutritious foods, to get plenty of sleep, and to take a brisk walk every morning, no matter how miserable the weather.

Under the guidance of the school's headmistress, Mademoiselle Souvestre (or "Sou"), she learned to ask searching questions and think for herself instead of just giving back on tests what teachers had said.

She also learned to speak French fluently, a skill she polished by traveling in France, living for a time with

a French family. Mademoiselle Souvestre arranged for
170 her to have a new red dress. Wearing it, after all of the
old, worn dresses Grandmother Hall had given her,
made her feel very proud.

Eleanor was growing up, and the joy of young
womanhood had begun to transform her personality.

In 1902, nearly eighteen years old, she left
Allenswood, not returning for her fourth year there.
Grandmother Hall insisted that, instead, she must be
introduced to society as a debutante—to go to dances
and parties and begin to take her place in the social
180 world with other wealthy young women.

Away from Allenswood, Eleanor's old uncertainty
about her looks came back again. She saw herself as too
tall, too thin, too plain. She worried about her buckteeth,
which she thought made her look horselike. The old
teasing began again, especially on the part of Uncle Ted's
daughter, "Princess" Alice Roosevelt, who seemed to take
pleasure in making Eleanor feel uncomfortable.

Eleanor, as always, did as she was told. She went to
all of the parties and dances. But she also began
190 working with poor children at the Rivington Street
Settlement House[4] on New York's Lower East Side.
She taught the girls gymnastic exercises. She took
children to museums and to musical performances. She
tried to get the parents interested in politics in order to
get better schools and cleaner, safer streets.

Pause & Reflect

. 4. **settlement house:** In the late 19th and early 20th century, settlement houses
provided services such as education, recreation, and health care to poor urban
neighborhoods such as New York's Lower East Side.

English Learner Support
Vocabulary

Word Origins The words
debutante and *debut* are
both from the French word
débuter, "to begin." All of
these words have related
meanings.
débuter (French)—to begin
debut (English)—the
beginning of something
debutante (English)—a
young woman beginning
her life in adult society

Pause & Reflect

1. **MARK IT UP** Review
the ways that Roosevelt
changed during her stay at
Allenswood. Star the one
that you think is most
important. (**Evaluate**)

2. **REREAD** the boxed
passage. What
do you learn
about Roosevelt's character
from this paragraph? (**Draw
Conclusions**)

She was obedient, but she

She was wealthy, but she

As the biography continues . . .

- Eleanor marries Franklin Delano Roosevelt.
- The couple start a family.
- Eleanor has problems with her mother-in-law and her husband.

English Learner Support
Culture

Marriage Customs To "give the bride away" is a custom in which a close relative or friend from the bride's family presents her to the groom. It is a way of saying, "We trust you with our loved one."

English Learner Support
Language

Figurative Language The highlighted passage has a figurative meaning—it means something different than the actual meanings of the words. Theodore Roosevelt was not really a bride or a corpse, but he wanted to be the center of attention wherever he went.

FOCUS

In this part Eleanor marries and has children. Read to learn about some of her problems as a young, married woman.

Meanwhile Eleanor's life reached a turning point. She fell in love! The young man was her fifth cousin, Franklin
200 Delano Roosevelt.

Eleanor and Franklin had known each other since childhood. Franklin recalled how once he had carried her piggyback in the nursery. When she was fourteen, he had danced with her at a party. Then, shortly after her return from Allenswood, they had met by chance on a train. They talked and almost at once realized how much they liked each other.

For a time they met secretly. Then they attended
210 parties together. Franklin—tall, strong, handsome— saw her as a person he could trust. He knew that she would not try to dominate him.

But did he really love her? Would he always? She wrote to him, quoting a poem she knew: "Unless you can swear, *'For life, for death!'* . . . Oh, never call it loving!"

Franklin promised that his love was indeed "for life," and Eleanor agreed to marry him. It was the autumn of 1903. He was twenty-one. She was nineteen.

On March 17, 1905, Eleanor and Franklin were
220 married. "Uncle Ted," by then president of the United States, was there to "give the bride away." It was sometimes said that the dynamic, energetic Theodore Roosevelt had to be "the bride at every wedding and the corpse at every funeral." And it was certainly true that day. Wherever the president went, the guests followed at his heels.

Before long Eleanor and Franklin found themselves standing all alone, deserted. Franklin seemed annoyed, but Eleanor didn't mind. She had found the ceremony
230 deeply moving. And she stood next to her husband in

a glow of idealism[5]—very serious, very grave, very much in love.

In May 1906 the couple's first child was born. During the next nine years Eleanor gave birth to five more babies, one of whom died in infancy. Still timid, shy, afraid of making mistakes, she found herself so busy that there was little time to think of her own drawbacks.

Still, looking back later on the early years of her marriage, Eleanor knew that she should have been a
240 stronger person, especially in the handling of Franklin's mother, or, as they both called her, "Mammá." Too often Mammá made the decisions about such things as where they would live, how their home would be furnished, how the children would be disciplined. Eleanor and Franklin let her pay for things they could not afford—extra servants, vacations, doctor bills, clothing. She offered, and they accepted.

Before long, trouble developed in the relationship between Eleanor and Franklin. Serious, shy, easily
250 embarrassed, Eleanor could not share Franklin's interests in golf and tennis. He enjoyed light talk and flirting with women. She could not be lighthearted. So she stayed on the sidelines. Instead of losing her temper, she bottled up her anger and did not talk to him at all. As he used to say, she "clammed up." Her silence only made things worse, because it puzzled him. Faced with her coldness, her <u>brooding</u> silence, he only grew angrier and more distant.

Pause & Reflect

How did Eleanor feel about making mistakes?

Pause & Reflect

1. Write an *E* beside the words below that describe Eleanor Roosevelt, and an *F* beside those that describe Franklin. **(Clarify)**

    __ energetic   __ outgoing
    __ serious   __ carefree
    __ timid   __ athletic
    __ shy   __ brooding

2. **| MARK IT UP >** What problems did Eleanor Roosevelt have with her mother-in-law? Circle the sentence on this page that contains the answer. **(Clarify)**

---

5. **idealism** (ī-dē′ə-lĭz′əm): the practice of forming ideals, or models to be imitated, and living under their influence.

WORDS TO KNOW
brooding (broo′dĭng) *adj.* full of worry; troubled **brood** *v.*

READING TIP The years between 1905 and 1921 were busy ones for the Roosevelts. Make a time line like the one below to record the major events that took place during those years.

Franklin and Eleanor marry.

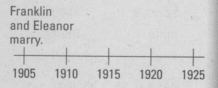

1905   1910   1915   1920   1925

MORE ABOUT . . .

(POLIO) Polio is caused by a viral infection. It can cause paralysis, or the inability to move part of one's body. Polio was widespread in the first half of the 20th century. By 1955, a strong vaccine was developed that eliminated the disease almost completely.

FOCUS
A disaster threatens Franklin's political career.

MARK IT UP Circle details that tell you about the disaster and Eleanor's response to it.

Meanwhile Franklin's career 260 in politics advanced rapidly. In 1910 he was elected to the New York State Senate. In 1913 President Wilson appointed him Assistant Secretary of the Navy—a powerful position in the national government, which required the Roosevelts to move to Washington, D.C.

In 1917 the United States entered World War I as an 270 active <u>combatant</u>. Like many socially <u>prominent</u> women, Eleanor threw herself into the war effort. Sometimes she worked fifteen and sixteen hours a day. She made sandwiches for soldiers passing through the nation's capital. She knitted sweaters. She used Franklin's influence to get the Red Cross to build a recreation room for soldiers who had been shell-shocked in combat. . . .

In 1920 the Democratic Party chose Franklin as its candidate for vice president of the United States. Even 280 though the Republicans won the election, Roosevelt became a well-known figure in national politics. All the time, Eleanor stood by his side, smiling, doing what was expected of her as a candidate's wife.

She did what was expected—and much more—in the summer of 1921 when disaster struck the Roosevelt family. While on vacation Franklin suddenly fell ill with infantile paralysis—polio—the horrible disease that each year used to kill or cripple thousands of children, and many adults as well. When Franklin 290 became a victim of polio, nobody knew what caused the disease or how to cure it.

WORDS TO KNOW
combatant (kəm-băt'nt) *n.* fighter
prominent (prŏm'ə-nənt) *adj.* well-known; widely recognized

Franklin lived, but the lower part of his body remained paralyzed. For the rest of his life he never again had the use of his legs. He had to be lifted and carried from place to place. He had to wear heavy steel braces from his waist to the heels of his shoes.

His mother, as well as many of his advisers, urged him to give up politics, to live the life of a country gentleman on the Roosevelt estate at Hyde Park, New 300 York. This time, Eleanor, calm and strong, stood up for her ideas. She argued that he should not be treated like a sick person, tucked away in the country, inactive, just waiting for death to come.

Franklin agreed. Slowly he recovered his health. His energy returned. In 1928 he was elected governor of New York. Then, just four years later, he was elected president of the United States.

Pause & Reflect

FOCUS

Eleanor fought strongly for various causes.

MARK IT UP > Put a star in the margin beside Eleanor's causes.

Meanwhile Eleanor had changed. To keep Franklin in 310 the public eye while he was recovering, she had gotten involved in politics herself. It was, she thought, her "duty." From childhood she had been taught "to do the thing that has to be done, the way it has to be done, when it has to be done."

With the help of Franklin's adviser Louis Howe, she made fund-raising speeches for the Democratic Party all around New York State. She helped in the work of 320 the League of Women Voters,[6] the Consumer's League,

---

6. **League . . . :** organizations devoted to national improvement through political education or improvement of working conditions.

Pause & Reflect

1. How did Eleanor Roosevelt help her husband cope with polio? (Summarize)

2. Review the details you circled. Why might Eleanor have become stronger after Franklin became ill with polio? (Draw Conclusions)

As the biography continues . . .

• Eleanor becomes more involved in politics.

• She fights for causes she believes in.

• She talks with Franklin, now President of the United States, about social change.

Pause & Reflect

1. REREAD the boxed paragraphs. How has Eleanor changed from when she was younger? (Compare and Contrast)

Eleanor Roosevelt used

to

Now she

2. Review the details you starred as you read. What kind of causes did Eleanor Roosevelt fight for? (Generalize)

and the Foreign Policy Association. After becoming interested in the problems of working women, she gave time to the Women's Trade Union League (WTUL).

It was through the WTUL that she met a group of remarkable women—women doing exciting work that made a difference in the world. They taught Eleanor about life in the slums. They awakened her hopes that something could be done to improve the condition of the poor. She dropped out of the "fashionable" society 330 of her wealthy friends and joined the world of reform—social change.

For hours at a time Eleanor and her reformer friends talked with Franklin. They showed him the need for new laws: laws to get children out of the factories and into schools; laws to cut down the long hours that women worked; laws to get fair wages for all workers.

By the time that Franklin was sworn in as president, the nation was facing its deepest depression[7]. One out of every four Americans was out of work, out of hope. 340 At mealtimes people stood in lines in front of soup kitchens for something to eat. Mrs. Roosevelt herself knew of once-prosperous families who found themselves reduced to eating stale bread from thrift shops or traveling to parts of town where they were not known to beg for money from house to house.

Pause & Reflect

7. **depression:** The Great Depression (1929–1941) was a period of drastic economic decline, widespread unemployment, and poverty in the United States and the rest of the world.

During her husband's presidency, Eleanor Roosevelt was known as the "president's conscience." Read on to learn more about the causes she supported.

Eleanor worked in the charity kitchens, ladling out soup. She visited slums. She crisscrossed the country 350 learning about the suffering of coal miners, shipyard workers, migrant farm workers, students, housewives—Americans caught up in the paralysis of the Great Depression. Since Franklin himself remained crippled, she became his eyes and ears, informing him of what the American people were really thinking and feeling.

Eleanor also was the president's conscience, 360 personally urging on him some of the most compassionate, forward-looking laws of his presidency, including, for example, the National Youth Administration (NYA), which provided money to allow impoverished young people to stay in school.

She lectured widely, wrote a regularly syndicated[8] newspaper column, "My Day," and spoke frequently on the radio. She fought for equal pay for women in industry. Like no other First Lady up to that time, she became a link between the president and the American 370 public.

Above all she fought against racial and religious prejudice. When Eleanor learned that the DAR (Daughters of the American Revolution)[9] would not

As the biography continues . . .

- Eleanor becomes a link between the president and the public.
- She fights racism and works hard to support her husband's presidency.

English Learner Support
Language

Idiom The words in blue mean that Eleanor saw and heard things during her travels alone that she reported to Franklin.

WHAT DOES IT MEAN?

Conscience means "sense of right and wrong" or "inner moral voice."

---

8. **syndicated:** sold to many newspapers for publication.

9. **DAR:** organization of women whose ancestors were in the Revolutionary War devoted to marking and preserving historic places associated with the Revolution.

WORDS TO KNOW
migrant (mī'grənt) *adj.* moving from place to place

allow the great black singer Marian Anderson to perform in their auditorium in Washington, D.C., she resigned from the organization. Then she arranged to have Miss Anderson sing in front of the Lincoln Memorial.

380 Similarly, when she entered a hall where, as often happened in those days, blacks and whites were seated in separate sections, she made it a point to sit with the blacks. Her example marked an important step in making the rights of blacks a matter of national <u>priority</u>.

On December 7, 1941, Japanese forces launched a surprise attack on the American naval base at Pearl Harbor, Hawaii, as well as on other American installations in the Pacific. The United States entered World War II, fighting not only against Japan but 390 against the brutal dictators who then controlled Germany and Italy.

Eleanor helped the Red Cross raise money. She gave blood, sold war bonds. But she also did the unexpected. In 1943, for example, she visited barracks and hospitals on islands throughout the South Pacific. When she visited a hospital, she stopped at every bed. To each soldier she said something special, something that a mother might say. Often, after she left, even battle-hardened men had tears in their eyes. Admiral 400 Nimitz, who originally thought such visits would be a nuisance, became one of her strongest admirers. Nobody else, he said, had done so much to help raise the spirits of the men.

By spring 1945 the end of the war in Europe seemed near. Then, on April 12, a phone call brought Eleanor the news that Franklin Roosevelt, who had gone to Warm Springs, Georgia, for a rest, was dead.

WHAT DOES IT MEAN? The *brutal dictators* were Adolf Hitler of Germany and Benito Mussolini of Italy.

READING CHECK

What did Eleanor do that was unexpected and special? Why were her actions appreciated by other people?

WORDS TO KNOW
priority (prī-ôr′ĭ-tē) *n.* something that must receive attention first

As Eleanor later declared, "I think that sometimes I
acted as his conscience. I urged him to take the harder
410 path when he would have preferred the easier way. In
that sense, I acted on occasion as a spur, even though
the spurring was not always wanted or welcome.

"Of course," said Eleanor, "I loved him, and I miss
him."

After Franklin's funeral, every day that Eleanor was
home at Hyde Park, without fail, she placed flowers
on his grave. Then she would stand very still beside
him there.

Pause & Reflect

Pause & Reflect

Number the following events
from 1 to 4 to show the order
in which they happened.
(Sequence of Events)

__ World War II begins.

__ Marion Anderson sings at
the Lincoln memorial.

__ President Roosevelt dies.

__ Eleanor Roosevelt visits
troops in the South Pacific.

FOCUS

After her husband's
death, Eleanor
Roosevelt continued to
be an important voice
for human rights.

MARK IT UP > As you
read, circle details that
help you understand her
accomplishments after
her husband's death.

With Franklin dead,
420 Eleanor Roosevelt might have
dropped out of the public eye,
might have been remembered
in the history books only as a
footnote to the president's
program of social reforms.
Instead she found new
strengths within herself, new
ways to live a useful,
interesting life—and to help
430 others. Now, moreover, her successes were her own,
not the result of being the president's wife.

**As the biography
ends . . .**

• Eleanor works tirelessly for
human rights.

• President Truman
encourages and supports
her work.

• Eleanor travels, writes, and
continues to work
throughout her lifetime.

WHAT DOES IT MEAN?

Wavering means "going back and forth" or "not making a decision."

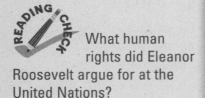

READING CHECK What human rights did Eleanor Roosevelt argue for at the United Nations?

In December 1945 President Harry S. Truman invited her to be one of the American delegates going to London to begin the work of the United Nations. Eleanor hesitated, but the president insisted. He said that the nation needed her; it was her duty. After that, Eleanor agreed.

In the beginning some of her fellow delegates from the United States considered her unqualified for the position, but after seeing her in action, they changed their minds.

It was Eleanor Roosevelt who, almost single-handedly, pushed through the United Nations General Assembly a resolution giving refugees from World War II the right *not* to return to their native lands if they did not wish to. The Russians angrily objected, but Eleanor's reasoning convinced wavering delegates. In a passionate speech defending the rights of the refugees she declared, "We [must] consider first the rights of man and what makes men more free—not governments, but man!"

Next Mrs. Roosevelt helped draft the United Nations Declaration of Human Rights. The Soviets wanted the declaration to list the duties people owed to their countries. Again Eleanor insisted that the United Nations should stand for individual freedom— the rights of people to free speech, freedom of religion, and such human needs as health care and education. In December 1948, with the Soviet Union and its allies refusing to vote, the Declaration of Human Rights won approval of the UN General Assembly by a vote of forty-eight to zero.

Even after retiring from her post at the UN, Mrs. Roosevelt continued to travel. In places around the world she dined with presidents and kings. But she also visited tenement slums[10] in Bombay, India; factories in Yugoslavia; farms in Lebanon and Israel.

Everywhere she met people who were eager to greet her. Although as a child she had been brought up to be
470 formal and distant, she had grown to feel at ease with people. They wanted to touch her, to hug her, to kiss her.

Eleanor's doctor had been telling her to slow down, but that was hard for her. She continued to write her newspaper column, "My Day," and to appear on television. She still began working at seven-thirty in the morning and often continued until well past midnight. Not only did she write and speak, she taught retarded children and raised money for health
480 care of the poor.

As author Clare Boothe Luce put it, "Mrs. Roosevelt has done more good deeds on a bigger scale for a longer time than any woman who ever appeared on our public scene. No woman has ever so comforted the distressed or so distressed the comfortable."

Gradually, however, she was forced to withdraw from some of her activities, to spend more time at home.

On November 7, 1962, at the age of seventy-eight,
490 Eleanor died in her sleep. She was buried in the rose garden at Hyde Park, alongside her husband.

Adlai Stevenson, the American ambassador to the United Nations, remembered her as "the First Lady of the World," as the person—male or female—most effective in working for the cause of human rights.

English Learner Support
Language

Fact and Opinion On this page, both Clare Boothe Luce and Adlai Stevenson share their *opinions* about Eleanor Roosevelt's achievements. An *opinion* is someone's personal belief about a subject, whereas a *fact* is a statement that is known to be true.

REREAD the boxed passage. Then restate it in your own words. **(Paraphrase)**

_____

10. **tenement slums:** parts of a city where poor people live in crowded, shabby buildings.

1. What do you think was Eleanor Roosevelt's greatest accomplishment after her husband's death? **(Evaluate)**

2. What questions do you have about Eleanor Roosevelt? List two. **(Question)**

CHALLENGE Adlai Stevenson said of Eleanor Roosevelt, "She would rather light a candle than curse the darkness." Using details from this selection, write a paragraph on another sheet of paper explaining what you think Stevenson meant. Share your paragraph with the class. **(Analyze)**

As Stevenson declared, "She would rather light a candle than curse the darkness."

And perhaps, in sum, that is what the struggle for human rights is all about. ❖

Pause & Reflect

⫿⫿⫿ MARK IT UP ⟩ Think back over the selection. Use the web provided here to complete the work you began on page 70. Add new ovals as necessary.

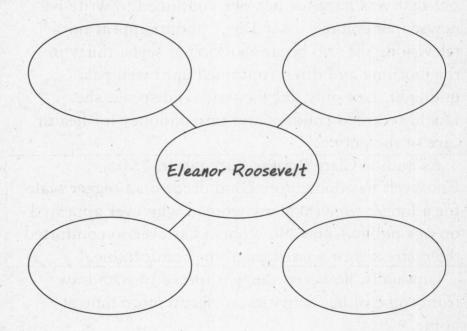

Eleanor Roosevelt

Active Reading SkillBuilder

Chronological Order

A time line helps you show the **chronological order** of events. The time line below lists important events in Eleanor Roosevelt's life. As you read, fill in a few details about Eleanor's life or feelings next to each event. The first item has been completed for you.

1884	Eleanor is born.	*October 11th in Manhattan, New York; mother, Anna Hall Roosevelt; father, Elliot Roosevelt; parents had hoped for a boy*
1892–1894	Eleanor's mother and father die.	
1902	Eleanor leaves boarding school.	
1905	Eleanor marries Franklin Delano Roosevelt.	
1917	United States enters World War I.	
1921	Franklin Roosevelt gets polio.	
1932	Franklin is elected President.	
1941	Japan attacks Pearl Harbor.	
1945	Franklin dies; Eleanor is a delegate to the United Nations.	

Literary Analysis SkillBuilder

Biography

A **biography** is the story of a person's life, written by someone else. As you read, use this chart to note signal words that the author has used to indicate chronological order, the events they relate to, and the effect the events have on Eleanor Roosevelt.

Signal Word	Event	Effect on Eleanor
then	Her father left.	She felt unloved, abandoned.

Follow Up: Write what you think Eleanor might have done if Franklin had decided to retire from public life when he contracted polio.

_____

_____

_____

Words to Know SkillBuilder

Words to Know

brooding   combatant   migrant   priority   prominent

A. For each word in the first column, find the phrase in the second column that is closest in meaning. Write the letter of that phrase in the blank.

_____ 1. combatant

_____ 2. migrant

_____ 3. brooding

_____ 4. priority

_____ 5. prominent

A. worried all the time

B. a mighty fighter

C. top of the to-do list

D. well-known

E. a wandering laborer

B. On each blank line, write the Word to Know that the verse describes.

1. In a duel there are two of these,
   In a war there may be many.
   The world would be more peaceful
   If there simply weren't any.

   _____

2. Though you may need to skip TV,
   And that may cause you sorrow,
   This describes the homework
   That you know is due tomorrow.

   _____

3. It would be silly, I would say,
   It would be quite absurd of you,
   To hope to be described as this
   When no one's ever heard of you.

   _____

4. A worried male will wear this look,
   A worried female too,
   If you get all your homework done,
   We won't see it on you.

   _____

5. A person goes from place to place,
   She never stays for long,
   She'll usually work for just awhile,
   And then she'll say "so long!"

   _____

Before You Read

Connect to Your Life

Is there a place in your neighborhood that is special to you and your friends? Picture the place in your mind. Then draw a picture of it. Write a caption naming the place and describing some of its special features.

Name of Place: _____

Special Features: _____

_____

_____

Key to the Story

WHAT YOU NEED TO KNOW In the 1960s, some African-American artists started a "wall of respect" movement. The artists worked to create special places by painting murals on walls in their communities as symbols of their respect for the neighborhoods. In the space below, list the names of some heroes of your own that you would include in a "wall of respect."

_____

_____

_____

_____

The War of the Wall

by
Toni Cade Bambara

PREVIEW One day a "painter lady" comes into the neighborhood and starts painting over a wall that is special to the community. How can the narrator and cousin Lou stop her from "messing" with their wall?

As the story begins . . .

• The narrator and Lou see a woman painting the wall of a building.

• They tell her the wall belongs to the neighborhood.

English Learner Support

Language

Dialect The character who tells this story speaks in dialect—the form of English spoken in a particular region. The narrator uses some words and phrases you would not see in formal written English, such as *me and Lou* instead of *Lou and I.*

REREAD the boxed passage. Is Lou right to say that the wall belongs to the kids? (Evaluate)

YES / NO, because

_____

_____

_____

FOCUS

In this section, the narrator and Lou discover a "painter lady" about to paint "their" wall.

MARK IT UP ▷ As you read, underline details that tell you why the wall is so special to the people in the neighborhood. An example is highlighted.

Me and Lou had no time for courtesies. We were late for school. So we just flat out told the painter lady to quit messing with the wall. It was our wall, and she had no right coming into our neighborhood painting on it. Stirring in the paint bucket

10 and not even looking at us, she mumbled something about Mr. Eubanks, the barber, giving her permission. That had nothing to do with it as far as we were concerned. We've been pitching pennies against that wall since we were little kids. Old folks have been dragging their chairs out to sit in the shade of the wall for years. Big kids have been playing handball against the wall since so-called integration[1] when the crazies 'cross town poured cement in our pool so we couldn't

20 use it. I'd sprained my neck one time boosting my cousin Lou up to chisel Jimmy Lyons's name into the wall when we found out he was never coming home from the war in Vietnam to take us fishing.

"If you lean close," Lou said, leaning hipshot against her beat-up car, "you'll get a whiff of bubble gum and kids' sweat. And that'll tell you something— that this wall belongs to the kids of Taliaferro Street." I thought Lou sounded very convincing. But the painter lady paid us no mind. She just snapped the

30 brim of her straw hat down and hauled her bucket up the ladder.

"You're not even from around here," I hollered up after her. The license plates on her old piece of car said

---

1. **since so-called integration:** from the time in the 1960s when segregation, the separation of the races in public places, was outlawed. The narrator is being sarcastic, suggesting that integration has not been successful.

"New York." Lou dragged me away because I was about to grab hold of that ladder and shake it. And then we'd really be late for school.

Pause & Reflect

FOCUS

Read on to find out what happens when the people in the neighborhood try to get to know the painter.

MARK IT UP As you read, underline details that tell how the painter reacts to the people in the neighborhood.

When we came from school, the wall was slick with white. The painter lady
40 was running string across the wall and taping it here and there. Me and Lou leaned against the gumball machine outside the pool hall and watched. She had strings up and down and back and forth. Then she began chalking them with a hunk of blue chalk.

The Morris twins crossed the street, hanging back at
50 the curb next to the beat-up car. The twin with the red ribbons was hugging a jug of cloudy lemonade. The one with yellow ribbons was holding a plate of dinner away from her dress. The painter lady began snapping the strings. The blue chalk dust measured off halves and quarters up and down and sideways too. Lou was about to say how hip it all was, but I dropped my book satchel on his toes to remind him we were at war.

Some good aromas were drifting our way from the
60 plate leaking pot likker[2] onto the Morris girl's white socks. I could tell from where I stood that under the tinfoil was baked ham, collard greens, and candied yams. And knowing Mrs. Morris, who sometimes

Pause & Reflect

Whose name is carved into the wall? What happened to this person? **(Clarify)**

As the story continues...

• The painter is making progress on the wall.

• The Morris twins offer her a plate of food.

English Learner Support
Culture

Food Food plays an important role in this story. The foods the narrator lists—baked ham, collard greens, and candied yams—are traditional foods of the southern United States. Collard greens are similar to spinach, and yams are sweet potatoes.

---

2. **pot likker:** cooking liquid that comes when pork is boiled with greens.

READING CHECK

What is the painter lady doing with the string and tape?

English Learner Support

Vocabulary

Idiom *He gave the painter lady the once-over* means "he looked at her very carefully."

English Learner Support

Language

Dialect The words spoken by the characters are often spelled the way people would say them. If you read the words aloud, you can figure out that *whatcha* means "what do you" and *suppah* means "supper." *Whatcha got there?* means "What do you have in your hands?"

English Learner Support

Language

Dialect *His best ain't-I-fine voice* means "his most polite way of speaking."

bakes for my mama's restaurant, a slab of buttered cornbread was probably up under there too, sopping up some of the pot likker. Me and Lou rolled our eyes, wishing somebody would send us some dinner. But the painter lady didn't even turn around. She was pulling the strings down and prying bits of tape loose.

70   Side Pocket came strolling out of the pool hall to see what Lou and me were studying so hard. He gave the painter lady the once-over, checking out her paint-spattered jeans, her chalky T-shirt, her floppy-brimmed straw hat. He hitched up his pants and glided over toward the painter lady, who kept right on with what she was doing.

"Whatcha got there, sweetheart?" he asked the twin with the plate.

"Suppah," she said all soft and countrylike.

80   "For her," the one with the jug added, jerking her chin toward the painter lady's back.

Still she didn't turn around. She was rearing back on her heels, her hands jammed into her back pockets, her face squinched up like the masterpiece she had in mind was taking shape on the wall by magic. We could have been gophers crawled up into a rotten hollow for all she cared. She didn't even say hello to anybody. Lou was muttering something about how great her concentration was. I butt him with my hip,

90   and his elbow slid off the gum machine.

"Good evening," Side Pocket said in his best ain't-I-fine voice. But the painter lady was moving from the milk crate to the step stool to the ladder, moving up and down fast, scribbling all over the wall like a crazy person. We looked at Side Pocket. He looked at the twins. The twins looked at us. The painter lady was

giving a show. It was like those old-timey music movies where the dancer taps on the tabletop and then starts jumping all over the furniture, kicking chairs
100 over and not skipping a beat. She didn't even look where she was stepping. And for a minute there, hanging on the ladder to reach a far spot, she looked like she was going to tip right over.

"Ahh," Side Pocket cleared his throat and moved fast to catch the ladder. "These young ladies here have brought you some supper."

"Ma'am?" The twins stepped forward. Finally the painter turned around, her eyes "full of sky," as my grandmama would say. Then she stepped down like
110 she was in a trance. She wiped her hands on her jeans as the Morris twins offered up the plate and the jug. She rolled back the tinfoil, then wagged her head as though something terrible was on the plate.

"Thank your mother very much," she said, sounding like her mouth was full of sky too. "I've brought my own dinner along." And then, without even excusing herself, she went back up the ladder, drawing on the wall in a wild way. Side Pocket whistled one of those oh-brother breathy whistles and
120 went back into the pool hall. The Morris twins shifted their weight from one foot to the other, then crossed the street and went home. Lou had to drag me away, I was so mad. We couldn't wait to get to the firehouse to tell my daddy all about this rude woman who'd stolen our wall.

Pause & Reflect

WHAT DOES IT MEAN? When the artist is described as being *full of sky,* it means that she is inspired and focused on her work.

Pause & Reflect

What does the painter lady do to make the narrator think she is rude? (Cause and Effect)

READING TIP From the painter lady's questions about food, Mama infers that this lady must belong to a religious group that forbids the eating of certain foods. For example, people of the Jewish and Muslim cultures do not eat pork.

English Learner Support

Language

Dialect *Sistuh* is the word *sister* pronounced with a regional accent. *T'other* is *the other* spoken in dialect.

English Learner Support

Vocabulary

Idioms *Cracking up* means "laughing." *Fix her wagon* means "yell at her" or "scold her."

FOCUS

Read to find out what happens when the painter lady visits Mama's restaurant.

All the way back to the block to help my mama out at the restaurant, me and Lou kept asking my daddy for 130 ways to run the painter lady out of town. But my daddy was busy talking about the trip to the country and telling Lou he could come too because Grandmama can always use an extra pair of hands on the farm.

Later that night, while me and Lou were in the back doing our chores, we found out that the painter lady was a liar. She came into the restaurant and leaned against the glass of the steam table, talking about how starved she was. I was scrubbing pots and Lou was 140 chopping onions, but we could hear her through the service window. She was asking Mama was that a ham hock in the greens, and was that a neck bone in the pole beans, and were there any vegetables cooked without meat, especially pork.

"I don't care who your spiritual leader is," Mama said in that way of hers. "If you eat in the community, sistuh, you gonna eat pig by-and-by, one way or t'other."

Me and Lou were cracking up in the kitchen, and 150 several customers at the counter were clearing their throats, waiting for Mama to really fix her wagon for not speaking to the elders when she came in. The painter lady took a stool at the counter and went right on with her questions. Was there cheese in the baked macaroni, she wanted to know? Were there eggs in the salad? Was it honey or sugar in the iced tea? Mama was fixing Pop Johnson's plate. And every time the painter lady asked a fool question, Mama would

dump another spoonful of rice on the pile. She was
160 tapping her foot and heating up in a dangerous way.
But Pop Johnson was happy as he could be. Me and
Lou peeked through the service window, wondering
what planet the painter lady came from. Who ever
heard of baked macaroni without cheese, or potato
salad without eggs?

"Do you have any bread made with unbleached
flour?" the painter lady asked Mama. There was a
long pause, as though everybody in the restaurant was
holding their breath, wondering if Mama would dump
170 the next spoonful on the painter lady's head. She
didn't. But when she set Pop Johnson's plate down, it
came down with a bang.

When Mama finally took her order, the starving
lady all of a sudden couldn't make up her mind
whether she wanted a vegetable plate or fish and a
salad. She finally settled on the broiled trout and a
tossed salad. But just when Mama reached for a plate
to serve her, the painter lady leaned over the counter
with her finger all up in the air.

180 "Excuse me," she said. "One more thing." Mama
was holding the plate like a Frisbee, tapping that foot,
one hand on her hip. "Can I get raw beets in that
tossed salad?"

"You will get," Mama said, leaning her face close to
the painter lady's, "whatever Lou back there tossed.
Now sit down." And the painter lady sat back down
on her stool and shut right up.

Pause & Reflect

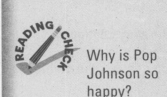

READING CHECK

Why is Pop
Johnson so
happy?

Pause & Reflect

1. Circle the phrase below
   that describes Mama's
   reaction to the painter lady.
   (Evaluate)

   warm and friendly

   angry and forceful

   curious and confused

2. Based on what you've
   read, do you think the
   painter lady and the people
   in the neighborhood will
   become friends? (Predict)
   YES / NO, because

As the story continues . . .

- Mama defends the painter lady.
- The narrator and Lou make secret plans to reclaim the wall.

English Learner Support

Vocabulary

Idiom The phrase *open fire on* means "criticize or insult."

WHAT DOES IT MEAN? An *easel* is an upright frame that supports an artist's canvas.

MORE ABOUT . . .

GRAFFITI In the early 1970s, many young artists in New York City used spray paint to create designs on walls and subway cars. This art is called graffiti. It often includes the artist's name in large, fancy, colorful letters.

FOCUS

Read to find out how the narrator and Lou plan to get their wall back from the painter lady.

MARK IT UP As you read, underline the details that help you to understand the scheme that the narrator and Lou think up.

All the way to the country, me and Lou tried to get
190 Mama to open fire on the painter lady. But Mama said that seeing as how she was from the North, you couldn't expect her to have any manners. Then Mama said she was sorry she'd been so impatient with the woman because she seemed like a decent person and was simply trying to stick to a very strict diet. Me and Lou didn't
200 want to hear that. Who did that lady think she was, coming into our neighborhood and taking over our wall?

"Welllll," Mama drawled, pulling into the filling station so Daddy could take the wheel, "it's hard on an artist, ya know. They can't always get people to look at their work. So she's just doing her work in the open, that's all."

Me and Lou definitely did not want to hear that. Why couldn't she set up an easel downtown or draw on the sidewalk in her own neighborhood? Mama told us to
210 quit fussing so much; she was tired and wanted to rest. She climbed into the back seat and dropped down into the warm hollow Daddy had made in the pillow.

All weekend long, me and Lou tried to scheme up ways to recapture our wall. Daddy and Mama said they were sick of hearing about it. Grandmama turned up the TV to drown us out. On the late news was a story about the New York subways. When a train came roaring into the station all covered from top to bottom, windows too, with writings and drawings
220 done with spray paint, me and Lou slapped five.

WORDS TO KNOW
drawl (drôl) *v.* to speak slowly, stretching the vowel sound
scheme (skēm) *v.* to plot or plan in a secretive way

Mama said it was too bad kids in New York had nothing better to do than spray paint all over the trains. Daddy said that in the cities, even grown-ups wrote all over the trains and buildings too. Daddy called it "graffiti." Grandmama called it a shame.

We couldn't wait to get out of school on Monday. We couldn't find any black spray paint anywhere. But in a junky hardware store downtown we found a can of white epoxy[3] paint, the kind you touch up old refrigerators with when they get splotchy and peely. We spent our whole allowance on it. And because it was too late to use our bus passes, we had to walk all the way home lugging our book satchels and gym shoes, and the bag with the epoxy.

Pause & Reflect

FOCUS

Read to find out about the painter lady's mural and how the community responds to it.

|MARK IT UP| > As you read, underline details that tell you about the lady's work.

When we reached the corner of Taliaferro and Fifth, it looked like a block party or something. Half the neighborhood was gathered on the sidewalk in front of the wall. I looked at Lou, he looked at me. We both looked at the bag with the epoxy and wondered how we were going to work our scheme. The painter lady's car was nowhere in sight. But there were too many people standing around to do anything. Side Pocket and his buddies were leaning on their cue sticks, hunching each other. Daddy was there with a lineman[4] he catches a ride with on Mondays.

---

3. **epoxy** (ĭ-pŏk'sē): a plastic used in glues and paints.
4. **lineman**: someone who installs telephone or electrical power lines.

Pause & Reflect

1. Check the sentence below that states Mama's view of artists. (Paraphrase)
   - ❏ They are stuck up.
   - ❏ They have a hard time getting people to notice their work.
   - ❏ They get paid too much.
   - ❏ It's best to stay away from them.

2. Why do the narrator and Lou buy a can of white epoxy paint? (Infer)

_____

_____

_____

As the story ends . . .

- The painter lady has finished her work.
- Many people gather to view the wall.
- The narrator and Lou are surprised by what they see.

250 Mrs. Morris had her arms flung around the shoulders of the twins on either side of her. Mama was talking with some of her customers, many of them with napkins still at the throat. Mr. Eubanks came out of the barbershop, followed by a man in a striped poncho, half his face shaved, the other half full of foam.

"She really did it, didn't she?" Mr. Eubanks huffed out his chest. Lots of folks answered right quick that she surely did when they saw the straight razor in his 260 hand.

READ ALOUD the boxed text. How do you think the narrator feels after seeing the African American heroes painted on the wall? (Connect)

Mama <u>beckoned</u> us over. And then we saw it. The wall. Reds, greens, figures outlined in black. Swirls of purple and orange. Storms of blues and yellows. It was something. I recognized some of the faces right off. There was Martin Luther King, Jr. And there was a man with glasses on and his mouth open like he was laying down a heavy rap.[5] Daddy came up alongside and reminded us that that was Minister Malcolm X. The serious woman with a rifle I knew was Harriet 270 Tubman because my grandmama has pictures of her all over the house. And I knew Mrs. Fannie Lou Hamer[6] 'cause a signed photograph of her hangs in the restaurant next to the calendar.

Then I let my eyes follow what looked like a vine. It trailed past a man with a horn, a woman with a big white flower in her hair, a handsome dude in a tuxedo seated at a piano, and a man with a goatee holding a book. When I looked more closely, I realized that what had looked like flowers were really faces. One face 280 with yellow petals looked just like Frieda Morris. One

MORE ABOUT . . .
FANNIE LOU HAMER In the 1960s, Fannie Lou Hamer joined other civil rights workers and fought for African Americans' right to vote. She continued working for civil rights throughout her life, despite being beaten and jailed once.

---

5. **laying down a heavy rap:** saying something serious.

6. **Martin Luther King, Jr., Minister Malcom X, Harriet Tubman, and Fannie Lou Hamer:** prominent civil rights leaders of the 19th and 20th centuries.

WORDS TO KNOW
beckon (bĕk'ən) v. to summon or call, usually by a gesture or nod

with red petals looked just like Hattie Morris. I could hardly believe my eyes.

"Notice," Side Pocket said, stepping close to the wall with his cue stick like a classroom pointer. "These are the flags of <u>liberation</u>," he said in a voice I'd never heard him use before. We all stepped closer while he pointed and spoke. "Red, black and green," he said, his pointer falling on the leaflike flags of the vine. "Our liberation flag.[7] And here Ghana, there
290 Tanzania. Guinea-Bissau, Angola, Mozambique." Side Pocket sounded very tall, as though he'd been waiting all his life to give this lesson.

Mama tapped us on the shoulder and pointed to a high section of the wall. There was a fierce-looking man with his arms crossed against his chest guarding a bunch of children. His muscles bulged, and he looked a lot like my daddy. One kid was looking at a row of books. Lou hunched me 'cause the kid looked like me. The one that looked like Lou was spinning a globe on
300 the tip of his finger like a basketball. There were other kids there with microscopes and compasses. And the more I looked, the more it looked like the fierce man was not so much guarding the kids as defending their right to do what they were doing.

Then Lou gasped and dropped the paint bag and ran forward, running his hands over a rainbow. He had to tiptoe and stretch to do it, it was so high. I couldn't breathe either. The painter lady had found the chisel marks and had painted Jimmy Lyons's name in a
310 rainbow.

---

7. **liberation flag:** designed early in the 20th century to symbolize the richness of skin color (black), the struggle for freedom (red), and hope (green).

WORDS TO KNOW
liberation (lĭb′ə-rā′shən) *n.* a state of freedom reached after a struggle

READING TIP Find the countries of Ghana, Tanzania, Guinea-Bissau, Angola, and Mozambique on a world map. On which continent are they located?

REREAD the boxed passage. How do you think Lou and the narrator feel when they see themselves in the painting? **(Connect)**

READING CHECK Who is Jimmy Lyons? If you can't remember, turn back to page 94.

Pause & Reflect

1. What does the mural show? Check three phrases below. **(Clarify)**

   ❑ heroes from African American history

   ❑ scenes from wars

   ❑ people in the neighborhood

   ❑ flags of African nations

2. Why does the name at the end of the rainbow particularly excite the narrator and Lou? **(Cause and Effect)**

   _____

   _____

   _____

3. Why does the painter lady offer her gift to the neighborhood? **(Infer)**

   _____

   _____

   _____

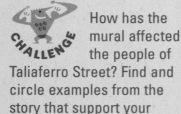

How has the mural affected the people of Taliaferro Street? Find and circle examples from the story that support your answer. **(Analyze)**

250 "Read the <u>inscription</u>, honey," Mrs. Morris said, urging little Frieda forward. She didn't have to urge much. Frieda marched right up, bent down, and in a loud voice that made everybody quit oohing and ahhing and listen, she read,

> *To the People of Taliaferro Street*
> *I Dedicate This Wall of Respect*
> *Painted in Memory of My Cousin*
> *Jimmy Lyons*

Pause & Reflect

WORDS TO KNOW
inscription (ĭn-skrĭp′shən) *n.* something written, carved, or engraved on a surface

Active Reading SkillBuilder

Cause and Effect

Two events are related as **cause and effect** if one brings about, or causes, the other. The event that happens first is the **cause,** the one that follows is the **effect.** Use the chart below to record causes and their effects as you read.

Cause	Effect
A stranger is painting the wall.	Lou and the narrator are angry because they feel that the wall was their wall.

Literary Analysis SkillBuilder

Climax

A story builds from its beginning to its moment of greatest intensity—the **climax.** At the climax of a story, the major **conflicts,** or struggles, reach a high point. On the chart below, list the conflicts you find in "The War of the Wall." Note who is in conflict with whom. Describe the climax of the story—when the conflict is the strongest—in the final box.

Conflict	Between Whom?
The narrator and Lou are upset that the painter lady is "messing" with their wall.	narrator and Lou vs. painter lady

Climax

Words to Know SkillBuilder

Words to Know

beckon   drawl   inscription   liberation   scheme

Fill in each set of blanks with the correct Word to Know. (Some words will be used more than once.) Then use the boxed letters to complete the sentence below the puzzle.

1. The American Revolution was fought to gain this from Britain.

   _ _ _ _ _ _ [ ] _ _ _

2. If you look at this on a penny, you will see it says "one cent."

   _ _ _ _ _ _ _ _ _ [ ] _

3. This is what you do when you make a sneaky plan.

   _ _ [ ] _ _ _ _

4. A police officer might do this to tell the traffic to move forward.

   _ _ _ _ [ ][ ] _

5. A nation that has won its freedom from another has achieved this.

   _ _ _ _ _ _ _ _ [ ] _

6. An actor playing a Southerner might have to learn to do this.

   _ [ ] _ _ _ _

7. One might do this in secret or in a whisper.

   _ _ _ [ ] _ _

8. This could be carved or painted or engraved.

   [ ] _ _ _ _ _ _ _ _ _

9. Shouting from the rooftops is not a good way to do this.

   _ _ _ _ [ ] _

10. Complete the following sentence with the three words that the boxed letters spell out.

    The artist dedicates the wall to her cousin _____.

Before You Read

Connect to Your Life

Have you ever seen a cat chase a bird, or a frog catch a bug? In the animal kingdom, some animals are the natural **prey,** or food, of other animals. Usually the prey's main defense is to run or to hide from its enemies, or **predators.** Sometimes the prey fights back. Connect each animal on the left with its natural enemy on the right. There may be more than one possible connection.

flying insects

jackrabbits

mice

red-tailed hawks

house cats

bats

Key to the Story

WHAT YOU NEED TO KNOW If you lived in India, you might know that the cobra and the mongoose are natural enemies. The **mongoose,** growing only as long as 16 inches, seems an unlikely hunter of the **cobra,** a poisonous snake about 6 feet in length and 6 inches around.

You will learn more about these animals in this story, set in India during the late 1800s. At that time the British ruled India. British families lived in open, airy one-story homes called bungalows. It was not uncommon to find snakes, insects, or wild animals near or even inside them.

Rikki-tikki-tavi

by Rudyard Kipling

PREVIEW In this story, the main characters are animals who talk, think, and behave like human beings. The hero is a fearless mongoose named Rikki-tikki-tavi. You will also meet Rikki-tikki's mortal enemies, the cobras Nag and Nagaina.

As the story begins . . .

- After a flood, Teddy and his parents find a mongoose in their yard.
- The mongoose becomes Teddy's pet.

English Learner Support

Language

Semicolons Many of the sentences in this story are long and punctuated with semicolons (;). Semicolons usually come at the end of a complete idea, so you should read sentences with semicolons in chunks. The sentence to the right has been broken into its four main ideas.

▌▌MARK IT UP ⧁ KEEP TRACK
Remember to use these marks to keep track of your reading.

* This is important.

? I have a question about this.

! This is a surprise.

FOCUS
In this part you will meet a mongoose named Rikki-tikki-tavi and the family that takes him in.

▌▌MARK IT UP ⧁ As you read, circle details that tell you what Rikki-tikki is like. An example is highlighted.

This is the story of the great war that Rikki-tikki-tavi fought single-handed, through the bathrooms of the big bungalow[1] in Segowlee cantonment.[2] Darzee, the tailorbird, helped him, and Chuchundra,[3] the muskrat,

10 who never comes out into the middle of the floor but always creeps round by the wall, gave him advice; but Rikki-tikki did the real fighting.

He was a mongoose, rather like a little cat in his fur and his tail but quite like a weasel in his head and his habits. ①His eyes and the end of his restless nose were pink; ②he could scratch himself anywhere he pleased with any leg, front or back, that he chose to use; ③he could fluff up his tail till it looked like a bottle-brush, ④and his war cry as he scuttled through the long grass

20 was: *Rikk-tikk-tikki-tikki-tchk!*

One day, a high summer flood washed him out of the burrow where he lived with his father and mother and carried him, kicking and clucking, down a roadside ditch. He found a little wisp of grass floating there and clung to it till he lost his senses. When he <u>revived</u>, he was lying in the hot sun on the middle of a garden path, very draggled indeed, and a small boy was saying, "Here's a dead mongoose. Let's have a funeral."

"No," said his mother, "let's take him in and dry

30 him. Perhaps he isn't really dead."

They took him into the house, and a big man picked him up between his finger and thumb and said he was

---

1. **bungalow** (bŭng′gə-lō′): in India, a house surrounded by a large outer porch.
2. **Segowlee cantonment** (sē-gô′lē kăn-tōn′mənt): Segowlee military base.
3. **Chuchundra** (chōō-chōōn′drə).

WORDS TO KNOW
revive (rĭ-vīv′) *v.* to become conscious; wake up

not dead but half choked; so they wrapped him in cotton wool and warmed him over a little fire, and he opened his eyes and sneezed. "Now," said the big man (he was an Englishman who had just moved into the bungalow), "don't frighten him, and we'll see what he'll do."

40 It is the hardest thing in the world to frighten a mongoose, because he is eaten up from nose to tail with curiosity. The motto of all the mongoose family is "Run and Find Out"; and Rikki-tikki was a true mongoose. He looked at the cotton wool, decided that it was not good to eat, ran all round the table, sat up and put his fur in order, scratched himself, and jumped on the small boy's shoulder.

"Don't be frightened, Teddy," said his father. "That's his way of making friends."

"Ouch! He's tickling under my chin," said Teddy.

50 Rikki-tikki looked down between the boy's collar and neck, snuffed at his ear, and climbed down to the floor, where he sat rubbing his nose.

"Good gracious," said Teddy's mother, "and that's a wild creature! I suppose he's so tame because we've been kind to him."

"All mongooses are like that," said her husband. "If Teddy doesn't pick him up by the tail or try to put him in a cage, he'll run in and out of the house all day long. Let's give him something to eat."

60 They gave him a little piece of raw meat. Rikki-tikki liked it immensely; and when it was finished, he went out into the veranda[4] and sat in the sunshine and fluffed up his fur to make it dry to the roots. Then he felt better.

"There are more things to find out about in this house," he said to himself, "than all my family could find out in all their lives. I shall certainly stay and find out."

English Learner Support

Vocabulary

Idiom In this sentence, *eaten up* means "filled."

MORE ABOUT . . .

MONGOOSE The Indian mongoose is a small animal similar to a weasel and known for killing snakes. Mongooses are easily tamed, and people often keep them as pets. They make their homes near streams or in burrows and eat small rodents, eggs, and insects.

---

4. **veranda** (və-răn′də): a long open porch.

Pause & Reflect

1. Check four words below that are true of Rikki-tikki. (Clarify)

   ❑ curious   ❑ playful
   ❑ timid   ❑ lazy
   ❑ friendly   ❑ restless

2. **REREAD** the boxed text. What do you think will happen now that the mongoose has entered the house? (Predict)

_____

_____

_____

_____

As the story continues . . .

• Rikki-tikki explores the garden.

• He meets an unhappy bird, Darzee, and his wife.

• He encounters Nag, the snake.

He spent all that day roaming over the house. He nearly drowned himself in the bathtubs, put his nose into the ink on a writing table, and burnt it on the end
70 of the big man's cigar, for he climbed up in the big man's lap to see how writing was done. At nightfall he ran into Teddy's nursery to watch how kerosene lamps were lighted, and when Teddy went to bed, Rikki-tikki climbed up too; but he was a restless companion, because he had to get up and attend to every noise all through the night and find out what made it. Teddy's mother and father came in, the last thing, to look at their boy, and Rikki-tikki was awake on the pillow.

"I don't like that," said Teddy's mother; "he may
80 bite the child."

"He'll do no such thing," said the father. "Teddy is safer with that little beast than if he had a bloodhound to watch him. If a snake came into the nursery now—"

But Teddy's mother wouldn't think of anything so awful.

Pause & Reflect

FOCUS

Rikki-tikki explores the garden surrounding the bungalow. Read to find out whom he meets.

MARK IT UP As you read, list in the margin each character that he meets.

Early in the morning Rikki-tikki came to early breakfast in the veranda, riding on Teddy's shoulder, and they
90 gave him banana and some boiled egg; and he sat on all their laps one after the other, because every well-brought-up mongoose always hopes to be a house mongoose some day and have rooms to run about in; and Rikki-tikki's mother (she used to live in the general's house at Segowlee) had carefully told

Rikki what to do if ever he came across white men.

Then Rikki-tikki went out into the garden to see
100 what was to be seen. It was a large garden, only half-
cultivated,[5] with bushes, as big as summerhouses, of
Marshal Niel roses, lime and orange trees, clumps of
bamboos, and thickets of high grass. Rikki-tikki licked
his lips. "This is a splendid hunting ground," he said,
and his tail grew bottlebrushy at the thought of it; and
he scuttled up and down the garden, snuffing here and
there till he heard very sorrowful voices in a thorn
bush. It was Darzee, the tailorbird, and his wife. They
had made a beautiful nest by pulling two big leaves
110 together and stitching them up the edges with fibers
and had filled the hollow with cotton and downy fluff.
The nest swayed to and fro, as they sat on the rim and
cried.

"What is the matter?" asked Rikki-tikki.

"We are very miserable," said Darzee. "One of our
babies fell out of the nest yesterday, and Nag[6] ate him."

"H'm!" said Rikki-tikki, "that is very sad—but I am
a stranger here. Who is Nag?"

Darzee and his wife only <u>cowered</u> down in the nest
120 without answering, for from the thick grass at the foot
of the bush there came a low hiss—a horrid, cold
sound that made Rikki-tikki jump back two clear feet.
Then inch by inch out of the grass rose up the head
and spread hood of Nag, the big black cobra, and he
was five feet long from tongue to tail. When he had
lifted one-third of himself clear of the ground, he
stayed, balancing to and fro exactly as a dandelion
tuft balances in the wind; and he looked at Rikki-tikki
with the wicked snake's eyes that never change their
130 expression, whatever the snake may be thinking of.

---

5. **cultivated:** cleared for the growing of garden plants.

6. **Nag** (näg).

WORDS TO KNOW
cower (kou'ər) *v.* to crouch or shrink down in fear

READING TIP To keep track of all the animals and people in the story, make a character chart like the one below. Include each character's name and details from the text that describe the character.

Character	Details from Text
Rikki-tikki-tavi	curious, well-bred, smart, restless, loyal
Darzee	
Nag	

MARK IT UP In the boxed passage, star words and phrases that help you picture Nag. **(Visualize)**

MORE ABOUT . . .

COBRAS The cobra is a large, poisonous snake. Before striking, a cobra lifts its head high off the ground and spreads its neck ribs to form a hood. The Indian cobra has an especially wide hood with markings that look like eyes. Indian cobras can grow to about 6 feet in length.

READING CHECK

What are Rikki-tikki and Nag afraid of?

"Who is Nag?" said he. "*I* am Nag. The great god Brahm[7] put his mark upon all our people when the first cobra spread his hood to keep the sun off Brahm as he slept. Look, and be afraid!"

He spread out his hood more than ever, and Rikki-tikki saw the spectacle mark on the back of it that looks exactly like the eye part of a hook-and-eye fastening.[8] He was afraid for the minute, but it is impossible for a mongoose to stay frightened for any length of time; and though Rikki-tikki had never met a live cobra before, his mother had fed him on dead ones, and he knew that all a grown mongoose's business in life was to fight and eat snakes. Nag knew that too, and at the bottom of his cold heart, he was afraid.

"Well," said Rikki-tikki, and his tail began to fluff up again, "marks or no marks, do you think it is right for you to eat fledgelings[9] out of a nest?"

Nag was thinking to himself and watching the least little movement in the grass behind Rikki-tikki. He knew that mongooses in the garden meant death sooner or later for him and his family; but he wanted to get Rikki-tikki off his guard. So he dropped his head a little, and put it on one side.

"Let us talk," he said. "You eat eggs. Why should not I eat birds?"

"Behind you! Look behind you!" sang Darzee.

Rikki-tikki knew better than to waste time in staring. He jumped up in the air as high as he could go, and just under him whizzed by the head of Nagaina,[10] Nag's wicked wife. She had crept up behind him as he was talking, to make an end of him; and he heard her savage hiss as the stroke missed. He came

---

7. **Brahm:** another name for Brahma, creator of the universe in the Hindu religion.

8. **hook-and-eye fastening:** a clothes fastener consisting of a small blunt metal hook that is inserted in a corresponding loop or eyelet.

9. **fledgelings** (flĕj'lĭngs): baby birds, as yet unable to fly.

10. **Nagaina** (näg-ä-ē'nə).

down almost across her back, and if he had been an old mongoose, he would have known that then was the time to break her back with one bite; but he was afraid of the terrible lashing return stroke of the cobra. He bit, indeed, but did not bite long enough; and he jumped clear of the whisking[11] tail, leaving Nagaina torn and angry.

170   "Wicked, wicked Darzee!" said Nag, lashing up as high as he could reach toward the nest in the thorn bush; but Darzee had built it out of reach of snakes, and it only swayed to and fro.

    Rikki-tikki felt his eyes growing red and hot (when a mongoose's eyes grow red, he is angry), and he sat back on his tail and hind legs like a little kangaroo and looked all around him and chattered[12] with rage. But Nag and Nagaina had disappeared into the grass. When a snake misses its stroke, it never says anything 180 or gives any sign of what it means to do next. Rikki-tikki did not care to follow them, for he did not feel sure that he could manage two snakes at once. So he trotted off to the gravel path near the house and sat down to think. It was a serious matter for him.

Pause & Reflect

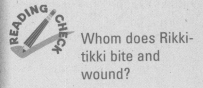

READING CHECK Whom does Rikki-tikki bite and wound?

Pause & Reflect

1. Cross out the one phrase below that is *not* true of Nag. **(Clarify)**

    is afraid of Rikki-tikki

    ate one of Darzee's babies

    has a wicked wife

    is bitten by Rikki-tikki

2. Why are the cobras able to escape from Rikki-tikki? **(Cause and Effect)**

---

11. **whisking** (hwĭsk-ĭng): moving quickly with a sweeping motion.

12. **chattered**: made a rapid series of clicking noises.

As the story continues . . .

• Rikki-tikki has his first fight with a snake.

English Learner Support

Language

Suffix The suffix *–ling* means "young or small." Karait is called a *snakeling* because he is a small snake.

snake + ling = snakeling (small snake)

duck + ling = duckling (young duck)

WHAT DOES IT MEAN? When Rikki-tikki is described as having *so perfectly balanced a gait,* it means he has a skillful way of moving on his feet.

FOCUS

In this part, Rikki-tikki comes upon another snake in the garden. Read on to find out what happens.

If you read the old books of natural history, you will find they say that when the mongoose fights the snake and happens to get bitten, he

190 runs off and eats some herb that cures him. That is not true. The victory is only a matter of quickness of eye and quickness of foot— snake's blow against mongoose's jump—and as no eye can follow the motion of a snake's head when it strikes, this makes things much more wonderful than any magic herb. Rikki-tikki knew he was a young mongoose, and it made him all the more pleased to think that he had managed to escape a blow from behind.

200 It gave him confidence in himself, and when Teddy came running down the path, Rikki-tikki was ready to be petted. But just as Teddy was stooping, something wriggled a little in the dust, and a tiny voice said, "Be careful. I am Death!" It was Karait,[13] the dusty brown snakeling that lies for choice on the dusty earth; and his bite is as dangerous as the cobra's. But he is so small that nobody thinks of him, and so he does the more harm to people.

Rikki-tikki's eyes grew red again, and he danced up

210 to Karait with the peculiar rocking, swaying motion that he had inherited from his family. It looks very funny, but it is so perfectly balanced a gait that you can fly off from it at any angle you please; and in dealing with snakes this is an advantage.

If Rikki-tikki had only known, he was doing a much more dangerous thing than fighting Nag; for Karait is so small and can turn so quickly, that unless Rikki bit him close to the back of the head, he would get the return stroke in his eye or his lip. But Rikki did not

13. **Karait** (kä-rīt´).

220 know: his eyes were all red, and he rocked back and forth, looking for a good place to hold. Karait struck out. Rikki jumped sideways and tried to run in, but the wicked little dusty gray head lashed within a fraction of his shoulder, and he had to jump over the body, and the head followed his heels close.

Teddy shouted to the house, "Oh, look here! Our mongoose is killing a snake"; and Rikki-tikki heard a scream from Teddy's mother. His father ran out with a stick, but by the time he came up, Karait had lunged
230 out once too far, and Rikki-tikki had sprung, jumped on the snake's back, dropped his head far between his forelegs, bitten as high up the back as he could get hold, and rolled away.

That bite paralyzed Karait, and Rikki-tikki was just going to eat him up from the tail, after the custom of his family at dinner, when he remembered that a full meal makes a slow mongoose; and if he wanted all his strength and quickness ready, he must keep himself thin. He went away for a dust bath under the castor-
240 oil bushes, while Teddy's father beat the dead Karait. "What is the use of that?" thought Rikki-tikki; "I have settled it all."

And then Teddy's mother picked him up from the dust and hugged him, crying that he had saved Teddy from death; and Teddy's father said that he was a providence,[14] and Teddy looked on with big scared eyes. Rikki-tikki was rather amused at all the fuss, which, of course, he did not understand. Teddy's mother might just as well have petted Teddy for playing
250 in the dust. Rikki was thoroughly enjoying himself.

Pause & Reflect

Pause & Reflect

1. █▌ **MARK IT UP** ▷ How does Rikki-tikki paralyze Karait? Circle descriptions on this page. Then write the answer. **(Clarify)**

2. Imagine you are in Rikki-tikki's situation. Why would you want to save all your strength and quickness after killing Karait? **(Connect)**

---

14. **providence:** blessing; something good given by God.

As the story continues . . .

- Rikki-tikki goes for a nighttime walk.
- He meets a fearful muskrat named Chuchundra and senses a snake nearby.

FOCUS

That night Rikki-tikki meets Chuchundra, the muskrat. Read on to find out about their meeting.

MARK IT UP > As you read, circle details that tell you what Chuchundra is like.

That night at dinner, walking to and fro among the wineglasses on the table, he might have stuffed himself three times over with nice things; but he remembered Nag and Nagaina, and though it was very pleasant to be patted and petted by 260 Teddy's mother and to sit on Teddy's shoulder, his eyes would get red from time to time, and he would go off into his long war cry of *"Rikk-tikk-tikki-tikki-tchk!"*

Teddy carried him off to bed and insisted on Rikki-tikki sleeping under his chin. Rikki-tikki was too well-bred to bite or scratch, but as soon as Teddy was asleep, he went off for his nightly walk around the house; and in the dark he ran up against Chuchundra, the muskrat, creeping around by the wall. Chuchundra is a brokenhearted little beast. He whimpers and 270 cheeps all the night, trying to make up his mind to run into the middle of the room; but he never gets there.

"Don't kill me," said Chuchundra, almost weeping. "Rikki-tikki, don't kill me!"

"Do you think a snake killer kills muskrats?" said Rikki-tikki scornfully.

"Those who kill snakes get killed by snakes," said Chuchundra, more sorrowfully than ever. "And how am I to be sure that Nag won't mistake me for you some dark night?"

280 "There's not the least danger," said Rikki-tikki; "but Nag is in the garden, and I know you don't go there."

"My cousin Chua,[15] the rat, told me—" said Chuchundra, and then he stopped.

"Told you what?"

---

15. **Chua** (chōō′ə).

"H'sh! Nag is everywhere, Rikki-tikki. You should have talked to Chua in the garden."

"I didn't—so you must tell me. Quick, Chuchundra, or I'll bite you!"

Chuchundra sat down and cried till the tears rolled
290 off his whiskers. "I am a very poor man," he sobbed. "I never had spirit enough to run out into the middle of the room. H'sh! I mustn't tell you anything. Can't you *hear*, Rikki-tikki?"

Rikki-tikki listened. The house was as still as still, but he thought he could just catch the faintest *scratch-scratch* in the world—a noise as faint as that of a wasp walking on a windowpane—the dry scratch of a snake's scales on brickwork.

"That's Nag or Nagaina," he said to himself, "and
300 he is crawling into the bathroom sluice.[16] You're right, Chuchundra; I should have talked to Chua."

Pause & Reflect

FOCUS

Nag and Nagaina make sly plans. Read to find out about these plans and how Rikki-tikki responds.

He stole off to Teddy's bathroom, but there was nothing there, and then to Teddy's mother's bathroom. At the bottom of the smooth plaster wall, there was a brick pulled out to make a sluice for the bath water, and as Rikki-tikki stole in by the masonry curb where the
310 bath is put, he heard Nag and Nagaina whispering together outside in the moonlight.

"When the house is emptied of people," said Nagaina to her husband, "*he* will have to go away,

---

16. **bathroom sluice** (slōōs): a channel and opening in a wall through which the water in a bathtub can be drained outdoors.

Pause & Reflect

1. How does Chuchundra's character differ from Rikki-tikki's? Put a "C" by qualities that apply to Chuchundra and an "R" by those that apply to Rikki-tikki. **(Compare and Contrast)**

___ timid

___ impatient

___ bold

___ helpless

___ sneaky

___ fearless

2. What is Chuchundra trying to warn Rikki-tikki about? **(Clarify)**

_____

_____

_____

As the story continues . . .

• Rikki-tikki overhears Nag and Nagaina plotting to kill the family.

• Rikki-tikki attacks Nag.

and then the garden will be our own again. Go in quietly, and remember that the big man who killed Karait is the first one to bite. Then come out and tell me, and we will hunt for Rikki-tikki together."

"But are you sure that there is anything to be gained by killing the people?" said Nag.

320 "Everything. When there were no people in the bungalow, did we have any mongoose in the garden? So long as the bungalow is empty, we are king and queen of the garden; and remember that as soon as our eggs in the melon bed hatch (as they may tomorrow), our children will need room and quiet."

"I had not thought of that," said Nag. "I will go, but there is no need that we should hunt for Rikki-tikki afterward. I will kill the big man and his wife, and the child if I can, and come away quietly. Then 330 the bungalow will be empty, and Rikki-tikki will go."

Rikki-tikki tingled all over with rage and hatred at this, and then Nag's head came through the sluice, and his five feet of cold body followed it. Angry as he was, Rikki-tikki was very frightened as he saw the size of the big cobra. Nag coiled himself up, raised his head, and looked into the bathroom in the dark, and Rikki could see his eyes glitter.

"Now, if I kill him here, Nagaina will know; and if I fight him on the open floor, the odds are in his favor. 340 What am I to do?" said Rikki-tikki-tavi.

Nag waved to and fro, and then Rikki-tikki heard him drinking from the biggest water jar that was used to fill the bath. "That is good," said the snake. "Now, when Karait was killed, the big man had a stick. He may have that stick still, but when he comes in to bathe in the morning, he will not have a stick. I shall wait here till he comes. Nagaina—do you hear me?— I shall wait here in the cool till daytime."

There was no answer from outside, so Rikki-tikki
350 knew Nagaina had gone away. Nag coiled himself
down, coil by coil, around the bulge at the bottom of
the water jar, and Rikki-tikki stayed still as death.
After an hour he began to move, muscle by muscle,
toward the jar. Nag was asleep, and Rikki-tikki looked
at his big back, wondering which would be the best
place for a good hold. "If I don't break his back at the
first jump," said Rikki, "he can still fight; and if he
fights—O Rikki!" He looked at the thickness of the
neck below the hood, but that was too much for him;
360 and a bite near the tail would only make Nag savage.

"It must be the head," he said at last; "the head
above the hood. And, when I am once there, I must
not let go."

Then he jumped. The head was lying a little clear of
the water jar, under the curve of it; and, as his teeth
met, Rikki braced his back against the bulge of the red
earthenware to hold down the head. This gave him
just one second's purchase,[17] and he made the most of
it. Then he was battered to and fro as a rat is shaken
370 by a dog—to and fro on the floor, up and down, and
round in great circles; but his eyes were red, and he
held on as the body cart-whipped over the floor,
upsetting the tin dipper and the soap dish and the flesh
brush, and banged against the tin side of the bath.

As he held, he closed his jaws tighter and tighter, for
he made sure he would be banged to death; and, for
the honor of his family, he preferred to be found with
his teeth locked. He was dizzy, aching, and felt
shaken to pieces when something went off like a
380 thunderclap just behind him; a hot wind knocked him
senseless, and red fire singed his fur. The big man had
been awakened by the noise and had fired both barrels
of a shotgun into Nag just behind the hood.

17. **purchase:** secure grasp or hold.

English Learner Support

Language

Simile A simile compares two things using the word *like* or *as*. The simile *still as death* compares Rikki-tikki to something dead. Rikki-tikki holds his body so still that he seems to be dead.

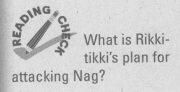 READING CHECK What is Rikki-tikki's plan for attacking Nag?

MARK IT UP Reread the boxed passage. Then circle details that help you picture the fight between Rikki-tikki and Nag. **(Visualize)**

Pause & Reflect

Why do Nag and Nagaina plan to kill the family rather than attack Rikki-tikki? (Cause and Effect)

As the story continues . . .

- Rikki-tikki makes a plan to destroy Nagaina's eggs.
- Darzee's wife warns Rikki-tikki that something has gone wrong.

Rikki-tikki held on with his eyes shut, for now he was quite sure he was dead; but the head did not move, and the big man picked him up and said, "It's the mongoose again, Alice; the little chap has saved *our* lives now."

390 Then Teddy's mother came in with a very white face and saw what was left of Nag, and Rikki-tikki dragged himself to Teddy's bedroom and spent half the rest of the night shaking himself tenderly to find out whether he really was broken into forty pieces, as he fancied.[18]

When morning came, he was very stiff but well pleased with his doings. "Now I have Nagaina to settle with, and she will be worse than five Nags, and there's no knowing when the eggs she spoke of will hatch. Goodness! I must go and see Darzee," he said.

Pause & Reflect

FOCUS

Rikki-tikki wants to find and destroy the cobra eggs. Read on to find out how Darzee's wife helps him.

MARK IT UP ❯ As you read, circle details that show you how Darzee's wife helps Rikki-tikki with his plan.

400 Without waiting for breakfast, Rikki-tikki ran to the thorn bush where Darzee was singing a song of triumph at the top of his voice. The news of Nag's death was all over the garden, for the sweeper[19] had thrown the body on the rubbish heap.

"Oh, you stupid tuft of 410 feathers!" said Rikki-tikki angrily. "Is this the time to sing?"

---

18. **fancied:** supposed.

19. **sweeper:** servant who sweeps out the bungalow.

"Nag is dead—is dead—is dead!" sang Darzee. "The valiant Rikki-tikki caught him by the head and held fast. The big man brought the bang stick, and Nag fell in two pieces! He will never eat my babies again."

"All that's true enough; but where's Nagaina?" said Rikki-tikki, looking carefully round him.

420 "Nagaina came to the bathroom sluice and called for Nag," Darzee went on; "and Nag came out on the end of a stick—the sweeper picked him up on the end of a stick and threw him upon the rubbish heap. Let us sing about the great, the red-eyed Rikki-tikki!" And Darzee filled his throat and sang.

"If I could get up to your nest, I'd roll your babies out!" said Rikki-tikki. "You don't know when to do the right thing at the right time. You're safe enough in your nest there, but it's war for me down here. Stop singing a minute, Darzee."

430 "For the great, the beautiful Rikki-tikki's sake I will stop," said Darzee. "What is it, O Killer of the terrible Nag?"

"Where is Nagaina, for the third time?"

"On the rubbish heap by the stables, mourning[20] for Nag. Great is Rikki-tikki with the white teeth."

"Bother my white teeth! Have you ever heard where she keeps her eggs?"

"In the melon bed, on the end nearest the wall, where the sun strikes nearly all day. She hid them 440 there weeks ago."

"And you never thought it worthwhile to tell me? The end nearest the wall, you said?"

"Rikki-tikki, you are not going to eat her eggs?"

"Not eat exactly, no. Darzee, if you have a grain of sense, you will fly off to the stables and pretend that

---

20. **mourning** (môrn′ĭng): showing grief for the death of someone.

READ ALOUD the boxed passage. How does Darzee describe Rikki-tikki? Check one. (Analyze)

❏ as a failure
❏ as a loved one who has died
❏ as a triumphant hero

English Learner Support
Vocabulary

Bother In this sentence, *bother* means "never mind" or "forget about." Rikki-tikki wants Darzee to stop talking about his white teeth and answer his question about Nagaina's eggs.

READING CHECK Why is Rikki-tikki annoyed with Darzee?

WHAT DOES IT MEAN? Darzee is described as being *featherbrained,* or "silly and lacking in good sense."

READING CHECK Why does Rikki-tikki want to reach Nagaina's eggs?

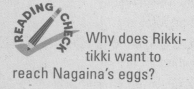

READ ALOUD the boxed passage. Work with a partner. One person should take the role of Darzee's wife and the other, Nagaina. Practice your lines several times. Then, with your partner, use your voices to express the drama of the situation.

your wing is broken and let Nagaina chase you away to this bush. I must get to the melon bed, and if I went there now, she'd see me."

Darzee was a featherbrained little fellow who could
450 never hold more than one idea at a time in his head; and just because he knew that Nagaina's children were born in eggs like his own, he didn't think at first that it was fair to kill them. But his wife was a sensible bird, and she knew that cobra's eggs meant young cobras later on; so she flew off from the nest and left Darzee to keep the babies warm and continue his song about the death of Nag. Darzee was very like a man in some ways.

She fluttered in front of Nagaina by the rubbish heap and cried out, "Oh, my wing is broken! The boy
460 in the house threw a stone at me and broke it." Then she fluttered more desperately than ever.

Nagaina lifted up her head and hissed, "You warned Rikki-tikki when I would have killed him. Indeed and truly, you've chosen a bad place to be lame in." And she moved toward Darzee's wife, slipping along over the dust.

"The boy broke it with a stone!" shrieked Darzee's wife.

"Well! It may be some <u>consolation</u> to you when
470 you're dead to know that I shall settle accounts with the boy. My husband lies on the rubbish heap this morning, but before night the boy in the house will lie very still. What is the use of running away? I am sure to catch you. Little fool, look at me!"

Darzee's wife knew better than to do *that,* for a bird who looks at a snake's eyes gets so frightened that she cannot move. Darzee's wife fluttered on, piping sorrowfully, and never leaving the ground, and Nagaina quickened her pace.

WORDS TO KNOW
consolation (kŏn'sə-lā'shən) *n.* something that comforts

480   Rikki-tikki heard them going up the path from the stables, and he raced for the end of the melon patch near the wall. There, in the warm litter[21] above the melons, very <u>cunningly</u> hidden, he found twenty-five eggs, about the size of a bantam's eggs[22] but with whitish skins instead of shells.

    "I was not a day too soon," he said, for he could see the baby cobras curled up inside the skin, and he knew that the minute they were hatched they could each kill a man or a mongoose. He bit off the tops of the eggs
490 as fast as he could, taking care to crush the young cobras, and turned over the litter from time to time to see whether he had missed any. At last there were only three eggs left, and Rikki-tikki began to chuckle to himself when he heard Darzee's wife screaming.

> "Rikki-tikki, I led Nagaina toward the house, and she has gone into the veranda and—oh, come quickly—she means killing!"

Pause & Reflect

FOCUS

Can Rikki-tikki save Teddy from Nagaina? Read to find out.

    Rikki-tikki smashed two eggs and tumbled backward
500 down the melon bed with the third egg in his mouth and <u>scuttled</u> to the veranda as hard as he could put foot to the ground. Teddy and his mother and father were there at early breakfast; but Rikki-tikki saw that they were not eating anything. They sat stone still, and their faces were white. Nagaina was coiled up on the

---

21. **litter:** upper layer of decayed leaves and other organic matter lying on the ground.

22. **bantam's eggs:** the eggs of a small hen.

WORDS TO KNOW
   cunningly (kŭn´ĭng-lē) *adv.* in a clever way that is meant to trick or deceive
   scuttle (skŭt´l) *v.* to run quickly, with hurried movements

Pause & Reflect

1. What does Rikki-tikki do to the cobra eggs? (Clarify)

2. **REREAD** the boxed sentence. What do you think Nagaina is planning to do? (Predict)

As the story continues . . .

- Rikki-tikki finds the family trapped by Nagaina.

- He tricks Nagaina, but she races off with her last egg.

matting by Teddy's chair, within easy striking distance of Teddy's bare leg; and she was swaying to and fro, singing a song of triumph.

510   "Son of the big man that killed Nag," she hissed, "stay still. I am not ready yet. Wait a little. Keep very still, all you three! If you move, I strike, and if you do not move, I strike. Oh, foolish people who killed my Nag!"

    Teddy's eyes were fixed on his father, and all his father could do was to whisper, "Sit still, Teddy. You mustn't move. Teddy, keep still."

    Then Rikki-tikki came up and cried, "Turn round, Nagaina; turn and fight!"

520   "All in good time," said she, without moving her eyes. "I will settle my account with you presently. Look at your friends, Rikki-tikki. They are still and white. They are afraid. They dare not move, and if you come a step nearer, I strike."

    "Look at your eggs," said Rikki-tikki, "in the melon bed near the wall. Go and look, Nagaina!"

    The big snake turned half round and saw the egg on the veranda. "Ah-h! Give it to me," she said.

    Rikki-tikki put his paws one on each side of the egg, 530 and his eyes were blood-red. "What price for a snake's egg? For a young cobra? For a young king cobra? For the last—the very last of the brood? The ants are eating all the others down by the melon bed."

    Nagaina spun clear round, forgetting everything for the sake of the one egg; and Rikki-tikki saw Teddy's father shoot out a big hand, catch Teddy by the shoulder, and drag him across the little table with the teacups, safe and out of reach of Nagaina.

    "Tricked! Tricked! Tricked! *Rikk-tck-tck!*" chuckled 540 Rikki-tikki. "The boy is safe, and it was I—I—I that

English Learner Support

Vocabulary

Idiom When Nagaina tells Rikki-tikki, *I will settle my account with you presently,* she means that she will fight Rikki-tikki after she has killed Teddy.

READ ALOUD the boxed passage. Imagine you are Rikki-tikki. Use the tone and volume of your voice to show that you are challenging Nagaina.

caught Nag by the hood last night in the bathroom."
Then he began to jump up and down, all four feet
together, his head close to the floor. "He threw me to
and fro, but he could not shake me off. He was dead
before the big man blew him in two. I did it! *Rikki-
tikki-tck-tck!* Come then, Nagaina. Come and fight
with me. You shall not be a widow long."

Nagaina saw that she had lost her chance of killing
Teddy, and the egg lay between Rikki-tikki's paws.
550 "Give me the egg, Rikki-tikki. Give me the last of my
eggs, and I will go away and never come back," she
said, lowering her hood.

"Yes, you will go away, and you will never come
back, for you will go to the rubbish heap with Nag.
Fight, widow! The big man has gone for his gun!
Fight!"

Rikki-tikki was bounding all round Nagaina,
keeping just out of reach of her stroke, his little eyes
like hot coals. Nagaina gathered herself together and
560 flung out at him. Rikki-tikki jumped up and
backwards. Again and again and again she struck, and
each time her head came with a whack on the matting
of the veranda, and she gathered herself together like a
watch spring. Then Rikki-tikki danced in a circle to get
behind her, and Nagaina spun round to keep her head
to his head, so that the rustle of her tail on the matting
sounded like dry leaves blown along by the wind.

He had forgotten the egg. It still lay on the veranda,
and Nagaina came nearer and nearer to it, till at last,
570 while Rikki-tikki was drawing breath, she caught it in
her mouth, turned to the veranda steps, and flew like
an arrow down the path, with Rikki-tikki behind her.
When the cobra runs for her life, she goes like a

WHAT DOES IT MEAN? A
widow is a woman whose
husband has died. Rikki-tikki
is referring to the fact that he
killed Nagaina's husband and
will soon try to kill her.

WHAT DOES IT MEAN? Inside
some watches, a tightly
wound wire called a *watch
spring* helps make the hands
move.

Pause & Reflect

Can Nagaina protect herself and her egg from Rikki-tikki? What do you think will happen next? (Predict)

As the story ends . . .

• Rikki-tikki chases Nagaina into the rat hole where she lives.

English Learner Support
Vocabulary

Multiple Meanings The word *care* often means "to be interested in something." In this sentence, *care* means "to like" or "to want." Most mongooses would not want to follow a cobra into its hole.

WHAT DOES IT MEAN? *Valiant* means "brave."

whiplash flicked across a horse's neck. Rikki-tikki knew that he must catch her, or all the trouble would begin again.

Pause & Reflect

FOCUS

Read to find out if your prediction is correct.

She headed straight for the long grass by the thorn bush, and as he was running, Rikki-
580 tikki heard Darzee still singing his foolish little song of triumph. But Darzee's wife was wiser. She flew off her nest as Nagaina came along and flapped her wings about Nagaina's head. If Darzee had helped, they might have turned her; but Nagaina only lowered her hood and went on. Still, the instant's delay brought Rikki-tikki up to her, and as she plunged into the rat hole where she and Nag used to live, his little white teeth were clenched on her tail, and he went down
590 with her—and very few mongooses, however wise and old they may be, care to follow a cobra into its hole.

It was dark in the hole; and Rikki-tikki never knew when it might open out and give Nagaina room to turn and strike at him. He held on savagely and stuck out his feet to act as brakes on the dark slope of the hot, moist earth.

Then the grass by the mouth of the hole stopped waving, and Darzee said, "It is all over with Rikki-tikki! We must sing his death song. Valiant Rikki-tikki
600 is dead! For Nagaina will surely kill him underground."

So he sang a very mournful song that he made up on the spur of the minute; and just as he got to the most touching part, the grass quivered again, and

Rikki-tikki, covered with dirt, dragged himself out of the hole leg by leg, licking his whiskers. Darzee stopped with a little shout. Rikki-tikki shook some of the dust out of his fur and sneezed. "It is all over," he said. "The widow will never come out again." And the red ants that live between the grass stems heard him
610 and began to troop down one after another to see if he had spoken the truth.

Rikki-tikki curled himself up in the grass and slept where he was—slept and slept till it was late in the afternoon, for he had done a hard day's work.

"Now," he said, when he awoke, "I will go back to the house. Tell the coppersmith, Darzee, and he will tell the garden that Nagaina is dead."

The coppersmith is a bird who makes a noise exactly like the beating of a little hammer on a copper
620 pot; and the reason he is always making it is because he is the town crier to every Indian garden and tells all the news to everybody who cares to listen. As Rikki-tikki went up the path, he heard his "attention" notes like a tiny dinner gong, and then the steady *"Ding-dong-tock!* Nag is dead—*dong!* Nagaina is dead! Ding-dong-tock!"* That set all the birds in the garden singing and the frogs croaking, for Nag and Nagaina used to eat frogs as well as little birds.

When Rikki got to the house, Teddy and Teddy's
630 mother (she looked very white still, for she had been fainting) and Teddy's father came out and almost cried over him; and that night he ate all that was given him till he could eat no more and went to bed on Teddy's shoulder, where Teddy's mother saw him when she came to look late at night.

"He saved our lives and Teddy's life," she said to her husband. "Just think, he saved all our lives."

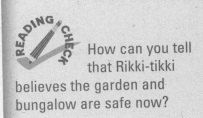

What happened between Rikki-tikki and Nagaina in the cobra's hole? Why do the red ants go into the hole?

How can you tell that Rikki-tikki believes the garden and bungalow are safe now?

Pause & Reflect

1. What qualities does Rikki-tikki show in his fight with Nagaina? (Infer)

2. How do you feel about Rikki-tikki by the end of the story? (Connect)

 How would the story be different if the author had told it from Nagaina's perspective? How would Nagaina describe events and characters differently? What details would stay the same? (Compare and Contrast)

Rikki-tikki woke up with a jump, for the mongooses are light sleepers.

640   "Oh, it's you," said he. "What are you bothering for? All the cobras are dead; and if they weren't, I'm here."

Rikki-tikki had a right to be proud of himself; but he did not grow too proud, and he kept that garden as a mongoose should keep it, with tooth and jump and spring and bite, till never a cobra dared show its head inside the walls. ❖

Pause & Reflect

▐▐▐ **MARK IT UP** ⟩ What was your favorite scene or event in the story? Draw it in the space below. (Visualize)

Active Reading SkillBuilder

Predicting

When you **make predictions,** you use what you already know to try to figure out
what will happen. Good readers gather information as they read and combine it with
things they know to predict events in a story. As you read "Rikki-tikki-tavi," pause after
each event listed in column 1 to make a prediction. Write the predictions in column 2.
Then read on and write what actually occurs in column 3.

Events	Predictions	What Actually Happens
1. Teddy's parents see Rikki-tikki on Teddy's pillow. (p. 112)	*They will shoo Rikki-tikki off the bed.*	
2. Rikki-tikki meets Nag in the garden. (p. 114)		
3. Rikki-tikki meets Karait in the garden. (p. 116)		
4. Nag sneaks into the house at night. (p. 120)		
5. Darzee's wife pretends to have a broken wing. (p. 124)		
6. Rikki-tikki is pulled down into Nagaina's hole. (p. 128)		

Literary Analysis SkillBuilder

Personification

In the story, Kipling **personifies,** or gives human traits to, animal characters. As you read, complete the chart below. Identify the type of animal each character is, the animal's traits, and the key actions or words you used to find those traits. See the example given.

Animal's Name	Type of Animal	Personality Traits	Key Actions or Words
Rikki-tikki-tavi	mongoose	confident, curious, brave, clever	fights all snakes, plots to kill cobras, protects the family
Darzee			
Darzee's wife			
Chuchundra			
Nag			
Nagaina			

Words to Know SkillBuilder

Words to Know

consolation cower cunningly revive scuttle

A. Fill in each blank with the correct Word to Know.

I'm allergic to the blossoms of most any sort of flower,

So I spend the spring and summer locked inside.

The presence of a tulip is enough to make me _____.
                                                        (1)

Do not ask me to be brave, for I have tried!

If I have to go outside, I _____ back into my dwelling,
                              (2)

Just as fast as I can scamper, for I fear each flowery bloom.

If I get too near a blossom, then my eyelids start their swelling,

And my sneezing blows the windows from my room.

B. Fill in each set of blanks with the correct Word to Know. The boxed letters
will spell out the kind of animal a mongoose looks most like.

1. A puppy may do this if it hears an angry voice
   or thinks it is in trouble.   __ __ ☐ __ __

2. After they faint, people must do this before
   they can stand up again.   __ __ __ __ ☐

3. This could be something like a pat on the back
   or a kind word.   __ __ , __ __ __ __ ☐ __ __ __ __

4. This is how mice might move when a cat is after them.   ☐ __ __ __ __ __ ☐

5. Someone who is trying to fool someone
   else may behave this way.   __ __ __ __ __ ☐ __ __

Animal: _____

Before You Read

Connect to Your Life

Think of a book or story you have read in which a character changes. What causes the change? Is the motive the kind that would change a real person? Use the chart to record your thoughts.

Character: _____   From: _____

Cause of Change: _____   Change: _____

_____   _____

_____   _____

Check one: Realistic ☐   Not Realistic ☐

Key to the Story

WHAT'S THE BIG IDEA? The noun **reformation** comes from the verb **reform**. A reformation is a reshaping of a person's character. Usually reformation means giving up harmful or bad behavior. Look in a dictionary for other words related to *reformation* and write them in the web.

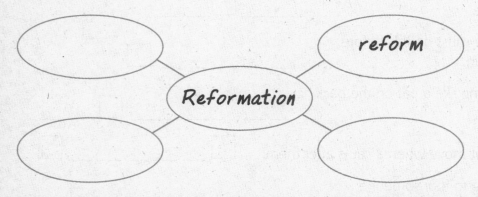

When you have finished the story, answer this question: How is the change that happens to Jimmy Valentine a **retrieved** reformation?

A Retrieved Reformation

by O. Henry

PREVIEW   The story you are about to read is about Jimmy Valentine, a criminal. He is an expert at breaking into safes. Can anything make him change his evil ways?

- Jimmy Valentine, a well-known bank robber, is released from prison.
- Jimmy travels to see an old friend.

English Learner Support

Vocabulary

Slang and Idioms *Brace up* means "get ready." *Cracking safes* means "breaking into locked vaults to steal money and other valuables." *Live straight* means "live an honest life."

READING TIP

Slang Words
O. Henry wrote this story in the late 1800s, and he uses many slang terms from that time. Examples include:

- *stir* = prison
- *high-toned* = superior
- *get sent up* = go to prison
- *rogue catcher* = person who captures criminals; police officer

Use the footnotes to help you understand such terms. If there is no footnote, use the context of the story to figure out the meaning.

FOCUS

In this part you will meet Jimmy Valentine as he gets ready to leave prison. Read on to find out about him:

MARK IT UP Circle details that help you get to know Jimmy. An example is highlighted.

A guard came to the prison shoe shop, where Jimmy Valentine was <u>assiduously</u> stitching uppers,[1] and escorted him to the front office. There the warden handed Jimmy his pardon, which had been signed that morning by the governor. Jimmy took it in a

10 tired kind of way. He had served nearly ten months of a four-year sentence. He had expected to stay only about three months, at the longest. When a man with as many friends on the outside as Jimmy Valentine had is received in the "stir" it is hardly worthwhile to cut his hair.

"Now, Valentine," said the warden, "you'll go out in the morning. Brace up, and make a man of yourself. You're not a bad fellow at heart. Stop cracking safes, and live straight."

20 "Me?" said Jimmy, in surprise. "Why, I never cracked a safe in my life."

"Oh, no," laughed the warden. "Of course not. Let's see, now. How was it you happened to get sent up on that Springfield job? Was it because you wouldn't prove an alibi for fear of compromising[2] somebody in extremely high-toned society? Or was it simply a case of a mean old jury that had it in for you? It's always one or the other with you innocent victims."

30 "Me?" said Jimmy, still blankly <u>virtuous</u>. "Why, warden, I never was in Springfield in my life!"

---

1. **upper:** the part of a shoe or boot above the sole.
2. **compromising** (kŏm′prə-mīz′ ing): exposing to danger or suspicion.

WORDS TO KNOW
assiduously (ə-sĭj′o͞o-əs-lē) *adv.* in a steady and hard-working way
virtuous (vûr′cho͞o-əs) *adj.* morally good; honorable

"Take him back, Cronin," smiled the warden, "and fix him up with outgoing clothes. Unlock him at seven in the morning, and let him come to the bull-pen. Better think over my advice, Valentine."

At a quarter past seven on the next morning Jimmy stood in the warden's outer office. He had on a suit of the villainously fitting, ready-made clothes and a pair of the stiff, squeaky shoes that the state furnishes to its
40 discharged <u>compulsory</u> guests.

The clerk handed him a railroad ticket and the five-dollar bill with which the law expected him to <u>rehabilitate</u> himself into good citizenship and prosperity. The warden gave him a cigar, and shook hands. Valentine, 9762, was chronicled on the books "Pardoned by Governor," and Mr. James Valentine walked out into the sunshine.

Disregarding the song of the birds, the waving green trees, and the smell of the flowers, Jimmy headed
50 straight for a restaurant. There he tasted the first sweet joys of liberty in the shape of a broiled chicken and a bottle of white wine—followed by a cigar a grade better than the one the warden had given him. From there he proceeded leisurely to the depot. He tossed a quarter into the hat of a blind man sitting by the door, and boarded his train. Three hours set him down in a little town near the state line. He went to the café of one Mike Dolan and shook hands with Mike, who was alone behind the bar.

Pause & Reflect

WORDS TO KNOW
   compulsory (kəm-pŭl'sə-rē) *adj.* that which must be done; required
   rehabilitate (rē'hə-bĭl'ĭ-tāt') *v.* to restore to useful life, as through therapy and education

Pause & Reflect

1. Jimmy Valentine serves time in prison for what crime? **(Clarify)**

2. How does having "many friends on the outside" help Jimmy? Circle one. **(Infer)**

   He is given excellent food in prison.

   He receives a pardon before serving his full sentence.

   He is given stylish clothes when he leaves prison.

As the story continues . . .

• Jimmy returns to his old apartment.
• Some bank robberies occur.
• Detective Ben Price investigates the robberies.

Why is there a button from Detective Ben Price's shirt on Jimmy's floor?

One way to better understand Jimmy is to create a character map like the one below. It will help you keep track of facts and details about Jimmy's actions and how he behaves with others. As you read, make additions and changes to your character map.

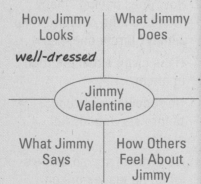

FOCUS

Jimmy takes up his old "profession."

MARK IT UP ▷ As you read, underline details that tell you about Jimmy's profession.

60 "Sorry we couldn't make it sooner, Jimmy, me boy," said Mike. "But we had that protest from Springfield to buck against, and the governor nearly <u>balked</u>. Feeling all right?"

"Fine," said Jimmy. "Got my key?"

He got his key and went upstairs, unlocking the door of a room at the rear. Everything was just as he 70 had left it. There on the floor was still Ben Price's collar-button that had been torn from that <u>eminent</u> detective's shirt-band when they had overpowered Jimmy to arrest him.

Pulling out from the wall a folding-bed, Jimmy slid back a panel in the wall and dragged out a dust-covered suitcase. He opened this and gazed fondly at the finest set of burglar's tools in the East. It was a complete set, made of specially tempered steel, the latest designs in drills, punches, braces and bits, 80 jimmies, clamps, and augers, with two or three novelties invented by Jimmy himself, in which he took pride. Over nine hundred dollars they had cost him to have made at _____, a place where they make such things for the profession.

In half an hour Jimmy went downstairs and through the café. He was now dressed in tasteful and well-fitting clothes, and carried his dusted and cleaned suitcase in his hand.

"Got anything on?" asked Mike Dolan, genially.

90 "Me?" said Jimmy, in a puzzled tone. "I don't understand. I'm representing the New York Amalgamated Short Snap Biscuit Cracker and Frazzled Wheat Company."

WORDS TO KNOW
balk (bôk) *v.* to refuse to move or act
eminent (ĕm′ə-nənt) *adj.* better than most others; very famous

This statement delighted Mike to such an extent that Jimmy had to take a seltzer-and-milk on the spot. He never touched "hard" drinks.

A week after the release of Valentine, 9762, there was a neat job of safe-burglary done in Richmond, Indiana, with no clue to the author. A scant eight 100 hundred dollars was all that was secured. Two weeks after that a patented, improved, burglar-proof safe in Logansport was opened like a cheese to the tune of fifteen hundred dollars, currency; securities and silver untouched. That began to interest the rogue catchers. Then an old-fashioned bank safe in Jefferson City became active and threw out of its crater an eruption of banknotes amounting to five thousand dollars. The losses were now high enough to bring the matter up into Ben Price's class of work. By comparing notes, a 110 remarkable similarity in the methods of the burglaries was noticed. Ben Price investigated the scenes of the robberies, and was heard to remark:

"That's Dandy Jim Valentine's autograph. He's resumed business. Look at that combination knob— jerked out as easy as pulling up a radish in wet weather. He's got the only clamps that can do it. And look how clean those tumblers were punched out! Jimmy never has to drill but one hole. Yes, I guess I want Mr. Valentine. He'll do his bit next time without 120 any short-time or clemency[3] foolishness."

Ben Price knew Jimmy's habits. He had learned them while working up the Springfield case. Long jumps, quick get-aways, no confederates,[4] and a taste for good society—these ways had helped Mr. Valentine to become noted as a successful dodger of <u>retribution</u>. It was given out that Ben Price had taken up the trail

---

3. **clemency:** a pardon.
4. **confederates** (kən-fĕd′ər-ĭts): accomplices or associates in crime.

WORDS TO KNOW
retribution (rĕt′rə-byōō′shən) *n.* punishment for bad behavior

English Learner Support
Language

Figurative Language The expression *opened like a cheese to the tune of fifteen hundred dollars* compares the safe to a piece of cheese. Opening the safe was as easy as slicing into a piece of cheese, and fifteen hundred dollars were stolen. The phrase *became active and threw out of its crater an eruption of banknotes* describes the safe as if it were an exploding volcano. This means that a lot of money was stolen all at once.

REREAD the boxed passage. How good is Jimmy at his profession? **(Evaluate)**

of the <u>elusive</u> cracksman, and other people with burglar-proof safes felt more at ease.

One afternoon Jimmy Valentine and his suitcase 130 climbed out of the mailhack in Elmore, a little town five miles off the railroad down in the blackjack country of Arkansas. Jimmy, looking like an athletic young senior just home from college, went down the board sidewalk toward the hotel.

Pause & Reflect

FOCUS

Something happens to change Jimmy's life. What do you think happens to him?

MARK IT UP ⟩ Circle details that help you understand why Jimmy's life changes.

A young lady crossed the street, passed him at the corner, and entered a door over which was the sign "The Elmore Bank." Jimmy Valentine looked 140 into her eyes, forgot what he was, and became another man. She lowered her eyes and colored slightly. Young men of Jimmy's style and looks were scarce in Elmore.

Jimmy collared a boy that was loafing on the steps of the bank as if he were one of the stockholders, and began to ask him questions about the town, feeding him dimes at intervals. By and by the young lady came out, looking royally unconscious of the young man 150 with the suitcase, and went her way.

"Isn't that young lady Miss Polly Simpson?" asked Jimmy, with specious guile.[5]

"Naw," said the boy. "She's Annabel Adams. Her pa owns this bank. What'd you come to Elmore for? Is that a gold watchchain? I'm going to get a bulldog.

---

5. **specious guile** (spē′shəs gīl): innocent charm masking real slyness.

WORDS TO KNOW
elusive (ĭ-lōō′sĭv) *adj.* escaping from capture as by daring, cleverness, or skill

---

Left sidebar

Pause & Reflect

Which of the following is a likely reason for Jimmy's coming to Elmore? Check one. **(Predict)**

❑ to rob the Elmore bank
❑ to take a vacation there
❑ to meet Ben Price

📝 **As the story continues . . .**

• Jimmy sees a young woman at the Elmore Bank.

• He changes his name and takes a room at the hotel.

WHAT DOES IT MEAN?
Feeding him dimes means "giving him dimes," or "paying for information."

Got any more dimes?"

Jimmy went to the Planters' Hotel, registered as
Ralph D. Spencer, and engaged a room. He leaned on
the desk and declared his platform to the clerk. He
160 said he had come to Elmore to look for a location to
go into business. How was the shoe business, now, in
the town? He had thought of the shoe business. Was
there an opening?

The clerk was impressed by the clothes and manner
of Jimmy. He, himself, was something of a pattern of
fashion to the thinly gilded youth of Elmore, but he
now perceived his shortcomings. While trying to figure
out Jimmy's manner of tying his four-in-hand[6] he
cordially gave information.

170 Yes, there ought to be a good opening in the shoe
line. There wasn't an exclusive shoe store in the place.
The dry-goods and general stores handled them.
Business in all lines was fairly good. Hoped Mr. Spencer
would decide to locate in Elmore. He would find it a
pleasant town to live in, and the people very sociable.

Mr. Spencer thought he would stop over in the town
a few days and look over the situation. No, the clerk
needn't call the boy. He would carry up his suitcase,
himself; it was rather heavy.

180 Mr. Ralph Spencer, the phoenix[7] that arose from
Jimmy Valentine's ashes—ashes left by the flame of a
sudden and alterative attack of love—remained in
Elmore, and prospered. He opened a shoe store and
secured a good run of trade.

Socially he was also a success and made many
friends. And he accomplished the wish of his heart. He
met Miss Annabel Adams, and became more and more
captivated by her charms.

---

6. **four-in-hand:** a necktie tied in the usual way, that is, in a slipknot with the ends
left hanging.

7. **phoenix** (fē′nĭks): a mythological bird that lived for over 500 years and then
burned itself to death, only to rise out of its own ashes to live another long life.

Create a two-column chart to show how Jimmy changes during the story. Write details that show what he was like before and after coming to Elmore.

Before	After

Pause & Reflect

1. Why does Jimmy change his life? (Cause and Effect)

_____

_____

_____

2. **REREAD** the letter Jimmy writes to his friend. Cross out any phrase below that is *not* part of Jimmy's plans. (Clarify)

move West

sell the shoe store

buy new tools

rob a bank

marry Annabel

At the end of a year the situation of Mr. Ralph Spencer was this: he had won the respect of the community, his shoe store was flourishing, and he and Annabel were engaged to be married in two weeks. Mr. Adams, the typical, plodding, country banker, approved of Spencer. Annabel's pride in him almost equaled her affection. He was as much at home in the family of Mr. Adams and that of Annabel's married sister as if he were already a member.

One day Jimmy sat down in his room and wrote this letter, which he mailed to the safe address of one of his old friends in St. Louis:

DEAR OLD PAL:

I want you to be at Sullivan's place, in Little Rock, next Wednesday night, at nine o'clock. I want you to wind up some little matters for me. And, also, I want to make you a present of my kit of tools. I know you'll be glad to get them—you couldn't duplicate the lot for a thousand dollars. Say, Billy, I've quit the old business—a year ago. I've got a nice store. I'm making an honest living, and I'm going to marry the finest girl on earth two weeks from now. It's the only life, Billy—the straight one. I wouldn't touch a dollar of another man's money now for a million. After I get married I'm going to sell out and go West, where there won't be so much danger of having old scores brought up against me. I tell you, Billy, she's an angel. She believes in me; and I wouldn't do another crooked thing for the whole world. Be sure to be at Sully's, for I must see you. I'll bring along the tools with me.

Your old friend,
JIMMY

Pause & Reflect

FOCUS

Someone from Jimmy's past reappears. He observes something terrible happen at the bank. Read on to find out what happens.

On the Monday night after Jimmy wrote this letter, Ben Price jogged <u>unobtrusively</u> into Elmore in a livery buggy. He lounged about town in his quiet way until he found out what he wanted to know.

From the drugstore across the street from Spencer's shoe store he got a good look at Ralph D. Spencer.

230 "Going to marry the banker's daughter are you, Jimmy?" said Ben to himself, softly. "Well, I don't know!"

The next morning Jimmy took breakfast at the Adamses. He was going to Little Rock that day to order his wedding suit and buy something nice for Annabel. That would be the first time he had left town since he came to Elmore. It had been more than a year now since those last professional "jobs," and he thought he could safely venture out.

240 After breakfast quite a family party went down together—Mr. Adams, Annabel, Jimmy, and Annabel's married sister with her two little girls, aged five and nine. They came by the hotel where Jimmy still boarded, and he ran up to his room and brought along his suitcase. Then they went on to the bank. There stood Jimmy's horse and buggy and Dolph Gibson, who was going to drive him over to the railroad station.

All went inside the high, carved oak railings into the 250 banking room—Jimmy included, for Mr. Adams's future son-in-law was welcome anywhere. The clerks were pleased to be greeted by the good-looking, agreeable young man who was going to marry Miss Annabel. Jimmy set his suitcase down. Annabel, whose heart was bubbling with happiness and lively youth,

As the story continues . . .

• Ben Price arrives in Elmore.

• As Jimmy prepares for a trip, a frightening incident occurs.

WHAT DOES IT MEAN?
A *livery buggy* is a cart pulled by a horse that can be rented or hired for traveling. It serves the same purpose as a modern taxi.

READING CHECK
Why does Ben Price question whether Jimmy will marry the banker's daughter?

WHAT DOES IT MEAN? A person's *son-in-law* is a man married to the person's daughter. When Jimmy marries Annabel, he will become Mr. Adams's son-in-law.

WORDS TO KNOW
unobtrusively (ŭn´əb-trōō´sĭv-lē) *adv.* in a way that attracts little or no attention

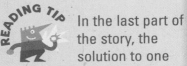
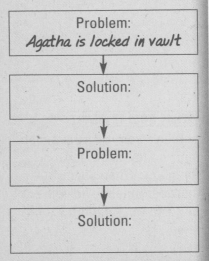
put on Jimmy's hat and picked up the suitcase. "Wouldn't I make a nice drummer[8]?" said Annabel.

"My! Ralph, how heavy it is. Feels like it was full of gold bricks."

260 "Lot of nickel-plated shoehorns in there," said Jimmy, coolly, "that I'm going to return. Thought I'd save express charges by taking them up. I'm getting awfully economical."

The Elmore Bank had just put in a new safe and vault. Mr. Adams was very proud of it, and insisted on an inspection by everyone. The vault was a small one, but it had a new patented door. It fastened with three solid steel bolts thrown simultaneously with a single handle, and had a time lock. Mr. Adams beamingly

270 explained its workings to Mr. Spencer, who showed a courteous but not too intelligent interest. The two children, May and Agatha, were delighted by the shining metal and funny clock and knobs.

While they were thus engaged Ben Price sauntered in and leaned on his elbow, looking casually inside between the railings. He told the teller that he didn't want anything; he was just waiting for a man he knew.

Suddenly there was a scream or two from the women, and a commotion. <u>Unperceived</u> by the elders,

280 May, the nine-year-old girl, in a spirit of play, had shut Agatha in the vault. She had then shot the bolts and turned the knob of the combination as she had seen Mr. Adams do.

The old banker sprang to the handle and tugged at it for a moment. "The door can't be opened," he groaned. "The clock hasn't been wound nor the combination set."

Agatha's mother screamed again, hysterically.

_____

8. **drummer:** a traveling salesman.

WORDS TO KNOW
unperceived (ŭn′pər-sēvd′) *adj.* not seen

"Hush!" said Mr. Adams, raising his trembling
290 hand. "All be quiet for a moment. Agatha!" he called
as loudly as he could. "Listen to me." During the
following silence they could just hear the faint sound
of the child wildly shrieking in the dark vault in a
panic of terror.

"My precious darling!" wailed the mother. "She will
die of fright! Open the door! Oh, break it open! Can't
you men do something?"

"There isn't a man nearer than Little Rock who can
open that door," said Mr. Adams, in a shaky voice.
300 "My God! Spencer, what shall we do? That child—she
can't stand it long in there. There isn't enough air, and,
besides, she'll go into convulsions from fright."

Pause & Reflect

FOCUS

Agatha's life is in danger.
What will Jimmy do?
Read to find out.

Agatha's mother, frantic
now, beat the door of the
vault with her hands.
Somebody wildly suggested
dynamite. Annabel turned to
Jimmy, her large eyes full of anguish, but not yet
despairing. To a woman nothing seems quite impossi-
310 ble to the powers of the man she worships.

"Can't you do something, Ralph—try, won't you?"

He looked at her with a queer, soft smile on his lips
and in his keen eyes.

"Annabel," he said, "give me that rose you are
wearing, will you?"

Hardly believing that she had heard him aright, she
unpinned the bud from the bosom of her dress, and
placed it in his hand. Jimmy stuffed it into his vest

Pause & Reflect

The door of the safe closes
on Agatha. This event puts
Jimmy in a difficult situation.
Why? (Analyze)

_____

_____

_____

_____

As the story ends . . .

• Annabel begs Jimmy to
help.

• Jimmy makes a quick and
fateful decision.

READING TIP Remember to complete the problem-solution chart you started on page 144. Add details from the end of the story.

Pause & Reflect

1. **REREAD** the boxed text. How does Jimmy think his decision to crack open the vault has changed his life? Check one. **(Infer)**

   ❏ He's now free to marry Annabel.

   ❏ He and Ben can now be friends.

   ❏ He's changed back to his old self, the bank robber.

2. Why does Ben Price pretend not to know Jimmy Valentine? **(Infer)**

 CHALLENGE At the end of some stories, you might feel that another story is about to begin. With a small group, tell a sequel to "A Retrieved Reformation." Explain what happens to the characters in the next 24 hours. **(Predict)**

pocket, threw off his coat and pulled up his shirt
320 sleeves. With that act Ralph D. Spencer passed away and Jimmy Valentine took his place.

"Get away from the door, all of you," he commanded, shortly.

He set his suitcase on the table, and opened it out flat. From that time on he seemed to be unconscious of the presence of anyone else. He laid out the shining, queer implements swiftly and orderly, whistling softly to himself as he always did when at work. In a deep silence and immovable, the others watched him as if
330 under a spell.

In a minute Jimmy's pet drill was biting smoothly into the steel door. In ten minutes—breaking his own burglarious record—he threw back the bolts and opened the door.

Agatha, almost collapsed, but safe, was gathered into her mother's arms.

Jimmy Valentine put on his coat, and walked outside the railings toward the front door. As he went he thought he heard a faraway voice that he once
340 knew call "Ralph!" But he never hesitated. At the door a big man stood somewhat in his way.

"Hello, Ben!" said Jimmy, still with his strange smile. "Got around at last, have you? Well, let's go. I don't know that it makes much difference, now."

And then Ben Price acted rather strangely.

"Guess you're mistaken, Mr. Spencer," he said. "Don't believe I recognize you. Your buggy's waiting for you, ain't it?"

And Ben Price turned and strolled down the street. ❖

Pause & Reflect

Active Reading SkillBuilder

Evaluating

During and after reading a story, you probably form opinions about its characters. Some of them you admire a great deal; others you may not admire at all. When you form these opinions, you are using the skill of **evaluating.** Think about the important characters in "A Retrieved Reformation." Then on the scale below, circle a number from 1 to 5 to reflect how much you admire each character, with 5 representing the greatest admiration and 1 the least. Write the reason for each opinion on the line in the third column.

Characters	Degree of Admiration	Reason
Jimmy Valentine	1 2 3 4 5	_____
Ben Price	1 2 3 4 5	_____
Annabel Adams	1 2 3 4 5	_____
Agatha	1 2 3 4 5	_____
Mr. Adams	1 2 3 4 5	_____

Literary Analysis SkillBuilder

Rising and Falling Action

Plot is the sequence of related events that make up a story. The events that lead up to the **climax,** or turning point, are a part of the **rising action.** Events after the climax are a part of the resolution, or **falling action.** In each box below, list an important event in the plot. Label each event *rising action, climax,* or *falling action.*

Sequence Chain for **"A Retrieved Reformation"**

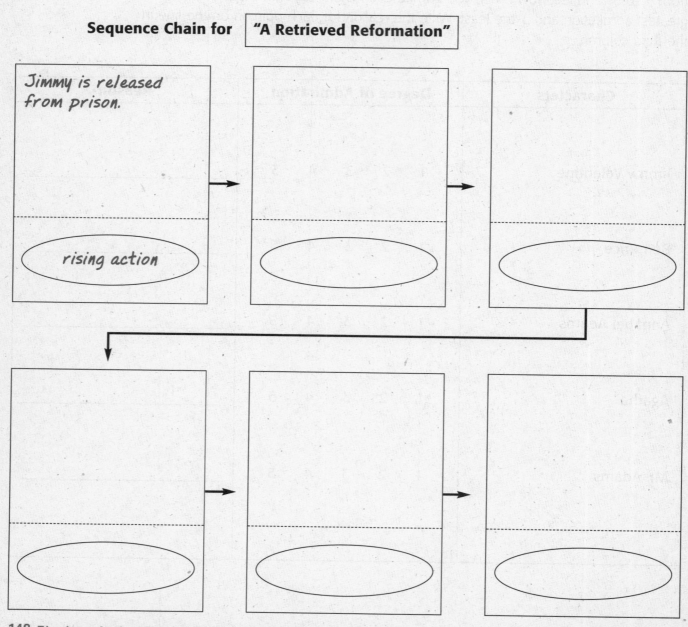

Jimmy is released from prison.

rising action

Words to Know SkillBuilder

Choose the word or phrase that best matches the meaning of each Word to Know.

1. In prison Jimmy worked **assiduously** at making shoes in the prison shoe factory.

   a. secretly   b. effortlessly   c. steadily   d. assertively

2. Work in the prison shoe factory had not been **compulsory.**

   a. voluntary   b. required   c. tedious   d. complicated

3. He had spent ten months in prison as **retribution** for the crime of safe cracking.

   a. punishment   b. tribute   c. confinement   d. restitution

4. Love helped to **rehabilitate** Jimmy to the ways of respectable society.

   a. relax   b. annoy   c. restore   d. refer

5. Jimmy fell in love with the daughter of an **eminent** citizen, Mr. Adams.

   a. bald   b. handsome   c. embarrassed   d. well-known

6. For a year he set aside his old "profession" and became the **virtuous** owner of a shoe store.

   a. friendly   b. indebted   c. honorable   d. strong

7. At the end of that year, the detective Ben Price arrived **unobtrusively** in Elmore.

   a. without asking directions   b. without obtaining permission

   c. without drawing attention   d. without much money

8. **Unperceived** by the adults, May locked Agatha in the bank's new safe.

   a. unnoticed   b. unpredicted   c. untaught   d. unasked

9. Jimmy did not **balk** at sacrificing everything in order to free the terrified child.

   a. walk   b. complain   c. hesitate   d. rejoice

10. The **elusive** safe cracker had changed.

    a. famous   b. in need of help   c. unpredictable   d. capable of avoiding capture

Before You Read

Connect to Your Life

Do you ever feel that you are too busy? Finding time to relax with friends is important. Write in the web some of the things that make time spent with others so valuable to you.

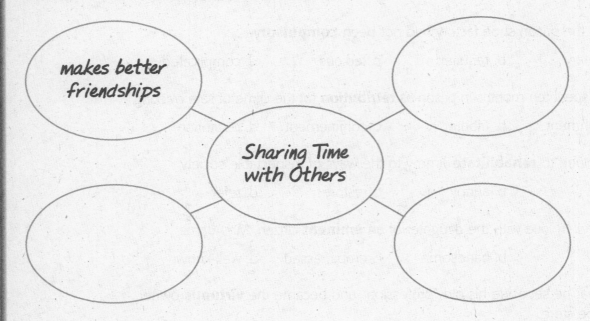

makes better friendships

Sharing Time with Others

Key to the Poems

WHAT TO LISTEN FOR Although Robert Frost's poems appear to be simple, they are actually full of meaning. In "The Pasture," the speaker describes a simple task—raking leaves away from a spring to let the water flow freely.

> *I'll only stop to rake the leaves away*
> *(And wait to watch the water clear, I may):*

Read the lines slowly. What scene comes to mind? Frost's image pulls the reader into the poem—to see the clear water of the spring bubbling out of the ground.

The Pasture

by Robert Frost

A Time to Talk

by Robert Frost

PREVIEW The poems you are about to read describe ordinary experiences on a farm. What feelings lie beneath the surface?

151

As the poem begins . . .

• The speaker describes two chores in the pasture.

MORE ABOUT . . .

(SPRINGS) A spring is a small pool of water that comes from the earth. Springs can supply farms with fresh water. Leaves can make this water dirty.

English Learner Support
Language

Word Order The words in the blue sentence are written in an unusual order. Poets sometimes do this to improve the way a line sounds. You could rewrite the line this way: "And I may wait to watch the water clear."

WHAT DOES IT MEAN? *Totters* means "sways" or "stands as if ready to fall."

Pause & Reflect

Why does the speaker invite the reader along? What does the speaker want the reader to notice or feel? **(Analyze)**

FOCUS

The speaker describes two chores he or she intends to do.

MARK IT UP As you read, underline the words that name each chore.

The Pasture

by Robert Frost

I'm going out to clean the pasture (spring;)
I'll only stop to rake the leaves away
(And wait to watch the water clear, I may):
I shan't be gone long.—You come too.

5   I'm going out to fetch the little calf
That's standing by the mother. It's so young
It totters when she licks it with her tongue.
I shan't be gone long.—You come too.

Pause & Reflect

As the poem begins . . .

• The speaker is working on a farm.
• A friend invites the speaker to talk.

FOCUS

The speaker is interrupted at work by a friend. Read to find out how the speaker reacts.

A Time to Talk

by Robert Frost

When a friend calls to me from the road
And slows his horse to a meaning walk,
I don't stand still and look around
On all the hills I haven't hoed,

5   And shout from where I am, "What is it?"
No, not as there is a time to talk.
I thrust my hoe in the mellow ground,
Blade-end up and five feet tall,
And plod: I go up to the stone wall

10 For a friendly visit.

Pause & Reflect

English Learner Support

Language

Meaning Walk This phrase means that the friend has slowed his horse's pace to a walk, signaling that he wants to talk.

READING CHECK How do you think the friend would feel if the speaker just stood still and shouted over at him?

Pause & Reflect

 READ ALOUD the boxed passage. Then check the phrase below that tells what is most important to the speaker. **(Infer)**

❏ making money
❏ keeping busy
❏ talking to friends

Active Reading SkillBuilder

Read Aloud

Reading aloud is a good way to enjoy a poem and to share it with others. These steps will help you present effective read-alouds:

• Read the poem to yourself to get a sense of its meaning.

• Try to imagine how the voice of the speaker might sound. Think about how to use your voice to convey the meaning of the words.

Copy "A Time to Talk" and use the key below to indicate cues you will use when you read the poem aloud. Some lines from "The Pasture" are provided as an example.

Key: ⊙ **pause**   ⤺ **don't pause**   *you* **emphasize**

◯	"The Pasture"
	I'm going out to clean the pasture spring ⊙
	I'll only stop to rake the leaves away ⤺
	(And wait to watch the water clear, I may) ⊙
	I shan't be gone long. ⊖ You come too.

_____

_____

_____

_____

_____

_____

_____

Literary Analysis SkillBuilder

Rhyme

Rhyme is a repetition of identical or similar sounds. **End rhyme,** the most common form of rhyme, occurs when the rhyming words come at the end of lines. A regular pattern of rhyming words is called a **rhyme scheme.** To chart the rhyme scheme of a poem, assign a letter of the alphabet to each line, beginning with the letter a. Lines that rhyme receive the same letter. For example, the rhyme scheme of the first four lines of "The Pasture" is *abbc.* Chart the rhyme schemes of "The Pasture" and "A Time To Talk."

"The Pasture"		"A Time to Talk"	
spring	a		
away	b		
may	b		
too	c		

Before You Read

Connect to Your Life

What does **self-control** mean to you? What would you do in the following situations? Put a check mark under the heading that applies to you.

	Let it slide	Discuss the situation	Lose your temper
Your friend borrows your sweater without asking.	_____	_____	_____
You overhear two people criticizing you.	_____	_____	_____
You find out that others know a secret you told to only one friend.	_____	_____	_____

Key to the Autobiography

JACKIE ROBINSON
outfield BROOKLYN DODGERS
Dodgers

WHAT YOU NEED TO KNOW Branch Rickey, the boss of the Brooklyn Dodgers, wanted to bring African Americans into Major League Baseball. He picked Robinson for his "noble experiment" to integrate baseball.

WHO: Jackie Robinson was a 26-year-old baseball player in the Negro Leagues.

WHEN: Robinson signed a contract with the Brooklyn Dodgers on April 10, 1947.

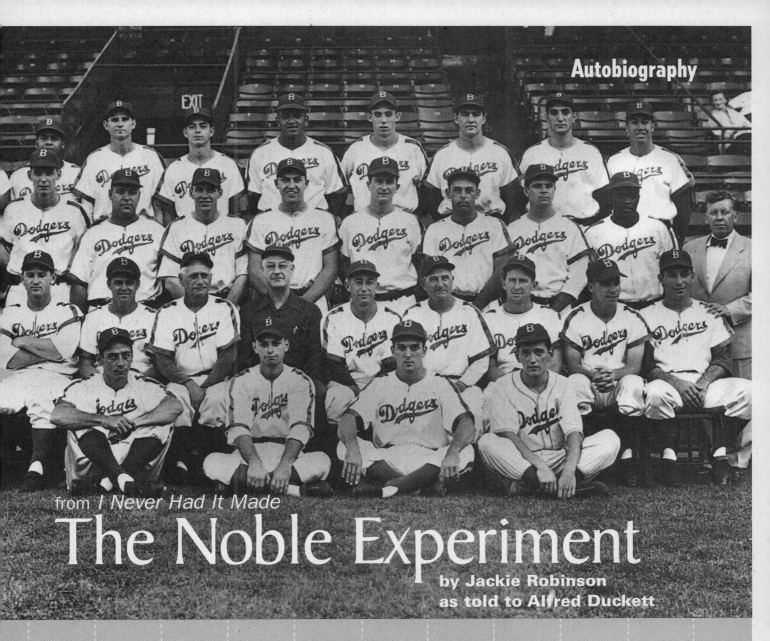

from *I Never Had It Made*

The Noble Experiment

**by Jackie Robinson
as told to Alfred Duckett**

PREVIEW You are about to read part of Jackie Robinson's account of his own life. He tells how he became the first African American ever to play baseball in the major leagues. He recalls the warnings about name-calling and physical attacks that would happen to him.

As the autobiography begins . . .

- Jackie Robinson tells what once happened to a black baseball player at a hotel.

- He describes how Branch Rickey reacted at the time.

- This event affected Mr. Rickey's future actions.

READING TIP In this true story, the author uses some difficult words. Use context and footnotes to help you determine meanings.

WHAT DOES IT MEAN?

A *compromise* is an end to a disagreement. Each side gives up something so that an agreement can be reached.

READING CHECK Why can't Charley sleep?

FOCUS

In this section you will meet Branch Rickey, a baseball coach. It is 1910, long before black players were allowed in the major leagues.

MARK IT UP As you read, underline details that show the unfair treatment of African Americans. An example is highlighted.

In 1910 Branch Rickey was a coach for Ohio Wesleyan. The team went to South Bend, Indiana, for a game. The hotel management registered the coach and team but refused to assign a room to a black player named Charley Thomas. In those
10 days college ball had a few black players. Mr. Rickey took the manager aside and said he would move the entire team to another hotel unless the black athlete was accepted. The threat was a bluff because he knew the other hotels also would have refused accommodations to a black man. While the hotel manager was thinking about the threat, Mr. Rickey came up with a compromise. He suggested a cot be put in his own room, which he would share
20 with the unwanted guest. The hotel manager wasn't happy about the idea, but he gave in.

Years later Branch Rickey told the story of the misery of that black player to whom he had given a place to sleep. He remembered that Thomas couldn't sleep.

"He sat on that cot," Mr. Rickey said, "and was silent for a long time. Then he began to cry, tears he couldn't hold back. His whole body shook with emotion. I sat and watched him, not knowing what to do until he began tearing at one hand with the other—
30 just as if he were trying to scratch the skin off his hands with his fingernails. I was alarmed. I asked him what he was trying to do to himself.

"'It's my hands,' he sobbed. 'They're black. If only they were white, I'd be as good as anybody then, wouldn't I, Mr. Rickey? If only they were white.'"

"Charley," Mr. Rickey said, "the day will come when they won't have to be white."

Thirty-five years later, while I was lying awake nights, frustrated, unable to see a future, Mr. Rickey, by now the president of the Dodgers, was also lying awake at night, trying to make up his mind about a new experiment.

He had never forgotten the agony of that black athlete. When he became a front-office executive in St. Louis, he had fought, behind the scenes, against the custom that consigned black spectators to the Jim Crow section[1] of the Sportsman's Park, later to become Busch Memorial Stadium. His pleas to change the rules were in vain. Those in power argued that if blacks were allowed a free choice of seating, white business would suffer.

Pause & Reflect

FOCUS

Branch Rickey begins a risky fight to bring blacks and whites together on pro-baseball teams.

MARK IT UP As you read, underline words and phrases that tell you about the risks and benefits of his fight.

Branch Rickey lost that fight, but when he became the boss of the Brooklyn Dodgers in 1943, he felt the time for equality in baseball had come. He knew that achieving it would be terribly difficult. There would be deep resentment, determined opposition, and perhaps even racial violence. He was convinced he was morally right, and he shrewdly sensed that making the game a truly

1. consigned . . . Jim Crow section: kept African Americans in different seats because of laws and rules that separated seating by race.

WORDS TO KNOW
shrewdly (shrōōd′lē) adv. wisely; in a clever way

English Learner Support
Language

Pronouns The pronoun I refers to the narrator, Jackie Robinson. The pronouns he and his continue the story of Branch Rickey.

English Learner Support
Vocabulary

Idiom A front-office executive is a manager who makes decisions in an organization.

WHAT DOES IT MEAN? In vain means "without success."

Pause & Reflect

Review the details you underlined as you read. Why did Charley Thomas cry and scratch at his hands? (Cause and Effect)

As the autobiography continues . . .

• Rickey gets permission to bring black players into baseball.

• He looks for the ideal player.

Baseball How much do you know about baseball? If you know only a little, ask a classmate for help with baseball terms, such as *coach* and *scout*.

WHAT DOES IT MEAN?

Insignificant means "having no importance." *Persecution* means "constant oppression or suffering."

Pause & Reflect

1. Review the words and phrases you underlined as you read. In the list below, mark an "R" beside each risk and a "B" beside each benefit of Rickey's fight. **(Evaluate)**

___ racial violence

___ healthy financial results

___ rejection by sportswriters

___ moral rightness

2. **REREAD** the boxed passage. Then circle the two words below that describe the qualities of Rickey's "ideal player." **(Infer)**

angry   strong

determined   selfish

national one would have healthy financial results. He took his case before the startled directors of the club, and using persuasive <u>eloquence</u>, he won the first battle in what would be a long and bitter campaign. He was voted permission to make the Brooklyn club the pioneer in bringing blacks into baseball.

70   Winning his directors' approval was almost insignificant in contrast to the task which now lay ahead of the Dodger president. He made certain that word of his plans did not leak out, particularly to the press. Next, he had to find the ideal player for his project, which came to be called "Rickey's noble experiment."

This player had to be one who could take abuse, name-calling, rejection by fans and sportswriters and by fellow players not only on opposing teams but on his own. He had to be able to stand up in the face of

80 merciless persecution and not <u>retaliate</u>. On the other hand, he had to be a contradiction in human terms; he still had to have spirit. He could not be an "Uncle Tom."[2] His ability to turn the other cheek had to be predicated[3] on his determination to gain acceptance.

Once having proven his ability as player, teammate, and man, he had to be able to cast off humbleness and stand up as a full-fledged participant whose triumph did not carry the poison of bitterness.

Pause & Reflect

2. "Uncle Tom": an offensive term for a black person who is regarded as trying too hard to please white people; from the novel *Uncle Tom's Cabin*, written by Harriet Beecher Stowe and published in 1852.

3. predicated (prĕd´ĭ-kā´tĭd): based.

WORDS TO KNOW
eloquence (ĕl´ə-kwəns) *n.* forceful, convincing speech
retaliate (rĭ-tăl´ē-āt´) *v.* to get revenge; get even

FOCUS

Branch Rickey searches for one athlete with dark skin who might break into the all-white leagues.

MARK IT UP As you read, circle the steps Rickey takes to find this athlete.

Unknown to most people 90 and certainly to me, after launching a major scouting program, Branch Rickey had picked me as that player. The Rickey talent hunt went beyond national borders. Cuba, Mexico, Puerto Rico, Venezuela, and other countries where dark-skinned people lived had been checked out. Mr. Rickey had learned that there were a 100 number of black players, war veterans mainly, who had gone to these countries, despairing of finding an opportunity in their own country. The manhunt had to be camouflaged. If it became known he was looking for a black recruit for the Dodgers, all hell would have broken loose. The gimmick he used as a cover-up was to make the world believe that he was about to establish a new Negro league. In the spring of 1945 he called a press conference and announced that the Dodgers were organizing the United States League, 110 composed of all black teams. This, of course, made blacks and prointegration whites indignant. He was accused of trying to uphold the existing segregation and, at the same time, capitalize on black players. Cleverly, Mr. Rickey replied that his league would be better organized than the current ones. He said its main purpose, eventually, was to be absorbed into the majors. It is ironic that by coming very close to telling the truth, he was able to conceal that truth from the enemies of <u>integrated</u> baseball. Most people assumed 120 that when he spoke of some distant goal of integration, Mr. Rickey was being a hypocrite[4] on this

---

4. **hypocrite** (hĭp′ə-krĭt′): someone who says one thing but does another; a liar.

WORDS TO KNOW
  integrated (ĭn′tĭ-grā′tĭd) *adj.* open to people of all races or ethnic groups
  without restriction; desegregated

As the autobiography continues . . .

- Rickey searches for a special black player.
- Rickey has clever ways of hiding the true purpose of his search.

English Learner Support
Language

Idiom The phrase *all hell would have broken loose* means that a lot of trouble would have occurred.

English Learner Support
Vocabulary

Word Families Many words are related to *integrate* (IHN-tih-GRAYT), a word that means "to bring in people of all races and ethnic groups." Use this meaning to help you figure out what these words mean:

- integrated
- integration / segregation (antonyms)
- prointegration ("for integration")

1. What trick did Rickey use to hide the fact that he was seeking a black player for the Dodgers? (**Summarize**)

He pretended that

2. Write the numbers 1, 2, 3, and 4 to show the order in which the events below occurred. (**Sequence of Events**)

__ Wendell Smith brought Robinson to a Red Sox tryout.

__ Councilman Muchneck wanted the Red Sox to hire black players.

__ Red Sox officials praised Robinson, but didn't call.

__ Smith told Rickey that Robinson was major-league material.

issue as so many of baseball's leaders had been.

Black players were familiar with this kind of hypocrisy. When I was with the Monarchs, shortly before I met Mr. Rickey, Wendell Smith, then sports editor of the black weekly Pittsburgh *Courier*, had arranged for me and two other players from the Negro league to go to a tryout with the Boston Red Sox. The tryout had been brought about because a Boston city
130 councilman had frightened the Red Sox management. Councilman Isadore Muchneck threatened to push a bill through banning Sunday baseball unless the Red Sox hired black players. Sam Jethroe of the Cleveland Buckeyes, Marvin Williams of the Philadelphia Stars, and I had been grateful to Wendell for getting us a chance in the Red Sox tryout, and we put our best efforts into it. However, not for one minute did we believe the tryout was sincere. The Boston club officials praised our performance, let us fill out application cards,
140 and said, "So long." We were fairly certain they wouldn't call us, and we had no intention of calling them.

Incidents like this made Wendell Smith as <u>cynical</u> as we were. He didn't accept Branch Rickey's new league as a genuine project, and he frankly told him so. During this conversation, the Dodger boss asked Wendell whether any of the three of us who had gone to Boston was really good major league material. Wendell said I was. I will be forever indebted to Wendell because, without his even knowing it, his
150 recommendation was in the end partly responsible for my career. At the time, it started a thorough investigation of my background.

Pause & Reflect

FOCUS

Jackie Robinson may be the end to Rickey's talent hunt. Read on to see how Robinson reacts when opportunity knocks.

In August 1945, at Comiskey Park in Chicago, I was approached by Clyde Sukeforth, the Dodger scout. Blacks have had to learn to protect themselves by being cynical but not cynical enough to slam the door on potential opportunities. We go through life walking a tightrope to prevent too much disillusionment.[5] I was out on the field when Sukeforth called my name and beckoned. He told me the Brown Dodgers were looking for top ballplayers, that Branch Rickey had heard about me and sent him to watch me throw from the hole.[6] He had come at an unfortunate time. I had hurt my shoulder a couple of days before that, and I wouldn't be doing any throwing for at least a week.

Sukeforth said he'd like to talk with me anyhow. He asked me to come to see him after the game at the Stevens Hotel.

Here we go again, I thought. Another time-wasting experience. But Sukeforth looked like a sincere person, and I thought I might as well listen. I agreed to meet him that night. When we met, Sukeforth got right to the point. Mr. Rickey wanted to talk to me about the possibility of becoming a Brown Dodger. If I could get a few days off and go to Brooklyn, my fare and expenses would be paid. At first I said that I couldn't leave my team and go to Brooklyn just like that. Sukeforth wouldn't take no for an answer. He pointed out that I couldn't play for a few days anyhow because of my bum arm. Why should my team object?

As the autobiography continues . . .

• Robinson is invited to try out for the Brown Dodgers.

• He explains why he was not very excited about this opportunity.

English Learner Support

Vocabulary

Idiom The phrase *Here we go again* means "I'm doing the same thing again that I have done before." Robinson means that he will not make the team even if he goes to the tryout. He has been to tryouts in the past and has never made the team.

READING CHECK Why wasn't Robinson delighted when Sukeforth asked him to try out for the Brown Dodgers?

---

5. **disillusionment** (dĭs-ĭ-lōō′zhən-mənt): shattered dreams, disappointment.

6. **throw from the hole**: to throw from deep in the infield to first base.

Pause & Reflect

Circle the word below that describes how Robinson felt about the offer to try out for the Brown Dodgers. (Evaluate)

happy   suspicious
angry   confused

As the autobiography continues . . .

• Branch Rickey asks Jackie Robinson some difficult questions.

• Rickey tells Robinson the truth about why he was invited to Brooklyn.

English Learner Support
Vocabulary

Hopeless Case When Robinson says that Rachel might consider him *a hopeless case,* he means that she may not want to be his girlfriend any longer.

I continued to hold out and demanded to know what would happen if the Monarchs fired me. The Dodger scout replied quietly that he didn't believe that would happen.

I shrugged and said I'd make the trip. I figured I had nothing to lose.

Pause & Reflect

FOCUS

Read to find out what happens when Branch Rickey and Jackie Robinson meet for the first time.

MARK IT UP > Underline details that show you how Branch Rickey treats Jackie Robinson.

190 Branch Rickey was an impressive-looking man. He had a classic face, an air of command, a deep, booming voice, and a way of cutting through red tape and getting down to basics. He shook my hand vigorously and, after a brief conversation, sprang the first question.

200 "You got a girl?" he demanded.

It was a hell of a question. I had two reactions: why should he be concerned about my relationship with a girl; and, second, while I thought, hoped, and prayed I had a girl, the way things had been going, I was afraid she might have begun to consider me a hopeless case. I explained this to Mr. Rickey and Clyde.

Mr. Rickey wanted to know all about Rachel. I told him of our hopes and plans.

"You know, you *have* a girl," he said heartily.

210 "When we get through today, you may want to call her up because there are times when a man needs a woman by his side."

My heart began racing a little faster again as I sat there <u>speculating</u>. First he asked me if I really understood why he had sent for me. I told him what Clyde Sukeforth had told me.

"That's what he was supposed to tell you," Mr. Rickey said. "The truth is you are not a candidate for the Brooklyn Brown Dodgers. I've sent for you
220 because I'm interested in you as a candidate for the Brooklyn National League Club. I think you can play in the major leagues. How do you feel about it?"

My reactions seemed like some kind of weird mixture churning in a blender. I was thrilled, scared, and excited. I was <u>incredulous</u>. Most of all, I was speechless.

"You think you can play for Montreal?" he demanded.

I got my tongue back. "Yes," I answered.

230 Montreal was the Brooklyn Dodgers' top farm club. The players who went there and made it had an excellent chance at the big time.

I was busy reorganizing my thoughts while Mr. Rickey and Clyde Sukeforth discussed me briefly, almost as if I weren't there. Mr. Rickey was questioning Clyde. Could I make the grade?

Abruptly, Mr. Rickey swung his swivel chair in my direction. He was a man who conducted himself with great drama. He pointed a finger at me.

240 "I know you're a good ballplayer," he barked. "What I don't know is whether you have the guts."

I knew it was all too good to be true. Here was a guy questioning my courage. That virtually amounted to him asking me if I was a coward. Mr. Rickey or no

MARK IT UP ⟩ Reread the boxed passage. How did Jackie Robinson react to Branch Rickey's idea? Circle words and phrases that tell the answer. **(Clarify)**

English Learner Support
Vocabulary
Idiom *I got my tohgue back* means that Robinson was now able to talk. Before this, he was so surprised that he could not speak.

WHAT DOES IT MEAN? In this sentence, *guts* means "courage and strength."

WORDS TO KNOW
speculating (spĕk'yə-lā'-tĭng) *adj.* thinking about different possibilities; guessing what might happen **speculate** *v.*
incredulous (ĭn-krĕj'ə-ləs) *adj.* unable or unwilling to believe something

WHAT DOES IT MEAN? The
sentence in blue means that
Robinson is feeling angry.

READING CHECK What were the
"big stakes"
Robinson and Rickey were
playing for?

Pause & Reflect

1. How did Branch Rickey
treat Jackie Robinson at
their first meeting? (Infer)

_____

_____

_____

_____

_____

2. Circle the two words
below that describe
Branch Rickey. (Evaluate)

calm   challenging

shy   brave

Mr. Rickey, that was an <u>insinuation</u> hard to take. I felt the heat coming up into my cheeks.

Before I could react to what he had said, he leaned forward in his chair and explained.

250 I wasn't just another athlete being hired by a ball club. We were playing for big stakes. This was the reason Branch Rickey's search had been so exhaustive. The search had spanned the globe and narrowed down to a few candidates, then finally to me. When it looked as though I might be the number-one choice, the investigation of my life, my habits, my reputation, and my character had become an intensified study.

"I've investigated you thoroughly, Robinson," Mr. Rickey said.

One of the results of this thorough screening were 260 reports from California athletic circles that I had been a "racial agitator"[7] at UCLA. Mr. Rickey had not accepted these criticisms on face value. He had demanded and received more information and came to the conclusion that if I had been white, people would have said, "Here's a guy who's a contender, a competitor."

Pause & Reflect

---

7. "racial agitator" (ăj'ĭ-tā'tər): a negative term used for someone who tries to stir up trouble between the races.

WORDS TO KNOW
insinuation (ĭn-sĭn'yōō-ā'shən) n. a suggestion or hint intended to insult

FOCUS

Rickey warns Robinson that he will need to be more than just a good ballplayer. Read to find out what else he must be.

After that he had some grim words of warning. "We can't fight our way through 270 this, Robinson. We've got no army. There's virtually nobody on our side. No owners, no umpires, very few newspapermen. And I'm afraid that many fans will be hostile. We'll be in a tough position. We can win only if we can convince the world that I'm doing this because you're a great ballplayer and a fine gentleman."

He had me transfixed[8] as he spoke. I could feel his sincerity, and I began to get a sense of how much this 280 major step meant to him. Because of his nature and his passion for justice, he had to do what he was doing. He continued. The rumbling voice, the theatrical gestures were gone. He was speaking from a deep, quiet strength.

"So there's more than just playing," he said. "I wish it meant only hits, runs, and errors—only the things they put in the box score. Because you know— yes, you would know, Robinson, that a baseball box score is a democratic thing. It doesn't tell how big you 290 are, what church you attend, what color you are, or how your father voted in the last election. It just tells what kind of baseball player you were on that particular day."

I interrupted. "But it's the box score that really counts—that and that alone, isn't it?"

"It's all that *ought* to count," he replied. "But it isn't. Maybe one of these days it *will* be all that counts. That is one of the reasons I've got you here, Robinson. If you're a good enough man, we can make

As the autobiography continues . . .

• Rickey tells Robinson some of the problems and challenges he will face.

MARK IT UP Reread the boxed passage. Underline the qualities in Rickey that held Robinson transfixed as Rickey spoke.

English Learner Support
Vocabulary

Box Score In baseball, a *box score* is a printed record of a game in the form of a chart. Players on each team are listed, and each player's individual performance is recorded.

WHAT DOES IT MEAN? When Rickey says, "It's all that *ought* to count," he means that people should judge ballplayers on their scores and not on their size, religion, color, or political beliefs.

---

8. **transfixed:** motionless because of strong emotion.

Pause & Reflect

According to Rickey, Robinson would need to be a great ballplayer and a fine _____. Check one. **(Clarify)**

❏ speaker
❏ husband
❏ teammate
❏ gentleman

As the autobiography ends . . .

• Branch Rickey tells Robinson exactly what kind of ballplayer he seeks.
• Robinson is told what could happen if he joins the team.
• He explains why he made his final decision.

WHAT DOES IT MEAN?
Retaliation means "doing something bad to someone who has done something bad to you."

300 this a start in the right direction. But let me tell you, it's going to take an awful lot of courage."

He was back to the crossroads question that made me start to get angry minutes earlier. He asked it slowly and with great care.

"Have you got the guts to play the game no matter what happens?"

"I think I can play the game, Mr. Rickey," I said.

Pause & Reflect

FOCUS

Rickey tells Robinson more about the challenges he will face.

MARK IT UP As you read, circle details that tell you about these challenges.

The next few minutes were tough. Branch Rickey had to 310 make absolutely sure that I knew what I would face. Beanballs[9] would be thrown at me. I would be called the kind of names which would hurt and infuriate any man. I would be physically attacked. Could I take all of this and control my temper, remain steadfastly loyal to our <u>ultimate</u> aim?

He knew I would have terrible problems and wanted 320 me to know the extent of them before I agreed to the plan. I was twenty-six years old, and all my life—back to the age of eight when a little neighbor girl called me a nigger—I had believed in payback, retaliation. The most luxurious possession, the richest treasure anybody has, is his personal dignity. I looked at Mr. Rickey guardedly, and in that second I was looking at

9. **beanballs:** pitches thrown purposefully at a batter's head.

WORDS TO KNOW
ultimate (ŭl′tə-mĭt) *adj.* final; most important

him not as a partner in a great experiment, but as the enemy—a white man. I had a question, and it was the age-old one about whether or not you sell your
330 birthright.

"Mr. Rickey," I asked, "are you looking for a Negro who is afraid to fight back?"

I never will forget the way he exploded.

"Robinson," he said, "I'm looking for a ballplayer with guts enough not to fight back."

After that, Mr. Rickey continued his lecture on the kind of thing I'd be facing.

He not only told me about it, but he acted out the part of a white player charging into me, blaming me
340 for the "accident" and calling me all kinds of foul racial names. He talked about my race, my parents, in language that was almost unendurable.

"They'll taunt and goad you," Mr. Rickey said. "They'll do anything to make you react. They'll try to provoke a race riot in the ballpark. This is the way to prove to the public that a Negro should not be allowed in the major league. This is the way to frighten the fans and make them afraid to attend the games."

If hundreds of black people wanted to come to the
350 ballpark to watch me play and Mr. Rickey tried to discourage them, would I understand that he was doing it because the emotional enthusiasm of my people could harm the experiment? That kind of enthusiasm would be as bad as the emotional opposition of prejudiced white fans.

Suppose I was at shortstop. Another player comes down from first, stealing, flying in with spikes high, and cuts me on the leg. As I feel the blood running down my leg, the white player laughs in my face.
360 "How do you like that, nigger boy?" he sneers.

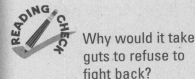

Why would it take guts to refuse to fight back?

WHAT DOES IT MEAN?
Unendurable means "so awful that a person cannot bear it."

English Learner Support
Language
Pronouns In this paragraph, the pronoun *they* refers to any people who verbally or physically attack Robinson because of his race.

WORDS TO KNOW
taunt (tônt) *v.* to make fun of; jeer

Pause & Reflect

1. What do you think was the greatest challenge Robinson would face? **(Evaluate)**

2. What do you admire most about Jackie Robinson? Explain. **(Connect)**

Branch Rickey said that he was "looking for a ballplayer with guts enough not to fight back." Write a definition of courage that you think Rickey would have agreed with. Support your definition with examples. **(Analyze)**

Could I turn the other cheek? I didn't know how I would do it. Yet I knew that I must. I had to do it for so many reasons. For black youth, for my mother, for Rae, for myself. I had already begun to feel I had to do it for Branch Rickey.

I was offered, and agreed to sign later, a contract with a $3,500 bonus and $600-a-month salary. I was officially a Montreal Royal. I must not tell anyone except Rae and my mother. ❖

Pause & Reflect

Active Reading SkillBuilder

Summarizing

When you **summarize** a story or an article, you write a short version of it in your own words. You restate only the main ideas and most important details. One way to recognize such details in an autobiography is by thinking about what happened, who was involved, and why it happened or why it was important. Use the diagram below to summarize the main ideas in "The Noble Experiment." Summarize each major event. The first one is done for you.

---

1. 1910, South Bend, Indiana
What happened? Who was involved? Why did it happen, or why was it important?
Branch Rickey saw the humiliation of Charley Thomas, an African-American player who was refused a room at a segregated hotel.

---

2. Considering a New Experiment
What happened? Who was involved? Why did it happen, or why was it important?

---

3. The Tryout
What happened? Who was involved? Why did it happen, or why was it important?

---

4. Meeting with Sukeforth
What happened? Who was involved? Why did it happen, or why was it important?

---

5. Meeting with Branch Rickey
What happened? Who was involved? Why did it happen, or why was it important?

Literary Analysis SkillBuilder

Motivation

To bring African-American players into major-league baseball, Branch Rickey had to take careful steps. Below is an outline of Rickey's steps. Next to each action, describe the reason, or **motivation,** Rickey had for taking it. See the example given.

Action	Reason
1. searched for a player who could take possible abuse	*Rickey expected that some people would treat the first black player badly.*
2. pretended that the Dodgers were organizing a new black league	
3. asked Wendell Smith if three leading black players were good enough to play in the major leagues	
4. sent a Dodger scout to bring Robinson to Brooklyn	
5. investigated all aspects of Robinson's life	
6. told Robinson about the problems he would face	
7. called Robinson foul names	
8. offered Robinson a contract to play on the Dodgers' farm team	

Words to Know SkillBuilder

Words to Know

cynical	incredulous	integrated	shrewdly	taunt
eloquence	insinuation	retaliate	speculating	ultimate

Read each statement. Circle the word or phrase that *best* completes it.

1. In fairy tales, the _____ is an animal that usually behaves **shrewdly.**

   a. gopher   b. fox   c. chicken   d. bear

2. The opposite of "to **retaliate**" is "to _____."

   a. get upset   b. recalculate   c. get even   d. forgive

3. An **integrated** neighborhood is _____ to people of all races.

   a. open   b. new   c. old   d. closed

4. If you are **speculating** about the future, you are _____ it.

   a. betting on   b. counting on   c. guessing about   d. forgetting about

5. **Cynical** people usually _____ the truth of things they hear.

   a. exaggerate   b. respect   c. doubt   d. contemplate

6. An **insinuation** is a particular type of _____.

   a. hint   b. ceremony   c. greeting   d. answer

7. If you suspected a story was not _____, you would be **incredulous.**

   a. long   b. false   c. short   d. true

8. If you **taunt** people, you tease them in a _____ way.

   a. harmless   b. kind   c. mean   d. absent-minded

9. Your **ultimate** goal is the one that is _____ important to you.

   a. most   b. somewhat   c. least   d. not

10. **Eloquence** is a quality that a _____ tries to have.

   a. speaker   b. umpire   c. swimmer   d. hunter

Before You Read

Connect to Your Life

We all admire athletes because they take on tough challenges. Who is your favorite? Complete the following sentences.

My favorite athlete is _____.

What I admire the most about him or her is _____

_____

_____.

When he or she is under pressure, I expect him or her to _____

_____

_____

_____.

Key to the Poem

WHAT'S THE BIG IDEA? During many team sporting events, there is a moment when success or failure depends upon the performance of a single person. If you were that person, what do you think would go through your mind at a moment like that?

_____

_____

_____

_____

_____

_____

_____

Casey at the Bat

by Ernest Lawrence Thayer

PREVIEW It looks as if the Mudville team is sure to lose the game. And the crowd knows that its only hope is "mighty Casey."

FOCUS

The game is almost lost. The Mudville fans are hoping for a miracle. Read to find out how they feel about Casey.

MARK IT UP Underline details that suggest how the fans feel toward Casey. An example is highlighted.

It looked extremely rocky for the Mudville nine that day;
The score stood two to four, with but an inning left to play.
So, when Cooney died at second, and Burrows did the same,
A pallor wreathed the features of the patrons of the game.

5   A straggling few got up to go, leaving there the rest,
With that hope which springs eternal within the human breast.
For they thought: "If only Casey could get a whack at that,"
They'd put even money now, with Casey at the bat.

But Flynn preceded Casey, and likewise so did Blake,
10   And the former was a pudd'n, and the latter was a fake.
So on that stricken multitude a deathlike silence sat;
For there seemed but little chance of Casey's getting to the bat.

But Flynn let drive a "single," to the wonderment of all.
And the much-despised Blakey "tore the cover off the ball."
15   And when the dust had lifted, and they saw what had occurred,
There was Blakey safe at second, and Flynn a-huggin' third.

Then from the gladdened multitude went up a joyous yell—
It rumbled in the mountaintops, it rattled in the dell;
It struck upon the hillside and rebounded on the flat;
20   For Casey, mighty Casey, was advancing to the bat.

Use this guide for help with unfamiliar words and difficult passages.

1 Mudville nine: the Mudville baseball team.

3 died at second: tagged out at second base.

4 pallor (păl'ər) **wreathed . . . the patrons:** The fans were so sad they were deathly pale.

5 A straggling few: a few scattered fans.

10 the former was a pudd'n: Flynn was weak; **the latter was a fake:** Blake only pretended to be good.

11–12 stricken multitude . . . to the bat: The fans are grim. If Flynn or Blake strikes out, Casey won't get to bat.

14 tore the cover off the ball: hit the ball hard and fast.

18–19 It rumbled . . . and rebounded on the flat: The roar of the crowd is so loud, it makes the countryside shake.

20 advancing: moving toward.

As the poem begins . . .

- The baseball game is almost over.
- The crowd is afraid that Casey won't get a chance to play.

English Learner Support
Vocabulary
Idiom *It looked extremely rocky* means that the team was not doing well.

 READING TIP The poem sometimes uses difficult or old-fashioned words and phrases. Read the side notes on this page and use context clues to learn what they mean.

 READING CHECK Why does the crowd want Casey at bat?

Pause & Reflect

1. How does the crowd feel about Casey? (Infer)

_____

_____

_____

2. **READ ALOUD** the boxed text. Use your voice to express how joyful the cheering is.

FOCUS

Casey steps up to bat.

| MARK IT UP ⟩ Circle details that
suggest what Casey looks like.

There was ease in Casey's manner as he stepped into his place,
There was pride in Casey's bearing and a smile on Casey's face;
And when responding to the cheers he lightly doffed his hat,
No stranger in the crowd could doubt 'twas Casey at the bat.

25 Ten thousand eyes were on him as he rubbed his hands with dirt,
Five thousand tongues applauded when he wiped them on his shirt;
Then when the writhing pitcher ground the ball into his hip,
Defiance glanced in Casey's eye, a sneer curled Casey's lip.

And now the leather-covered sphere came hurtling through the air,
30 And Casey stood a-watching it in haughty grandeur there.
Close by the sturdy batsman the ball unheeded sped;
"That ain't my style," said Casey. "Strike one," the umpire said.

From the benches, filled with people, there went up a muffled roar,
Like the beating of the storm waves on the stern and distant shore.
35 "Kill him! Kill the umpire!" shouted someone on the stand;
And it's likely they'd have killed him had not Casey raised his hand.

With a smile of honest charity great Casey's visage shone;
He stilled the rising tumult, he made the game go on;
He signaled to the pitcher, and once more the spheroid flew;
40 But Casey still ignored it, and the umpire said, "Strike two."

"Fraud!" cried the maddened thousands, and the echo answered
    "Fraud!"
But one scornful look from Casey and the audience was awed;
They saw his face grow stern and cold, they saw his muscles strain,
And they knew that Casey wouldn't let the ball go by again.

22 pride in Casey's bearing: Casey walks and stands as if he is really proud of himself.
23 doffed: took off.

26 tongues applauded: everyone cheered.
27 writhing (rīth'ĭng): twisting as in pain.
28 sneer: a look meant to make fun of someone.
29 sphere: ball; **hurtling:** flying.
30 haughty grandeur: being above it all.
31 the ball unheeded sped: The ball flew past Casey without his "heeding" or responding to it.

37 smile of honest charity: smile as if doing the umpire a favor; **visage** (vĭz'ĭj): face.
38 tumult (tōō'mŭlt'): disorderly disturbance.

As the poem continues . . .

• The suspense builds as Casey steps to the plate to face the pitcher.

English Learner Support
Vocabulary

Idiom The expression *ten thousand eyes were on him* is an idiom—it does not mean exactly what the words say. It means that all five thousand people in the stadium were watching Casey.

MORE ABOUT . . .

BENCHES Old ballparks had benches instead of seats for the fans.

WHAT DOES IT MEAN? *Fraud* means "someone who cheats." The fans are angry with the umpire because they disagree with the umpire's calls.

Pause & Reflect

Cross out one phrase that does not describe Casey. (**Summarize**)

ease in his manner
smile on his face
tears in his eyes
pride in his bearing

45 The sneer is gone from Casey's lips, his teeth are clenched in hate,
He pounds with cruel vengeance his bat upon the plate;
And now the pitcher holds the ball, and now he lets it go,
And now the air is shattered by the force of Casey's blow.

Oh, somewhere in this favored land the sun is shining bright,
50 The band is playing somewhere, and somewhere hearts are light;
And somewhere men are laughing, and somewhere children shout,
But there is no joy in Mudville: Mighty Casey has struck out. ❖

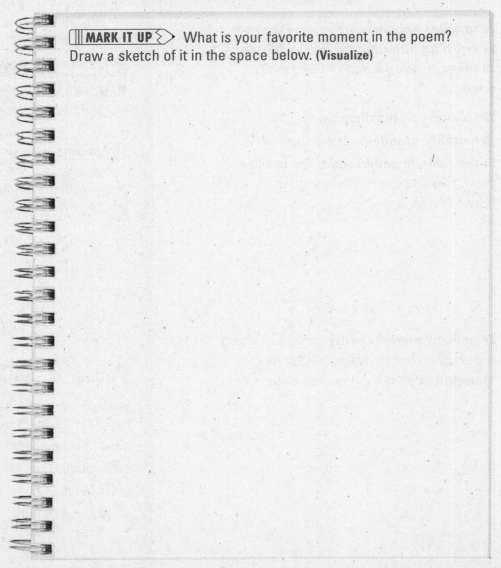

MARK IT UP ▷ What is your favorite moment in the poem?
Draw a sketch of it in the space below. (Visualize)

46 with cruel vengeance (věn'jəns): as if getting back at the pitcher and the umpire.

48 the air is shattered . . . : Casey swings so hard that it's as if the fans can feel the force of it in the air.

As the poem ends . . .

• Casey finally swings at a ball.

Did Casey hit the last ball? How can you tell?

Pause & Reflect

1. the final stanza, lines 49–52. How does the crowd feel at the end of the game? Why? **(Infer)**

_____

_____

_____

_____

2. Do you think that Casey did his best? **(Evaluate)**

   YES / NO, because

_____

_____

_____

Throughout the poem, the author uses **exaggeration,** making things seem greater or more important than they really are. Mark examples of this technique in the poem. How does exaggeration affect the way you view Casey? **(Analyze)**

Active Reading SkillBuilder

Questioning

Questioning is an important part of reading. Good readers ask **questions** both before and as they read. Reading a narrative poem is a lot like reading a story; it has characters, setting, and plot. As you read the narrative poem "Casey at the Bat," use the chart below to write down questions.

Stanza	Question
two	How does the crowd feel about Casey?

Literary Analysis SkillBuilder

Sound Devices

Poets use **sound devices** such as rhyme, rhythm, and repetition to create certain moods, emphasize ideas, and communicate meaning. **Rhyme** is the repetition of the same sound at the ends of words. **Rhythm** is the pattern of stressed and unstressed syllables that gives a poem its musical quality. **Repetition** is the repeated use of a sound, word, phrase, or line.

To explore the use of rhyme, rhythm, and repetition in "Casey at the Bat," copy one of the last four stanzas of the poem and mark the rhythm, using the symbols shown in the sample below. Also circle any repetitions.

/ ˘ / ˘ / ˘ / ˘ / ˘ / ˘ /
"Kill him! Kill the umpire!" shouted someone on the stand;

˘ ˘ / ˘ / ˘ / ˘ / ˘ / ˘ / ˘ /
And it's likely they'd have killed him had not Casey raised his hand.

Follow Up: Use your marked-up copy as a script and read the stanza to your classmates.

Before You Read

Connect to Your Life

Suppose you had to compete against a close friend for something you really wanted, like a sports trophy or a class election. How would you feel about it?

I would feel _____ because _____

_____

_____

Key to the Story

WHAT DO YOU THINK? In the story you are about to read, two best friends are about to compete in a boxing match. One says to the other:

"We gotta be like two heavy strangers that want the same thing, and only one can have it."

How would you have replied if you were this character's friend?

AMIGO BROTHERS

by Piri Thomas

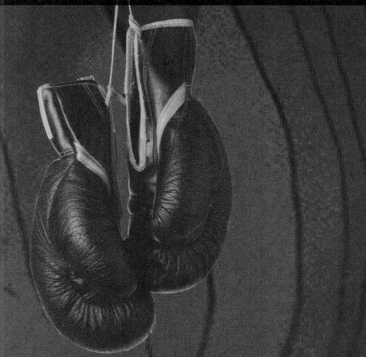

PREVIEW Of all the amateur boxing contests, none is more famous than the Golden Gloves tournament. Felix Vargas and Antonio Cruz both want to win the Golden Gloves. Felix and Antonio are best friends. Can they face each other in the ring and still be friends?

As the story begins . . .

- Two friends, Antonio and Felix, are both excellent boxers.
- Both want to be lightweight champion.

English Learner Support

Vocabulary

Spanish Words In this story, you will sometimes find Spanish words and slang expressions. Be sure to check the footnotes if you need help understanding these terms.

MORE ABOUT . . .

LIGHTWEIGHT To keep matches fair, boxers are classified by their weights. Lightweights weigh between 130 and 135 pounds.

English Learner Support

Vocabulary

Idioms *Street negatives* are activities that are bad for a person or for a community.

FOCUS

In this section you will meet Antonio Cruz and Felix Vargas, two lifelong friends who love boxing.

MARK IT UP As you read, underline details that show the boys' feelings toward boxing. An example is highlighted.

Antonio Cruz and Felix Vargas were both seventeen years old. They were so together in friendship that they felt themselves to be brothers. They had known each other since childhood, growing up on the lower east side of Manhattan in the
10 same tenement building on Fifth Street between Avenue A and Avenue B.

Antonio was fair, lean, and lanky, while Felix was dark, short, and husky. Antonio's hair was always falling over his eyes, while Felix wore his black hair in a natural Afro style.

Each youngster had a dream of someday becoming lightweight champion of the world. Every chance they had the boys worked out, sometimes at the Boys Club on 10th Street and Avenue A and sometimes at the
20 pro's gym on 14th Street. Early morning sunrises would find them running along the East River Drive, wrapped in sweatshirts, short towels around their necks, and handkerchiefs Apache style around their foreheads.

While some youngsters were into street negatives, Antonio and Felix slept, ate, rapped, and dreamt positive. Between them, they had a collection of *Fight* magazines second to none, plus a scrapbook filled with torn tickets to every boxing match they had ever
30 attended and some clippings of their own. If asked a question about any given fighter, they would immediately zip out from their memory banks divisions,[1] weights, records of fights, knockouts, technical knockouts, and draws or losses.

---

1. **divisions:** weight groups into which boxers are separated.

Each had fought many bouts representing their community and had won two gold-plated medals plus a silver and bronze medallion. The difference was in their style. Antonio's lean form and long reach made him the better boxer, while Felix's short and muscular frame made him the better slugger. Whenever they had met in the ring for sparring sessions, it had always been hot and heavy.

Now, after a series of elimination bouts,[2] they had been informed that they were to meet each other in the division finals that were scheduled for the seventh of August, two weeks away—the winner to represent the Boys Club in the Golden Gloves Championship Tournament.

Pause & Reflect

FOCUS

The two boys are scheduled to fight each other. Read to find out how they feel about that fight and what they promise each other.

The two boys continued to run together along the East River Drive. But even when joking with each other, they both sensed a wall rising between them.

One morning less than a week before their bout, they met as usual for their daily workout. They fooled around with a few jabs at the air, slapped skin, and then took off, running lightly along the dirty East River's edge.

Antonio glanced at Felix, who kept his eyes purposely straight ahead, pausing from time to time to do some fancy leg work while throwing one-twos followed by upper cuts to an imaginary jaw. Antonio then beat the air with a <u>barrage</u> of body blows and

2. **elimination bouts:** matches to determine which boxers advance in a competition.

WORDS TO KNOW
barrage (bə-räzh´) n. a rapid, heavy attack

Pause & Reflect

Cross out one statement below that is *not* true about Antonio and Felix. (Summarize)

They each want to be lightweight champion.

They just want to have fun.

They work out every chance they get.

They read boxing magazines.

As the story continues . . .

• The friends know that only one of them will win.

• They decide to act like strangers while they train and fight.

WHAT DOES IT MEAN? The phrase *sensed a wall rising between them* means they no longer felt as close as before; something now separated them.

short devastating lefts with an overhand, jawbreaking right.

After a mile or so, Felix puffed and said, "Let's stop for awhile, bro. I think we both got something to say to each other."

70 Antonio nodded. It was not natural to be acting as though nothing unusual was happening when two ace boon buddies were going to be blasting . . . each other within a few short days.

They rested their elbows on the railing separating them from the river. Antonio wiped his face with his short towel. The sunrise was now creating day.

Felix leaned heavily on the river's railing and stared across to the shores of Brooklyn. Finally, he broke the silence.

". . . , man. I don't know how to come out with it."

80 Antonio helped. "It's about our fight, right?"

"Yeah, right." Felix's eyes squinted at the rising orange sun.

"I've been thinking about it too, *panin*.[3] In fact, since we found out it was going to be me and you, I've been awake at night, pulling punches[4] on you, trying not to hurt you."

"Same here. It ain't natural not to think about the fight. I mean, we both are *cheverote*[5] fighters, and we both want to win. But only one of us can win. There

90 ain't no draws in the eliminations."[6]

Felix tapped Antonio gently on the shoulder. "I don't mean to sound like I'm bragging, bro. But I wanna win, fair and square."

Antonio nodded quietly. "Yeah. We both know that in the ring the better man wins. Friend or no friend, brother or no . . ."

---

3. *panin* (pä'nēn) *American Spanish:* pal; buddy.

4. **pulling punches:** holding back in delivering blows.

5. *cheverote* (chĕ-vĕ-rō'tĕ) *American Spanish:* really cool.

6. **There . . . eliminations:** There are no ties; there has to be a winner.

Felix finished it for him. "Brother. Tony, let's promise something right here. Okay?"

"If it's fair, *hermano*,[7] I'm for it." Antonio admired
100 the courage of a tugboat pulling a barge five times its welterweight[8] size.

"It's fair, Tony. When we get into the ring, it's gotta be like we never met. We gotta be like two heavy strangers that want the same thing, and only one can have it. You understand, don'tcha?"

"*Sí*, I know." Tony smiled. "No pulling punches. We go all the way."

"Yeah, that's right. Listen, Tony. Don't you think it's a good idea if we don't see each other until the day of
110 the fight? I'm going to stay with my Aunt Lucy in the Bronx. I can use Gleason's Gym for working out. My manager says he got some sparring partners with more or less your style."

Tony scratched his nose <u>pensively</u>. "Yeah, it would be better for our heads." He held out his hand, palm upward. "Deal?"

"Deal." Felix lightly slapped open skin.

"Ready for some more running?" Tony asked lamely.

120 "Naw, bro. Let's cut it here. You go on. I kinda like to get things together in my head."

"You ain't worried, are you?" Tony asked.

"No way, man." Felix laughed out loud. "I got too much smarts for that. I just think it's cooler if we split right here. After the fight, we can get it together again like nothing ever happened."

The amigo brothers were not ashamed to hug each other tightly.

---

7. *hermano* (ĕr-mä′nō) *Spanish:* brother.

8. **welterweight:** one of boxing's weight divisions, with a minimum weight of 140 and a maximum weight of 147 pounds.

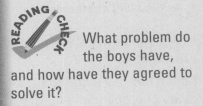
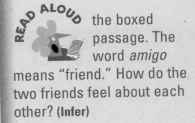

WHAT DOES IT MEAN?

Psyching up means "mental preparation."

Pause & Reflect

What do the two boys promise each other? Circle one phrase below. **(Clarify)**

to be gentle during the fight

to flip a coin to see who wins

to just wait and see what happens

to fight as if they never met

As the story continues . . .

- Tony and Felix get ready for the fight.
- Each boy has a different way of preparing to fight his friend.

MORE ABOUT . . .

THE CHAMPION The movie *The Champion* showed professional boxing, not amateur boxing. Professional boxers do not wear protective headgear and they use smaller gloves than amateurs do. As a result, their injuries are often worse.

"Guess you're right. Watch yourself, Felix. I hear
130 there's some pretty heavy dudes up in the Bronx.
Suavecito,[9] okay?"

"Okay. You watch yourself too, *sabe?*"[10]

Tony jogged away. Felix watched his friend disappear from view, throwing rights and lefts. Both fighters had a lot of psyching up to do before the big fight.

Pause & Reflect

FOCUS

How do Antonio and Felix get ready for the fight?

MARK IT UP > As you read, underline details that show you what each boy does to try to prepare for the fight.

The days in training passed much too slowly. Although they kept out of each other's way, they were aware of each
140 other's progress via the ghetto grapevine.

The evening before the big fight, Tony made his way to the roof of his tenement. In the quiet early dark, he peered over the ledge. Six stories below, the lights of the city blinked, and the sounds of cars mingled with the curses and the laughter of children in the street. He tried not to think of Felix, feeling he had succeeded in psyching his mind. But only in the ring would he really know. To spare Felix hurt, he would
150 have to knock him out, early and quick.

Up in the South Bronx, Felix decided to take in a movie in an effort to keep Antonio's face away from his fists. The flick was The Champion with Kirk Douglas, the third time Felix was seeing it.

The champion was getting . . . beat . . . , his face being pounded into raw, wet hamburger. His eyes were

---

9. *Suavecito* (swä-vĕ-sē′tō) *American Spanish:* Take it easy.
10. *sabe?* (sä′bĕ) *Spanish:* you know?

cut, jagged, bleeding, one eye swollen, the other almost shut. He was saved only by the sound of the bell.

160 Felix became the champ and Tony the challenger.

The movie audience was going out of its head, roaring in blood lust at the butchery going on. The champ hunched his shoulders, grunting and sniffing red blood back into his broken nose. The challenger, confident that he had the championship in the bag, threw a left. The champ countered with a dynamite right that exploded into the challenger's brains.

Felix's right arm felt the shock. Antonio's face, superimposed on the screen, was shattered and split 170 apart by the awesome force of the killer blow. Felix saw himself in the ring, blasting Antonio against the ropes. The champ had to be forcibly restrained. The challenger was allowed to crumble slowly to the canvas, a broken, bloody mess.

When Felix finally left the theatre, he had figured out how to psyche himself for tomorrow's fight. It was Felix the Champion vs. Antonio the Challenger.

He walked up some dark streets, deserted except for small pockets of wary-looking kids wearing gang 180 colors. Despite the fact that he was Puerto Rican like them, they eyed him as a stranger to their turf. Felix did a last shuffle, bobbing and weaving, while letting loose a torrent of blows that would demolish whatever got in its way. It seemed to impress the brothers, who went about their own business.

Finding no takers, Felix decided to split to his aunt's. Walking the streets had not relaxed him, neither had the fight flick. All it had done was to stir him up. He let himself quietly into his Aunt Lucy's 190 apartment and went straight to bed, falling into a fitful sleep with sounds of the gong for Round One.

Antonio was passing some heavy time on his rooftop. How would the fight tomorrow affect his

WHAT DOES IT MEAN?
Superimposed means "covering something else." In other words, Felix saw Antonio's face in place of the challenger's.

English Learner Support
Culture

Gangs In some cities, *gangs,* or groups of young people, band together for social and often unlawful behavior. They often wear certain colors that identify their gangs. A gang mainly stays in one area, called its *turf.* Gang members may attack other people who enter their turf.

WHAT DOES IT MEAN? The *gong* is a bell that signals the beginning and end of each round.

Pause & Reflect

Describe how each boy prepares for the fight. (Summarize)

Felix:

_____

_____

_____

_____

Antonio:

_____

_____

_____

_____

As the story continues . . .

- Many people think Antonio will win, while others believe Felix will win.
- A large crowd gathers to watch the fight.
- Antonio and Felix change into their fighting gear.

WHAT DOES IT MEAN?
Dynamite-packed means "having as much power as dynamite" or "ready to explode."

relationship with Felix? After all, fighting was like any other profession. Friendship had nothing to do with it. A gnawing doubt crept in. He cut negative thinking real quick by doing some speedy fancy dance steps, bobbing and weaving like mercury.[11] The night air was blurred with <u>perpetual</u> motions of left hooks and right crosses. Felix, his *amigo* brother, was not going to be Felix at all in the ring. Just an opponent with another face. Antonio went to sleep, hearing the opening bell for the first round. Like his friend in the South Bronx, he prayed for victory via a quick, clean knockout in the first round.

Pause & Reflect

FOCUS
Read to find out how the whole neighborhood gets ready for the big fight.

MARK IT UP As you read, underline details that show you how the neighborhood prepares.

Large posters plastered all over the walls of local shops announced the fight between Antonio Cruz and Felix Vargas as the main bout.

The fight had created great interest in the neighborhood. Antonio and Felix were well liked and respected. Each had his own loyal following. Betting fever was high and ranged from a bottle of Coke to cold, hard cash on the line.

Antonio's fans bet with <u>unbridled</u> faith in his boxing skills. On the other side, Felix's admirers bet on his dynamite-packed fists.

---

11. **mercury:** a liquid metallic element, also called quicksilver.

WORDS TO KNOW
perpetual (pər-pĕch′ōō-əl) *adj.* continual; unending
unbridled (ŭn-brīd′ld) *adj.* lacking in restraint or control

220   Felix had returned to his apartment early in the morning of August 7th and stayed there, hoping to avoid seeing Antonio. He turned the radio on to salsa music sounds and then tried to read while waiting for word from his manager.

    The fight was scheduled to take place in Tompkins Square Park. It had been decided that the gymnasium of the Boys Club was not large enough to hold all the people who were sure to attend. In Tompkins Square Park, everyone who wanted could view the fight,
230 whether from ringside or window fire escapes or tenement rooftops.

    The morning of the fight, Tompkins Square was a beehive of activity with numerous workers setting up the ring, the seats, and the guest speakers' stand. The scheduled bouts began shortly after noon, and the park had begun filling up even earlier.

    The local junior high school across from Tompkins Square Park served as the dressing room for all the fighters. Each was given a separate classroom, with
240 desktops, covered with mats, serving as resting tables. Antonio thought he caught a glimpse of Felix waving to him from a room at the far end of the corridor. He waved back just in case it had been him.

    The fighters changed from their street clothes into fighting gear. Antonio wore white trunks, black socks, and black shoes. Felix wore sky blue trunks, red socks, and white boxing shoes. Each had dressing gowns to match their fighting trunks with their names neatly stitched on the back.

250   The loudspeakers blared into the open window of the school. There were speeches by dignitaries, community leaders, and great boxers of yesteryear. Some were well prepared, some <u>improvised</u> on the spot. They all carried the same message of great

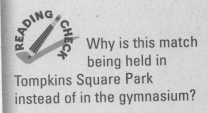

READING CHECK   Why is this match being held in Tompkins Square Park instead of in the gymnasium?

WORDS TO KNOW
improvise (ĭm′prə-vīz′) *v.* to speak or perform without preparation

If you lived in the
neighborhood, how would
you feel about the fight?
(Connect)

_____

_____

_____

As the story continues . . .

• The friends face each other
  before the fight.
• The crowd is screaming
  with excitement.
• The fight begins quickly.

English Learner Support

Language

Metaphor A metaphor
compares two things. The
metaphor *the crowd
exploded with a roar*
compares the people's
sudden, loud yelling to an
explosion.

pleasure and honor at being part of such a historic
event. This great day was in the tradition of champions
emerging from the streets of the lower east side.

Interwoven with the speeches were the sounds of the
other boxing events. After the sixth bout, Felix was

260 much relieved when his trainer, Charlie, said, "Time
change. Quick knockout. This is it. We're on."

Pause & Reflect

FOCUS

Felix and Antonio are
about to begin the match.

MARK IT UP As you
read, underline details
that help you visualize
what happens when the
two boys enter the ring.

Waiting time was over.
Felix was escorted from the
classroom by a dozen fans in
white T-shirts with the word
FELIX across their fronts.

Antonio was escorted down
a different stairwell and guided
through a roped-off path.

270   As the two climbed into the ring, the crowd exploded
with a roar. Antonio and Felix both bowed gracefully
and then raised their arms in acknowledgment.

Antonio tried to be cool, but even as the roar was in
its first birth, he turned slowly to meet Felix's eyes
looking directly into his. Felix nodded his head and
Antonio responded. And both as one, just as quickly,
turned away to face his own corner.

Bong, bong, bong. The roar turned to stillness.

"Ladies and Gentlemen, *Señores y Señoras.*"

280   The announcer spoke slowly, pleased at his bilingual
efforts.

"Now the moment we have all been waiting for—
the main event between two fine young Puerto Rican
fighters, products of our lower east side."

"Loisaida,"[12] called out a member of the audience.

"In this corner, weighing 131 pounds, Felix Vargas. And in this corner, weighing 133 pounds, Antonio Cruz. The winner will represent the Boys Club in the tournament of champions, the Golden Gloves. There
290 will be no draw. May the best man win."

The cheering of the crowd shook the windowpanes of the old buildings surrounding Tompkins Square Park. At the center of the ring, the referee was giving instructions to the youngsters.

"Keep your punches up. No low blows. No punching on the back of the head. Keep your heads up. Understand. Let's have a clean fight. Now shake hands and come out fighting."

Both youngsters touched gloves and nodded. They
300 turned and danced quickly to their corners. Their head towels and dressing gowns were lifted neatly from their shoulders by their trainers' nimble fingers. Antonio crossed himself. Felix did the same.

BONG! BONG! ROUND ONE. Felix and Antonio turned and faced each other squarely in a fighting pose. Felix wasted no time. He came in fast, head low, half hunched toward his right shoulder, and lashed out with a straight left. He missed a right cross as Antonio slipped the punch and countered with one-two-three
310 lefts that snapped Felix's head back, sending a mild shock coursing through him. If Felix had any small doubt about their friendship affecting their fight, it was being neatly underlined.

Pause & Reflect

---

12. **Loisaida** (lō′ē-sī′dä): a Hispanic slang pronunciation of *Lower East Side*.

WORDS TO KNOW
   dispel (dĭ-spĕl′) *v.* to scatter; get rid of

Pause & Reflect

1. What do you think might be going through each boy's mind when they see each other for the first time in the ring? (Infer)

Felix:

_____

_____

Antonio:

_____

_____

_____

2. What does Felix realize after Antonio's first punch? Check one sentence below. (Draw Conclusions)

❑ Antonio will be easy to beat.

❑ The crowd is on Antonio's side.

❑ Antonio is not thinking about their friendship.

❑ Antonio is not fighting fair.

As the story continues . . .

- Both fighters give and receive many blows.
- Both are hurt and glad when the second round ends.

WHAT DOES IT MEAN?

Bobbed means "moved up and down," and *weaved* means "moved from side to side."

English Learner Support

Language

Metaphor In this sentence, *dynamite* is a metaphor comparing Felix's powerful fist to explosive material.

MORE ABOUT . . .

TRAINERS Trainers, who are like coaches, help fighters see what they must do to win.

FOCUS

The first two rounds are fast and furious.

MARK IT UP As you read, circle the details that help you form impressions of the two boys as fighters.

Antonio danced, a joy to behold. His left hand was like a piston pumping jabs one right after another with seeming ease. Felix bobbed and weaved and never

320 stopped boring in. He knew that at long range he was at a disadvantage. Antonio had too much reach on him. Only by coming in close could Felix hope to achieve the dreamed-of knockout.

Antonio knew the dynamite that was stored in his amigo brother's fist. He ducked a short right and missed a left hook. Felix trapped him against the ropes just long enough to pour some punishing rights and lefts to Antonio's hard midsection. Antonio slipped

330 away from Felix, crashing two lefts to his head, which set Felix's right ear to ringing.

Bong! Both *amigos* froze a punch well on its way, sending up a roar of approval for good sportsmanship.

Felix walked briskly back to his corner. His right ear had not stopped ringing. Antonio gracefully danced his way toward his stool none the worse, except for glowing glove burns, showing angry red against the whiteness of his midribs.

"Watch that right, Tony." His trainer talked into his

340 ear. "Remember Felix always goes to the body. He'll want you to drop your hands for his overhand left or right. Got it?"

Antonio nodded, spraying water out between his teeth. He felt better as his sore midsection was being firmly rubbed.

Felix's corner was also busy.

"You gotta get in there, fella." Felix's trainer poured water over his curly Afro locks. "Get in there or he's gonna chop you up from way back."

³⁵⁰ *Bong! Bong!* Round two. Felix was off his stool and rushed Antonio like a bull, sending a hard right to his head. Beads of water exploded from Antonio's long hair.

Antonio, hurt, sent back a blurring barrage of lefts and rights that only meant pain to Felix, who returned with a short left to the head followed by a looping right to the body. Antonio countered with his own flurry, forcing Felix to give ground. But not for long.

Felix bobbed and weaved, bobbed and weaved,
³⁶⁰ occasionally punching his two gloves together.

Antonio waited for the rush that was sure to come. Felix closed in and <u>feinted</u> with his left shoulder and threw his right instead. Lights suddenly exploded inside Felix's head as Antonio slipped the blow and hit him with a pistonlike left, catching him flush on the point of his chin.

<u>Bedlam</u> broke loose as Felix's legs momentarily buckled. He fought off a series of rights and lefts and came back with a strong right that taught Antonio
³⁷⁰ respect.

Antonio danced in carefully. He knew Felix had the habit of playing possum when hurt, to sucker an opponent within reach of the powerful bombs he carried in each fist.

A right to the head slowed Antonio's pretty dancing. He answered with his own left at Felix's right eye that began puffing up within three seconds.

Antonio, a bit too eager, moved in too close, and Felix had him entangled into a rip-roaring, punching
³⁸⁰ toe-to-toe slugfest that brought the whole Tompkins Square Park screaming to its feet.

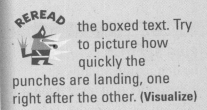

REREAD the boxed text. Try to picture how quickly the punches are landing, one right after the other. **(Visualize)**

WHAT DOES IT MEAN?

Playing possum means "pretending to be asleep or dead." Antonio wonders if Felix is trying to trick him into moving closer so that Felix can attack him.

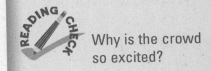

Why is the crowd so excited?

WORDS TO KNOW
feint (fānt) *v.* to make a pretended attack in order to draw attention away from one's real purpose or target
bedlam (bĕd′ləm) *n.* a noisy confusion

MORE ABOUT . . .

RING DOCTORS During a boxing match, judges sit outside the ring, as does the ring doctor. When fighters have been cut or injured, this doctor decides if they can safely continue to fight.

Pause & Reflect

1. MARK IT UP Review the details you circled. Star the ones that made the strongest impression. **(Evaluate)**

2. Do you think that the fight will affect the friendship between Felix and Antonio? **(Predict)**

YES / NO, because

Rights to the body. Lefts to the head. Neither fighter was giving an inch. Suddenly a short right caught Antonio squarely on the chin. His long legs turned to jelly, and his arms flailed out desperately. Felix, grunting like a bull, threw wild punches from every direction. Antonio, groggy, bobbed and weaved, <u>evading</u> most of the blows. Suddenly his head cleared. His left flashed out hard and straight catching Felix on
390 the bridge of his nose.

Felix lashed back with a haymaker, right off the ghetto streets. At the same instant, his eye caught another left hook from Antonio. Felix swung out, trying to clear the pain. Only the frenzied screaming of those along ringside let him know that he had dropped Antonio. Fighting off the growing haze, Antonio struggled to his feet, got up, ducked, and threw a smashing right that dropped Felix flat on his back.

Felix got up as fast as he could in his own corner,
400 groggy but still <u>game</u>. He didn't even hear the count. In a fog, he heard the roaring of the crowd, who seemed to have gone insane. His head cleared to hear the bell sound at the end of the round. He was . . . glad. His trainer sat him down on the stool.

In his corner, Antonio was doing what all fighters do when they are hurt. They sit and smile at everyone.

The referee signaled the ring doctor to check the fighters out. He did so and then gave his okay. The cold-water sponges brought clarity to both *amigo*
410 brothers. They were rubbed until their circulation ran free.

Pause & Reflect

WORDS TO KNOW
evading (ĭ-vā′dĭng) *adj.* avoiding; escaping **evade** *v.*
game (gām) *adj.* ready and willing to proceed

FOCUS

Read to find out how the fight ends.

Bong! Round three—the final round. Up to now it had been tick-tack-toe, pretty much even. But everyone knew there could be no draw and that this round would decide the winner.

This time, to Felix's surprise, it was Antonio who came out fast, charging across the ring. Felix braced
420 himself but couldn't ward off the barrage of punches. Antonio drove Felix hard against the ropes.

The crowd ate it up. Thus far the two had fought with *mucho corazón*.[13] Felix tapped his gloves and commenced his attack anew. Antonio, throwing boxer's caution to the winds, jumped in to meet him.

Both pounded away. Neither gave an inch, and neither fell to the canvas. Felix's left eye was tightly closed. Claret red blood poured from Antonio's nose. They fought toe-to-toe.

430 The sounds of their blows were loud in contrast to the silence of a crowd gone completely mute. The referee was stunned by their savagery.

Bong! Bong! Bong! The bell sounded over and over again. Felix and Antonio were past hearing. Their blows continued to pound on each other like hailstones.

Finally the referee and the two trainers pried Felix and Antonio apart. Cold water was poured over them to bring them back to their senses.

440 They looked around and then rushed toward each other. A cry of alarm surged through Tompkins Square Park. Was this a fight to the death instead of a boxing match?

The fear soon gave way to wave upon wave of cheering as the two amigos embraced.

As the story ends . . .

• The boys fight a final third round.

• They continue fighting, even after the final bell.

• Before the winner is announced, something surprising happens.

English Learner Support
Vocabulary

Idiom *The crowd ate it up* means "the crowd loved it."

WHAT DOES IT MEAN? *Mute* means "silent."

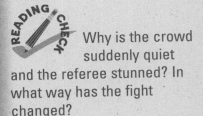

READING CHECK Why is the crowd suddenly quiet and the referee stunned? In what way has the fight changed?

---

13. *mucho corazón* (mōo'chô kō-rä-sōn') *Spanish:* a lot of heart; great courage.

READING CHECK
The last sentence refers to *the champions,* not to a single champion. What does this mean?

Pause & Reflect

1. Why do you think the two boys leave the ring together before the winner is announced? (Infer)

2. Who do you think is the winner of the match? (Infer)

CHALLENGE
How well do you think Antonio and Felix handle the tension involved in competing for a prize they both want? Mark passages in the story that support your views. (Evaluate)

No matter what the decision, they knew they would always be champions to each other.

Bong! Bong! Bong! "Ladies and Gentlemen. *Señores* and *Señoras.* The winner and representative to the
450 Golden Gloves Tournament of Champions is . . ."

The announcer turned to point to the winner and found himself alone. Arm in arm, the champions had already left the ring. ❖

Pause & Reflect

MARK IT UP How do you imagine the two fighters look as they leave the ring? Draw a sketch in the space below. (Visualize)

Active Reading SkillBuilder

Predicting

When you **predict,** you are trying to figure out what will happen next. Good readers use information from the story as well as their own knowledge to form predictions. As you read, use the chart below to note details about the character, plot, and setting that help you predict the answers to the questions. Write your predictions next to the clues.

Question	Detail from the Story	Your Prediction
Will they fight hard?	They work out at the gym every chance they get.	
Will they remain friends after the fight?		

Literary Analysis SkillBuilder

Suspense

The feeling of growing tension and excitement that makes you curious about the outcome of a story is called **suspense.** As you read, be aware of questions you would like to see answered, and write them down in the diagram below. Also note details about how the author increases the suspense in the story.

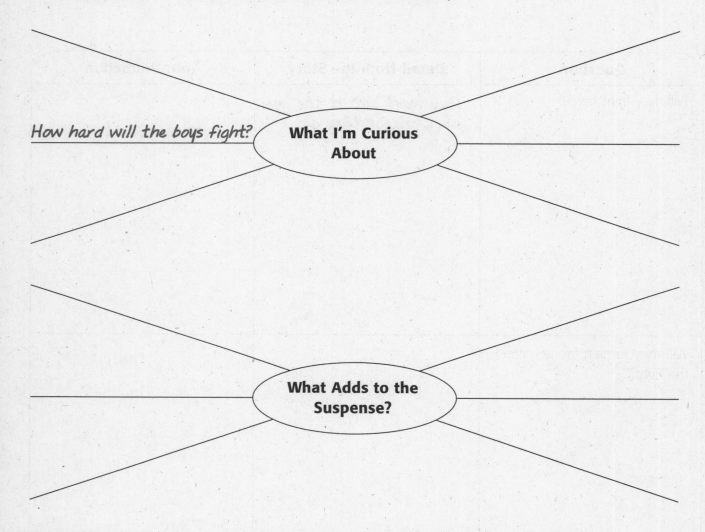

How hard will the boys fight?

What I'm Curious About

What Adds to the Suspense?

Follow Up: How were you left in suspense at the end of the story? Tell why you think the author made that choice.

Words to Know SkillBuilder

Words to Know

barrage	dispel	feint	improvise	perpetual
bedlam	evading	game	pensively	unbridled

A. Write on each line below a Word to Know that completes the sentence logically.

1. Some community leaders, when asked to talk to the audience, had to _____ a speech on the spot.

2. Antonio threw a _____ of blows at the punching bag.

3. Felix bobbed and weaved, _____ most of his opponent's blows.

4. Both boys tried to _____ doubts about their friendship.

5. When Felix practiced, he looked like a _____ motion machine.

6. Antonio scratched his nose _____ as he thought about the upcoming bout.

7. Each of the boys was _____ to fight his best.

8. When the match ended, _____ broke loose in the audience.

9. Felix would _____ with his left shoulder but punch with his right hand.

10. Antonio's fans had _____ faith in his abilities to win the fight.

B. Imagine that the fight between Antonio and Felix is on TV. You are the sportscaster. Write what you might say. Use at least **five** of the Words to Know.

Before You Read

Connect to Your Life

When you come up against something strange and unknown, how do you react? What do you do when you think danger is near? Fill out these charts. List the ways in which you and other people react to danger.

How I React to Danger	How Groups React
1. run as fast as I can	1. stick together
2.	2.
3.	3.
4.	4.

Key to the Drama

WHAT DO YOU THINK? This sentence gives you insight into the theme of the drama. What do you think the sentence means? Think of related words to help you unlock the meaning.

For the record, (prejudices) *can kill and* (suspicion) *can destroy.*

The Monsters Are Due on Maple Street

BY ROD SERLING

PREVIEW   In this television drama, something strange happens on Maple Street, a quiet street in a small American town. The people are sitting on their front porches talking. Suddenly a strange roar and flash of light briefly disturb the peace of the scene. What will happen when ordinary people have to face the unknown?

As the play begins . . .

- Maple Street is a quiet, ordinary street in a small town.

- The people living there hear a noise and see a flash of light.

MORE ABOUT . . .

TELEPLAYS A teleplay is a play written for television. Like other plays, the script usually contains a list of characters, dialogue (the words the characters speak), and stage directions. Stage directions are written in *italic* type. They describe how the stage looks, how the actors speak and move, and what the (camera) should be doing.

 READING TIP Read the stage directions carefully. They are printed in italic type. In this play, important events are described in the stage directions.

Cast of Characters

Narrator	Voice Five
Tommy	Pete Van Horn
Steve Brand	Charlie
Don Martin	Sally, *Tommy's mother*
Myra Brand, *Steve's wife*	Man One
Woman	Les Goodman
Voice One	Ethel Goodman, *Les's wife*
Voice Two	Man Two
Voice Three	Figure One
Voice Four	Figure Two

FOCUS

Maple Street is a typical suburban street in the 1950s. On this street, ordinary people do ordinary activities on a late summer evening.

MARK IT UP As you read, underline details that describe these activities. An example is highlighted.

Act One

(*Fade in on a shot of the night sky. The various heavenly bodies stand out in sharp, sparkling relief. The* (camera) *moves slowly across the heavens until it passes the horizon and stops on a sign that reads "Maple Street." It is daytime. Then we see the*
10 *street below. It is a quiet, tree-lined, small-town American street. The houses have front porches on which people sit and swing on gliders, talking across from house to house. Steve Brand is polishing his car, which is parked in front of his house. His neighbor, Don Martin, leans against the fender watching him. An ice-cream vendor[1] riding a bicycle is just in the process of stopping to sell some ice cream to a couple of kids. Two women gossip on the front lawn. Another man is watering*
20 *his lawn with a garden hose. As we see these various activities, we hear the* Narrator's *voice.*)

---

1. **vendor:** a person who sells.

Narrator. Maple Street, U.S.A., late summer. A tree-lined little world of front-porch gliders, hopscotch, the laughter of children, and the bell of an ice-cream vendor.

(*There is a pause, and the camera moves over to a shot of the ice-cream vendor and two small boys who are standing alongside just buying ice cream.*)

Narrator. At the sound of the roar and the flash of
30   the light, it will be precisely six-forty-three P.M. on Maple Street.

(*At this moment* Tommy, *one of the two boys buying ice cream from the vendor, looks up to listen to a tremendous screeching roar from overhead. A flash of light plays on the faces of both boys and then moves down the street and disappears. Various people leave their porches or stop what they are doing to stare up at the sky.* Steve Brand, *the man who has been polishing his car, stands there transfixed,[2] staring*
40   *upwards. He looks at* Don Martin, *his neighbor from across the street.*)

Steve. What was that? A meteor?

Don. That's what it looked like. I didn't hear any crash though, did you?

Steve. Nope. I didn't hear anything except a roar.

Myra (*from her porch*). What was that?

Steve (*raising his voice and looking toward the porch*). Guess it was a meteor, honey. Came awful close, didn't it?

50   **Myra.** Too close for my money! Much too close.

(*The camera moves slowly across the various porches to people who stand there watching and talking in low conversing tones.*)

---

2. **transfixed:** unable to move.

||| MARK IT UP > Reread the boxed passage. A strange thing happens on Maple Street at 6:43 P.M. Circle details that describe how the people react to this event. **(Clarify)**

English Learner Support
Vocabulary

Idiom This sentence means that a light briefly shines on both boys.

English Learner Support
Vocabulary

Meteor A *meteor* is a piece of rock or other debris from outer space that burns up as it enters Earth's atmosphere, causing a streak of light across the sky.

English Learner Support
Vocabulary

Idiom *Too close for my money* is a way of saying, "The meteor came so close that I feel frightened."

Pause & Reflect

Look over the details you underlined as you read. Do you think you would like to live on Maple Street? **(Connect)**

YES / NO, because

_____

_____

_____

_____

📖 **As the play continues . . .**

- The power goes off and all machines stop working.
- People try to figure out why things aren't working.

REREAD the boxed stage directions. What information do they give about what is happening on Maple Street? **(Summarize)**

_____

_____

READING TIP Characters that do not have real names—such as Woman, Voice One, and Voice Two—are usually not important characters. They are used to give more information about the story's setting or events.

Narrator. Maple Street. Six-forty-four P.M. on a late September evening. (*He pauses.*) Maple Street in the last calm and reflective moment (*pause*) before the monsters came!

Pause & Reflect

FOCUS

After the screeching roar and the flash of light, several strange events happen on Maple Street.

✏️ **MARK IT UP** > As you read, underline details that tell you about these events.

(*The camera takes us across the porches again. A man is* 60 *replacing a light bulb on a front porch. He gets off his stool to flick the switch and finds that nothing happens. Another man is working on an electric power mower. He plugs in the plug, flicks the switch of the mower off and on, but nothing happens. Through a window we see a woman pushing her finger up and down on the dial hook* 70 *of a telephone. Her voice sounds far away.*)

Woman. Operator, operator, something's wrong on the phone, operator! (*Myra Brand comes out on the porch and calls to* Steve.)

Myra (*calling*). Steve, the power's off. I had the soup on the stove, and the stove just stopped working.

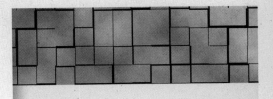

Woman. Same thing over here. I can't get anybody on the phone either. The phone seems to be dead.

(*We look down again on the street. Small, mildly disturbed voices are heard coming from below.*)

80 **Voice One.** Electricity's off.

Voice Two. Phone won't work.

Voice Three. Can't get a thing on the radio.

Voice Four. My power mower won't move, won't work at all.

Voice Five. Radio's gone dead!

(*Pete Van Horn, a tall, thin man, is seen standing in front of his house.*)

Pete. I'll cut through the back yard to see if the power's still on, on Floral Street. I'll be right back!

90 (*He walks past the side of his house and disappears into the back yard. The camera pans down slowly until we are looking at ten or eleven people standing around the street and overflowing to the curb and sidewalk. In the background is Steve Brand's car.*)

Steve. Doesn't make sense. Why should the power go off all of a sudden and the phone line?

Don. Maybe some kind of an electrical storm or something.

Charlie. That don't seem likely. Sky's just as blue as 100 anything. Not a cloud. No lightning. No thunder. No nothing. How could it be a storm?

Woman. I can't get a thing on the radio. Not even the portable.

(*The people again begin to murmur softly in wonderment.*)

The Monsters . . . 209

 REREAD the boxed passage. What do you think might be the cause of the power failures? (**Cause and Effect**)

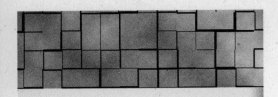

Why does everyone watch Steve when he tries to start his car?

WHAT DOES IT MEAN?
Sluggishly means "very slowly."

Pause & Reflect

1. Look over the details you underlined as you read. Cross out the one event below that does *not* happen on Maple Street. **(Clarify)**

   A radio doesn't work.

   Steve's car won't start.

   A phone line is dead.

   A fire burns out of control.

2. How do the people on Maple Street react to the strange events? **(Infer)**

Charlie. Well, why don't you go downtown and check with the police, though they'll probably think we're crazy or something. A little power failure and right away we get all <u>flustered</u> and everything—

110 **Steve.** It isn't just the power failure, Charlie. If it was, we'd still be able to get a broadcast on the portable.

(*There is a murmur of reaction to this.* Steve *looks from face to face and then at his car.*)

Steve. I'll run downtown. We'll get this all straightened out.

(*He gets in the car and turns the key. Looking through the open car door, we see the crowd watching* Steve *from the other side. He starts the engine. It turns over* sluggishly *and then stops dead. He tries it again,*
120 *and this time he can't get it to turn over. Then very slowly he turns the key back to "off" and gets out of the car. The people stare at* Steve. *He stands for a moment by the car and then walks toward them.*)

Steve. I don't understand it. It was working fine before—

Don. Out of gas?

Steve (*shakes his head*). I just had it filled.

Woman. What's it mean?

Charlie. It's just as if (*pause*) as if everything had
130 stopped. (*Then he turns toward* Steve.) We'd better walk downtown.

(*Another murmur of assent to this.*)

Steve. The two of us can go, Charlie. (*He turns to look back at the car.*) It couldn't be the meteor. A meteor couldn't do this.

Pause & Reflect

WORDS TO KNOW
flustered (flŭs′tərd) *adj.* nervous or confused **fluster** *v.*

Steve and Charlie start to walk downtown. Suddenly, a boy named Tommy stops them with his own explanation of the strange events. Read to find out about Tommy's explanation.

(*He and* Charlie *exchange a look. Then they start to walk away from the group.* Tommy *comes into view. He*
140 *is a serious-faced young boy in spectacles. He stands halfway between the group and the two men, who start to walk down the sidewalk.*)

Tommy. Mr. Brand—you'd better not!

Steve. Why not?

Tommy. They don't want you to.

(Steve *and* Charlie *exchange a grin, and* Steve *looks back toward the boy.*)

150 **Steve.** Who doesn't want us to?

Tommy (*jerks his head in the general direction of the distant horizon*). Them!

Steve. Them?

Charlie. Who are them?

Tommy (*intently*). Whoever was in that thing that came by overhead.

(Steve *knits his brows for a moment, cocking his head questioningly. His voice is* <u>intense</u>.)

Steve. What?

160 **Tommy.** Whoever was in that thing that came over. I don't think they want us to leave here.

(Steve *leaves* Charlie, *walks over to the boy, and puts his hand on the boy's shoulder. He forces his voice to remain gentle.*)

Steve. What do you mean? What are you talking about?

- Tommy warns Steve and Charlie about "them."
- According to Tommy, "they" send down people who look like humans but aren't.
- People try to act calm, but they are very frightened.

READ ALOUD the boxed passage. As you read these lines, use your voice to show the different and changing emotions of the characters.

WORDS TO KNOW
intense (ĭn-tĕns') *adj.* showing great concentration or determination

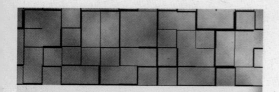

Idiom When used alone, the word *shut* means "close," as in "shut the door." *Shut off* means to cause something to stop working.

READING TIP   The three dots in the middle of a sentence show that a character hesitates, or pauses briefly, while speaking. In the highlighted sentence, Steve hesitates when speaking about the meteor.

WHAT DOES IT MEAN?

Picking up the cue means that Don understands Steve is trying to sound confident, so he tries to sound the same way.

Tommy. They don't want us to leave. That's why they shut everything off.

Steve. What makes you say that? Whatever gave you 170 that idea?

Woman (*from the crowd*). Now isn't that the craziest thing you ever heard?

Tommy (*persistent but a little frightened*). It's always that way, in every story I ever read about a ship landing from outer space.

Woman (*to the boy's mother*, Sally, *who stands on the fringe of the crowd*). From outer space yet! Sally, you better get that boy of yours up to bed. He's been reading too many comic books or seeing 180 too many movies or something!

Sally. Tommy, come over here and stop that kind of talk.

Steve. Go ahead, Tommy. We'll be right back. And you'll see. That wasn't any ship or anything like it. That was just a . . . a meteor or something. Likely as not— (*He turns to the group, now trying very hard to sound more optimistic than he feels.*) No doubt it did have something to do with all this power failure and the rest of it. Meteors can do 190 some crazy things. Like sunspots.

Don (*picking up the cue*). Sure. That's the kind of thing—like sunspots. They raise Cain[3] with radio reception all over the world. And this thing being so close—why, there's no telling the sort of stuff it can do. (*He wets his lips and smiles nervously.*) Go ahead, Charlie. You and Steve go into town and see if that isn't what's causing it all.

---

3. **raise Cain:** cause trouble; create a disturbance.

WORDS TO KNOW
persistent (pər-sĭs'tənt) *adj.* refusing to give up; continuing stubbornly
optimistic (ŏp'tə-mĭs'tĭk) *adj.* hopeful about the future; confident

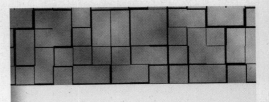

(Steve *and* Charlie *walk away from the group down the sidewalk as the people watch silently.* Tommy *stares* 200 *at them, biting his lips, and finally calls out again.*)

Tommy. Mr. Brand!

(*The two men stop.* Tommy *takes a step toward them.*)

Tommy. Mr. Brand . . . please don't leave here.

(Steve *and* Charlie *stop once again and turn toward the boy. In the crowd there is a murmur of irritation and concern, as if the boy's words—even though they didn't make sense—were* bringing up *fears that shouldn't be brought up.* Tommy *is both frightened and* <u>defiant</u>.)

210 **Tommy.** You might not even be able to get to town. It was that way in the story. Nobody could leave. Nobody except—

Steve. Except who?

Tommy. Except the people they sent down ahead of them. They looked just like humans. And it wasn't until the ship landed that— (*The boy suddenly stops, conscious of the people staring at him and his mother and of the sudden hush of the crowd.*)

Sally (*in a whisper, sensing the* <u>antagonism</u> *of the* 220 *crowd*). Tommy, please son . . . honey, don't talk that way—

Man One. That kid shouldn't talk that way . . . and we shouldn't stand here listening to him. Why this is the craziest thing I ever heard of. The kid tells us a comic book plot, and here we stand listening—

(Steve *walks toward the camera and stops beside the boy.*)

Steve. Go ahead, Tommy. What kind of story was this? What about the people they sent out ahead?

WORDS TO KNOW
  defiant (dĭ-fī′ənt) *adj.* willing to stand up to opposition; bold
  antagonism (ăn-tăg′ə-nĭz′əm) *n.* hostility; unfriendliness

Pause & Reflect

1. The people on Maple Street take Tommy's story very seriously. Why do you think they react this way? (Infer)

2. Do you think Tommy's explanation of the strange sighting over Maple Street is logical? (Evaluate)

YES / NO, because

▷ As the play continues . . .

• One car starts on its own, and the group wonders why.

• They suspect the car's owner of something, even though he is also confused by events.

230 **Tommy.** That was the way they prepared things for the landing. They sent four people. A mother and a father and two kids who looked just like humans . . . but they weren't.

(*There is another silence as Steve looks toward the crowd and then toward* Tommy. *He wears a tight grin.*)

Steve. Well, I guess what we'd better do then is to run a check on the neighborhood and see which ones of us are really human.

(*There is laughter at this, but it's a laughter that*
240 *comes from a desperate[4] attempt to lighten the atmosphere. The people look at one another in the middle of their laughter.*)

Pause & Reflect

FOCUS

The people of Maple Street single out one of their neighbors. Read to find out why.

▯▮ MARK IT UP ▷ As you read, circle details that tell why they find Les Goodman suspicious.

Charlie (*rubs his jaw nervously*). I wonder if Floral Street's got the same deal we got. (*He looks past the houses.*) Where is Pete Van Horn anyway? Isn't he back yet?

250 (*Suddenly there is the sound of a car's engine starting to turn over. We look across the street toward the driveway of Les Goodman's house. He is at the wheel trying to start the car.*)

4. desperate: without hope.

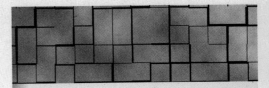

Sally. Can you get started, Les?

(Les Goodman *gets out of the car, shaking his head.*)

Les. No dice.

(*He walks toward the group. He stops suddenly as, behind him, the car engine starts up all by itself. Les* 260 *whirls around to stare at the car. The car idles roughly, smoke coming from the exhaust, the frame shaking gently. Les's eyes go wide, and he runs over to his car. The people stare at the car.*)

Man One. He got the car started somehow. He got *his* car started!

(*The people continue to stare, caught up by this revelation and wildly frightened.*)

Woman. How come his car just up and started like that?

270 **Sally.** All by itself. He wasn't anywheres near it. It started all by itself.

(Don Martin *approaches the group and stops a few feet away to look toward* Les's *car.*)

Don. And he never did come out to look at that thing that flew overhead. He wasn't even interested. (*He turns to the group, his face taut and serious.*) Why? Why didn't he come out with the rest of us to look?

Charlie. He always was an oddball. Him and his whole family. Real oddball.

280 **Don.** What do you say we ask him?

(*The group starts toward the house. In this brief fraction of a moment, it takes the first step toward changing from a group into a mob. The group members begin to head purposefully across the street toward the house. Steve* stands in front of them. For a moment their fear almost turns their walk into a*

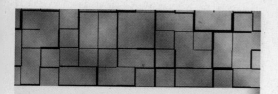

READING TIP As you read, think about what happens and the effect that it has. Sometimes, one action can have more than one effect. You can use a flow chart like the one below to track causes and effects.

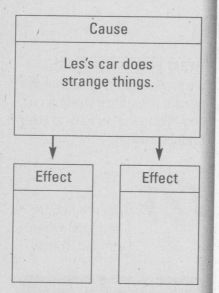

Cause
Les's car does strange things.

Effect	Effect

wild stampede, but Steve's voice, loud, incisive,[5] and commanding, makes them stop.)

Steve. Wait a minute . . . wait a minute! Let's not be
290 a mob!

(*The people stop, pause for a moment, and then, much more quietly and slowly, start to walk across the street. Les stands alone facing the people.*)

Les. I just don't understand it. I tried to start it, and it wouldn't start. You saw me. All of you saw me.

(*And now, just as suddenly as the engine started, it stops, and there is a long silence that is gradually intruded upon by the frightened murmuring of the people.*)

300 **Les.** I don't understand. I swear . . . I don't understand. What's happening?

Don. Maybe you better tell us. Nothing's working on this street. Nothing. No lights, no power, no radio, (*then meaningfully*) nothing except one car—yours!

(*The people's murmuring becomes a loud chant filling the air with accusations and demands for action. Two of the men pass Don and head toward Les, who backs away from them against his car. He is cornered.*)

Les. Wait a minute now. You keep your distance—all
310 of you. So I've got a car that starts by itself—well, that's a freak thing—I admit it. But does that make me a criminal or something? I don't know why the car works—it just does!

(*This stops the crowd momentarily, and Les, still backing away, goes toward his front porch. He goes up the steps and then stops, facing the mob.*)

---

5. **incisive:** sharp and clear; penetrating.

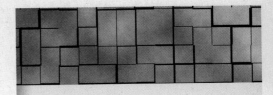

Les. What's it all about, Steve?

Steve (*quietly*). We're all on a monster kick, Les.
Seems that the general impression holds that maybe
320   one family isn't what we think they are. Monsters
from outer space or something. Different from us.
Aliens from the vast beyond. (*He chuckles.*) You
know anybody that might fit that description
around here on Maple Street?

Les. What is this, a gag? (*He looks around the group
again.*) This a practical joke or something?

(*Suddenly the car engine starts all by itself, runs for a
moment, and stops. One woman begins to cry. The
eyes of the crowd are cold and accusing.*)

330 **Les.** Now that's supposed to <u>incriminate</u> me, huh?
The car engine goes on and off, and that really
does it, doesn't it? (*He looks around at the faces of
the people.*) I just don't understand it . . . any more
than any of you do! (*He wets his lips, looking from
face to face.*) Look, you all know me. We've lived
here five years. Right in this house. We're no
different from any of the rest of you! We're no
different at all. . . . Really . . . this whole thing is
just . . . just weird—

340 **Woman.** Well, if that's the case, Les Goodman,
explain why— (*She stops suddenly, clamping her
mouth shut.*)

Les (*softly*). Explain what?

Steve (*interjecting*). Look, let's forget this—

Charlie (*overlapping him*). Go ahead, let her talk.
What about it? Explain what?

WORDS TO KNOW
incriminate (ĭn-krĭm′ə-nāt′) *v.* to cause to appear guilty

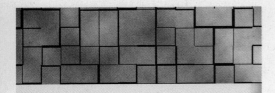

Pause & Reflect

1. Check the statement below that is *not* a reason why the neighbors are suspicious of Les. **(Clarify)**

   ❏ He's considered an "oddball."

   ❏ He works on his own car.

   ❏ He watches the sky by himself.

   ❏ His car stops and starts by itself.

2. Do you think the neighbors have good reasons for being suspicious? Why or why not? **(Evaluate)**

   _____

   _____

   _____

3. Why might someone look up at the night sky? **(Cause and Effect)**

   _____

   _____

   _____

   _____

Woman (*a little reluctantly*). Well . . . sometimes I go to bed late at night. A couple of times . . . a couple of times I'd come out here on the porch, and I'd see
350 Mr. Goodman here in the wee hours of the morning standing out in front of his house . . . looking up at the sky. (*She looks around the circle of faces.*) That's right, looking up at the sky as if . . . as if he were waiting for something, (*pauses*) as if he were looking for something.

(*There's a murmur of reaction from the crowd again as* Les *backs away.*)

Les. She's crazy. Look, I can explain that. Please . . . I can really explain that. . . . She's making it up
360 anyway. (*Then he shouts.*) I tell you she's making it up!

(*He takes a step toward the crowd, and they back away from him. He walks down the steps after them, and they continue to back away. Suddenly he is left completely alone, and he looks like a man caught in the middle of a menacing circle as the scene slowly fades to black.*)

Pause & Reflect

FOCUS

As night falls, the terror grows. Read to find out how the neighbors treat one another.

Act Two

Scene One

(*Fade in on Maple Street at night. On the sidewalk, little* 370 *knots of people stand around talking in low voices. At the end of each conversation they look toward* Les Goodman's *house. From the various houses, we can see candlelight but no electricity. The quiet that blankets the whole area is disturbed only by the almost whispered voices of the people standing around. In one group* Charlie *stands staring across at the* Goodmans' *house. Two men stand across the street from it in almost sentrylike[6] poses.*)

Sally (*in a small, hesitant voice*). It just doesn't seem 380 right, though, keeping watch on them. Why . . . he was right when he said he was one of our neighbors. Why, I've known Ethel Goodman ever since they moved in. We've been good friends—

Charlie. That don't prove a thing. Any guy who'd spend his time lookin' up at the sky early in the morning—well, there's something wrong with that kind of person. There's something that ain't legitimate. Maybe under normal circumstances we could let it go by, but these aren't normal 390 circumstances. Why, look at this street! Nothin' but candles. Why, it's like goin' back into the Dark Ages or somethin'!

(Steve *walks down the steps of his porch, down the street to the* Goodmans' *house, and then stops at the foot of the steps.* Les *is standing there;* Ethel Goodman *behind him is very frightened.*)

---

6. **sentrylike:** like a sentry, a person, especially a soldier, who keeps watch.

WORDS TO KNOW
 legitimate (lə-jĭt′ə-mĭt) *adj.* in accordance with accepted practices; reasonable

As the play continues . . .

• The neighbors are now suspicious of any action that seems "different."

• The group starts to panic, and one person does something awful.

READING CHECK How are Sally's feelings about watching Ethel and Les different from Charlie's feelings?

MORE ABOUT . . .

THE DARK AGES This name refers to the early part of the Middle Ages, between 400 A.D. and 1000 A.D. In some ways, this period in Europe was a time of ignorance, superstition, and social unrest.

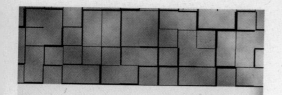

READING TIP Ethel is supporting Les because she is his wife. If you have trouble remembering how characters are related to each other, refer to the cast list on page 206.

English Learner Support

Vocabulary

Informal English The word *ain't* is a short, informal form of "are not" or "is not." When Charlie says that Steve "ain't exactly above suspicion," he means that people are also suspicious of Steve.

English Learner Support

Culture

Playing Cards The phrase in blue comes from card games. A player "tips his or her hand" by accidentally holding the cards in a way that allows other players to see them. Charlie means "Someone will do something that proves he's the monster."

Les. Just stay right where you are, Steve. We don't want any trouble, but this time if anybody sets foot on my porch—that's what they're going to get— 400 trouble!

Steve. Look, Les—

Les. I've already explained to you people. I don't sleep very well at night sometimes. I get up and I take a walk and I look up at the sky. I look at the stars!

Ethel. That's exactly what he does. Why, this whole thing, it's . . . it's some kind of madness or something.

Steve (*nods grimly*). That's exactly what it is—some 410 kind of madness.

Charlie's Voice (*shrill, from across the street*). You best watch who you're seen with, Steve! Until we get this all straightened out, you ain't exactly above suspicion yourself.

Steve (*whirling around toward him*). Or you, Charlie. Or any of us, it seems. From age eight on up!

Woman. What I'd like to know is—what are we gonna do? Just stand around here all night?

Charlie. There's nothin' else we *can* do! (*He turns* 420 *back, looking toward* Steve *and* Les *again.*) One of 'em'll tip their hand.[7] They got to.

Steve (*raising his voice*). There's something you can do, Charlie. You can go home and keep your mouth shut. You can quit strutting around like a self-appointed judge and climb into bed and forget it.

Charlie. You sound real anxious to have that happen, Steve. I think we better keep our eye on you, too!

---

7. **tip their hand:** reveal themselves.

Don (*as if he were taking the bit in his teeth,*[8] *takes a hesitant step to the front*). I think everything might
430 as well come out now. (*He turns toward* Steve.) Your wife's done plenty of talking, Steve, about how odd you are!

Charlie (*picking this up, his eyes widening*). Go ahead, tell us what she's said.

(Steve *walks toward them from across the street.*)

> **Steve.** Go ahead, what's my wife said? Let's get it all out. Let's pick out every <u>idiosyncrasy</u> of every single man, woman, and child on the street. And then we might as well set up some kind of citizens'
> 440 court. How about a firing squad at dawn, Charlie, so we can get rid of all the suspects. Narrow them down. Make it easier for you.

Don. There's no need gettin' so upset, Steve. It's just that . . . well . . . Myra's talked about how there's been plenty of nights you spent hours down in your basement workin' on some kind of radio or something. Well, none of us have ever seen that radio—

(*By this time* Steve *has reached the group. He stands*
450 *there defiantly.*)

Charlie. Go ahead, Steve. What kind of "radio set" you workin' on? I never seen it. Neither has anyone else. Who do you talk to on that radio set? And who talks to you?

Steve. I'm surprised at you, Charlie. How come you're so dense all of a sudden? (*He pauses.*) Who do I talk to? I talk to monsters from outer space.

English Learner Support
Vocabulary

Idiom In the sentence in blue, the phrase *come out* means "be discussed." Don means to say, "I think we should talk about everything, including everyone's odd behavior."

READ ALOUD the boxed passage. Make sure the tone of your voice shows Steve's real feelings about what he is suggesting.

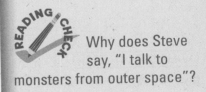 **READING CHECK** Why does Steve say, "I talk to monsters from outer space"?

---

8. **taking the bit in his teeth:** taking the initiative to do or say something.

WORDS TO KNOW
   idiosyncrasy (ĭd'ē-ō-sĭng'krə-sē) *n.* a personal way of acting; odd mannerism

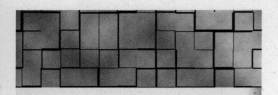

I talk to three-headed green men who fly over here in what look like meteors.

460 (*Myra Brand steps down from the porch, bites her lip, calls out.*)

Myra. Steve! Steve, please. (*Then looking around, frightened, she walks toward the group.*) It's just a ham radio set, that's all. I bought him a book on it myself. It's just a ham radio set. A lot of people have them. I can show it to you. It's right down in the basement.

Steve (*whirls around toward her*). Show them nothing! If they want to look inside our house—let 470 them go and get a search warrant.

Charlie. Look, buddy, you can't afford to—

Steve (*interrupting him*). Charlie, don't start telling me who's dangerous and who isn't and who's safe and who's a menace. (*He turns to the group and shouts.*) And you're with him, too—all of you! You're standing here all set to crucify—all set to find a scapegoat[9]—all desperate to point some kind of a finger at a neighbor! Well now, look, friends, the only thing that's gonna happen is that we'll eat 480 each other up alive—

(*He stops abruptly as Charlie suddenly grabs his arm.*)

Charlie (*in a hushed voice*). That's not the only thing that can happen to us.

(*Down the street, a figure has suddenly materialized in the gloom. In the silence we hear the clickety-clack of slow, measured footsteps on concrete as the figure walks slowly toward them. One of the women lets out a stifled cry. Sally grabs her boy, as do a couple of other mothers.*)

---

9. **scapegoat:** a person who is made to bear the blame of others.

HAM RADIO A ham radio is a two-way radio that allows people to talk to each other across long distances. Many people build and use ham radios as a hobby.

READ ALOUD the boxed passage. Do you think that people tend to look for someone to blame when things go wrong? Give an example. (**Connect**)

❑ yes ❑ no

WHAT DOES IT MEAN? *Crucify* means "torture or torment."

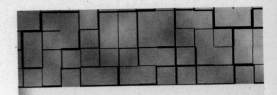

490 **Tommy** (*shouting, frightened*). It's the monster! It's the monster!

(*Another woman lets out a wail, and the people fall back in a group staring toward the darkness and the approaching figure. The people stand in the shadows watching. Don Martin joins them, carrying a shotgun. He holds it up.*)

Don. We may need this.

Steve. A shotgun? (*He pulls it out of Don's hand.*) No! Will anybody think a thought around here!
500 Will you people wise up. What good would a shotgun do against—

(*The dark figure continues to walk toward them as the people stand there, fearful, mothers clutching children, men standing in front of their wives.*)

Charlie (*pulling the gun from Steve's hands*). No more talk, Steve. You're going to talk us into a grave! You'd let whatever's out there walk right over us, wouldn't yuh? Well, some of us won't!

(*Charlie swings around, raises the gun, and suddenly
510 pulls the trigger. The sound of the shot explodes in the stillness. The figure suddenly lets out a small cry, stumbles forward onto his knees, and then falls forward on his face. Don, Charlie, and Steve race forward to him. Steve is there first and turns the man over. The crowd gathers around them.*)

Steve (*slowly looks up*). It's Pete Van Horn.

Don (*in a hushed voice*). Pete Van Horn! He was just gonna go over to the next block to see if the power was on—
520 **Woman.** You killed him, Charlie. You shot him dead!

WHAT DOES IT MEAN? *You're going to talk us into a grave* means "Because you talk instead of act, we will all be killed."

 REREAD the boxed passage. What important event is described in these stage directions? **(Clarify)**

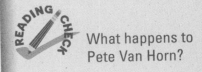 **READING CHECK** What happens to Pete Van Horn?

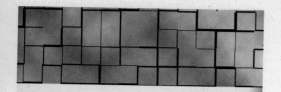

Pause & Reflect

How would you **evaluate** the way the people on Maple Street treat one another? Write the answer below. Then circle evidence in the play that helped you reach your answer.

Charlie (*looks around at the circle of faces, his eyes frightened, his face* <u>contorted</u>). But . . . but I didn't know who he was. I certainly didn't know who he was. He comes walkin' out of the darkness—how am I supposed to know who he was? (*He grabs* Steve.) Steve—you know why I shot! How was I supposed to know he wasn't a monster or something? (*He grabs* Don.) We're all scared of the same thing. I was just tryin' to . . . tryin' to protect my home, that's all! Look, all of you, that's all I was tryin' to do. (*He looks down wildly at the body.*) I didn't know it was somebody we knew! I didn't know—

530

(*There's a sudden hush and then an intake of breath in the group. Across the street all the lights go on in one of the houses.*)

Pause & Reflect

As the play continues . . .

- The neighbors accuse one another of being the monster.
- The mob begins to attack those who are accused.

FOCUS

Read to find out what happens when Charlie tries to justify his actions.

Woman (*in a hushed voice*). Charlie . . . Charlie . . . the lights just went on in your house. Why did the lights just go on?

540

Don. What about it, Charlie? How come you're the only one with lights now?

Les. That's what I'd like to know.

(*Pausing, they all stare toward* Charlie.)

Les. You were so quick to kill, Charlie, and you were so quick to tell us who we had to be careful of. Well, maybe you had to kill. Maybe Pete there was

WORDS TO KNOW
contorted (kən-tôr′tĭd) *adj.* twisted or pulled out of shape **contort** *v.*

550 trying to tell us something. Maybe he'd found out something and came back to tell us who there was amongst us we should watch out for—

(Charlie *backs away from the group, his eyes wide with fright.*)

Charlie. No . . . no . . . it's nothing of the sort! I don't know why the lights are on. I swear I don't. Somebody's pulling a gag or something.

(*He bumps against* Steve, *who grabs him and whirls him around.*)

Steve. A gag? A gag? Charlie, there's a dead man on
560 the sidewalk, and you killed him! Does this thing look like a gag to you?

(Charlie *breaks away and screams as he runs toward his house.*)

Charlie. No! No! Please!

(*A man breaks away from the crowd to chase* Charlie. *As the man tackles him and lands on top of him, the other people start to run toward them.* Charlie *gets up, breaks away from the other man's grasp, and lands a couple of desperate punches that push the*
570 *man aside. Then he forces his way, fighting, through the crowd and jumps up on his front porch.* Charlie *is on his porch as a rock thrown from the group smashes a window beside him, the broken glass flying past him. A couple of pieces cut him. He stands there perspiring, rumpled, blood running down from a cut on the cheek. His wife breaks away from the group to throw herself into his arms. He buries his face against her. We can see the crowd converging on the porch.*)

Voice One. It must have been him.

580 **Voice Two.** He's the one.

Voice Three. We got to get Charlie.

REREAD the boxed passage. Then write the words *accuser* and *accused* in the right slots in the following sentence: (Draw Conclusions)

Les Goodman

has become the

_____, and

Charlie has become

the _____.

English Learner Support

Vocabulary

Idiom A *gag* is a joke. *Pulling a gag* means "playing a joke on someone."

READING TIP As you read the stage directions, remember that this script was written for a television audience. **Visualize** the action as if it were appearing on a television screen.

(*Another rock lands on the porch.* Charlie *pushes his wife behind him, facing the group.*)

Charlie. Look, look I swear to you. . . . it isn't me . . . but I do know who it is . . . I swear to you, I do know who it is. I know who the monster is here. I know who it is that doesn't belong. I swear to you I know.

Don (*pushing his way to the front of the crowd*). All
590   right, Charlie, let's hear it!

(Charlie's *eyes dart around wildly.*)

Charlie. It's . . . it's . . .

Man Two (*screaming*). Go ahead, Charlie.

Charlie. It's . . . it's the kid. It's Tommy. He's the one!

(*There's a gasp from the crowd as we see* Sally *holding the boy.* Tommy *at first doesn't understand and then, realizing the eyes are all on him, buries his face against his mother.*)

Sally (*backs away*). That's crazy! He's only a boy.

600   **Woman.** But he knew! He was the only one! He told us all about it. Well, how did he know? How could he have known?

(*Various people take this up and repeat the question.*)

Voice One. How could he know?

Voice Two. Who told him?

Voice Three. Make the kid answer.

(*The crowd starts to* converge *around the mother, who grabs* Tommy *and starts to run with him. The crowd starts to follow, at first walking fast, and then*
610   *running after him. Suddenly* Charlie's *lights go off and the lights in other houses go on, then off.*)

Man One (*shouting*). It isn't the kid . . . it's Bob Weaver's house.

READING CHECK

What **motive**, or reason, might Charlie have for saying that Tommy is the monster?

WHAT DOES IT MEAN?
Converge means "come together."

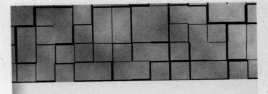

Woman. It isn't Bob Weaver's house, it's Don Martin's place.

Charlie. I tell you it's the kid.

Don. It's Charlie. He's the one.

(People shout, accuse, and scream as the lights go on and off. Then, slowly, in the middle of this
620 *nightmarish confusion of sight and sound, the camera starts to pull away until, once again, we have reached the opening shot looking at the Maple Street sign from high above.)*

Pause & Reflect

FOCUS

What is really happening on Maple Street? Read on to find the answer.

Scene Two

(The camera continues to move away while gradually bringing into focus a field. We see the metal side of a spacecraft that sits shrouded in darkness. An open door throws out a beam of light from the illuminated
630 *interior. Two figures appear, silhouetted against the bright lights. We get only a vague feeling of form.)*

Figure One. Understand the procedure now? Just stop a few of their machines and radios and telephones and lawn mowers. . . . Throw them into darkness for a few hours, and then just sit back and watch the pattern.

Figure Two. And this pattern is always the same?

Pause & Reflect

How have the people on Maple Street changed in this play? **(Compare and Contrast)**

As the play ends . . .

• You learn who the monsters on Maple Street are.

English Learner Support

Language

Stage Directions *We get only a vague feeling of form* means that television viewers don't see clearly what the two figures look like; they are just dim shapes.

Figure One. With few variations. They pick the most dangerous enemy they can find . . . and it's
640 themselves. And all we need do is sit back . . . and watch.

Figure Two. Then I take it this place . . . this Maple Street . . . is not unique.

Figure One (*shaking his head*). By no means. Their world is full of Maple Streets. And we'll go from one to the other and let them destroy themselves. One to the other . . . one to the other . . . one to the other—

Scene Three

(*The camera slowly moves up for a shot of the starry
650 sky, and over this we hear the* Narrator's *voice.*)

Narrator. The tools of conquest do not necessarily come with bombs and explosions and fallout.[10] There are weapons that are simply thoughts, attitudes, prejudices—to be found only in the minds of men. For the record, prejudices can kill and suspicion can destroy. A thoughtless, frightened search for a scapegoat has a fallout all its own for the children . . . and the children yet unborn, (*a pause*) and the pity of it is . . . that these things
660 cannot be confined to . . . The Twilight Zone!

(*Fade to black.*) ❖

Pause & Reflect

WHAT DOES IT MEAN? *Unique* means "the only one of its kind."

Pause & Reflect

1. **MARK IT UP** Who is the most dangerous enemy of the people on Maple Street? Circle the answer at the top of this page. **(Clarify)**

2. **REREAD** the boxed sentence. **Paraphrase,** or restate it in your own words.

CHALLENGE What does the narrator contribute to this play? Mark passages in the play to support your views. **(Analyze)**

---

10. **fallout:** radioactive particles that fall to Earth after a nuclear explosion.

Active Reading SkillBuilder

Author's Purpose

The reason for creating a particular work is the **author's purpose.** An author may write to **entertain,** to **explain** or **inform,** to **express an opinion,** or to **persuade** readers to do or believe something. To determine the purpose of a work, look at the details. Think about why the author might have included each detail. As you read *The Monsters Are Due on Maple Street,* use the chart below to record details about plot, setting, and characters. Note how the details relate to Rod Serling's purpose for writing the drama.

Details	Purpose
The Narrator opens the play, describes the setting, and sets up suspense.	to explain to entertain

Literary Analysis SkillBuilder

Teleplay

A **teleplay** is a play written for television. In a teleplay the stage directions include directions for the camera. Camera directions specify the focus of a shot and tell when the camera should fade in or out of a scene. Paying attention to the camera directions can help you visualize what the drama might look like on television. Camera directions can also tell you what details the author wants to focus on. As you read *The Monsters Are Due on Maple Street,* use the chart to jot down notes about the camera directions and what they help you to visualize.

Camera Directions	Visual Impression
Fade in on shot of night sky.	*puts focus on "outer space"*

Follow Up: With a partner, discuss how the camera directions help you to picture the action. Why does the camera show a shot of the starry sky at the end of the play?

Words to Know SkillBuilder

Words to Know

antagonism	defiant	idiosyncrasy	intense	optimistic
contorted	flustered	incriminate	legitimate	persistent

A. Read the following statements. Indicate whether each is true or false.   **True** **False**

1. Someone who is so upset by a question that he or she cannot answer it is **flustered** by it.   ❏   ❏

2. An **intense** voice is one that is soothing and carefree.   ❏   ❏

3. When you have a suspicion that just won't go away, it is a **persistent** one.   ❏   ❏

4. If you are **optimistic** about your future, you are confident that things will work out well.   ❏   ❏

5. A **defiant** response to an order means that you are willing to carry the order out.   ❏   ❏

6. Good friends are likely to express a lot of **antagonism** toward each other.   ❏   ❏

7. A person's fingerprints found at the scene of a crime might **incriminate** him or her.   ❏   ❏

8. A **legitimate** answer to a question is one that is reasonable.   ❏   ❏

9. A person who has a behavior that is out of the ordinary might be said to have an **idiosyncrasy.**   ❏   ❏

10. A face that reveals calm self-assurance is likely to be a **contorted** face.   ❏   ❏

B. Imagine that you are the director for *The Monsters Are Due on Maple Street*.
What will you be looking for in choosing actors? Use at least **four** of the Words to Know.

Before You Read

Connect to Your Life

An important survival skill is the ability to adapt. To adapt means to change in ways that are appropriate to your surroundings. Can you think of a time when you had to adapt? Use the concept web below to tell how you changed, or adapted.

I learned _____

_____

_____

I noticed _____

_____

I had to adapt
when _____
_____

I changed _____

_____

_____

I watched _____

_____

Key to the Story

WHAT'S THE BIG IDEA? Write three words that the theme of *colonization* suggests to you. Then use each word in a sentence.

1. [ ] _____

2. [ ] _____

3. [ ] _____

DARK THEY WERE,
AND GOLDEN-EYED

BY RAY BRADBURY

PREVIEW You are about to read a short story about Mars. Landing on this planet, a family from Earth looks out on a strange, new world. Will this family be able to survive in these surroundings?

As the story begins . . .

- A family arrives on Mars from Earth.
- The man wants to return to Earth.
- Instead, the family walks into town.

English Learner Support
Language

Word Forms *Martian* is the adjective form of *Mars*. The *Martian meadow* means "the meadow of Mars."

Proper Noun	→	Proper Adjective
Mars	→	Martian

English Learner Support
Language

Metaphor When the author calls the children "small seeds," he is using a metaphor—a comparison that says one thing is something else. The children are like seeds because they have traveled far from home and will grow up in a new place.

MARK IT UP KEEP TRACK
Remember to use these marks to keep track of your reading.

- ***** This is important.
- **?** I have a question about this.
- **!** This is a surprise.

FOCUS

A man, his wife, and their children have just landed on Mars. Read to find out how the man feels about the new environment.

MARK IT UP As you read, circle details that tell you about his feelings. An example is highlighted.

The rocket metal cooled in the meadow winds. Its lid gave a bulging *pop*. From its clock interior stepped a man, a woman, and three children. The other passengers whispered away across the Martian meadow, leaving the man alone among his family.

10 The man felt his hair flutter and the tissues of his body draw tight as if he were standing at the center of a vacuum. His wife, before him, seemed almost to whirl away in smoke. The children, small seeds, might at any instant be sown to all the Martian climes.[1]

The children looked up at him, as people look to the sun to tell what time of their life it is. His face was cold.

"What's wrong?" asked his wife.

"Let's get back on the rocket."

20 "Go back to Earth?"

"Yes! Listen!"

The wind blew as if to flake away their identities. At any moment the Martian air might draw his soul from him, as marrow comes from a white bone. He felt submerged in a chemical that could dissolve his intellect and burn away his past.

They looked at Martian hills that time had worn with a crushing pressure of years. They saw the old cities, lost in their meadows, lying like children's

30 delicate bones among the blowing lakes of grass.

"Chin up,[2] Harry," said his wife. "It's too late. We've come over sixty million miles."

The children with their yellow hair hollered at the deep dome of Martian sky. There was no answer but

---

1. **climes:** regions.

2. **chin up:** slang meaning "Don't be discouraged."

the racing hiss of wind through the stiff grass.

He picked up the luggage in his cold hands. "Here we go," he said—a man standing on the edge of a sea, ready to wade in and be drowned.

They walked into town.

Pause & Reflect

FOCUS

A nagging fear troubles Harry and his wife. Read to find out more about this fear.

40   Their name was Bittering. Harry and his wife Cora; Dan, Laura, and David. They built a small white cottage and ate good breakfasts there, but the fear was never gone. It lay with Mr. Bittering and Mrs. Bittering, a third unbidden partner at every midnight talk, at every dawn awakening.

"I feel like a salt crystal," he said, "in a mountain stream, being washed away. We don't belong here. We're
50 Earth people. This is Mars. It was meant for Martians. For heaven's sake, Cora, let's buy tickets for home!"

But she only shook her head. "One day the (atom bomb) will fix Earth. Then we'll be safe here."

"Safe and insane!"

Tick-tock, seven o'clock sang the voice-clock; *time to get up.* And they did.

Something made him check everything each morning—warm hearth, potted blood-geraniums—precisely as if he expected something to be <u>amiss</u>. The
60 morning paper was toast-warm from the 6 A.M. Earth rocket. He broke its seal and tilted it at his breakfast place. He forced himself to be convivial.[3]

---

3. **convivial** (kən-vĭv′ē-əl): merry, festive.

WORDS TO KNOW
amiss (ə-mĭs′) *adj.* out of proper order; wrong

Pause & Reflect

How does Harry feel about Mars? Circle three words below. (Clarify)

threatened   amused

frightened   comforted

calm   worried

As the story continues . . .

- Harry Bittering keeps feeling that they don't belong on Mars.
- His son David wonders about the Martians and their cities.
- Harry warns him to stay away from the cities.

MORE ABOUT . . .

(ATOM BOMB) This story was written in 1949. Only a few years earlier, atomic bombs were first used in warfare. After the world had seen the awful power of such bombs, people feared they could destroy Earth if they were used again.

Pause & Reflect

What do you think Harry and his wife are afraid of? (Infer)

"Colonial days⁴ all over again," he declared. "Why, in ten years there'll be a million Earthmen on Mars. Big cities, everything! They said we'd fail. Said the Martians would resent our invasion. But did we find any Martians? Not a living soul! Oh, we found their empty cities, but no one in them. Right?"

70 A river of wind submerged the house. When the windows ceased rattling Mr. Bittering swallowed and looked at the children.

"I don't know," said David. "Maybe there're Martians around we don't see. Sometimes nights I think I hear 'em. I hear the wind. The sand hits my window. I get scared. And I see those towns way up in the mountains where the Martians lived a long time ago. And I think I see things moving around those towns, Papa. And I wonder if those Martians *mind* us living here. I wonder if they won't do something to us for coming here."

80 "Nonsense!" Mr. Bittering looked out the windows. "We're clean, decent people." He looked at his children. "All dead cities have some kind of ghosts in them. Memories, I mean." He stared at the hills. "You see a staircase and you wonder what Martians looked like climbing it. You see Martian paintings and you wonder what the painter was like. You make a little ghost in your mind, a memory. It's quite natural. Imagination." He stopped. "You haven't been prowling up in those ruins, have you?"

90 "No, Papa." David looked at his shoes.

"See that you stay away from them. Pass the jam."

"Just the same," said little David, "I bet something happens."

Pause & Reflect

---

4. **colonial days:** the period when Europeans began to settle in North America.

FOCUS
Read to find out about
the news Laura brings
and Harry's reaction to it.

MARK IT UP > Underline
the news.

Laura stumbled through the
settlement, crying. She dashed
blindly onto the porch.

"Mother, Father—the war,

100 Earth!" she sobbed. "A radio flash just came. Atom
bombs hit New York! All the space rockets blown up.
No more rockets to Mars, ever!"

"Oh, Harry!" The mother held onto her husband
and daughter.

"Are you sure, Laura?" asked the father quietly.

Laura wept. "We're stranded on Mars, forever and
ever!"

For a long time there was only the sound of the
wind in the late afternoon.

110   Alone, thought Bittering. Only a thousand of us
here. No way back. No way. No way. Sweat poured
from his face and his hands and his body; he was
drenched in the hotness of his fear. He wanted to
strike Laura, cry, "No, you're lying! The rockets will
come back!" Instead, he stroked Laura's head against
him and said, "The rockets will get through someday."

"Father, what will we do?"

"Go about our business, of course. Raise crops and
children. Wait. Keep things going until the war ends

120 and the rockets come again."

The two boys stepped out onto the porch.

"Children," he said, sitting there, looking beyond
them, "I've something to tell you."

"We know," they said.

Pause & Reflect

As the story continues . . .

• There has been a war on
Earth.

• Harry says the family will
have to wait until the war
ends before they can return
to Earth.

English Learner Support
Vocabulary

Idiom *Blown up* means
"exploded."

Pause & Reflect

1. How does the war on Earth
affect the Earth people on
Mars? (Cause and Effect)

_____

_____

_____

_____

2. REREAD the boxed
passage.
Although Harry
is afraid, how does he act?
Circle the word below.
(Infer)

sad   angry

scared   brave

- Harry wonders what will happen to his family.
- He thinks about the names Earth people have given to the places on Mars.
- He becomes upset when he notices something odd in his garden.

MARK IT UP > Underline a sentence in the last two paragraphs that tells how the settlers from Earth felt about renaming things on Mars. (Clarify)

FOCUS

The Earth people are stranded on Mars. Read to find out what Harry thinks about and discovers as he works in his garden.

In the following days, Bittering wandered often through the garden to stand alone in his fear. As long as the rockets had spun a silver web
130 across space, he had been able to accept Mars. For he had always told himself: Tomorrow, if I want, I can buy a ticket and go back to Earth.

But now: The web gone, the rockets lying in jigsaw heaps of molten girder[5] and unsnaked wire. Earth people left to the strangeness of Mars, the cinnamon dusts and wine airs, to be baked like gingerbread shapes in Martian summers, put into harvested storage by Martian winters. What would happen to him, the
140 others? This was the moment Mars had waited for. Now it would eat them.

He got down on his knees in the flower bed, a spade in his nervous hands. Work, he thought, work and forget.

He glanced up from the garden to the Martian mountains. He thought of the proud old Martian names that had once been on those peaks. Earthmen, dropping from the sky, had gazed upon hills, rivers, Martian seas left nameless in spite of names. Once Martians had built cities, named cities; climbed
150 mountains, named mountains; sailed seas, named seas. Mountains melted, seas drained, cities tumbled. In spite of this, the Earthmen had felt a silent guilt at putting new names to these ancient hills and valleys.

Nevertheless, man lives by symbol and label. The names were given.

---

5. **molten girder:** a metal structural support that has melted under extreme heat.

Mr. Bittering felt very alone in his garden under the Martian sun, anachronism[6] bent here, planting Earth flowers in a wild soil.

Think. Keep thinking. Different things. Keep your
160 mind free of Earth, the atom war, the lost rockets.

He perspired. He glanced about. No one watching. He removed his tie. Pretty bold, he thought. First your coat off, now your tie. He hung it neatly on a peach tree he had imported as a sapling from Massachusetts.

He returned to his philosophy of names and mountains. The Earthmen had changed names. Now there were Hormel Valleys, Roosevelt Seas, Ford Hills, Vanderbilt Plateaus, Rockefeller[7] Rivers, on Mars. It wasn't right. The American settlers had shown
170 wisdom, using old Indian prairie names: Wisconsin, Minnesota, Idaho, Ohio, Utah, Milwaukee, Waukegan, Osseo. The old names, the old meanings.

Staring at the mountains wildly, he thought: Are you up there? All the dead ones, you (Martians?) Well, here we are, alone, cut off! Come down, move us out! We're helpless!

The wind blew a shower of peach blossoms.

He put out his sun-browned hand and gave a small cry. He touched the blossoms and picked them up. He
180 turned them, he touched them again and again. Then he shouted for his wife.

"Cora!"

She appeared at a window. He ran to her.

"Cora, these blossoms!"

She handled them.

"Do you see? They're different. They've changed! They're not peach blossoms any more!"

"Look all right to me," she said.

---

6. **anachronism** (ə-năk′rə-nĭz′əm): something out of its normal time period or sequence.

7. **Hormel, Roosevelt, Ford, Vanderbilt, Rockefeller:** names of wealthy Americans.

Why does Harry start pulling up vegetables from his garden? Circle the best answer. (Draw Conclusions)

They need to be thinned.

He is hungry.

He is afraid the vegetables have changed.

As the story continues . . .

• Harry is frightened when he looks at what is growing in his garden.

• He fears the fruits and vegetables will cause him and his family to change.

"They're not. They're wrong! I can't tell how. An
190 extra petal, a leaf, something, the color, the smell!"

The children ran out in time to see their father hurrying about the garden, pulling up radishes, onions, and carrots from their beds.

Pause & Reflect

FOCUS

Read to find out about the things from Earth that have changed on Mars.

MARK IT UP Circle the things that have changed in the Martian climate.

"Cora, come look!"

They handled the onions, the radishes, the carrots among them.

"Do they look like carrots?"

200 "Yes . . . no." She hesitated. "I don't know."

"They're changed."

"Perhaps."

"You know they have! Onions but not onions, carrots but not carrots. Taste: the same but different. Smell: not like it used to be." He felt his heart pounding, and he was afraid. He dug his fingers into the earth. "Cora, what's happening? What is it? We've got to get away from this." He ran across the garden.
210 Each tree felt his touch. "The roses. The roses. They're turning green!"

And they stood looking at the green roses.

And two days later Dan came running. "Come see the cow. I was milking her and I saw it. Come on!"

They stood in the shed and looked at their one cow.

It was growing a third horn.

And the lawn in front of their house very quietly and slowly was coloring itself like spring violets. Seed from Earth but growing up a soft purple.

220 "We must get away," said Bittering. "We'll eat this stuff and then we'll change—who knows to what? I can't let it happen. There's only one thing to do. Burn this food!"

"It's not poisoned."

"But it is. Subtly, very subtly. A little bit. A very little bit. We mustn't touch it."

He looked with dismay at their house. "Even the house. The wind's done something to it. The air's burned it. The fog at night. The boards, all warped

230 out of shape. It's not an Earthman's house any more."

"Oh, your imagination!"

He put on his coat and tie. "I'm going into town. We've got to do something now. I'll be back."

"Wait, Harry!" his wife cried.

But he was gone.

Pause & Reflect

Pause & Reflect

What is happening to the plants and animals brought from Earth? (Summarize)

As the story continues . . .

- Harry is scared that the planet will change them all.
- He makes a plan to build a rocket and leave.
- Harry notices that people's eyes are changing color.

FOCUS

Harry goes to town to talk to the other people from Earth. Read to find out what happens and what Harry decides to do.

In town, on the shadowy step of the grocery store, the men sat with their hands on their knees, conversing with

240 great leisure and ease.

Mr. Bittering wanted to fire a pistol in the air.

What are you doing, you fools! he thought. Sitting here! You've heard the news—we're stranded on this planet. Well, move! Aren't you frightened? Aren't you afraid? What are you going to do?

"Hello, Harry," said everyone.

"Look," he said to them. "You did hear the news, the other day, didn't you?"

250 They nodded and laughed. "Sure. Sure, Harry."

English Learner Support

Culture

Pistols A gun that is fired with one hand is called a pistol. Guns are sometimes used to get people's attention. For example, a pistol is often used to signal the start of a race.

READING TIP Read the dialogue on this page carefully. It contains a lot of information about the characters and about the plot.

WHAT DOES IT MEAN? When Sam says the words in blue, he is teasing Harry. He is suggesting that no one will help Harry and that without help, the job will take many years.

READ ALOUD the boxed passage on this page. Why is Harry so amazed? (Clarify)

"What are you going to do about it?"

"Do, Harry, do? What *can* we do?"

"Build a rocket, that's what!"

"A rocket, Harry? To go back to all that trouble? Oh, Harry!"

"But you *must* want to go back. Have you noticed the peach blossoms, the onions, the grass?"

"Why, yes, Harry, seems we did," said one of the men.

"Doesn't it scare you?"

260 "Can't recall that it did much, Harry."

"Idiots!"

"Now, Harry."

Bittering wanted to cry. "You've got to work with me. If we stay here, we'll all change. The air. Don't you smell it? Something in the air. A Martian virus, maybe; some seed, or a pollen. Listen to me!"

They stared at him.

"Sam," he said to one of them.

"Yes, Harry?"

270 "Will you help me build a rocket?"

"Harry, I got a whole load of metal and some blueprints. You want to work in my metal shop on a rocket, you're welcome. I'll sell you that metal for five hundred dollars. You should be able to construct a right pretty rocket, if you work alone, in about thirty years."

Everyone laughed.

"Don't laugh."

Sam looked at him with quiet good humor.

"Sam," Bittering said. "Your eyes—"

280 "What about them, Harry?"

"Didn't they used to be gray?"

"Well now, I don't remember."

"They were, weren't they?"

"Why do you ask, Harry?"

"Because now they're kind of yellow-colored."

"Is that so, Harry?" Sam said, casually.

"And you're taller and thinner—"

"You might be right, Harry."

"Sam, you shouldn't have yellow eyes."

290 "Harry, what color eyes have *you* got?" Sam said.

"My eyes? They're blue, of course."

"Here you are, Harry." Sam handed him a pocket mirror. "Take a look at yourself."

Mr. Bittering hesitated, and then raised the mirror to his face.

There were little, very dim flecks of new gold captured in the blue of his eyes.

"Now look what you've done," said Sam a moment later. "You've broken my mirror."

300 Harry Bittering moved into the metal shop and began to build the rocket. Men stood in the open door and talked and joked without raising their voices. Once in a while they gave him a hand on lifting something. But mostly they just idled and watched him with their yellowing eyes.

"It's suppertime, Harry," they said.

His wife appeared with his supper in a wicker basket.

"I won't touch it," he said. "I'll eat only food from our Deepfreeze. Food that came from Earth. Nothing
310 from our garden."

His wife stood watching him. "You can't build a rocket."

"I worked in a shop once, when I was twenty. I know metal. Once I get it started, the others will help," he said, not looking at her, laying out the blueprints.

"Harry, Harry," she said, helplessly.

"We've *got* to get away, Cora. We've got to!"

Pause & Reflect

English Learner Support

Vocabulary

Deepfreeze A *Deepfreeze* is freezer that holds a large amount of food.

Pause & Reflect

1. How does Harry Bittering's attitude differ from that of the other Earth people? (**Compare and Contrast**)

Bittering: We must

Others: We would

rather

2. Why does Harry drop the mirror? (**Cause and Effect**)

As the story continues . . .

- Harry still feels frightened and works on his rocket.
- One day he says a strange word.
- Harry's friends say that he's thinner, and he's used up all the Earth food.

English Learner Support

Language

Story Title In this paragraph, you will read part of a sentence that sounds very much like the title of this story. Story titles often give you clues about what is important in a story.

READ ALOUD the boxed passage. Why does Harry suddenly speak a Martian word? **(Infer)**

FOCUS

Harry Bittering and his wife are changing. Read to find out how.

▮▮▮ **MARK IT UP** ⟫ As you read, circle details that help you understand these changes.

320 The nights were full of wind that blew down the empty moonlit sea meadows past the little white chess cities lying for their twelve-thousandth year in the shallows. In the Earthmen's settlement, the Bittering house shook with a feeling of change.

Lying abed, Mr. Bittering felt his bones shifted, shaped, melted like gold. His wife, lying beside him, was dark 330 from many sunny afternoons. Dark she was, and golden-eyed, burnt almost black by the sun, sleeping, and the children metallic in their beds, and the wind roaring <u>forlorn</u> and changing through the old peach trees, the violet grass, shaking out green rose petals.

The fear would not be stopped. It had his throat and heart. It dripped in a wetness of the arm and the temple and the trembling palm.

A green star rose in the east.

A strange word emerged from Mr. Bittering's lips.
340 "*Iorrt. Iorrt.*" He repeated it.

It was a Martian word. He knew no Martian.

In the middle of the night he arose and dialed a call through to Simpson, the archaeologist.

"Simpson, what does the word *Iorrt* mean?"

"Why that's the old Martian word for our planet Earth. Why?"

"No special reason."

The telephone slipped from his hand.

"Hello, hello, hello, hello," it kept saying while he 350 sat gazing out at the green star. "Bittering? Harry, are you there?"

The days were full of metal sound. He laid the frame of the rocket with the reluctant help of three

WORDS TO KNOW
forlorn (fôr-lôrn´) *adj.* appearing lonely and sad

indifferent men. He grew very tired in an hour or so and had to sit down.

"The altitude," laughed a man.

"Are you *eating*, Harry?" asked another.

"I'm eating," he said, angrily.

"From your Deepfreeze?"

360   "Yes!"

"You're getting thinner, Harry."

"I'm not!"

"And taller."

"Liar!"

His wife took him aside a few days later. "Harry, I've used up all the food in the Deepfreeze. There's nothing left. I'll have to make sandwiches using food grown on Mars."

He sat down heavily.

370   "You must eat," she said. "You're weak."

"Yes," he said.

He took a sandwich, opened it, looked at it, and began to nibble at it.

"And take the rest of the day off," she said. "It's hot. The children want to swim in the canals[8] and hike. Please come along."

"I can't waste time. This is a crisis!"

"Just for an hour," she urged. "A swim'll do you good."

380   He rose, sweating. "All right, all right. Leave me alone. I'll come."

"Good for you, Harry."

Pause & Reflect

8. **canal:** Mars was once believed to be crisscrossed by canals. This image occurs frequently in science fiction set on Mars.

English Learner Support
Language

Direct Address Often, when you see the name of a character with a comma before or after it, the speaker is talking directly to that person. This speaker is talking to Harry when he says, "Are you *eating*, Harry?" The pronoun *he* in the reply refers to Harry.

Pause & Reflect

1. How would you describe the way Harry's wife and children look now? (Visualize)

2. Why do you think Harry's wife tries to get him away from building the rocket? (Infer)

As the story continues . . .

• Harry and his family spend a pleasant day swimming.

• Dan uses a Martian word.

• The Bitterings visit a deserted Martian home and notice how pleasant it is.

 READ ALOUD the boxed dialogue. How would you explain why the children's eyes have changed color? (Cause and Effect)

FOCUS

Harry and his family go for a swim. Read to find out about his son Dan's surprising request.

The sun was hot, the day quiet. There was only an immense staring burn upon the land. They moved along the canal, the father, the mother, the racing children in their swimsuits. They stopped and ate meat
390 sandwiches. He saw their skin baking brown. And he saw the yellow eyes of his wife and his children, their eyes that were never yellow before. A few tremblings shook him, but were carried off in waves of pleasant heat as he lay in the sun. He was too tired to be afraid.

"Cora, how long have your eyes been yellow?"
She was bewildered. "Always, I guess."
"They didn't change from brown in the last three months?"
She bit her lips. "No. Why do you ask?"
400 "Never mind."
They sat there.
"The children's eyes," he said. "They're yellow, too."
"Sometimes growing children's eyes change color."
"Maybe *we're* children, too. At least to Mars. That's a thought." He laughed. "Think I'll swim."

They leaped into the canal water, and he let himself sink down and down to the bottom like a golden statue and lie there in green silence. All was water-
410 quiet and deep, all was peace. He felt the steady, slow current drift him easily.

If I lie here long enough, he thought, the water will work and eat away my flesh until the bones show like coral. Just my skeleton left. And then the water can build on that skeleton—green things, deep water things, red things, yellow things. Change. Change. Slow, deep, silent change. And isn't that what it is up *there?*

He saw the sky submerged above him, the sun made
420 Martian by atmosphere and time and space.

Up there, a big river, he thought, a Martian river; all
of us lying deep in it, in our pebble houses, in our
sunken boulder houses, like crayfish hidden, and the
water washing away our old bodies and lengthening
the bones and—

He let himself drift up through the soft light.

Dan sat on the edge of the canal, regarding his
father seriously.

"*Utha*," he said.

430 "What?" asked his father.

The boy smiled. "You know. *Utha's* the Martian
word for 'father.'"

"Where did you learn it?"

"I don't know. Around. *Utha!*"

"What do you want?"

The boy hesitated. "I—I want to change my name."

"Change it?"

"Yes."

His mother swam over. "What's wrong with Dan for
440 a name?"

Dan fidgeted. "The other day you called Dan, Dan,
Dan. I didn't even hear. I said to myself, That's not my
name. I've a new name I want to use."

Mr. Bittering held to the side of the canal, his body
cold and his heart pounding slowly. "What is this new
name?"

"Linnl. Isn't that a good name? Can I use it? Can't
I, please?"

Mr. Bittering put his hand to his head. He thought
450 of the silly rocket, himself working alone, himself
alone even among his family, so alone.

He heard his wife say, "Why not?"

He heard himself say, "Yes, you can use it."

"Yaaa!" screamed the boy. "I'm Linnl, Linnl!"

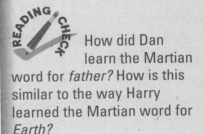

READING CHECK How did Dan
learn the Martian
word for *father?* How is this
similar to the way Harry
learned the Martian word for
Earth?

WHAT DOES IT MEAN?
Fidgeted means "moved
nervously."

 REREAD the boxed
passage. Why
does Harry feel
so alone? **(Infer)**

Racing down the meadowlands, he danced and shouted.

Mr. Bittering looked at his wife. "Why did we do that?"

"I don't know," she said. "It just seemed like a good
460 idea."

They walked into the hills. They strolled on old mosaic paths, beside still pumping fountains. The paths were covered with a thin film of cool water all summer long. You kept your bare feet cool all the day, splashing as in a creek, wading.

They came to a small deserted Martian villa⁹ with a good view of the valley. It was on top of a hill. Blue marble halls, large murals, a swimming pool. It was refreshing in this hot summertime. The Martians
470 hadn't believed in large cities.

"How nice," said Mrs. Bittering, "if we could move up here to this villa for the summer."

"Come on," he said. "We're going back to town. There's work to be done on the rocket."

But as he worked that night, the thought of the cool blue marble villa entered his mind. As the hours passed, the rocket seemed less important.

Pause & Reflect

Pause & Reflect

1. Why does Dan want to change his name? Circle one sentence below. **(Infer)**

   He wants to defy his parents.

   He is changing into a Martian.

2. ▌MARK IT UP⟩ Do you think Harry is going to work on the rocket again? Write your prediction below. Then circle clues in the story that led you to your answer. **(Predict)**

9. **villa:** a large, luxurious country house of a wealthy person.

FOCUS

Harry makes a major decision. Read to find out what it is and why he makes it.

In the flow of days and weeks, the rocket <u>receded</u> and
480 <u>dwindled</u>. The old fever was gone. It frightened him to think he had let it slip this way. But somehow the heat, the air, the working conditions—

He heard the men murmuring on the porch of his metal shop.

"Everyone's going. You heard?"

"All going. That's right."

Bittering came out. "Going where?" He saw a
490 couple of trucks, loaded with children and furniture, drive down the dusty street.

"Up to the villas," said the man.

"Yeah, Harry. I'm going. So is Sam. Aren't you, Sam?"

"That's right, Harry. What about you?"

"I've got work to do here."

"Work! You can finish that rocket in the autumn, when it's cooler."

He took a breath. "I got the frame all set up."

500 "In the autumn is better." Their voices were lazy in the heat.

"Got to work," he said.

"Autumn," they reasoned. And they sounded so sensible, so right.

"Autumn would be best," he thought. "Plenty of time, then."

> No! cried part of himself, deep down, put away, locked tight, suffocating. No! No!
>
> "In the autumn," he said.

510 "Come on, Harry," they all said.

WORDS TO KNOW
recede (rĭ-sēd') v. to become fainter and more distant
dwindle (dwĭn'dl) v. to become less, until little remains

As the story continues . . .

- People are moving to houses in the mountains, where it's cool.
- They invite the Bitterings.
- Harry agrees, planning to return to town in the fall.

WHAT DOES IT MEAN? *The old fever was gone* means "The desire to quickly build a rocket was gone."

 Why does Harry not join the others immediately?

 the boxed passage. Notice that these lines show a **conflict** within Harry.

Dark They Were . . . **249**

"Yes," he said, feeling his flesh melt in the hot liquid air. "Yes, in the autumn. I'll begin work again then."

"I got a villa near the Tirra Canal," said someone.

"You mean the Roosevelt Canal, don't you?"

"Tirra. The old Martian name."

"But on the map—"

"Forget the map. It's Tirra now. Now I found a place in the Pillan Mountains—"

520 "You mean the Rockefeller Range," said Bittering.

"I mean the Pillan Mountains," said Sam.

"Yes," said Bittering, buried in the hot, swarming air. "The Pillan Mountains."

Everyone worked at loading the truck in the hot, still afternoon of the next day.

Laura, Dan, and David carried packages. Or, as they preferred to be known, Ttil, Linnl, and Werr carried packages.

The furniture was abandoned in the little white
530 cottage.

"It looked just fine in Boston," said the mother. "And here in the cottage. But up at the villa? No. We'll get it when we come back in the autumn."

Bittering himself was quiet.

"I've some ideas on furniture for the villa," he said after a time. "Big, lazy furniture."

"What about your encyclopedia? You're taking it along, surely?"

Mr. Bittering glanced away. "I'll come and get it
540 next week."

They turned to their daughter. "What about your New York dresses?"

The bewildered girl stared. "Why, I don't want them any more."

They shut off the gas, the water, they locked the doors and walked away. Father peered into the truck.

"Gosh, we're not taking much," he said. "Considering all we brought to Mars, this is only a handful!"

550 He started the truck.

Looking at the small white cottage for a long moment, he was filled with a desire to rush to it, touch it, say good-bye to it, for he felt as if he were going away on a long journey, leaving something to which he could never quite return, never understand again.

Just then Sam and his family drove by in another truck.

"Hi, Bittering! Here we go!"

560 The truck swung down the ancient highway out of town. There were sixty others traveling in the same direction. The town filled with a silent, heavy dust from their passage. The canal waters lay blue in the sun, and a quiet wind moved in the strange trees.

"Good-bye, town!" said Mr. Bittering.

"Good-bye, good-bye," said the family, waving to it.

They did not look back again.

Pause & Reflect

FOCUS

Time passes at the villa. Read to find out how Harry and his wife now feel about the Earth settlement.

MARK IT UP > As you read, circle details that reveal their feelings.

Summer burned the canals dry. Summer moved like 570 flame upon the meadows. In the empty Earth settlement, the painted houses flaked and peeled. Rubber tires upon which children had swung in back yards hung suspended like stopped clock pendulums in the blazing air.

Pause & Reflect

1. Why do you think Harry decides to move to the villa? (Infer)

2. REREAD the boxed passage. What does leaving the cottage mean to Harry? (Infer)

As the story continues . . .

• Harry and his wife are happy at the villa.
• They have no plans to return to town.

WHAT DOES IT MEAN? A pendulum is an object that hangs from a fixed support so that it moves back and forth under the force of gravity. A clock pendulum swings back and forth as the clock ticks.

Pause & Reflect

1. Use your own words to describe the Martian summer and how people spent their time. **(Visualize)**

2. **REREAD** the boxed text. Then circle the two statements that are true of Harry Bittering. **(Infer)**

   He longs to return to Earth.

   He has forgotten that he is from Earth.

   He is getting younger looking.

   He thinks the Earth people built beautiful houses.

At the metal shop, the rocket frame began to rust.

In the quiet autumn Mr. Bittering stood, very dark 580 now, very golden-eyed, upon the slope above his villa, looking at the valley.

"It's time to go back," said Cora.

"Yes, but we're not going," he said quietly. "There's nothing there any more."

"Your books," she said. "Your fine clothes."

"Your *llles* and your fine *ior uele rre*," she said.

"The town's empty. No one's going back," he said. "There's no reason to, none at all."

The daughter wove tapestries and the sons played 590 songs on ancient flutes and pipes, their laughter echoing in the marble villa.

Mr. Bittering gazed at the Earth settlement far away in the low valley. "Such odd, such ridiculous houses the Earth people built."

"They didn't know any better," his wife mused. "Such ugly people. I'm glad they've gone."

They both looked at each other, startled by all they had just finished saying. They laughed.

"Where did they go?" he wondered. He glanced at 600 his wife. She was golden and slender as his daughter. She looked at him, and he seemed almost as young as their eldest son.

"I don't know," she said.

"We'll go back to town maybe next year, or the year after, or the year after that," he said, calmly. "Now— I'm warm. How about taking a swim?"

They turned their backs to the valley. Arm in arm they walked silently down a path of clear-running spring water.

Pause & Reflect

FOCUS

A rocket from Earth lands on Mars five years later. Read to find out what has happened to the Bitterings and the other Earth people.

MARK IT UP > As you read, circle details that help you figure out what has happened.

610 Five years later a rocket fell out of the sky. It lay steaming in the valley. Men leaped out of it, shouting.

"We won the war on Earth! We're here to rescue you! Hey!"

But the American-built town of cottages, peach trees, and theaters was silent. They 620 found a <u>flimsy</u> rocket frame rusting in an empty shop.

The rocket men searched the hills. The captain established headquarters in an abandoned bar. His lieutenant came back to report.

"The town's empty, but we found native life in the hills, sir. Dark people. Yellow eyes. Martians. Very friendly. We talked a bit, not much. They learn English fast. I'm sure our relations will be most friendly with them, sir."

"Dark, eh?" mused the captain. "How many?"

630 "Six, eight hundred, I'd say, living in those marble ruins in the hills, sir. Tall, healthy. Beautiful women."

"Did they tell you what became of the men and women who built this Earth settlement, Lieutenant?"

"They hadn't the foggiest notion of what happened to this town or its people."

"Strange. You think those Martians killed them?"

"They look surprisingly peaceful. Chances are a plague did this town in, sir."

"Perhaps. I suppose this is one of those mysteries 640 we'll never solve. One of those mysteries you read about."

The captain looked at the room, the dusty windows, the blue mountains rising beyond, the canals moving in the light, and he heard the soft wind in the air. He

As the story ends . . .

• A new group from Earth arrives on Mars.

• The original Earth settlement is empty, but the group finds some life forms.

• As the new group makes plans, the wind sends shivers through them.

English Learner Support

Culture

The Lost Colony The situation at the end of this story mirrors a real one that occurred in the 1500s. An English settlement at Roanoke, Virginia, vanished. Even now, no one knows if they died or if they joined Native Americans who lived nearby.

WHAT DOES IT MEAN? When the lieutenant says, "Chances are a plague did this town in," he is guessing that a horrible disease killed all the people who lived there.

WORDS TO KNOW
flimsy (flĭm'zē) adj. not solid or strong

Pause & Reflect

1. What has happened to Harry and his family? **(Infer)**

2. the boxed passage. What do you predict will happen to the new arrivals from Earth? **(Predict)**

They will

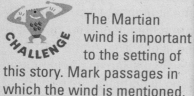
The Martian wind is important to the setting of this story. Mark passages in which the wind is mentioned. What **mood**, or feeling, does the wind create? **(Analyze)**

shivered. Then, recovering, he tapped a large fresh map he had thumbtacked to the top of an empty table.

"Lots to be done, Lieutenant." His voice droned on and quietly on as the sun sank behind the blue hills. "New settlements. Mining sites, minerals to be looked 650 for. Bacteriological specimens taken. The work, all the work. And the old records were lost. We'll have a job of remapping to do, renaming the mountains and rivers and such. Calls for a little imagination.

"What do you think of naming those mountains the Lincoln Mountains, this canal the Washington Canal, those hills—we can name those hills for you, Lieutenant. Diplomacy. And you, for a favor, might name a town for me. Polishing the apple. And why not make this the Einstein Valley, and farther over . . . are 660 you *listening*, Lieutenant?"

The lieutenant snapped his gaze from the blue color and the quiet mist of the hills far beyond the town.

"What? Oh, *yes*, sir!" ❖

Pause & Reflect

Active Reading SkillBuilder

Visualize

Many writers use vivid descriptions to help tell their stories. From these descriptive details, which appeal to the senses, readers can **visualize,** or form mental pictures of, characters, events, or settings. Ray Bradbury's vivid descriptions in "Dark They Were, and Golden-Eyed" evoke strong mental images of Mars and the transformation of the humans. Write down details that help you to visualize the different elements of the story.

Description

Setting	Characters	Events
"... the lawn in front of their house ... was coloring itself like spring violets"		

Literary Analysis SkillBuilder

Circular Plot Structure

Writers plan the sequence of events in their stories to show development of character, to contribute to mood, and to convey theme. Sometimes the events are organized into a **circular plot structure.** This arrangement means that details and events that occur at the beginning of the story are reflected in similar events that occur at the end. Fill in the diagram with key events from the story.

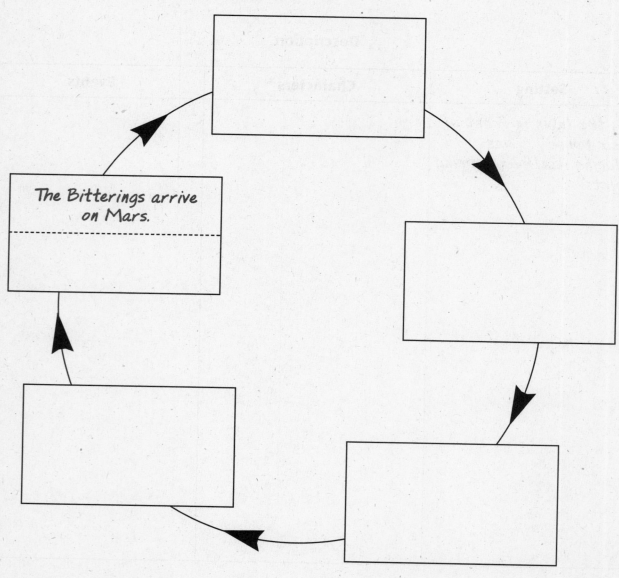

The Bitterings arrive on Mars.

Words to Know SkillBuilder

Words to Know

amiss   dwindle   flimsy   forlorn   recede

A. For each word in the first column, find the phrase in the second column that is closest in meaning. Write the letter of that phrase in the blank.

_____ 1. amiss   A. wrong, out of order

_____ 2. dwindle   B. feeling sad

_____ 3. flimsy   C. become fainter and more distant

_____ 4. forlorn   D. become fewer until not many remain

_____ 5. recede   E. not solid, weak

B. Complete each sentence with the correct choice from the Words to Know above.

1. The rocket he was trying to build seemed too _____ to withstand the pressure of the atmosphere.

2. Thoughts of home tended to _____ after so many months on Mars.

3. The supply of food in the freezer was going to _____ to nothing if Bittering continued to eat it for every meal.

4. When he looked at the peach blossom, he couldn't point out what was wrong exactly, but he knew something was _____.

5. Bittering was feeling quite _____ as he watched his family slowly begin to change.

C. On a sheet of paper, write a diary entry from Harry Bittering's perspective about his efforts to build his rocket. Use at least **four** Words to Know.

Before You Read

Connect to Your Life

Do you know of a case where someone sacrificed something valuable or meaningful for someone he or she loved? Describe the sacrifice in the space below.

_____

_____

_____

_____

_____

Key to the Poem

WHAT'S THE BIG IDEA? Highwaymen were robbers on horseback in England during the 1700s. They were colorful figures who robbed from the rich and often gave what they took to the poor. Their adventures were told and retold in stories, songs, and poems like the one you are about to read. What would you like to learn about "the highwayman" who rides in this poem?

<u>What he looked like</u>_____

_____

_____

_____

_____

The Highwayman

BY ALFRED NOYES

PREVIEW The highwayman promises Bess, his love, that he will come back for her "before the morning light." Will he be able to keep his promise?

FOCUS

In these stanzas you will meet the highwayman, a brave and handsome robber on horseback.

MARK IT UP As you read, underline details that describe the highwayman. An example is highlighted.

Part One

The wind was a torrent of darkness among
    the gusty trees.
The moon was a ghostly galleon tossed upon
    cloudy seas.
The road was a ribbon of moonlight over
    the purple moor,
And the highwayman came riding—
5   Riding—riding—
The highwayman came riding, up to
    the old inn-door.

He'd a French cocked-hat on his forehead,
    a bunch of lace at his chin,
A coat of the claret velvet, and breeches
    of brown doeskin.
They fitted with never a wrinkle. His boots
    were up to the thigh.
10 And he rode with a jeweled twinkle,
    His pistol butts a-twinkle.
His rapier hilt a-twinkle, under the jeweled sky.

Pause & Reflect

Use this guide for help with unfamiliar
words and difficult passages.

1 torrent: a storm.

2 galleon: a large sailing ship.

3 moor: an open, rolling wasteland, usually
covered with low-growing shrubs.

7 a French cocked-hat: a hat with a
three-cornered brim, popular in the 1700s;
a bunch of lace at his chin: a lacy tie on
the front of his shirt.
8 claret: dark red, like red wine;
breeches: pants.

12 rapier hilt: sword handle.

As the poem begins . . .

- On a windy night, a highwayman rides to
  the door of an inn.
- The highwayman is handsome and well
  dressed.

READING TIP   The sidenotes in the Guide
for Reading explain many
difficult words and phrases.

English Learner Support

Language

Metaphors The poet uses metaphors
to compare the wind to a river, the
moon to a ship, and the road to a
ribbon.

MORE ABOUT . . .

(HIGHWAYMEN) During the 1700s in
England, a highwayman was a person
who robbed highway travelers. A few
highwaymen, like the one in this poem,
acted and dressed like gentlemen.

Pause **&** Reflect

Which detail does *not* describe the
highwayman? Cross it out. **(Clarify)**

a velvet coat

brown doeskin breeches

a gold compass

thigh-high boots

FOCUS

Read on to find out about the meeting
between the highwayman and Bess.

▐▐▐ **MARK IT UP** 〉 As you read,
underline details that help you to get
to know how the highwayman and
Bess feel about each other.

Over the cobbles he clattered and clashed in
   the dark inn-yard.
He tapped with his whip on the shutters,
   but all was locked and barred.
15 He whistled a tune to the window, and who
   should be waiting there
But the landlord's black-eyed daughter,
   Bess, the landlord's daughter,
Plaiting a dark red love-knot into
   her long black hair.

And dark in the dark old inn-yard a stable
   wicket creaked
20 Where Tim the ostler listened. His face was
   white and peaked.
His eyes were hollows of madness, his hair
   like moldy hay,
But he loved the landlord's daughter,
   The landlord's red-lipped daughter.
Dumb as a dog he listened, and he heard
   the robber say—

25 "One kiss, my bonny sweetheart, I'm after
   a prize tonight,
But I shall be back with the yellow gold before
   the morning light;
Yet, if they press me sharply, and harry me
   through the day,

13 cobbles: rounded stones used for paving roads; **clattered and clashed:** his horse's hooves rattled the stones.

18 plaiting: braiding; **a dark red love-knot:** a red bow worn by young women in the 1700s to show their love for a young man.

19 wicket: a small door or gate.

20 ostler: a worker who takes care of horses at an inn.

21 His eyes . . . madness: his eyes showed that he was insane.

24 Dumb as a dog: without making a sound.

25 bonny: beautiful; **after a prize:** going out to steal something.

27 press me sharply . . . harry me: follow me closely, chase me.

As the poem continues . . .

- The highwayman kisses Bess.
- He says nothing will stop him from seeing her again.
- A worker who loves Bess overhears this.

READING TIP This poem tells a story. Use a simple story map, like the one below, to keep track of characters and events.

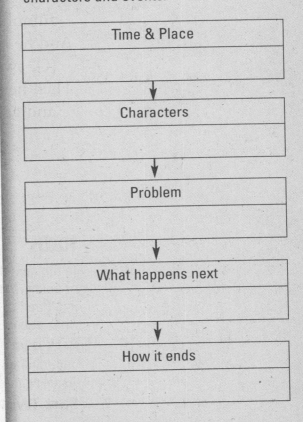

Time & Place

↓

Characters

↓

Problem

↓

What happens next

↓

How it ends

WHAT DOES IT MEAN? *Peaked* (PEE-kihd) means "thin, tense, or unhealthy."

READING CHECK How do you think Tim feels when he hears the highwayman and Bess?

Then look for me by moonlight,
    Watch for me by moonlight,
30 I'll come to thee by moonlight, though hell
    should bar the way."

He rose upright in the stirrups. He scarce
    could reach her hand,
But she loosened her hair in the casement.
    His face burnt like a brand
As the black cascade of perfume came
    tumbling over his breast;
And he kissed its waves in the moonlight,
35   (O, sweet black waves in the moonlight!)
Then he tugged at his rein in the moonlight,
    and galloped away to the west.

Pause & Reflect

FOCUS

In the next three stanzas, redcoats, or soldiers of the king, march to the inn. Read to find out what they do to Bess and why.

MARK IT UP As you read, underline details that help you to visualize the redcoats.

Part Two

He did not come in the dawning. He did not
    come at noon;
And out of the tawny sunset, before the rise
    of the moon,
When the road was a gypsy's ribbon, looping
    the purple moor,

32 **casement:** a window that opens outward on side hinges.

33 **black cascade of perfume:** the poet compares Bess's hair to a waterfall of perfume.

38 **tawny:** brownish orange.

39 **gypsy's ribbon:** the poet uses figurative language to show that the road leading to the inn is winding and has turned a bright color in the sunset.

English Learner Support

Vocabulary

Pronouns The word *thee* is an older form of *you*.

Pause & Reflect

1. How do the highwayman and Bess feel about each other? **(Infer)**

_____

_____

2. What does the highwayman tell Bess? Circle the correct statement. **(Clarify)**

He will never see her again.

He will return no matter what happens.

If he does not return before morning, he will never return.

She should forget that she ever knew him.

▶ As the poem continues . . .

• The next evening, soldiers arrive and take over the inn.

• Bess knows that the soldiers are waiting for the highwayman to return.

• She realizes that he will ride into a trap.

40 A redcoat troop came marching—
   Marching—marching—
King George's men came marching, up to
   the old inn-door.

They said no word to the landlord. They
   drank his ale instead.
But they gagged his daughter, and bound her,
   to the foot of her narrow bed.
45 Two of them knelt at her casement, with
   muskets at their side!
There was death at every window;
   And hell at one dark window;
For Bess could see, through her casement,
   the road that *he* would ride.

They had tied her up to attention, with
   many a sniggering jest.
50 They had bound a musket beside her, with
   the muzzle beneath her breast!
"Now, keep good watch!" and they kissed her.
   She heard the doomed man say—
Look for me by moonlight;
   Watch for me by moonlight;
I'll come to thee by moonlight, though hell
   should bar the way!

Pause & Reflect

40 redcoat troop: British troops in the 1700s wore bright red uniforms.

42 King George's men: soldiers of King George III of England.

45 muskets: rifles used in the 1700s that could fire only one shot before they had to be reloaded.

49 sniggering jest: mocking joke.

50 muzzle: the tip of the barrel of a rifle or pistol.

English Learner Support

Language

Figurative Language *There was death at every window* means "Soldiers had guns at every window, waiting to kill the highwayman."

Pause & Reflect

1. How do you think the redcoats could have found out that the highwayman would ride to the inn? **(Infer)**

2. How do the redcoats set a trap for the highwayman? **(Summarize)**

3. What was your reaction to the conduct of the redcoats? **(Evaluate)**

FOCUS

Read on to find out what Bess does to warn the highwayman about the ambush.

55 She twisted her hands behind her; but all the
        knots held good!
    She writhed her hands till her fingers were wet
        with sweat or blood!
    They stretched and strained in the darkness,
        and the hours crawled by like years,
    Till, now, on the stroke of midnight,
        Cold, on the stroke of midnight,
60 The tip of one finger touched it! The trigger
        at least was hers!

    The tip of one finger touched it. She strove
        no more for the rest.
    Up, she stood up to attention, with the muzzle
        beneath her breast.
    She would not risk their hearing; she would
        not strive again;
    For the road lay bare in the moonlight;
65   Blank and bare in the moonlight;
    And the blood of her veins, in the moonlight,
        throbbed to her love's refrain.

    Tlot-tlot; tlot-tlot! Had they heard it? The
        horse hoofs ringing clear;
    Tlot-tlot, tlot-tlot, in the distance? Were they
        deaf that they did not hear?
    Down the ribbon of moonlight, over the brow
        of the hill,
70 The highwayman came riding—
        Riding—riding—

- Although she tries very hard, Bess cannot escape.
- Bess hears the hoofbeats of the highwayman's horse.
- As he approaches, she takes action.

56 writhed (rīthd): twisted.

57 They: Bess's fingers.

61 strove: tried.

English Learner Support

Language

Pronouns When the author writes, "The trigger at least was hers," *hers* is a pronoun that shows ownership. Bess now owns, or has control of, the trigger. The word *it* in the next line refers to the trigger.

66 refrain: repeated words.

READ ALOUD the boxed passage. How do you think Bess feels when she hears the sounds of the horse's hoofs? Why does she feel this way? **(Evaluate)**

The redcoats looked to their priming! She stood
    up, straight and still.

Tlot-tlot, in the frosty silence! *Tlot-tlot,* in the
    echoing night!
Nearer he came and nearer. Her face was like
    a light.
75 Her eyes grew wide for a moment; she drew
        one last deep breath,
    Then her finger moved in the moonlight,
        Her musket shattered the moonlight,
    Shattered her breast in the moonlight and
        warned him—with her death.

Pause & Reflect

FOCUS

Read to find out what happens to
the highwayman at the end of the
poem.

He turned. He spurred to the west; he did
    not know who stood
80 Bowed, with her head o'er the musket,
        drenched with her own blood!
    Not till the dawn he heard it, his face grew
        grey to hear
    How Bess, the landlord's daughter,
        The landlord's black-eyed daughter,
    Had watched for her love in the moonlight,
        and died in the darkness there.

72 looked to their priming: prepared their muskets by pouring in the explosive used to fire them.

79 spurred to the west: rode toward the west.

81 his face grew grey: his face turned pale.

Pause & Reflect

1. What does Bess do to warn the highwayman about the redcoats? **(Cause and Effect)**

2. Why does Bess warn him in this way? **(Infer)**

As the poem ends . . .

• The highwayman reacts to the news about Bess.

85 Back, he spurred like a madman, shouting a
     curse to the sky,
  With the white road smoking behind him and his
     rapier brandished high.
  Blood-red were his spurs in the golden noon;
     wine-red was his velvet coat;
  When they shot him down on the highway,
     Down like a dog on the highway,
90 And he lay in his blood on the highway, with
     a bunch of lace at his throat.

  *And still of a winter's night, they say, when the
     wind is in the trees,*
  *When the moon is a ghostly galleon tossed upon
     cloudy seas,*
  *When the road is a ribbon of moonlight over the
     purple moor,*
  A highwayman comes riding—
95   *Riding—riding—*
  A highwayman comes riding, up to the old inn-door.

  *Over the cobbles he clatters and clangs in the
     dark inn-yard.*
  *He taps with his whip on the shutters, but all is
     locked and barred.*
  *He whistles a tune to the window, and who
     should be waiting there*
100 *But the landlord's black-eyed daughter,*
     Bess, the landlord's daughter,
  *Plaiting a dark red love-knot into her long black
     hair.* ❖

  ## Pause & Reflect

91–101 ***And still...long black hair:*** The highwayman and Bess live on as legendary figures in the minds of the people.

WHAT DOES IT MEAN? *Brandished* means "displayed or waved in a threatening way."

Pause & Reflect

1. What do the redcoats do to the highwayman? Circle one phrase below. **(Clarify)**

hang him

shoot him

capture him

reward him

2. What images stayed in your mind after you finished reading the poem? **(Writer's Style)**

How would your response to the poem be different if the last two stanzas were left out? **(Analyze)**

Active Reading SkillBuilder

Responding to the Writer's Style

A **writer's style** is his or her manner of writing. It involves *how* something is said rather than *what* is said. The style of this poem is vivid and dramatic. As you read, try to notice aspects of the writer's style such as *mood, tone, images, figurative language, sound devices,* and *word choice*. Note examples of these aspects on this chart.

Examples	Aspect of Style
lines 1-6	mood (spooky, mysterious)
moon was a ghostly galleon	metaphor

Literary Analysis SkillBuilder

Word Choice

"The Highwayman" is full of vivid writing containing powerful, memorable images. Notice the poet's **word choices,** including verbs, metaphors, and similes. Use this chart to write down important events in the poem. Note vivid words or phrases that add to the impact of each event.

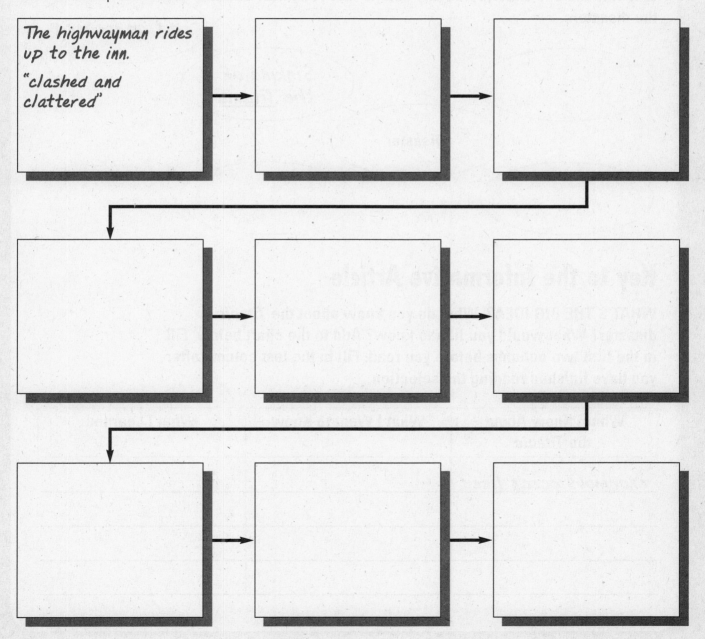

The highwayman rides up to the inn.

"clashed and clattered"

Before You Read

Connect to Your Life

The sinking of the great ship *Titanic* on April 14–15, 1912 shocked the world. What other large-scale disasters do you know about? Brainstorm with your classmates, and list the disasters in a web like the one shown. Add any details that you know about the disasters.

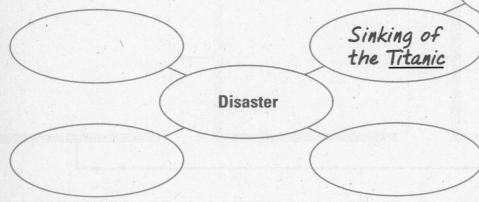

hit an iceberg

Sinking of the *Titanic*

Disaster

Key to the Informative Article

WHAT'S THE BIG IDEA? What do you know about the *Titanic* disaster? What would you like to know? Add to the chart below. Fill in the first two columns before you read. Fill in the last column after you have finished reading the selection.

What I Know About the *Titanic*	What I Want to Know	What I Learned
enormous ocean liner		

FROM · EXPLORING THE TITANIC

BY ROBERT D. BALLARD

PREVIEW The "unsinkable" *Titanic* was an example of the best technology of the early 1900s. Despite its builders' great confidence in technology, the huge ocean liner sank on its first voyage. The story of the disaster became front-page news around the world.

FOCUS
How did the idea of building the *Titanic* come about? Read to find out.

The story of the *Titanic* began before anyone had even thought about building the great ship. In 1898, fourteen years before the *Titanic* sank, an American writer named Morgan Robertson wrote a book called *The Wreck of the Titan*.[1] In his story, the *Titan*, a passenger ship almost identical to the *Titanic*, and labeled "unsinkable," sails
10 from England headed for New York. With many rich and famous passengers on board, the *Titan* hits an iceberg in the North Atlantic and sinks. Because there are not enough lifeboats, many lives are lost.

The story of the *Titan* predicted exactly what would happen to the *Titanic* fourteen years later. It was an eerie prophecy of terrible things to come.

In 1907, nearly ten years after *The Wreck of the Titan* was written, two men began making plans to build a real titanic ship. At a London dinner party, as
20 they relaxed over coffee and cigars, J. Bruce Ismay, president of the White Star Line of passenger ships, and Lord Pirrie, chairman of Harland & Wolff shipbuilders, discussed a plan to build three enormous ocean liners. Their goal was to give the White Star Line a competitive edge in the Atlantic passenger trade with several gigantic ships whose accommodations would be the last word in comfort and elegance.

The two men certainly dreamed on a grand scale. When these floating palaces were finally built, they
30 were so much bigger than other ships that new docks

---

1. *Titanic* (tī-tăn′ĭk) . . . *Titan* (tīt′n): In Greek mythology, the Titans were a race of giants. *Titanic* has come to be applied to any person or thing of great size or power.

WORDS TO KNOW
eerie (îr′ē) *adj.* weird, especially in a frightening way
prophecy (prŏf′ĭ-sē) *n.* a prediction; foretelling of future events
accommodations (ə-kŏm′ə-dā′shənz) *n.* a room and food, especially in hotels or on ships or trains

had to be built on each side of the Atlantic to service them. Four years after that London dinner party, the first of these huge liners, the *Olympic,* safely completed her maiden voyage.[2]

Pause & Reflect

Pause & Reflect

What were the goals of the men who built the *Titanic*? Cross out the one *wrong* answer below. (Clarify)

to build three enormous ocean liners

to help immigrants

to add comfort and elegance to ocean travel

to beat the competition

FOCUS

In this part you will learn about the size of the *Titanic.*

|||MARK IT UP〉 As you read, circle details that tell you about the size of the *Titanic.* An example is highlighted.

On May 31, 1911, the hull of the *Titanic* was launched at the Harland & Wolff shipyards in Belfast, Ireland, before a cheering crowd of 100,000.
40 Bands played, and people came from miles around to see this great wonder of the sea. Twenty-two tons of soap, grease, and train oil were used to slide her into the water. In the words of one eyewitness, she had "a rudder as big as an elm tree . . . propellers as big as a windmill. Everything was on a nightmare scale."

For the next ten months the *Titanic* was outfitted
50 and carefully prepared down to the last detail. The final size and richness of this new ship was astounding. She was 882 feet long, almost the length of four city blocks. With nine decks, she was as high as an eleven-story building.

Among her gigantic features, she had four huge funnels[3], each one big enough to drive two trains through. During construction an astonishing three million rivets had been hammered into her hull. Her three enormous anchors weighed a total of thirty-one

☞ As the article continues . . .

• A large crowd cheers as the *Titanic* is put into the water.

• The huge ship is elegantly decorated and has an experienced captain.

WHAT DOES IT MEAN?
Outfitted means "provided with the necessary equipment." A ship's *hull* is its frame or body.

|||MARK IT UP〉 KEEP TRACK
Remember to use these marks to keep track of your reading.

＊ This is important.

？ I have a question about this.

！ This is a surprise.

---

2. **maiden voyage:** very first trip.
3. **funnel:** the smokestack of a ship.

Pause & Reflect

1. What **fact** about the size of the *Titanic* impressed you most? Explain. **(Fact and Opinion)**

_____

_____

_____

_____

2. 🖊 **MARK IT UP** ⟩ On this page, circle details that tell you about Captain Smith. **(Clarify)**

_____

_____

_____

_____

_____

📑 As the article continues . . .

• Passengers begin to board the ship.

• Ruth Becker and Jack Thayer describe who and what they saw on the *Titanic*.

WHAT DOES IT MEAN? A *missionary* is a person sent by a church to teach its religion in a foreign country.

60 tons—the weight of twenty cars. And for her maiden voyage, she carried enough food to feed a small town for several months.

As her name boasted, the *Titanic* was indeed the biggest ship in the world. Nicknamed "the Millionaires' Special," she was also called "the Wonder Ship," "the Unsinkable Ship," and "the Last Word in Luxury" by newspapers around the world.

The command of this great ocean liner was given to the senior captain of the White Star Line, Captain 70 Edward J. Smith. This proud, white-bearded man was a natural leader and was popular with both crew members and passengers. Most important, after thirty-eight years' service with the White Star Line, he had an excellent safety record. At the age of fifty-nine, Captain Smith was going to retire after this last trip, a perfect final <u>tribute</u> to a long and successful career.

Pause & Reflect

FOCUS

In this part you will meet some of the passengers on the *Titanic*. Read to find out their impressions of the "floating palace."

🖊 **MARK IT UP** ⟩ Circle details that reveal how lavish and "modern" the *Titanic* was.

On Wednesday, April 10, 1912, the *Titanic*'s passengers began to arrive in 80 Southampton for the trip to New York. Ruth Becker was <u>dazzled</u> as she boarded the ship with her mother, her younger sister, and two-year-old brother, Richard. Ruth's father was a missionary in India. The rest of the family was sailing to New York to find medical help for

WORDS TO KNOW
 tribute (trĭb′yŏŏt) *n.* an action or gift that honors a deserving individual
 dazzled (dăz′əld) *adj.* amazed or overwhelmed by a spectacular display
   dazzle *v.*

young Richard, who had developed a serious illness in India. They had booked second-class tickets on the
90 *Titanic.*

Twelve-year-old Ruth was delighted with the ship. As she pushed her little brother about the decks in a stroller, she was impressed with what she saw. "Everything was new. New!" she recalled. "Our cabin was just like a hotel room, it was so big. The dining room was beautiful—the linens, all the bright, polished silver you can imagine."

Meanwhile, seventeen-year-old Jack Thayer from Philadelphia was trying out the soft mattress on the
100 large bed in his cabin. The first-class rooms his family had reserved for themselves and their maid had thick carpets, carved wooden panels on the walls, and marble sinks. As his parents were getting settled in their adjoining stateroom,[4] Jack decided to explore this fantastic ship.

On A Deck, he stepped into the Verandah and Palm Court and admired the white wicker furniture and the ivy growing up the trellised walls. On the lower decks, Jack discovered the squash court,[5] the swimming pool,
110 and the Turkish bath[6] decorated like a room in a sultan's palace. In the gymnasium, the instructor was showing passengers the latest in exercise equipment, which included a mechanical camel you could ride on, stationary bicycles, and rowing machines.

Daylight shone through the huge glass dome over the Grand Staircase as Jack went down to join his parents in the first-class reception room.

There, with the ship's band playing in the background, his father pointed out some of the other
120 first-class passengers. "He's supposed to be the world's

---

4. **stateroom:** a private cabin on a ship.
5. **squash court:** a walled court or room for playing squash, in which a rubber ball is hit off the walls.
6. **Turkish bath:** a steam bath.

WHAT DOES IT MEAN? On a ship, the *decks* are platforms that extend from one side to the other. They are like floors in a house or building.

READING TIP Use a sequence chain like the one below to keep track of important details in the article. After you finish reading each section, add one or two boxes to the chain.

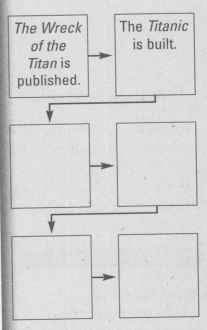

READING CHECK Ismay and Pirrie, who planned the *Titanic,* wanted the ship to be comfortable and elegant. Did they accomplish their goal? Explain.

Pause & Reflect

Why do you think the author names both regular passengers and rich people who sailed aboard the *Titanic*? (Author's Purpose)

_____

_____

_____

_____

📑 **As the article continues ...**

- People from different social classes are treated very differently on the *Titanic*.

- As the ship leaves the dock, its enormous size nearly causes a disaster.

English Learner Support

Language

Word Parts The word *unsinkable* contains a prefix (*un–*) and a suffix (*–able*). The base word, sink, means "go under the water." You can use these parts to figure out the meaning of *unsinkable*:

un (not) + sink + able = unsinkable (not able to be sunk)

richest man," said his father of Colonel John Jacob Astor, who was escorting the young Mrs. Astor. He also identified Mr. and Mrs. Straus, founders of Macy's of New York, the world's largest department store. Millionaire Benjamin Guggenheim was aboard, as were Jack's parents' friends from Philadelphia, Mr. and Mrs. George Widener and their son, Harry. Mr. Widener had made a fortune building streetcars. Mr. and Mrs. William Carter were also friends of the
130 Thayers. Stowed in one of the holds below was a new Renault car that they were bringing back from England.

Pause & Reflect

FOCUS

Read on to find out about the social classes of the passengers and about what happened when the *Titanic* cast off.

J. Bruce Ismay, president of the White Star Line, moved about the room saying hello to people. He wanted to make sure that his wealthy passengers were comfortable, that they would feel relaxed and safe aboard his
140 floating palace.

Indeed, when Ruth Becker's mother had asked one of the second-class staff about the safety of the ship, she had been told that there was absolutely nothing to worry about. The ship had watertight[7] compartments that would allow her to float <u>indefinitely</u>. There was much talk among the passengers about the *Titanic* being unsinkable.

---

7. **watertight:** made so water cannot enter or escape.

WORDS TO KNOW
   indefinitely (ĭn-dĕf′ə-nĭt-lē) *adv.* for an unlimited length of time

In 1912, people were divided into social classes according to background, wealth, and education. Because of these class lines, the *Titanic* was rather like a big floating layer cake. The bottom layer consisted of the lowly manual workers sweating away in the heat and grime of the boiler rooms and engine rooms. The next layer was the third-class passengers, people of many nationalities hoping to make a new start in America. After that came the second class—teachers, merchants, and professionals of moderate means like Ruth's family. Then, finally, there was the icing on the cake in first class: the rich and the aristocratic. The differences between these groups were enormous. While the wealthy brought their maids and valets[8] and mountains of luggage, most members of the crew earned such tiny salaries that it would have taken them years to save the money for a single first-class ticket.

At noon on Wednesday, April 10, the *Titanic* cast off. The whistles on her huge funnels were the biggest ever made. As she began her journey to the sea, they were heard for miles around.

Moving majestically down the River Test, and watched by a crowd that had turned out for the occasion, the *Titanic* slowly passed two ships tied up to a dock. All of a sudden, the mooring ropes holding the passenger liner *New York* snapped with a series of sharp cracks like fireworks going off. The enormous pull created by the *Titanic* moving past her had broken the *New York*'s ropes and was now drawing her stern toward the *Titanic*. Jack Thayer watched in horror as the two ships came closer and closer. "It looked as though there surely would be a collision," he later wrote. "Her stern could not have been more than a yard or two from our side. It almost hit us."

MARK IT UP Reread the boxed text. Circle details that show how the different social classes were treated on the *Titanic*. (Clarify)

English Learner Support
Language

Simile A simile compares two things using the word *like* or *as*. The simile in blue type compares the *Titanic*, which has many decks stacked on top of each other, to a *layer cake*. A layer cake has several layers, or levels, of cake with frosting between the layers.

WHAT DOES IT MEAN? The *stern* is the rear end of a ship.

8. **valets** (vă-lāz′): gentlemen's personal servants.

Pause & Reflect

Number the following groups from 1 (highest) to 4 (lowest) according to the class system aboard the *Titanic*. **(Clarify)**

__ immigrants

__ teachers, professionals, merchants

__ manual workers

__ wealthy aristocrats

📄 **As the article continues . . .**

• Three days have passed and the *Titanic* is at sea.

• Reports of iceberg sightings are not treated seriously.

• A lookout sees danger ahead.

MORE ABOUT . . .

ICEBERGS An iceberg is a floating chunk of ice. Icebergs can be huge—bigger than the state of Rhode Island—and can damage or sink ships that crash into them. Most of an iceberg is hidden underwater, so it may be hard to spot from a distance. Ships' crews must keep a constant watch for icebergs in certain parts of the ocean.

At the last moment, some quick action by Captain Smith and a tugboat captain nearby allowed the *Titanic* to slide past with only inches to spare.

It was not a good sign. Did it mean that the *Titanic* might be too big a ship to handle safely? Those who knew about the sea thought that such a close call at the beginning of a maiden voyage was a very bad omen.

Pause & Reflect

FOCUS

The *Titanic* starts receiving reports of icebergs. Read to find out about the events that follow.

✏️ **MARK IT UP** As you read, circle each iceberg report.

190 Jack Phillips, the first wireless operator on the *Titanic*, quickly jotted down the message coming in over his headphones. "It's another iceberg warning," he said wearily to his young assistant, Harold Bride. "You'd better take it up to the bridge." Both men had been at work

200 for hours in the *Titanic*'s radio room, trying to get caught up in sending out a large number of personal messages. In 1912, passengers on ocean liners thought it was a real <u>novelty</u> to send postcard-style messages to friends at home from the middle of the Atlantic.

Bride picked up the iceberg message and stepped out onto the boat deck. It was a sunny but cold Sunday morning, the fourth day of the *Titanic*'s maiden voyage. The ship was steaming at full speed across a calm sea. Harold Bride was quite pleased with himself

210 at having landed a job on such a magnificent new ship. After all, he was only twenty-two years old and had just nine months' experience at operating a

WORDS TO KNOW
novelty (nŏv'əl-tē) *n.* something new, original, or unusual

"wireless set," as a ship's radio was then called. As he entered the bridge area, he could see one of the crewmen standing behind the ship's wheel steering her course toward New York.

Captain Smith was on duty in the bridge,[9] so Bride handed the message to him. "It's from the *Caronia,* sir. She's reporting icebergs and pack ice ahead." The
220 captain thanked him, read the message, and then posted it on the bulletin board for other officers on watch to read. On his way back to the radio room, Bride thought the captain had seemed quite unconcerned by the message. But then again, he had been told that it was not unusual to have ice floating in the sea lanes during an April crossing. Besides, what danger could a few pieces of ice present to an unsinkable ship?

Elsewhere on board, passengers relaxed on deck
230 chairs, reading or taking naps. Some played cards, some wrote letters, while others chatted with friends. As it was Sunday, church services had been held in the morning, the first-class service led by Captain Smith. Jack Thayer spent most of the day walking about the decks getting some fresh air with his parents.

Two more ice warnings were received from nearby ships around lunch time. In the chaos of the radio room, Harold Bride only had time to take one of them to the bridge. The rest of the day passed quietly. Then,
240 in the late afternoon, the temperature began to drop rapidly. Darkness approached as the bugle call announced dinner.

Jack Thayer's parents had been invited to a special dinner for Captain Smith, so Jack ate alone in the first-class dining room. After dinner, as he was having a cup of coffee, he was joined by Milton Long, another passenger going home to the States. Long was

---

9. **bridge:** enclosed area above the main deck of the ship from which the ship is controlled.

WHAT DOES IT MEAN? *Pack ice* is frozen seawater that forms on the surface of the ocean.

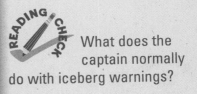 What does the captain normally do with iceberg warnings?

WHAT DOES IT MEAN? *Sea lanes* are permanent routes that many ships follow through the ocean.

English Learner Support
Culture

Sunday Services Many Christian religions hold religious services every Sunday morning.

older than Jack, but in the easy-going atmosphere of shipboard travel, they struck up a conversation and
250 talked together for an hour or so.

At 7:30 P.M., the radio room received three more warnings of ice about fifty miles ahead. One of them was from the steamer *Californian* reporting three large icebergs. Harold Bride took this message up to the bridge, and it was again politely received. Captain Smith was attending the dinner party being held for him when the warning was delivered. He never got to see it. Then, around 9:00 P.M., the captain excused himself and went up to the bridge. He and his officers
260 talked about how difficult it was to spot icebergs on a calm, clear, moonless night like this with no wind to kick up white surf around them. Before going to bed, the captain ordered the lookouts to keep a sharp watch for ice.

After trading travel stories with Milton Long, Jack Thayer put on his coat and walked around the deck. "It had become very much colder," he said later. "It was a brilliant, starry night. There was no moon, and I have never seen the stars shine brighter . . . sparkling
270 like diamonds. . . . It was the kind of night that made one feel glad to be alive." At eleven o'clock, he went below to his cabin, put on his pajamas, and got ready for bed.

In the radio room, Harold Bride was exhausted. The two operators were expected to keep the radio working twenty-four hours a day, and Bride lay down to take a much-needed nap. Phillips was so busy with the passenger messages that he actually brushed off the final ice warning of the night. It was from the
280 *Californian.* Trapped in a field of ice, she had stopped for the night about nineteen miles north of the *Titanic.* She was so close that the message literally blasted in Phillips's ears. Annoyed by the loud interruption, he

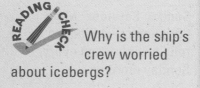

REREAD the boxed text. Why is it so hard to see icebergs this night? (**Cause and Effect**)

READING CHECK Why is the ship's crew worried about icebergs?

WHAT DOES IT MEAN?
Brushed off means "refused to take seriously."

cut off the *Californian*'s radio operator with the words, "Shut up, shut up. I'm busy."

The radio room had received a total of seven ice warning messages in one day. It was quite clear that floating icebergs lay ahead of the *Titanic*.

290 High up in the crow's nest[10] on the forward mast, Fred Fleet had passed a quiet watch. It was now 11:40 P.M., and he and his fellow lookout were waiting to be relieved so they could head below, perhaps for a hot drink before hopping into their warm bunks. The sea was dead calm. The air was bitterly cold.

Suddenly, Fleet saw something. A huge, dark shape loomed out of the night directly ahead of the *Titanic*. An iceberg! He quickly sounded the alarm bell three times and picked up the telephone.

"What did you see?" asked the duty officer.

300 "Iceberg right ahead," replied Fleet.

Immediately, the officer on the bridge ordered the wheel turned as far as it would go. The engine room was told to reverse the engines, while a button was pushed to close the doors to the watertight compartments in the bottom of the ship.

The lookouts in the crow's nest braced themselves for a collision. Slowly the ship started to turn. It looked as though they would miss it. But it was too late. They had avoided a head-on crash, but the

310 iceberg had struck a glancing blow along the *Titanic*'s starboard bow.[11] Several tons of ice fell on the ship's decks as the iceberg brushed along the side of the ship and passed into the night. A few minutes later, the *Titanic* came to a stop.

Pause & Reflect

---

10. **crow's nest:** a small lookout platform located near the top of a mast or other high place on a ship.

11. **starboard bow:** the right side of the front of the ship.

English Learner Support
Vocabulary

Multiple Meanings Many words can have different meanings in different sentences. In this sentence, *passed* means "experienced" and *watch* means "time spent looking for possible dangers." Fleet has been looking for icebergs, but he has seen nothing.

WHAT DOES IT MEAN? A *glancing blow* means "a forceful hit along the side."

Pause & Reflect

1. How many times was the *Titanic* warned about icebergs? **(Clarify)**

2. Cross out the phrase that is *not* true about the *Californian*. **(Clarify)**

   trapped in an ice field

   had radio problems

   stopped 19 miles north of the *Titanic*

   warned the *Titanic*

As the article continues . . .

- At first, few people realize that the *Titanic* has hit an iceberg.
- Seawater begins to flood parts of the ship.
- The ship's crew sends a call for help.

English Learner Support

Language

Time Words As you read, notice words and phrases that tell you when things happen. Here are a few words and phrases that you will find on this page:

- already
- no longer
- when
- as
- while

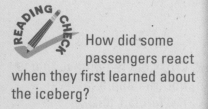

How did some passengers react when they first learned about the iceberg?

FOCUS

Read to learn what happens in the first twenty minutes after the collision.

MARK IT UP As you read, circle details that tell you what happens.

Many of the passengers didn't know the ship had hit anything. Because it was so cold, almost everyone was inside, and most people had

320 already gone to bed. Ruth Becker and her mother were awakened by the dead silence. They could no longer hear the soothing hum of the vibrating engines from below. Jack Thayer was about to step into bed when he felt himself sway ever so slightly. The engines stopped. He was startled by the sudden quiet.

Sensing trouble, Ruth's mother looked out of the door of their second-class cabin and asked a steward[12]

330 what had happened. He told her that nothing was the matter, so Mrs. Becker went back to bed. But as she lay there, she couldn't help feeling that something was very wrong.

Jack heard running feet and voices in the hallway outside his first-class cabin. "I hurried into my heavy overcoat and drew on my slippers. All excited, but not thinking anything serious had occurred, I called in to my father and mother that I was going up on deck to see the fun."

340 On deck, Jack watched some third-class passengers playing with the ice that had landed on the forward deck as the iceberg had brushed by. Some people were throwing chunks at each other, while a few skidded about playing football with pieces of ice.

Down in the very bottom of the ship, things were very different. When the iceberg had struck, there had been a noise like a big gun going off in one of the boiler rooms. A couple of stokers[13] had been

---

12. **steward:** a worker on a ship who attends to the needs of the passengers.

13. **stokers:** workers who tended the boilers that powered steamships.

immediately hit by a jet of icy water. The noise and the
350 shock of cold water had sent them running for safety.

Twenty minutes after the crash, things looked very
bad indeed to Captain Smith. He and the ship's
builder, Thomas Andrews, had made a rapid tour
below decks to inspect the damage. The mail room
was filling up with water, and sacks of mail were
floating about. Water was also pouring into some of
the forward holds and two of the boiler rooms.

Captain Smith knew that the *Titanic*'s hull was
divided into a number of watertight compartments.
360 She had been designed so that she could still float if
only the first four compartments were flooded, but not
any more than that. But water was pouring into the
first five compartments. And when the water filled
them, it would spill over into the next compartment.
One by one all the remaining compartments would
flood, and the ship would eventually sink. Andrews
told the captain that the ship could last an hour, an
hour and a half at the most.

Harold Bride had just awakened in the radio room
370 when Captain Smith stuck his head in the door. "Send
the call for assistance," he ordered.

"What call should I send?" Phillips asked.

"The regulation international call for help. Just
that." Then the captain was gone. Phillips began to
send the Morse code "CQD" distress call, flashing
away and joking as he did it. After all, they knew the
ship was unsinkable.

Five minutes later, the captain was back. "What are
you sending?" he asked.

380 "CQD," Phillips answered. Then Bride cut in and
suggested that they try the new SOS signal that was
just coming into use. They began to send out the new
international call for help—it was one of the first SOS
calls ever sent out from a ship in distress.

REREAD the boxed passage. Why was the *Titanic* doomed to sink? (Cause and Effect)

MORE ABOUT . . .

MORSE CODE Morse code uses patterns of electrical pulses to stand for letters, numbers, and punctuation marks. In the early 1900s, many radio operators used the letters *CQD* to call for help. By 1908 a new distress signal, *SOS*, had been adopted. *SOS* is easy to remember in Morse code. It is made up of three short pulses ("dots"), three long pulses ("dashes"), and three more short pulses. It would be written this way:

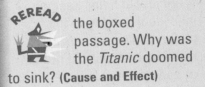

WHAT DOES IT MEAN?

A *life jacket* helps keep an individual floating in the water, while *lifeboats* are small boats that hold groups of people.

Pause & Reflect

1. What did Captain Smith do to respond to the accident? Cross out the *wrong* answer. (Clarify)

   got the lifeboats ready

   calmed Ruth's mother

   inspected the damage

   ordered distress rockets fired

2. Why did the people in the bottom of the ship react differently to the collision than passengers on other decks? (Cause and Effect)

Ruth and her family had stayed in their bunks for a good fifteen minutes or so after the room steward had told them nothing was wrong. But Ruth's mother couldn't stop worrying as she heard the sound of running feet and shouting voices in the hallway.
390 Poking her head out of the cabin, she found a steward and asked what the matter was.

"Put on your things and come at once," said the steward.

"Do we have time to dress?" she asked.

"No, madam. You have time for nothing. Put on your life jackets and come up to the top deck."

Ruth helped her mother dress the children quickly. But they only had time to throw their coats over their nightgowns and put on their shoes and stockings. In
400 their rush, they forgot to put on their life jackets.

Just after midnight, Captain Smith ordered the lifeboats uncovered. The ship's squash court, which was thirty-two feet above the keel, was now completely flooded. Jack Thayer and his father came into the first-class lounge to try to find out exactly what the matter was. When Thomas Andrews, the ship's builder, passed by, Mr. Thayer asked him what was going on. He replied in a low voice that the ship had not much more than an hour to live. Jack and his
410 father couldn't believe their ears.

From the bridge of the *Titanic,* a ship's lights were observed not far away, possibly the *Californian*'s. Captain Smith then ordered white distress rockets fired to get the attention of the nearby ship. They burst high in the air with a loud boom and a shower of stars. But the rockets made no difference. The mystery ship in the distance never answered.

Pause & Reflect

FOCUS

Read to find out more about what the captain and his crew do as the ship continues to sink.

MARK IT UP > As you read, circle details that help you visualize the lowering of the lifeboats.

In the radio room, Bride and Phillips now knew how
420 serious the accident was and were <u>feverishly</u> sending out calls for help. A number of ships heard and responded to their calls, but most were too far away to come to the rescue in time. The closest ship they had been able to reach was the *Carpathia,* about fifty-eight miles away. Immediately, the *Carpathia* reported that she was racing full steam to
430 the rescue. But could she get there in time?

Not far away, the radio operator of the *Californian* had gone to bed for the night and turned off his radio. Several officers and crewmen on the deck of the *Californian* saw rockets in the distance and reported them to their captain. The captain told them to try to contact the ship with a Morse lamp. But they received no answer to their flashed calls. No one thought to wake up the radio operator.

On board the *Titanic,* almost an hour after the
440 crash, most of the passengers still did not realize the seriousness of the situation. But Captain Smith was a very worried man. He knew that the *Titanic* only carried lifeboats for barely half the estimated twenty-two hundred people on board. He would have to make sure his officers kept order to avoid any panic among the passengers. At 12:30 Captain Smith gave the orders to start loading the lifeboats—women and children first. Even though the *Titanic* was by now quite noticeably down at the bow and <u>listing</u> slightly
450 to one side, many passengers still didn't want to leave

WORDS TO KNOW
feverishly (fē'vər-ĭsh-lē) *adv.* in a highly emotional or nervous way
list (lĭst) *v.* to tilt; lean

As the article continues . . .

- No nearby ships respond to the *Titanic*'s distress signals.
- Captain Smith knows there are not enough lifeboats to save everyone.
- Many third-class passengers are trapped below decks.

 REREAD the boxed passage. Why didn't the *Californian* hear the *Titanic*'s calls for help? **(Clarify)**

 READING CHECK Why was Captain Smith "a very worried man"?

English Learner Support

Culture

Women and Children First
Men were supposed to be brave and strong. They were expected to take care of women and children, even if it meant sacrificing their own lives.

Exploring the *Titanic* **291**

the huge, brightly lit ship. The ship's band added to a kind of party feeling as the musicians played lively tunes.

About 12:45 the first lifeboat was lowered. It could carry sixty-five people, but left with only twenty-eight aboard. Indeed, many of the first boats to leave were half empty. Ruth Becker noticed that there was no panic among the crowds of passengers milling about on the decks. "Everything was calm, everybody was orderly." But the night air was now biting cold. Ruth's
460 mother told her to go back to their cabin to get some blankets. Ruth hurried down to the cabin and came back with several blankets in her arms. The Beckers walked toward one of the lifeboats, and a sailor picked up Ruth's brother and sister and placed them in the boat.

"That's all for this boat," he called out. "Lower away!"

"Please, those are my children!" cried Ruth's mother. "Let me go with them!"
470 The sailor allowed Mrs. Becker to step into the lifeboat with her two children. She then called back to Ruth to get into another lifeboat. Ruth went to the next boat and asked the officer if she could get in. He said, "Sure," picked her up, and dumped her in.

Boat No. 13 was so crowded that Ruth had to stand up. Foot by foot it was lowered down the steep side of the massive ship. The new pulleys shrieked as the ropes passed through them, creaking under the weight of the boat and its load of sixty-four people. After
480 landing in the water, Ruth's lifeboat began to drift. Suddenly Ruth saw another lifeboat coming down right on top of them! Fearing for their lives, the men in charge of her boat shouted, "Stop!" to the sailors

up on the deck. But the noise was so great that nobody noticed. The second lifeboat kept coming down, so close that they could actually touch the bottom of it. All of a sudden, one of the men in Ruth's boat jumped up, pulled out a knife, and cut them free of their lowering ropes. Ruth's boat pushed away from 490 the *Titanic* just as boat No. 15 hit the water inches away from them.

Below, in the third-class decks of the ship, there was much more confusion and alarm. Most of these passengers had not yet been able to get above decks. Some of those who did finally make it out had to break down the barriers between third and first class.

By 1:30 the bow was well down, and people were beginning to notice the slant of the decks. In the radio room, Bride and Phillips were still desperately sending 500 out calls for help: "We are sinking fast . . . women and children in boats. We cannot last much longer." The radio signal gradually got weaker and weaker as the ship's power faded out. Out on the decks, most passengers now began to move toward the stern area, which was slowly lifting out of the water.

Pause & Reflect

FOCUS

Read to learn about the *Titanic*'s final moments.

‖ MARK IT UP ⟩ As you read, circle details that help you imagine the horror.

By 2:05 there were still over 1,500 people left on the sinking ship. All the lifeboats were now away, and a strange 510 stillness took hold. People stood quietly on the upper decks, bunching together for

Pause & Reflect

1. For the first hour after the collision, what was the atmosphere on deck like? Check the *false* statement. (Clarify)
   - ❏ The passengers panicked.
   - ❏ The crew tried to maintain calm.
   - ❏ The passengers didn't realize the seriousness of the situation.
   - ❏ Captain Smith was very worried.

2. What might have happened if the man in Ruth's boat had not cut the lowering ropes? (Draw Conclusions)

⟩ **As the article ends . . .**

• Survivors describe the horrible events just before and after the *Titanic* sank.

WHAT DOES IT MEAN? *Now it's every man for himself* means "You no longer have to take care of the passengers; you must look after your own safety."

English Learner Support

Vocabulary

Idioms *Let's clear out* means "Let's leave here immediately!"

READING CHECK Why did people jump overboard into the icy water?

warmth, trying to keep away from the side of the tilting ship.

Captain Smith now made his way to the radio room and told Harold Bride and Jack Phillips to save themselves. "Men, you have done your full duty," he told them. "You can do no more. Abandon your cabin. Now it's every man for himself." Phillips kept
520 working the radio, hanging on until the very last moment. Suddenly Bride heard water gurgling up the deck outside the radio room. Phillips heard it, too, and cried, "Come on, let's clear out."

Near the stern, Father Thomas Byles had heard confession and given absolution[14] to over one hundred passengers. Playing to the very end, the members of the ship's brave band finally had to put down their instruments and try to save themselves. In desperation, some of the passengers and crew began to jump over-
530 board as the water crept up the slant of the deck.

Jack Thayer stood with his friend Milton Long at the railing to keep away from the crowds. He had become separated from his father in the confusion on deck. Now Jack and his friend heard muffled thuds and explosions deep within the ship. Suddenly the *Titanic* began to slide into the water. The water rushed up at them. Thayer and Long quickly said goodbye and good luck to each other. Then they both jumped.

540 As he hit the water, Jack Thayer was sucked down. "The cold was terrific. The shock of the water took the breath out of my lungs. Down and down I went, spinning in all directions." When he finally surfaced, gasping for air and numbed by the water, the ship was about forty feet away from him. His friend Milton

---

14. **heard confession . . . absolution:** Father Byles has conducted a Roman Catholic religious practice in which a priest listens to people confess their sins and then declares them forgiven.

Long was nowhere to be seen. Jack would never see him again.

Jack Thayer was lucky. As he struggled in the water, his hand came to rest on an overturned lifeboat. He
550 grabbed hold and hung on, barely managing to pull himself up out of the water. Harold Bride had been washed overboard and now also clung to this same boat.

Both Jack and Harold witnessed the mighty ship's last desperate moments. "We could see groups of . . . people aboard, clinging in clusters or bunches, like swarming bees; only to fall in masses, pairs, or singly, as the great part of the ship . . . rose into the sky. . . ." said Thayer. "I looked upwards—we were right under
560 the three enormous propellers. For an instant, I thought they were sure to come right down on top of us. Then . . . she slid quietly away from us into the sea."

Out in the safety of her lifeboat, Ruth Becker also witnessed the end of the *Titanic*. "I could look back and see this ship, and the decks were just lined with people looking over. Finally, as the *Titanic* sank faster, the lights died out. You could just see the stern remaining in an upright position for a couple of
570 minutes. Then . . . it disappeared."

Then, as Ruth recalled, "there fell upon the ear the most terrible noise that human beings ever listened to—the cries of hundreds of people struggling in the icy cold water, crying for help with a cry we knew could not be answered." In Thayer's words, they became "a long continuous wailing chant." Before long this ghastly wailing stopped, as the freezing water took its toll.

 REREAD the boxed passage on this page. How might you feel if you were in the position of Jack or Harold? **(Connect)**

MORE ABOUT . . .

HYPOTHERMIA People cannot survive in freezing water for very long. When a person's body temperature falls to 95°F or below, a condition called hypothermia occurs. The body's functions slow down, and the person will eventually lose consciousness and die from organ failure.

WORDS TO KNOW
toll (tōl) *n.* the amount of loss or destruction caused by a disaster

Pause & Reflect

1. Why did the captain say, "Now it's every man for himself"?

Cause

↓

Effect

The captain gave his final command.

2. What was your reaction when you finished the selection? **(Connect)**

_____

_____

_____

_____

_____

Do you have any **questions** that are unanswered by the article? Work with a partner to brainstorm a list of questions that begin with *why, how, where, when, who,* and *what.*

580 Jack Thayer and Harold Bride and a number of other survivors clung to their overturned lifeboat, inches away from an icy death in the North Atlantic. Numb from the cold and not daring to move in case the boat sank under their weight, they prayed and waited for help. Then, as the first light of dawn crept on the horizon, a rocket was seen in the distance. The *Carpathia* had come to their rescue. ❖

Pause & Reflect

MARK IT UP ⟩ Use the following chart to complete the lists you began on page 276. Write what you knew, what you wanted to know, and what you learned about the *Titanic*.

What I Know about the *Titanic*
What I Want to Know
What I Learned

Active Reading SkillBuilder

Fact and Opinion

Statements of **fact** can be proved to be true. **Opinions**—personal feelings or beliefs—cannot. However, opinions supported by facts carry more weight than unsupported opinions. Note on this chart examples of fact and of opinion from the selection.

Fact	Opinion
The <u>Titanic</u> was the biggest ship in the world.	"The dining room was beautiful . . ."

Literary Analysis SkillBuilder

Setting: Time

When thinking about the **setting** of a work, keep in mind the actual **time** period (*e.g.,* time of day, year) in which it takes place. Also think about the particular historical period, with its social structure, beliefs, and customs. The *Titanic* was built at a time when some things were changing dramatically while others were staying the same. Use this chart to note what was new and what was old about the *Titanic*.

New	Old
the size of the ship	the division into passengers and crew

Words to Know SkillBuilder

Words to Know

accommodations	eerie	indefinitely	novelty	toll
dazzled	feverishly	list	prophecy	tribute

A. Fill in each set of blanks with the correct Word to Know. The boxed letters will spell out a quality that the *Titanic* was famous for before it sailed.

1. This is how you do something when you are frantically trying to get it done.

   __ __ __ __ __ __ ☐ __ __

2. This is how you might feel when a lot of fireworks go off, especially if they're really great.

   __ ☐ __ __ __ __ __

3. This is how long something goes on when it goes on *and on and on.*

   __ __ __ ☐ __ __ __ __ __ __ __

4. This is something that's unusual but not *just* unusual. It's usually kind of creepy, too.

   __ ☐ __ __ __

5. This is what a pair of glasses would be if they had little wipers for when it rained.

   __ __ __ __ __ ☐☐ __ __

Quality of the *Titanic*: _____

B. For each phrase in the first column, find the phrase in the second column that is closest in meaning. Write the letter of that phrase on the line.

_____ 1. a terrible toll   A. prevent a prediction

_____ 2. acres of accommodations B. a large loss

_____ 3. a tremendous tribute   C. tilting tots

_____ 4. prohibit a prophecy   D. lots and lots of lodging

_____ 5. little lads who list   E. a huge honor

Before You Read

Connect to Your Life

List five words you associate with the concept of freedom. Then write a sentence using each word.

1. Responsibility _____

2. [ ] _____

3. [ ] _____

4. [ ] _____

5. [ ] _____

Key to the Memoir

WHAT YOU NEED TO KNOW Nelson Mandela was the first black South African to become president of his country. South Africa had been ruled for many years under a policy of racial segregation called apartheid (ə-pärt'hīt'). Apartheid meant that by law black South Africans had to live separately from whites. Black South Africans were told where to live, work, go to school, shop, and many other things.

Nelson Mandela and the organization which he headed, the African National Congress, opposed apartheid. Mandela spent 27 years in prison as punishment. When South Africa's first free elections took place in 1994, Mandela was elected president by a majority of South Africans.

Freedom

to

Walk

from

Long

by Nelson Mandela

PREVIEW You are about to read part of the memoir, or autobiography, of Nelson Mandela. Mandela sums up the lessons he learned during the long struggle against apartheid in South Africa.

As the memoir begins . . .

• Nelson Mandela explains how apartheid produced heroes in South Africa.

• During difficult times, his ideas about love gave him hope and courage.

WHAT DOES IT MEAN? In this sentence, *oppression* means "governing in an unjust way" or "taking away people's freedom."

READING TIP In this memoir, you will read some unfamiliar names of people and places. Don't worry about them. Instead, look for the author's main ideas. If you read a word that you want to look up later, write it in the margin.

READING CHECK How does Mandela define courage?

WHAT DOES IT MEAN? *This great transformation* means the end of apartheid in South Africa.

FOCUS

In this part Mandela describes the effects of apartheid and the courage of those who fought against it.

The policy of apartheid created a deep and lasting wound in my country and my people. All of us will spend many years, if not generations, recovering from that profound hurt. But the decades of oppression and brutality had another, unintended effect, and that was that it produced the Oliver Tambos, the Walter
10 Sisulus, the Chief Luthulis, the Yusuf Dadoos, the Bram Fischers, the Robert Sobukwes[1] of our time—men of such extraordinary courage, wisdom, and generosity that their like may never be known again. Perhaps it requires such depth of oppression to create such heights of character. My country is rich in the minerals and gems that lie beneath its soil, but I have always known that its greatest wealth is its people, finer and truer than the purest diamonds.

It is from these comrades in the struggle that I learned
20 the meaning of courage. Time and again, I have seen men and women risk and give their lives for an idea. I have seen men stand up to attacks and torture without breaking, showing a strength and <u>resiliency</u> that defies the imagination. I learned that courage was not the absence of fear, but the triumph over it. I felt fear myself more times than I can remember, but I hid it behind a mask of boldness. The brave man is not he who does not feel afraid, but he who conquers that fear.

I never lost hope that this great transformation[2]
30 would occur. Not only because of the great heroes I have already cited, but because of the courage of the

---

1. **Oliver Tambos . . . Robert Sobukwes:** South Africans who, like Mandela, had fought against apartheid.

2. **transformation:** an important change.

WORDS TO KNOW
    resiliency (rĭ-zĭl'yən-sē) *n.* the ability to recover quickly from illness, change, or misfortune

ordinary men and women of my country. I always knew that deep down in every human heart, there is mercy and generosity. No one is born hating another person because of the color of his skin, or his background, or his religion. People must learn to hate, and if they can learn to hate, they can be taught to love, for love comes more naturally to the human heart than its opposite. Even in the grimmest times in prison, when 40 my comrades and I were pushed to our limits, I would see a glimmer of humanity in one of the guards, perhaps just for a second, but it was enough to reassure me and keep me going. Man's goodness is a flame that can be hidden but never extinguished.

Pause & Reflect

FOCUS

The struggle against apartheid forced Mandela to make a difficult choice. Read on to learn about the choice he made as his desire for freedom grew.

We took up the struggle with our eyes wide open, under no illusion that the path would be an easy one. As a young man, when I 50 joined the African National Congress,[3] I saw the price my comrades paid for their beliefs, and it was high. For myself, I have never regretted my commitment to the struggle, and I was always prepared to face the hardships that affected me personally. But my family paid a terrible price, perhaps too dear a price for my commitment.

In life, every man has twin obligations[4]—obligations to his family, to his parents, to his wife and children; 60 and he has an obligation to his people, his community,

---

3. **African National Congress:** the political party opposed to apartheid that Mandela helped found.

4. **obligations:** duties.

Pause & Reflect

1. What were some of the effects of apartheid on South Africa? (**Main Idea**)

2. What does Mandela believe about love? Cross out the wrong answer below. (**Clarify**)

   Love comes naturally to people.

   Love is weaker than hate.

   Love can be learned.

   Love can never be completely destroyed.

As the memoir continues . . .

- Mandela discusses what a man owes both to his family and to his people.
- He evaluates how well he fulfilled his duties.
- He explains how his ideas about freedom changed over time.

WHAT DOES IT MEAN? Here, *dear* means "expensive."

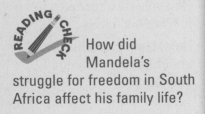

How did Mandela's struggle for freedom in South Africa affect his family life?

his country. In a civil and humane society, each man is able to fulfill those obligations according to his own inclinations and abilities. But in a country like South Africa, it was almost impossible for a man of my birth and color to fulfill both of those obligations. In South Africa, a man of color who attempted to live as a human being was punished and isolated. In South Africa, a man who tried to fulfill his duty to his people was inevitably ripped from his family and his home

70 and was forced to live a life apart, a twilight existence of secrecy and rebellion. I did not in the beginning choose to place my people above my family, but in attempting to serve my people, I found that I was prevented from fulfilling my obligations as a son, a brother, a father, and a husband.

In that way, my commitment to my people, to the millions of South Africans I would never know or meet, was at the expense of the people I knew best and loved most. It was as simple and yet as <u>incomprehensible</u> as the

80 moment a small child asks her father, "Why can you not be with us?" And the father must utter the terrible words: "There are other children like you, a great many of them . . ." and then one's voice trails off.

I was not born with a hunger to be free. I was born free—free in every way that I could know. Free to run in the fields near my mother's hut, free to swim in the clear stream that ran through my village, free to roast mealies⁵ under the stars and ride the broad backs of slow-moving bulls.⁶ As long as I obeyed my father and

90 abided by the customs of my tribe, I was not troubled by the laws of man or God.

It was only when I began to learn that my boyhood

---

5. **mealies:** *South African,* corn.

6. **bulls:** domesticated water buffalo, imported from South Asia, used in South Africa for farm work such as plowing.

WORDS TO KNOW

incomprehensible (ĭn´kŏm-prĭ-hĕn´sə-bəl) *adj.* not understandable

freedom was an illusion, when I discovered as a young man that my freedom had already been taken from me, that I began to hunger for it. At first, as a student, I wanted freedom only for myself, the <u>transitory</u> freedoms of being able to stay out at night, read what I pleased, and go where I chose. Later, as a young man in Johannesburg, I yearned for the basic and

100 honorable freedoms of achieving my potential, of earning my keep, of marrying and having a family— the freedom not to be obstructed in a lawful life.

But then I slowly saw that not only was I not free, but my brothers and sisters were not free. I saw that it was not just my freedom that was <u>curtailed</u>, but the freedom of everyone who looked like I did. That is when I joined the African National Congress, and that is when the hunger for my own freedom became the greater hunger for the freedom of my people. It was

110 this desire for the freedom of my people to live their lives with dignity and self-respect that animated[7] my life, that transformed a frightened young man into a bold one, that drove a law-abiding attorney to become a criminal, that turned a family-loving husband into a man without a home, that forced a life-loving man to live like a monk. I am no more virtuous or self-sacrificing than the next man, but I found that I could not even enjoy the poor and limited freedoms I was allowed when I knew my people were not free.

120 Freedom is <u>indivisible</u>; the chains on any one of my people were the chains on all of them, the chains on all of my people were the chains on me.

Pause & Reflect

---

7. **animated:** gave life to; inspired to action.

WORDS TO KNOW
transitory (trăn′sĭ-tôr′ē) *adj.* lasting only a short time; temporary
curtail (kər-tāl′) *v.* to cut short
indivisible (ĭn′də-vĭz′ə-bəl) *adj.* incapable of being divided

Pause & Reflect

1. **MARK IT UP** > Circle the sentences that express Mandela's ideas about freedom. What did he think as a boy, as a student, as a young man, and later? **(Main Idea)**

2. How did Mandela change after joining the African National Congress? Check three answers below. **(Clarify)**
   ❑ He became bold.
   ❑ He became homeless.
   ❑ He became law-abiding.
   ❑ He lived like a monk.

3. the boxed sentence. Restate the main idea in your own words. **(Paraphrase)**

As the memoir ends . . .

- Mandela explains why the oppressor, as well as the oppressed, needs to be freed.
- He tells the secret he learned about the journey to freedom.

English Learner Support

Vocabulary

Word Endings A word's ending can change its meaning. An *oppressor* is someone who oppresses. The *oppressed* are people who are victims of oppression.

Pause & Reflect

According to Mandela, why is the oppressor not free? Check the correct answer. **(Clarify)**

❏ He loses his humanity.

❏ Someone else takes his freedom away.

❏ He cannot leave prison.

CHALLENGE

In this memoir, Mandela sometimes uses **repetition,** or states something more than once. Mark examples of this technique in one or more passages. What effect does the repetition have on you as a reader? **(Analyze)**

FOCUS

Mandela explains how under apartheid no one can be free.

It was during those long and lonely years that my hunger for the freedom of my own people became a hunger for the freedom of all people, white and black. I knew as well as I knew anything that the oppressor must be liberated just as surely as the oppressed. A man who
130 takes away another man's freedom is a prisoner of hatred, he is locked behind the bars of prejudice and narrow-mindedness. I am not truly free if I am taking away someone else's freedom, just as surely as I am not free when my freedom is taken from me. The oppressed and the oppressor alike are robbed of their humanity.

When I walked out of prison, that was my mission, to liberate the oppressed and the oppressor both. Some say that has now been achieved. But I know that that is not the case. The truth is that we are not yet free;
140 we have merely achieved the freedom to be free, the right not to be oppressed. We have not taken the final step of our journey, but the first step on a longer and even more difficult road. For to be free is not merely to cast off one's chains, but to live in a way that respects and enhances the freedom of others. The true test of our devotion to freedom is just beginning.

I have walked that long road to freedom. I have tried not to falter; I have made missteps along the way. But I have discovered the secret that after climbing a great hill,
150 one only finds that there are many more hills to climb. I have taken a moment here to rest, to steal a view of the glorious vista[8] that surrounds me, to look back on the distance I have come. But I can rest only for a moment, for with freedom come responsibilities, and I dare not linger, for my long walk is not yet ended. ❖

Pause & Reflect

---

8. **vista:** a broad, distant view.

Active Reading SkillBuilder

Main Idea and Details

The **main idea** of a passage is the writer's most important message. It may be stated directly, or may be implied. Choose one paragraph from the selection. Write the main idea and any supporting details on this chart. As an example, here are the main idea and **supporting details** from the second paragraph.

Main idea: Bravery is not fearlessness, but overcoming fear.

Supporting details: I have often seen men risk their lives for an idea.

Men have stood up to attack and torture.

I have felt fear more times than I can remember.

Supporting Details

Main Idea

Literary Analysis SkillBuilder

Memoir

A **memoir** is a form of autobiography in which the person retells key events in his or her life. Use this chart to note significant experiences in Mandela's life and what he learned from them.

Experiences in Mandela's Life	What He Learned from Them
Struggle alongside his comrades against apartheid	Learned the meaning of courage

Follow Up: How did these experiences link Mandela more and more to his countrymen and to all people?

_____

_____

_____

Words to Know SkillBuilder

Words to Know

curtail   incomprehensible   indivisible   resiliency   transitory

A. Complete each analogy with a Word to Know.

1. WONDERFUL : TERRIBLE : : understandable : _____

2. HAPPY : CHEERFUL : : united : _____

3. BUOYANT : BUOYANCY : : resilient : _____

4. LASTING : PASSING : : permanent : _____

5. FIRE : EXTINGUISH : : freedom : _____

B. Using information from the selection, write up a mock interview with Nelson Mandela. Use all **five** Words to Know.

Interviewer:_____

_____

Mandela:_____

_____

Interviewer:_____

_____

Mandela:_____

_____

Interviewer:_____

_____

Mandela:_____

_____

Before You Read

Connect to Your Life

When times are stressful or difficult in your life, who are the people that you think about? List three examples below. One has been done for you.

People I Care About <u>My Parents</u>

_____

_____

_____

Key to the Biography

WHAT YOU NEED TO KNOW Between the 1500s and the 1800s, some 12 million Africans were brought to the Western Hemisphere as slaves. Because conditions were harsh, many tried to escape. In 1850, Congress passed the Fugitive Slave Law in which the United States government claimed the right to rule—or the jurisdiction—over the return of runaway slaves to their masters. Anthony Burns was one such runaway slave. List some things you would like to know about him.

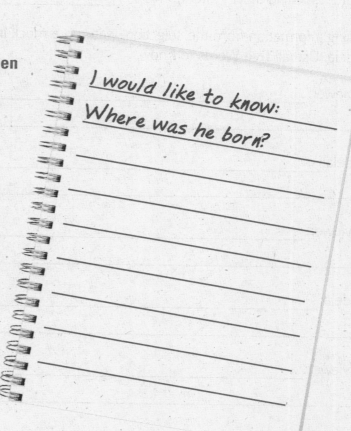

I would like to know:
Where was he born?

FROM
ANTHONY BURNS:
THE DEFEAT AND TRIUMPH OF A FUGITIVE SLAVE

BY VIRGINIA HAMILTON

PREVIEW In May of 1854, Anthony Burns, an escaped slave from Virginia, was captured on the streets of Boston. As more and more people heard about what had happened, the trial of Anthony Burns became the trial of slavery itself. Here are some of the people you will read about who were a part of the trial.

Anthony Burns: Fugitive slave who ran away from Virginia to Boston, Massachusetts

Asa Butman: Deputy U.S. Marshal known for capturing fugitive slaves

Richard Henry Dana: Abolitionist lawyer for Anthony Burns

Leonard Grimes: Pastor of the 12th Baptist Church of Boston, known as the fugitive slave church

Edward Greely Loring: Judge of Probate and Commissioner, presider over trial of Anthony Burns

Robert Morriss: Abolitionist lawyer

Edward G. Parker: Lawyer for Charles Suttle

Theodore Parker: Abolitionist, minister of the 28th Congregational Society, Tremont Temple

Deputy Marshal John H. Riley: One of the Marshal's men guarding Anthony Burns

Thomas Sims: Fugitive slave, captured by Asa Butman in 1851, tried and returned to slavery

Charles F. Suttle (Colonel Suttle): Son of John Suttle, owner of Anthony Burns

John Suttle: Called "Mars John," father of Charles Suttle, owner of child Anthony Burns

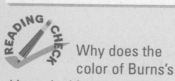

READING CHECK Why does the color of Burns's skin make him wonder if "Mars John" is his father?

WHAT DOES IT MEAN? A *freeman* was an African American who was not a slave.

FOCUS

Meet Anthony Burns, an escaped slave from Virginia. He sits in a Boston jail about to stand trial for his escape.

MARK IT UP Underline details that help you understand what Burns is thinking and feeling while he awaits trial. An example is highlighted.

MAY 25, 1854
The weight of the past and the darkness of its night enclosed Anthony until slowly, with the growing light of day, he returned to the present.

The windows of the jury room where he was kept under guard were covered
10 with iron bars that seemed to break the day into welts of pain. If he could somehow keep his eyes from those bright stripes, he might keep his suffering at bay. But it was no use.

Here I be! he despaired. Caught, I am, and no longer a man. Father, protect me!

He tried retreating again into the past, but all that would come to him was the time of sadness in Mamaw's cabin. With him these many years was the
20 same question, born out of that night. "Who am I?" For the thousandth time he asked himself, "Be I the slave owner's own boy or the slave driver's son? He Mars John's or Big Walker's?"

Again, he lifted his good hand, as he had so many times before. Held it close to his eyes to see it better. There was no denying his skin was light brown. Big Walker had been a dark man, his mamaw a very black woman.

It had been whispered about the plantation that Big
30 Walker Burns was once a freeman. That he had been tricked, caught, and brought down South. But Anthony never knew for certain if this was true, nor did any other of Mars John's black folks. Big Walker never said anything about it directly.

What matter any of it now? Anthony thought. Here I be, like a starved dog in his pen.

Anthony's stomach ached him, he was so hungry. He hadn't eaten since sometime in the dayclean before this. The room stank from the odor of stale ale and
40 sweat. Anthony felt dizzy, then sick to his stomach from the stench. He would have to have something to eat and soon, or he would faint dead away.

Pause & Reflect

FOCUS

Read to find out Anthony Burns's condition as he is brought into a Boston courtroom.

MARK IT UP As you read, underline details that tell you about his physical and mental pain.

Presently the heavy door to the jury room swung open. A man entered. He went over to Asa Butman. "Get him ready," he said. "We have to take him down now."

He came over to Anthony.
50 "Deputy Marshal Riley," he said, introducing himself. "You are going to court now, Anthony. Go with Asa here. He will see that you fix yourself up a bit."

Anthony did as he was told. In a small room off to the side he washed his face and smoothed his hair. There was no comb or brush for him. He straightened his clothing. He took a tin cup of cold water that Asa offered him, but that was all he was given. When he and Butman came out again, Deputy Riley ordered
60 irons closed around his wrists.

Anthony went numb into himself. He moved down the steps like a sleepwalker. When he entered the room set aside in this state Court House as a Federal

WHAT DOES IT MEAN?

Dayclean is the part of the day just before the sun rises.

Pause & Reflect

Which statement below is *not* true of Anthony Burns? Cross it out. **(Clarify)**

He is in a room with bars on the windows.

He plans his escape.

He prays to God for protection.

He isn't sure who his father is.

As the biography continues . . .

• Burns enters the courtroom.

• His former owner, Colonel Suttle, is in the courtroom, along with many other men who want to return Burns to slavery.

MORE ABOUT . . .

MARSHALS Marshals are officers who make sure that laws are followed. A deputy marshal helps another marshal. Riley and Asa Butman are both deputy marshals.

READING TIP This biography contains the names of many people. If you become confused, refer to the list of characters on page 311. William Brent is Colonel Suttle's agent—he helps Suttle buy and sell slaves.

WHAT DOES IT MEAN? When Colonel Suttle says *Tony,* he is referring to Anthony Burns. His statement is meant to intimidate and frighten Burns.

Pause & Reflect

1. Whom does Burns *not* see in the courtroom? Cross out the answer. **(Monitor)**

Colonel Suttle

Marshal Freeman

his mother

William Brent

2. REREAD the boxed paragraph. How would you describe Anthony's feelings? **(Infer)**

He feels

courtroom, he made no response to seeing Colonel Suttle and William Brent there flanked by men he had never seen before—their lawyers. Also present was the one called Marshal Freeman. Some ten of his men, deputies, were with him.

Anthony took the prisoner's seat across from the judge's bench as he was directed by Asa.

"I'm makin' no promises, Tony," Colonel Suttle said to him calmly as he seated himself, "and I'm makin' no threats."

Anthony heard what Suttle said but could give no answer. He was aware of all that went on around him, but it was hard now for him to keep his mind on any one thing for long. His head felt light. He wanted so much just to lie down. The wrist irons and the chain that connected them grew heavier by the minute. Anthony couldn't find the strength or will to lift a finger even to scratch his nose, which itched him. The itching became a dull aching. It in turn spread into a <u>throbbing</u> loneliness throughout his body. He felt miserably hot in his shoulders and deathly cold in his legs.

Anthony bowed his head. For the rest of the time he sat as if hypnotized.

Pause & Reflect

WORDS TO KNOW
throb (thrŏb) *v.* to beat strongly (as though hurting)

FOCUS

Read to find out why
Anthony Burns's captors
want to keep his trial a
secret.

MARK IT UP As you
read, underline details
that help you to
understand their reasons.

Asa Butman and one of his
men took their seats on either
90 side of Anthony. Also present
and seated was the U.S.
Attorney for the Federal
Government, District of
Massachusetts, Benjamin
Hallett. Hallett was a
politician who believed his
position as U.S. District Attorney gave him the right to
oversee the government's policy of rigidly executing
the Fugitive Slave Act. He agreed with that policy, in
100 fact. He and the other officials present hoped that the
examination would be completed as soon as possible.
There had been no inkling of a fugitive arrest in the
morning papers. Reporters knew nothing yet about
what was going on. Colonel Suttle and Mr. Brent
intended to take the prisoner out of Boston and down
South before the dreaded Boston "radicals"[1] knew
about his capture. Ben Hallett hoped they would, too.
For if the abolitionists[2] found out, they had a hundred
ways in which they might come to Burns's defense.
110 They might try to mob Colonel Suttle or even have
him prosecuted for kidnapping.

The prisoner was definitely the slave Anthony
Burns. He had admitted as much when he had first
faced the Colonel. It was a simple matter, then, of
going through the proceeding according to law.
Colonel Suttle had provided an affidavit[3] of
ownership, and Commissioner Loring had issued a
warrant for Burns's arrest. There would be a hearing
as soon as possible, it was hoped—all strictly

---

1. **Boston "radicals":** citizens of Boston who fought to end slavery.
2. **abolitionists** (ăb′ə-lĭsh′ən-ĭsts): people who wanted slavery to be abolished.
3. **affidavit** (ăf′ĭ-dā′vĭt): a written declaration made under oath before a notary public or other authorized officer.

**As the biography
continues . . .**

• An official from the U.S.
government, Benjamin
Hallett, hopes to make
Burns's trial go quickly.

MORE ABOUT . . .

FUGITIVE SLAVE ACT The
Fugitive Slave Law of 1850
gave the U.S. government
control over returning
runaway slaves to their
owners. The law was
intended to replace state
laws in the North that gave
runaway slaves more rights,
including the right to a lawyer
and a jury trial. In this
selection, people argue about
these laws at Anthony
Burns's trial.

English Learner Support
Culture

U.S. Laws The United
States is a country
governed by laws, or rules
that should apply equally to
every citizen in every
situation. Hallett feels that
what should happen to
Anthony Burns is clear
because there is a law that
explains what must be
done.

WHAT DOES IT MEAN?

A *warrant for Burns's arrest*
is an official paper that says
he can be taken to jail.

Pause & Reflect

Why did Burns's captors want to keep his trial a secret?
(Cause and Effect)

_____

_____

_____

As the biography continues . . .

- Burns's landlord, Coffin Pitts, notices that Burns is missing.

- He seeks help from Reverend Theodore Parker, a well-known abolitionist.

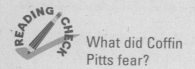

What did Coffin Pitts fear?

_____

120 according to provisions[4] of the Fugitive Slave Act. The Commissioner would then issue the Colonel a certificate allowing him to take the prisoner back to Virginia. But unknown to the Colonel or anyone else in the courtroom, the Boston abolitionists were already informed.

Pause & Reflect

FOCUS

In this section some of the Boston abolitionists learn of Anthony Burns's arrest.

⬚ **MARK IT UP** ▷ As you read, underline the names of the abolitionists.

Coffin Pitts, Anthony's employer and landlord, had been looking for him all the previous night.

130 "Anthony? Anthony!" Coffin Pitts called. When he couldn't find him anywhere in his house, he went out at once in search of him. He looked everywhere in the fugitives' quarter he could think of, but Anthony seemed to have disappeared into thin air. Fearing the worst, he went straight to Exeter Place, the home of the abolitionist Reverend Theodore Parker.

Reverend Parker was the minister of the 28th 140 Congregational Society. He believed, he always said, in an Almighty God and the equality and dignity of all who were God's children. He had gained national attention for the sermons he preached to thousands each Sunday in the enormous music hall called Tremont Temple.

"I know that men urge in argument," Theodore Parker preached, "that the Constitution of the United States is the supreme law of the land, and that it

4. **provisions:** stipulations of the law.

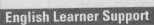

sanctions[5] slavery. There is no supreme law but that
150 made by God; if our laws <u>contradict</u> that, the sooner
they end or the sooner they are broken, why, the better."

Almost every word that Parker uttered made Coffin
Pitts smile in agreement. Yet he couldn't bring himself
to awaken Reverend Parker when he got to his home.
He waited, nodding and dozing, on Theodore Parker's
front steps all night long.

Reverend Parker found him there Thursday morning
when he opened the door to let in the morning air.
"Good Lord, man, come in, come in!" he said, and
160 ushered Deacon Pitts inside. "You must be chilled
through. Here, let us have coffee." Parker proceeded
to the kitchen and prepared coffee while Deacon Pitts
told him of the missing Anthony Burns.

"I am sorry to have to tell you this," said Parker,
"but there are Virginia slavers in town."

"Oh, no!" Deacon Pitts said.

"Yes, I'm afraid so," Parker answered. "Tuesday
morning another colored man, a waiter from the
Revere House, came to see me. Said he had waited on
170 two Virginia slave hunters at breakfast.

"He gave me useful information," Parker continued.
"The slavers are a Colonel Suttle and William Brent.
But the man didn't know which slave it was they were
after. So for two days I asked everyone I could think
of, and nobody knew! Not even Reverend Grimes of
your church—and he dared not question his
congregation, lest they panic and run away north
toward Canada."

Reverend Leonard Grimes had been born in Virginia
180 of free parents who had bought their freedom from a
sympathetic owner. As an adult there he ran a livery

---

5. **sanctions:** permits.

WORDS TO KNOW
contradict (kŏn'trə-dĭkt') *v.* to express the opposite of; to be contrary to

Pause & Reflect

1. Put an "S" beside the characters who are for slavery and an "A" beside those who are against it. **(Clarify)**

__ Coffin Pitts

__ Theodore Parker

__ Colonel Suttle

__ William Brent

__ Leonard Grimes

2. What **questions** do you have at this point in the selection? Write one below.

_____

_____

_____

_____

As the biography continues . . .

• Theodore Parker meets a member of a secret society outside the Court House.

• The two men make plans to help Anthony Burns.

WHAT DOES IT MEAN? Here, *intensive* means "very thorough and complete."

stable, and he used his horse-drawn carriages to transport fugitives farther north under cover of darkness. Once he went deep into Virginia and carried out an entire slave family; three months later he was caught and sent to prison for two years for the crime of aiding runaways. After his release Reverend Grimes moved to Boston, where he continued his work as a minister and friend to all escaped slaves.

190 "The slavers have been among us, hunting, and we had no wind of it for two days!" exclaimed Deacon Pitts. "They caught us unawares."

"Yes, and I daresay the slavers are here after your Anthony," replied Reverend Parker. "Well. You may stay as long as you like, Deacon Pitts, but I must be off. Have yourself another of my brew. Get yourself warmed! I'm going to the Court House."

Pause & Reflect

FOCUS

Reverend Parker goes to the courthouse to help Burns. Read to find out about his attitude toward the Fugitive Slave Act.

With that, Parker hurried out. He had not let Deacon 200 Pitts see it, but he was seething with anger. That some men would even think to enslave other men made his blood boil. That was why, when the Fugitive Slave Act had become law in 1850, he had slapped a revolver down on his desk and left it there as clear warning to all slave hunters.

He knew that for the South, passage of the Fugitive Slave Act was a signal for an intensive manhunt in the 210 North. And it was not long before Southern authorities sent people North to bring back fugitives and to spy on abolitionist groups. In response to this,

Northern blacks and whites took direct action to head off <u>compliance</u> with the law. Theodore Parker found the rising tension and possibility of violence quite unpleasant. He was not a violent man himself. But if forced to, he would without question defend a fugitive with his life.

> As he neared the Court House, Parker happened to
> 220 meet Charles Mayo Ellis, a lawyer and member of the Boston Vigilance Committee. The Vigilance Committee was a large, secret body of abolitionists organized to operate on a moment's notice. Its main purpose was "to secure the fugitives and colored inhabitants of Boston and vicinity from any invasion of their rights."
> Parker quickly explained the situation to Ellis. He then asked Ellis to go to the Court House to observe what was taking place and to keep watch over the fugitive. "I'll go find Richard Dana," Reverend Parker
> 230 said. Richard Henry Dana was another member of the Vigilance Committee, a well-known novelist as well as an attorney.

Pause & Reflect

FOCUS

One of the abolitionists, the Reverend Leonard Grimes, speaks with Burns. Read to find out what he learns about the prisoner's state of mind.

But it was Reverend Leonard Grimes of the 12th Baptist Church who was the first of the Vigilance Committee to see Anthony Burns handcuffed in the prisoner's box. Passing by the

240 Court House, he had noticed unusual activity and had gone inside, only to see Anthony surrounded by armed guards. Alarmed, Reverend Grimes approached Anthony.

WORDS TO KNOW
compliance (kəm-plī'əns) *n.* the act of obeying a request or a command

---

WHAT DOES IT MEAN?
Vigilance means "watching closely at all times." *Vicinity* means "the surrounding area."

Pause & Reflect

1. In what situation would Reverend Parker be willing to use violence? (Infer)

_____

_____

2. [MARK IT UP ⟩] Reread the boxed passage. Circle the names of two members of the Boston Vigilance Committee. (Clarify)

As the biography continues . . .

• Reverend Grimes, another member of the Boston Vigilance Committee, tries to help Anthony Burns.

• Asa Butman and Ben Hallett disagree over whether Grimes should be allowed to stay in the courtroom.

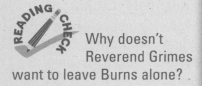

READING CHECK

Why doesn't Reverend Grimes want to leave Burns alone?

WHAT DOES IT MEAN? *Yassir* means "Yes, sir." In this sentence, *give the word* means "tell me to remove Grimes from the courtroom." *Conspirators* are people who work together in an illegal or immoral activity.

Pause & Reflect

Circle the sentence below that best describes how the guards and Asa Butman acted toward Reverend Grimes. **(Summarize)**

They treated him with respect.

They looked at him with suspicion.

They joked with him.

They ignored him.

"My son, are you all right?" he asked. "Please, tell me what I may do for you now."

Anthony made no reply, and looked through space at nothing. Sadness and fear, poor soul! the reverend thought. Anthony appeared to be in a trance, unmindful or unknowing of his situation. I can't leave him alone in his condition, the reverend decided.

250 One of the guards at Anthony's side stood up, menacing the reverend. He put his hand on his gun butt, and Reverend Grimes backed away from the prisoner's dock. He knew it was best to act timidly before such <u>petty</u> officials. Quickly, bowing his head slightly, he took a seat in the rear of the court to wait and see what would happen next.

The slave catchers watched him sit down. So did District Attorney Ben Hallett. Asa Butman whispered to Hallett, "Sir, might I throw that preacher out? He
260 ain't got any business at all bein' in here."

"No, leave him alone," Hallett said. He knew Reverend Grimes to be a respected colored minister, able enough at fund-raising to have raised ten thousand dollars and built himself a church. "Better to have him in here where we can keep an eye on him than outside where he might make trouble," he explained.

"Yassir, as you wish, then," Asa said. "But give the word and he's out as quick as you please." He winked at Hallett as if they were conspirators.

270 Ben Hallett looked pained. To think he must depend on the lowest life, such as Butman, to see that the Federal law was enforced! He turned away in distaste and busied himself with his court papers as Asa hurried back to his post beside Anthony.

Pause & Reflect

WORDS TO KNOW
petty (pĕt'ē) *adj.* of little importance, trivial

FOCUS

In this section you will meet Richard Henry Dana, an abolitionist lawyer, who learns about Anthony Burns's arrest.

MARK IT UP ⟩ As you read, underline details that help you get to know Richard Henry Dana.

MAY 25, 1854

Richard Henry Dana was not in his office when Theodore Parker went there looking for him. He had
280 learned early that morning, as had Reverend Grimes, that a fugitive was about to appear in court before Commissioner Edward G. Loring. While passing the Court House on his way to work, Dana had been approached by a stranger and told the bad news.

"Good God!" he had said. "I need a runner!" He soon found a Negro youth he knew well, one of the
290 many among the growing community of free persons and fugitives who lived in Boston.

Without further delay Dana sent the youth to find members of the Boston Vigilance Committee. For it was the Committee's sworn duty to defend, without fee, all black inhabitants of Boston and vicinity against slavers and bounty hunters.

Dana, one of the Committee's most <u>illustrious</u> members, had helped defend the fugitive slave Thomas Sims in court in 1851. As a young man he had
300 withdrawn from Harvard when measles had weakened his eyesight, and had, in 1834, shipped out to California as a sailor to regain his health. After calling at California's ports loading cargo, his ship sailed around Cape Horn and returned home to Boston in 1835.

Dana's travel experiences cured him physically and also taught him sympathy for the less fortunate. He reentered Harvard and was admitted to the Massachusetts bar in 1840. That same year he published *Two Years Before the Mast*, a novel written

As the biography continues . . .

• News of Anthony Burns's trial reaches more members of the Boston Vigilance Committee.

• Richard Henry Dana prepares to defend Burns.

WHAT DOES IT MEAN?

A *runner* is a person who does errands for another. In this case, Richard Dana needs a runner to take messages to other members of the Boston Vigilance Committee.

English Learner Support
Culture

Harvard Harvard College, the oldest American college, was founded in 1636. Harvard is located in Cambridge, Massachusetts, just north of Boston.

WHAT DOES IT MEAN? The word *bar* here refers to the law profession. The *Massachusetts bar* is the group of lawyers who practice law in that state.

WORDS TO KNOW
illustrious (ĭ-lŭs′trē-əs) *adj.* well-known or distinguished

Political Parties The United States has always had numerous political parties. Free Soil, which lasted a short time, later became part of the Republican party.

Slavery in New States At the time of Burns's trial, the United States was still growing. As settlers moved into western areas, Americans debated whether the new states created in these areas should allow slavery.

Pause & Reflect

Cross out the one phrase that is *not* true about Richard Henry Dana. **(Clarify)**

had been a sailor

had defended two fugitive slaves

opposed slavery in the North

sometimes put aside his beliefs to keep his law clients

310 from diaries he'd kept at sea about "the life of a common sailor as it really is." In it he revealed the awful abuses endured by his fellow seamen at the hands of their superiors. The book made him famous.

When the slavery question moved North with the fugitives, Dana put novel writing aside. His political party was Free Soil, which meant he did not oppose slavery in the South. But he vowed to fight against its spread into the western land tracts, such as Kansas and Nebraska. He lost many of his wealthy, proslavery 320 clients because of this "moderate" view, but he didn't care.

"I am against slavery in the North," he said again and again.

By 1854 Dana no longer put much faith in justice. He had defended two slaves already, Sims and another popularly known as Shadrach, and neither case had ended well. Sims had lost his case and was returned to Georgia, where he died. Shadrach had been "stolen," from the very Court House that now held Anthony 330 Burns, by black abolitionists who managed to get him away to freedom.

Justice and law both had come out scarred and battered, Dana observed grimly at the time. But he believed that gentlemen must behave with justice. And if slave hunters wished to take back a slave, then they would have to proceed at every turn strictly according to the law.

Let them make a single wrong explanation, and I will have them! Richard Dana thought.

340 Now he braced himself and entered the courtroom.

Pause & Reflect

FOCUS

Read on to find out how Richard Henry Dana tries to help Anthony Burns.

Dana swiftly took in the scene, observing the armed guards around the prisoner. So that's Burns, he thought. And as pitiful-looking a fugitive as I've ever seen. Not the man Sims was, surely. This one looks lost witted.[6]

The slave had a small scar on his cheek—a brand of some kind, Dana supposed. One hand, his right, was hideously deformed, and Dana assumed at once that Burns had been awfully mistreated by his owner. He glanced over at the man within the bar—the railing that separated the public from the rest of the courtroom—who he rightly guessed was Colonel Charles Suttle, slave owner of Virginia, surrounded by his agent and lawyers.[7]

So then, Dana thought, they mean to have it all their way, and quickly. But not so fast!

He walked over to Anthony, ignoring the guards and Marshal Freeman. "I'm a lawyer," he said to Anthony. "Richard Dana is my name. Let me help you. And there will be no fee."

Anthony was shocked to hear the learned voice of a white man speaking to him. Who? . . . A buckra[8] again. Seems to care . . . kind voice. But the colonel, he standing up. Glaring so at me.

Colonel Suttle, hearing what Dana had said, had risen to his feet. His face was red with fury.

Anthony dared not answer Richard Dana.

"Anthony," Dana persisted, "there are certain papers from Virginia that an owner must have in order. These might have mistakes. And you might get off if you have a lawyer."

---

6. **lost witted:** completely bewildered.

7. **agent and lawyers:** Colonel Suttle is accompanied by his agent, William Brent, a man who helps him buy and sell slaves, and his lawyers.

8. **buckra:** *old slang,* a white person.

As the biography continues . . .

- Colonel Suttle is enraged when Dana offers to help Burns.
- Burns is afraid to ask for help, which means Dana may not be able to do anything.

WHAT DOES IT MEAN? A *brand* is a symbol or mark burned into the skin. *Deformed* means "having an unnatural shape."

English Learner Support
Vocabulary

Slang *Not so fast* means "Do not act so quickly." The phrase suggests that Dana wants to block the actions of Suttle and his lawyers.

READING CHECK

Why is Colonel Suttle's face red with fury?

English Learner Support
Vocabulary

Idiom In this sentence, *get off* means "avoid being sent back to slavery."

READING TIP Remember that the author not only tells what is happening in the courtroom but also describes Burns's thoughts and feelings. As you read, look for passages that tell what Burns is thinking and feeling. An example is highlighted on this page.

Pause & Reflect

1. What does Dana want to do to help Anthony Burns? **(Clarify)**

_____

_____

_____

2. How does Burns feel while Dana is talking to him? Circle one phrase below. **(Infer)**

angry and resentful

afraid and confused

There was a long silence. Anthony was thinking, Oh, I feel so ashamed. I should have said something to Reverend Grimes first, when Mr. Grimes come to talk to me. Should have said how sorry I was to have got myself captured. How I should've gone to the dedication of Reverend Grimes' church. Then maybe

380 none of this would have happened.

Oh, so many shoulds!

The white man still stood there before him.

"I . . . I . . ." Anthony began.

"Yes?" Dana said quickly.

"I . . . don't know," Anthony finished, murmuring so low that Dana had to come even closer to hear.

Anthony didn't know what to do. He did know that Mars Charles would make his life miserable if it cost him extra time and money to get Anthony back down South.

390 "Anthony? Tell me what you want," Dana said.

"It's of no use," Anthony responded, finally. "They know me. Mars Charles, the Colonel, knows me. I will fare worse if I resist."

Dana straightened up. He reasoned that Anthony was frightened out of his wits by the numbers of hostile white men in the room—a dozen guards, all armed, the Marshal, the District Attorney, his owner, and the others. Clearly, Anthony was threatened by them.

I can't defend him unless he wants me to, Dana kept

400 thinking. The fugitive must ask to be represented. Dana could not otherwise take his case. I need time! he was thinking.

At that instant four other abolitionist lawyers, members of the Vigilance Committee, entered the court: Charles Mayo Ellis, Theodore Parker, Wendell Phillips, and a black lawyer, Robert Morriss.

Pause & Reflect

FOCUS

Judge Edward G. Loring begins the trial of Anthony Burns.

MARK IT UP ⟩ Underline details that help you to understand how the trial begins.

Not two minutes later the Commissioner, Judge Edward Loring, walked briskly in.

410 Immediately, Marshal Freeman spoke loudly, "The court. All rise."

Anthony was made to stand, as everyone in the courtroom got to his feet. After the judge sat down, Anthony and the rest sat.

Judge Loring looked askance at all the guards in the room. He asked Marshal Freeman why there were so many and was told how difficult were the circum-
420 stances surrounding the capture of Burns. Judge Loring then asked whether the defendant was in the prisoner's dock.

"Yes, Your Honor," the Marshal answered.

"Is the claimant[9] here, or his agent?" Loring asked.

"Both of them are here, Judge," Marshal Freeman answered.

"Then we may begin," Judge Loring said.

At that point Richard Dana asked to speak to Loring privately.

430 Loring agreed, and Dana explained how frightened the prisoner, Anthony Burns, was. "He cannot act even in his own behalf," Dana said. "I suggest that you call him up to the bench instead of addressing him in the prisoner's dock. He will then be out of the way of the gaze of the claimant, Colonel Suttle. And so we might know what he wants to do."

"I intend to do that," Judge Loring said. "But now I must proceed."

"Yes, of course," Dana said, "thank you, Your
440 Honor." And he sat down.

---

9. **claimant:** a person who makes a claim in court.

As the biography continues . . .

• Dana speaks to the judge privately.

• The judge explains what Suttle and his lawyers must prove before Burns can be returned to slavery.

WHAT DOES IT MEAN?
Askance means "with disapproval."

MORE ABOUT . . .

LEGAL LANGUAGE

Defendants are people who defend themselves against charges brought against them in a court of law. Often, they stand in a special area, the *prisoner's dock,* where everyone in court can see them. Defendants who are called up to the *bench,* where the judge sits, leave the dock and walk up close to the judge. They can then speak to the judge more privately.

Judge Loring started the proceedings by saying that he was presiding as a U.S. Commissioner, that his duties were executive, and that the hearing was an inquiry.[10] The question before the court, he said, was whether he should award to Charles F. Suttle a certificate authorizing him to take to Virginia the slave Anthony Burns. The claim was that Anthony Burns owed Mr. Suttle service and labor.

"There are three facts that are to be proved," Loring
450 said. "And these are: that Anthony Burns escaped from slavery from the state of Virginia; that Anthony Burns was by the law of Virginia the slave of Charles F. Suttle; that the prisoner is indeed Anthony Burns.

"If counsel for Charles Suttle can prove these facts," the judge continued, "I am empowered to issue a certificate stating the proofs; this will allow the rendition[11] of Anthony Burns."

Anthony listened now and understood. He knew what rendition was. Means me, he thought, taken
460 back home by Mars Charles. Means me, a slave again.

He swallowed hard and felt himself retreat within. But there was no comfort now. His loneliness and fear, his <u>wretched</u> hunger, wouldn't permit him to bring the memory of Mamaw into this harsh place. Neither could he bring forth the child he had been. Where was that young Anthony now? he wondered, for he could not summon the image of the boy he had been.

Pause & Reflect

---

10. **U.S. Commissioner . . . inquiry:** Judge Loring is enforcing the law by acting as a representative of the President of the United States and acting without a jury.

11. **rendition:** return to slavery.

READING CHECK

What three facts must be proved, and what will happen to Anthony Burns if they are proved?

Pause & Reflect

1. What does Richard Henry Dana say to Judge Loring? **(Clarify)**

   Burns is too stupid to get his own lawyer.

   Burns is dangerous.

   Burns should have a better view of Colonel Suttle.

   Burns should be called up to the bench.

2. What do you think Anthony Burns is feeling as he watches and listens to the court proceedings? **(Infer)**

FOCUS

The lawyers for Charles Suttle, Burns's former master, begin their case. Read on to find out how they proceed.

The second counsel for Charles Suttle, Edward G. Parker, now rose, and read from the warrant for Anthony's arrest:

470

"In the name of the President of the United States of America, you are hereby commanded forthwith to apprehend Anthony Burns, a negro man, alleged now to be in your District, charged with being a fugitive from labor, and with having escaped from service in the State of Virginia, and have him forthwith before me, Edward G. Loring,

480 *one of the Commissioners of the Circuit Court of the United States, there to answer to the complaint of Charles F. Suttle, of Alexandria, alleging under oath that said Burns, on the twenty-fourth day of March last, and for a long time prior thereto had owed service and labor to him in the State of Virginia and that, while held to service there by said Suttle, the said Burns escaped into the said State of Massachusetts. . . ."*

He next read the record of the Virginia Court as required by the Fugitive Slave Act:

490 *"In Alexandria Circuit Court, May 16, 1854. On the application of Charles F. Suttle, who this day appeared in Court and made satisfactory proof to the Court that Anthony Burns was held to service and labor by him in the State of Virginia, and service and labor are due to him from the said Anthony, and that the said Anthony has escaped. Anthony is a man of dark complexion, about six feet high, with a scar on one of his cheeks, and also a scar on the back of his right hand, and about twenty-three or four years of*

500 *age—it is therefore ordered, in pursuance of an act of Congress, 'An Act respecting Fugitives from Justice and Persons escaping from the Service of their*

As the biography continues . . .

- Suttle's lawyer, Edward G. Parker, reads aloud legal documents.
- An abolitionist lawyer, Charles Mayo Ellis, urges Dana to act quickly.

WHAT DOES IT MEAN?
Counsel is another word for *lawyer.*

WHAT DOES IT MEAN? In legal documents, *said* means "mentioned previously." *Said Burns* means "the same Anthony Burns described earlier in this document."

English Learner Support
Language

Legal Documents The sections in *italic* type on this page are legal documents—official papers relating to the law. Such documents are often difficult to read because they contain words not normally used in speech. The first document is an order from the U.S. government for Burns's arrest. The second is a report from the state of Virginia that describes Burns and says he is a fugitive, or runaway, slave.

masters,' that the matter set forth be entered on the record of this Court."

The abolitionist lawyer Charles Mayo Ellis watched the proceedings closely. When he saw Richard Dana speak privately to Judge Loring, he supposed Dana meant to make himself the lawyer for Anthony Burns. But when this did not seem to be his purpose, Mr. Ellis 510 made his way to Dana's side as quietly as he could.

As Edward Parker went on with the Alexandria Circuit Court record, Ellis spoke urgently to Richard Dana. "Loring is sitting as a *judge*, Richard. You must *do* something. Massachusetts law clearly forbids judges sitting on slave cases.

"There's no jury," Ellis added. "The armed guards sitting illegally in the jury box are plainly petty thieves being used to terrify an already frightened man."

Richard Dana shrugged. "What can I do?" he said. 520 "Anthony Burns would seem to want to go back without trouble to his master. He won't accept my aid."

Pause & Reflect

FOCUS

Theodore Parker pleads with Anthony Burns to accept his help. Read to find out whether Burns agrees.

Reverend Theodore Parker got to his feet. He could stand it no longer. It was clear to him that the poor fugitive was being tried without a lawyer. He marched angrily to the front of the courtroom just as Edward Parker was finishing and before Marshal Freeman could testify.

530 He strode up to the witness box and <u>peered</u> into it. On seeing that Anthony was handcuffed, he glared

WORDS TO KNOW
peer (pîr) *v.* to look intently

indignantly at Judge Loring. Next, he spoke to Anthony.

"I am Theodore Parker," he said. "I am a minister. Surely you want me to help you."

He could see that Anthony was frozen with fear. "Let us give you counsel," Parker said. "Richard Dana there is the best lawyer in Boston. He is on your side! The black man over there is Robert Morriss and a fine
540 lawyer, too. Will you not let us defend you?"

Anthony began to shake all over. Lord, oh, Lord! Tell me what I must do! he thought.

But he couldn't help seeing that Mars Charles Suttle watched him, that Mars Brent watched him. Anthony commenced stammering, "Mars . . . Mars . . . Colonel . . . he know . . . he knows me . . . I shall have to go back. Mars Brent . . . know me."

"But it can do you no harm to make a defense," urged Parker.
550 "I shall have to go back," Anthony said again. "If I must . . . go back, I want ter go back as easy as I can—but—do as you have a mind to."

Theodore Parker strode back to his seat. He was thinking that if Charles Suttle's lawyers put a nervous witness on the stand and the witness made a false statement, they might have a case. He gave a nod to Richard Dana, to say that Dana had the prisoner's permission to defend him.

Colonel Suttle's other lawyer, Seth Thomas, now
560 rose. He was upset that Theodore Parker had interrupted, but he did not show it. He at once put William Brent upon the stand as a witness to prove the identity of the prisoner with the person named in the arrest warrant. Brent gave his testimony confidently.

English Learner Support
Language

Metaphor A metaphor compares two things. When water is frozen, it becomes hard and does not move. *Frozen with fear* means that Burns was so frightened he could not move.

English Learner Support
Vocabulary

Idiom When people are *on your side,* they support your cause and will help you.

 READ ALOUD the boxed passage. Why is Burns afraid to ask for legal help? **(Infer)**

WHAT DOES IT MEAN? The words in blue mean that Theodore Parker is worried that Suttle's lawyers might put Anthony Burns on the stand. Burns is so upset and confused that Suttle's lawyers might be able to trick him into saying something that would send him back to slavery.

WHAT DOES IT MEAN? The word *reciting* suggests that Brent practiced his statement before coming to court.

MORE ABOUT . . .

IMPROPER TESTIMONY

Testimony means the statements people make in a court of law. Under the Fugitive Slave Act, fugitives were not allowed to give testimony. Suttle's lawyers want to get around this rule by having Brent repeat something Burns said.

Pause & Reflect

1. Who watches Burns as Parker talks to him? Circle two. **(Monitor)**

   Colonel Suttle

   William Brent

   Robert Morriss

   Big Walker

2. Why is William Brent put on the stand? **(Clarify)**

He was a merchant from Richmond, Virginia, he said. And he was a close friend of Colonel Suttle.

"Do you know Anthony Burns?" Mr. Thomas asked.

"Yes, I know him well," he said. And he stated that
570 Anthony Burns was the prisoner in the prisoner's box.

"Can you tell us something about Anthony Burns?" Thomas asked.

Brent began speaking as if reciting: "Anthony Burns was owned by the Colonel's mother. Colonel Suttle has owned him for some fourteen years. I paid the Colonel for the services of Anthony Burns in 1846, '47, and '48."

"Good. Now then," the lawyer said, "can you tell me what you know about his escape?"

"In March," said Brent, "Anthony was missing from
580 Richmond. I didn't see him again until last day past, when he spoke to his master."

"Kindly repeat what was said then," said Thomas.

Theodore Parker rose to his feet again. Brent's statements concerning this conversation would be improper testimony. "You've got to defend him now," he told Richard Dana as he stood. "And if you won't, I will!"

Pause & Reflect

FOCUS

Richard Henry Dana steps in to ask for a delay. Read on to find out what Judge Loring decides to do.

Judge Loring struck with his gavel in an effort to quiet 590 Reverend Parker. Before the Marshal and his deputies could think to restrain the pastor, Richard Dana rose to address the court. It was clear to him that the prisoner would have to have his aid at once. Under the Fugitive Slave Act, the testimony of the <u>alleged</u> fugitive could not be admitted as evidence. Despite this, Anthony's testimony was about to be admitted. Dana had to prevent this.

600 He presented himself to Judge Loring as *amicus curiae*, or friend of the court—one who is called in to advise the court. "I urge Your Honor that there be a delay so that the prisoner can decide what would be his best course," he said.

"I oppose this motion, Your Honor," responded Seth Thomas. "The prisoner by his own statement has admitted that he is Charles Suttle's slave. He does not want a lawyer, nor does he want a defense."

"The prisoner is in no condition to determine whether 610 he would have counsel or not!" Dana said heatedly. "He does not know what he is saying. He must be given time to recover himself and to talk with a lawyer."

Over the objections of both of Suttle's lawyers, Judge Loring had Anthony Burns brought before him. Marshal Freeman hurriedly unlocked Anthony's wrist irons before leading him to the judge.

Loring spoke to Anthony in a kindly manner, explaining what the claim against him was. "Anthony, do you wish to make a defense to this claim?" he 620 asked. "If you do, you can have counsel to aid you, and you shall have time to make a defense. You have a right to a defense if you wish for one."

As the biography continues . . .

- Dana ask Judge Loring to give Burns time to decide whether he wants a lawyer.
- Judge Loring speaks privately to Burns before making a decision.

English Learner Support

Vocabulary

Multiple Meanings The author has used two different meanings of the word *admitted. Admitted as evidence* means "allowed as part of an argument in a court of law." When Thomas says that the prisoner has *admitted* he is Suttle's slave, it means that Burns has confessed or said that this is true.

Why is Seth Thomas against the delay?

WORDS TO KNOW
alleged (ə-lĕjd´) *adj.* supposed

Anthony finally dared look around the room slowly. His gaze rested on Richard Dana and then on Robert Morriss, but he made no reply.

Dana thought it was all over then. But Judge Loring said to Anthony reassuringly. "Anthony, do you wish for time to think about this? Do you wish to go away and meet me here tomorrow or next day, and tell me
630 what you will do?"

All in the courtroom watched Anthony. He gave a slight twitching of his deformed hand, but no one knew whether he meant yes or no by the movement. He did not know himself.

I will have to go back, he was thinking. I will be whipped unto an inch of my life. I will die a slave.

Judge Loring looked doubtful, but at last he said to Anthony, "I understand you to say that you would."

Very faintly, Anthony said, "I would."
640 "Then you shall have it," Loring said.

Marshal Freeman whispered to the judge. Judge Loring replied out loud, "No sir, he must have the time necessary."

Again the Marshal whispered. Judge Loring replied sternly, "I can't help that, sir—he shall have the proper time."

The day was Thursday. "You shall have until Saturday morning," Judge Loring told Anthony and his defenders, and struck his (gavel) down.
650 Anthony was taken back to the jury room high up in the court building. There four men, including Deputy Asa Butman, guarded him.

"Tony, boy," Butman said to him, mimicking words spoken by Charles Suttle, "now we here are curious. Did the Colonel just *raise* you up or did he *buy* you from somebody?"

The other guards nodded encouragement. "Come on, lad, you know us here for your friends."

READING CHECK What does Judge Loring mean when he says, "Then you shall have it"? What will Burns have?

MORE ABOUT . . .

(GAVEL) A gavel is a small wooden hammer. A judge strikes a gavel on a block of wood to call for silence, to get people's attention, or to show that some action has been completed.

Anthony knew they thought him a fool. He had
660 figured out that they hoped to get information from
him for Mars Charles and Mars Brent. He knew there
must be a reward for him. Every runaway slave had a
price on his head.

Wonder how much Mars Charles think me worth?

Anthony played dumb; he acted confused, stared off
into space, and told his jailers nothing.

Pause & Reflect

FOCUS

Read on to learn why
many citizens of Boston
supported Anthony Burns.

||| MARK IT UP >> Underline
the details that help you
understand their reasons.

The court had emptied,
and almost at once news
of Anthony's arrest spread
670 throughout Boston. The
concerned public learned
that slave hunters were in
the city, hoping to force
another wretched soul back into bondage.

All sympathetic citizens, and there were thousands,
felt duty bound to disobey the Fugitive Slave Act on
behalf of the captured fugitive in their midst. But there
was another factor that <u>mobilized</u> them: for months
there had been a proposal before Congress that would
680 allow slavery in the Great Plains lands of Kansas and
Nebraska. The two tracts were to be territories within
the Louisiana Purchase, the enormous parcel of land,
stretching from the Gulf of Mexico to Canada, bought
from France in 1803. The Missouri Compromise of
1820 had closed the Louisiana Purchase to slavery
"forever." But people on the proslavery as well as the
antislavery sides had been sending their settlers into

Pause & Reflect

REREAD the boxed
passage. Why is it
smart for Anthony
Burns to "play dumb"? (Draw
Conclusions)

_____

_____

_____

As the biography
continues . . .

• News of Burns's situation
spreads across the country.

• Reverend Parker writes
leaflets to stir the emotions
of all Americans who
oppose slavery.

WHAT DOES IT MEAN?
Wretched means "very
unhappy or unfortunate."

English Learner Support
Language

Prefixes The prefix pro–
means "for." The prefix
anti– means "against."
Therefore, people who
supported slavery were
proslavery; people who
were against it were
antislavery.

WORDS TO KNOW
mobilize (mō′bə-līz′) v. to assemble for a purpose

Kansas and Nebraska to <u>agitate</u> and to be in a position to vote for their sides once the territories were 690 divided into states.

On May 25, 1854, the very same day that Anthony appeared in court, the Kansas-Nebraska Bill passed in the United States Senate. It permitted slavery in states that would be carved from the two territories if it was provided for in the state constitutions. So in effect it repealed[12] the Missouri Compromise. After these victories for slavery, the jailing of a poor fugitive in a Boston court house at the bidding of a slave owner was the very last straw for those against slavery. Thus 700 had the slavocracy[13] rocked the cradle of liberty.

By evening the news that Anthony Burns had escaped from the South only to be captured in the free North moved from town to town and newspaper to newspaper across the country.

KIDNAPPING AGAIN! read the first leaflet out of Boston that told the tale:

A man was stolen Last Night
By the Fugitive Slave Bill Commissioner
He will have His

710 MOCK TRIAL

On Saturday, May 27, in the Kidnapper's Court
Before the Honorable Slave Bill Commissioner
At the Court House in Court Square
SHALL BOSTON STEAL ANOTHER MAN?

Thursday, May 25, 1854

---

12. **repealed:** taken back or reversed.

13. **slavocracy:** the political power of slavery.

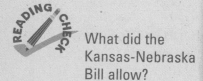

English Learner Support

Vocabulary

Idiom The phrase *last straw* means "the event that finally causes someone to take action."

REREAD the boxed passage. Why did the Kansas-Nebraska Bill affect how antislavery people felt about Anthony Burns and his trial? **(Draw Conclusions)**

WHAT DOES IT MEAN? A *leaflet* is a sheet of paper printed with information about a specific topic. A leaflet is meant to be distributed or handed out.

Written by Reverend Parker, the leaflet was printed by the antislavery press and carried across Massachusetts by volunteers who worked on trains, stagecoaches, and trucks. As it was being distributed, 720 Theodore Parker had time to fire off another leaflet:

SEE TO IT THAT NO FREE CITIZEN OF MASSACHUSETTS IS DRAGGED INTO SLAVERY

Pause & Reflect

English Learner Support
Vocabulary

Idiom In this sentence, *fire off* means "quickly write and publish."

Pause & Reflect

Why do you think Parker included the time and place of the trial in his leaflets? What did he want his readers to do? **(Draw Conclusions)**

FOCUS

Read to find out what his supporters were doing while Anthony Burns was under guard.

Overnight, without his ever knowing it, Anthony Burns became a symbol of freedom. But high up in the Court House he was a tired, miserable prisoner, alone save for his guard of petty criminals.

730 Anthony felt he had no one to turn to. He had no way of knowing that all through the night men watched the three massive doors of his granite prison Court House. It was a different time from 1851, when Thomas Sims was taken. The watchers made certain the authorities knew of their presence. Their message was clear: Anthony Burns was cared for.

Anthony was unaware that abolitionist ministers and lawyers argued fiercely hour upon hour over their next course of action on his behalf. There was no one 740 to inform him that the slavers, Suttle and Brent, were followed everywhere by black men who never looked at them but were always in their sight. Suttle became so terrified that these blacks would try to lynch him,

As the biography ends . . .

- Anthony Burns's many supporters fight for his freedom.
- Suttle and Brent find that they are very unpopular in Boston.
- Judge Loring makes his ruling.

English Learner Support
Vocabulary

Lynch To *lynch* means to kill someone as punishment for a crime without holding a legal trial first. The threat of being lynched can make people afraid to act as they wish.

Pause & Reflect

1. Which statement below is *not* true about Colonel Suttle and William Brent after the first day of Anthony Burns's trial? Cross it out. **(Clarify)**

   They were followed.

   They changed rooms in their hotel.

   They changed their minds and set Anthony free.

   They hired bodyguards.

2. What were your feelings about the ordeal of Anthony Burns after you finished reading the selection? **(Connect)**

CHALLENGE Why do you think Anthony Burns became "a symbol to freedom lovers"? What facts about him or his case raised such strong feelings? Mark passages in the selection that support your views. **(Analyze)**

he and Brent moved to quarters in the Revere House attic and hired bodyguards.

In two short days Anthony had become a symbol to freedom lovers and a devilish token of danger to slavers like Suttle. But the courteous Reverend Leonard Grimes and his deacon, Coffin Pitts, never for an instant confused the man, the fugitive, with his cause. They agreed that Reverend Grimes must try to see Anthony the next morning.

Anthony knew none of this. He wished to shut out the prying questions of guards hoping to trick him. He did what he knew how to do best of all: He retreated within, taking comfort in his unchanging past. ❖

Pause & Reflect

[*When the trial resumed, witnesses came forward to testify for both sides, but finally Judge Loring ruled that Anthony must return to slavery. As he was led to the ship that would take him away, many of Anthony's supporters feared that he was soon to face severe punishment and possibly death. Upon Anthony's arrival in Richmond, Virginia, Colonel Suttle had him imprisoned and then sold him to a man named David McDaniel. Soon, word of Anthony's whereabouts reached Reverend Grimes back in Boston. Grimes convinced McDaniel to sell Anthony to him. McDaniel brought Anthony to Baltimore where Grimes was waiting. Money was exchanged, and Anthony was a free man at last. Anthony Burns went on to attend Oberlin College in Ohio and later became a minister. He served as pastor of the Mount Zion Baptist Church in Saint Catherines, Ontario, Canada where he died on July 27, 1862.*]

Active Reading SkillBuilder

Monitor

When you read, it is important to **monitor** your understanding of the material. You can do that by using all the familiar strategies, such as those shown in the chart. Complete the chart by responding to one event from the story. In the center, a key event has been written. Follow the strategy shown on each connecting line, and write your response in the box.

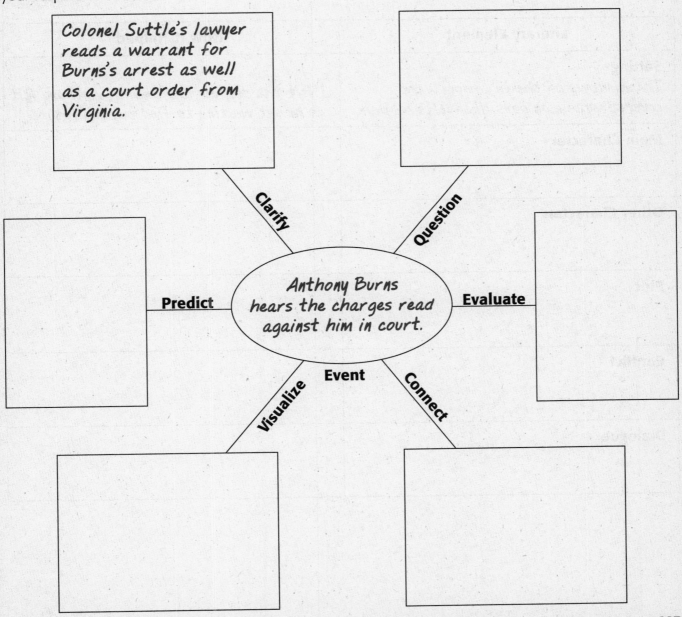

Colonel Suttle's lawyer reads a warrant for Burns's arrest as well as a court order from Virginia.

Clarify

Question

Predict

Evaluate

Anthony Burns hears the charges read against him in court.

Visualize

Event

Connect

Literary Analysis SkillBuilder

Literary Nonfiction

Literary nonfiction—biographies, essays, memoirs—tells the story of a real person and/or event, but in a creative way. The author may imagine some dialogue and minor characters. Other elements of fiction, such as plot and setting also apply. Complete the chart below, listing literary elements from the story. Tell how they helped to bring Anthony Burns's story to life.

Literary Element	How it Helped
Setting The windows of the jury room were covered with iron bars like welts of pain.	I felt the despair and anguish Anthony felt as he sat waiting to find out his future.
Main Character	
Other Characters	
Plot	
Conflict	
Dialogue	

Words to Know SkillBuilder

Words to Know

agitate	compliance	illustrious	peer	throbbing
alleged	contradict	mobilize	petty	wretched

A. Complete each sentence with the Word to Know that best fits the context.

1. Dana tried to _____ Colonel Suttle's lawyers with opposing views.

2. Anthony's chains were so tight that his wrists were _____ with pain.

3. Theodore Parker had to _____ into the witness box for a few seconds to get a good look at Anthony.

4. Reverend Grimes considered Anthony's guards to be _____ officials and refused to be bothered by such people of no importance.

5. Until proven, Anthony's escape was an _____ crime.

B. For each phrase in the first column, find the word in the second column that is closest in meaning. Write the letter of that word in the blank.

___	1. to stare intently	A. wretched
___	2. not for sure, supposed	B. contradict
___	3. to stir up interest for a cause	C. alleged
___	4. beating strongly with pain	D. petty
___	5. of little importance	E. peer
___	6. miserable, horrible	F. compliance
___	7. to assemble for a purpose	G. illustrious
___	8. the act of obeying a request	H. throbbing
___	9. well-known	I. mobilize
___	10. to express the opposite of	J. agitate

Academic and Informational Reading

In this section you'll find strategies to help you read all kinds of informational materials. The examples here range from magazines you read for fun to textbooks and bus schedules. Applying these simple and effective techniques will help you be a successful reader of the many texts you encounter every day.

Reading a Magazine Article

A magazine article is designed to catch and hold your interest. Learning how to recognize the items on a magazine page will help you read even the most complicated articles. Look at the sample magazine article as you read each strategy below.

A Study **visuals**—photos, pictures, maps—together with their **captions**. Visuals help bring the topic to life.

B Read the **title** and other **headings** to get an idea of the article's topic. The title and headings will often try to grab your attention with a question, an exclamation, or a play on words.

C Note sections of text that are set off in some way, such as an **indented paragraph** or a passage in a **larger typeface**. This text often summarizes the article's main subject.

D Pay attention to terms in different typefaces, such as **italics** or **boldface**. Look for definitions or explanations before or after these terms.

E Look for special features, such as **charts** or **sidebars**, that provide additional or related information on the topic.

∥ MARK IT UP ⟩ Use the sample magazine page and the tips above to help you answer the following questions.

1. Circle the photos that represent "talking" animals.

2. Underline the title or heading that uses a play on the word *language*. Circle the title or heading that uses a question to grab your attention.

3. What is the magazine article's main subject? _____

4. Find the text that summarizes the main subject. How is it set off?

   _____

5. Underline the boldface term that refers to the sounds dolphins make. Double-underline the term that means "chemicals."

6. Who or what is the subject of the sidebar? _____

Roar!

Sorry. I don't speak lion.

Say What? Dogs bark, cows moo, horses neigh. You can hear the languages these animals speak. Now find out about some of the more unusual ways creatures communicate.

Dolphins

These water-loving mammals use a variety of ways to talk to each other. For example, dolphins communicate by slapping their flukes, or tail fins, on the water. They also use a series of whistles and clicks to exchange information. These sounds are called **phonations**. Scientists believe that dolphins use different sounds in different situations. When dolphins are in trouble, for instance, they seem to voice a special distress call.

Now You're Speaking My Language

Animals that talk to each other is one thing, but how about animals that can talk to humans? Two gorillas named Koko and Michael can do just that. Since the 1970s, they have been taught to understand spoken English and use sign language to talk to their human trainers. Koko, in particular, has made amazing progress. Today, the female lowland gorilla can understand about 2,000 spoken words and can use more than 500 signs.

Bees

Most animals have a better sense of smell than humans. Some animals even make chemicals called **pheromones** to talk with smells. Bees, for example, have a chemical language of at least 36 pheromones. They use these chemicals to send smell-messages. One smell may warn other bees about trouble. Another may tell where the best flowers are.

Reading a Textbook

The first page of a textbook lesson introduces you to a particular topic. The page also provides important information that will help guide you through the rest of the lesson. Look at the sample textbook page as you read each strategy below.

A Preview the **title** and **subheadings** to find out the lesson's main topic and related subtopics.

B Read the **objectives** that often appear at the top of the page. These objectives establish a purpose for your reading.

C Look for a list of **vocabulary terms.** These words will be identified and defined throughout the lesson.

D Find words set in special type, such as **italics** or **boldface.** Unfamiliar words are often set in italics and defined in the text. Boldface is often used to identify the vocabulary terms in the lesson.

E Study any **graphics,** such as tables or charts, on the page. Graphics provide more detailed information on the topic.

F Examine **visuals,** such as drawings and diagrams, and their **captions.** Visuals can sometimes present information more clearly than words can.

MARK IT UP Use the sample textbook page and the tips above to help you answer the following questions.

1. What is the lesson's main topic? _____

What subtopic is covered on this page? _____

2. Underline the lesson objectives.

3. Circle the vocabulary terms for this lesson.

4. Which vocabulary term is defined on this page? _____

5. Find the prefix *milli* in Table 1-4 and underline it. What does the prefix mean?

_____

6. Circle the caption that explains the picture of the metric ruler. What do the numbers on the ruler measure? _____ What do the lines between each pair of numbers measure? _____

1.4 *Scientific Measurement*

Lesson Objectives

▶ *Identify* the standard units of measurement used in science.

▶ *Name* some tools used to make scientific measurements.

▶ **Activity** *Measure* length, mass, volume, temperature, and time in scientific units.

New Terms

meter	liter
mass	degree Celsius
gram	second
volume	

Like most people, you probably enjoy buying new clothes. But how do you make sure your new clothes fit? You probably look for the right size. Sizes are a special system of measurement used for clothes.

A special system of measurement is used in science too. The system of measurement used by scientists all over the world is the International System of Units, or SI. By using the same system of measurement, scientists all over can share their data, repeat experiments, and compare results.

SI is a decimal system. This means that it is based on the number 10. The system is easy to use because units can be made larger or smaller by moving the decimal point. Prefixes are used to show the size of a unit. When a prefix is added to the beginning of a unit, the unit size changes by a multiple of 10. Look at the prefixes in Table 1-4. Notice that each prefix has its own meaning. For example, *kilo* means 1000 and *deci* means 1/10. What does *hecto* mean? **D**

Table 1-4 Prefixes for Scientific Units

Prefix	Symbol	Meaning	Example
kilo	k	1000	kilogram (kg)
hecto	h	100	hectometer (hm)
deca	da	10	decaliter (daL)
deci	d	1/10	decigram (dg)
centi	c	1/100	centimeter (cm)
milli	m	1/1000	milliliter (mL)
micro	μ	1/1 000 000	micrometer (μm)

Length **D**

The SI unit of length is the **meter.** A doorknob is about 1 meter above the floor. The top of a door is about 2 meters above the floor. You will use a meterstick or metric ruler to measure length.

Look at the metric ruler in Figure 1-7. The numbers on the ruler are centimeters. Find the prefix *centi* in Table 1-4. Centi means 1/100, so a centimeter is 1/100 of a meter. That means there are 100 centimeters in 1 meter.

Figure 1-7 A metric ruler. Each centimeter is divided into 10 millimeters.

Reading Graphs and Charts

Charts and graphs help readers understand key ideas. Line graphs, like the one below, represent data over a period of time. Use these tips and the examples below to help you read charts and graphs more quickly and accurately.

A Read the **title** to help you understand what the graph is about.

B Look to see how the data from the chart and graph relate to each other.

C Read the **headings** to see what kind of information is given.

D Read **across the horizontal lines** and **up the vertical lines** of a graph to get an estimate, or value, of the data.

E Make sure you understand any **symbols or abbreviations,** such as °F (temperature in Fahrenheit).

F Look at the **credit** to see if the information is up-to-date and from a respected source.

The chart and graph below show the average monthly temperatures (°F) for Juneau, Alaska.

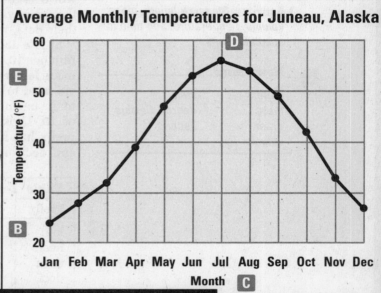

A Average Monthly Temperatures for Juneau, Alaska

ALASKA
★Juneau

Source: National Oceanic and Atmospheric Administration **F**

A Average Monthly Temperatures for Juneau, Alaska											
B Month	JAN	FEB	MAR	APR	MAY	JUN	JUL	AUG	SEP	OCT	NOV	DEC
Temp (°F)	24	28	32	39	47	53	56	54	49	42	33	27

∥ MARK IT UP ⟩ Answer the following questions, using the chart and line graph above.

1. What information does the line graph show?

_____

2. Draw a circle around the point in the line graph that shows the highest temperatures.

3. On the chart, shade the boxes that show the highest and lowest temperatures in Juneau, Alaska.

What is the difference between the two temperatures? _____

Reading a Weather Map

To read a map correctly, you have to identify and understand its elements. Look at the example as you read each strategy in this list.

A Scan the **title** to find the content of the map.

B Study the **key,** or **legend,** to find out what the symbols and colors on the map stand for.

C Look at **geographic labels** to understand specific places on the map.

D Notice the **scale** and **pointer** to determine distance and direction.

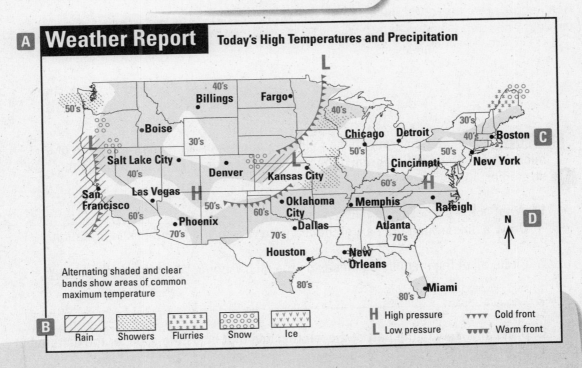

A Weather Report — Today's High Temperatures and Precipitation

Alternating shaded and clear bands show areas of common maximum temperature

B Rain | Showers | Flurries | Snow | Ice

H High pressure ▾▾▾ Cold front
L Low pressure ▾▾▾ Warm front

MARK IT UP → Use the map above to answer the following questions or statements.

1. What is the purpose of this map? _____

2. What does the symbol ⬚ mean?

_____

3. Underline Billings, Detroit, and Memphis on the map.

4. Circle the areas on the map where snow is predicted.

5. Describe the weather predicted for Kansas City. _____

_____

Reading a Diagram

Diagrams combine pictures with a few words to provide a lot of information. Look at the example on the opposite page as you read each of the following strategies.

A Look at the the **title** to get a quick idea of what the diagram is about.

B Study the **image** closely to understand each part of the diagram.

C Look at the **captions** and the **labels** for more information.

MARK IT UP The diagram on the following page shows the different parts of a microscope. Study the diagram, then answer the following questions using the strategies above.

1. What is the purpose of a microscope? _____
   Draw a box around the part of the diagram where you found this information.

2. Circle all of the magnifying lenses on the microscope. What are their names?

   _____

3. Draw an arrow to the part of the microscope that holds the slide, or the material to be magnified.

4. Put an asterisk (*) next to the parts of the microscope that have to do with lighting the slide.

5. Where on the microscope can you adjust your vision? _____

6. Find the high-power objective and the low-power objective. Which of the two gives you a closer view?

   _____

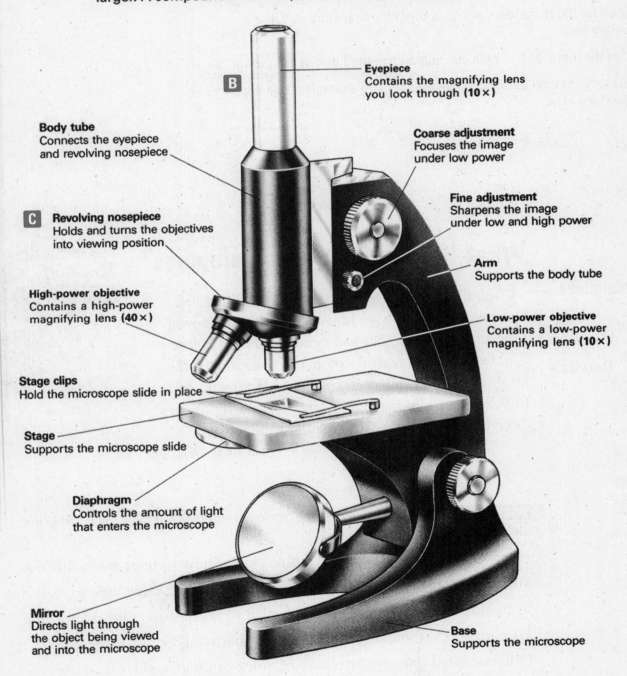

A **COMPOUND MICROSCOPE**
A microscope is a tool used to make tiny objects look larger. A compound microscope has two or more lenses.

B

Eyepiece
Contains the magnifying lens you look through (**10×**)

Body tube
Connects the eyepiece and revolving nosepiece

Coarse adjustment
Focuses the image under low power

Fine adjustment
Sharpens the image under low and high power

C **Revolving nosepiece**
Holds and turns the objectives into viewing position

Arm
Supports the body tube

High-power objective
Contains a high-power magnifying lens (**40×**)

Low-power objective
Contains a low-power magnifying lens (**10×**)

Stage clips
Hold the microscope slide in place

Stage
Supports the microscope slide

Diaphragm
Controls the amount of light that enters the microscope

Mirror
Directs light through the object being viewed and into the microscope

Base
Supports the microscope

Main Idea and Supporting Details

The main idea in a paragraph is its most important point. Details in the paragraph support the main idea. Identifying the main idea will help you understand a paragraph's message without having to memorize all of the details. Use the following strategies to help you identify a paragraph's main idea and supporting details.

- Look for the **main idea,** which is often the first sentence in a paragraph.

- Use the main idea to help you **summarize** the point of the paragraph.

- Identify specific details, including facts and examples, that **support** the main idea.

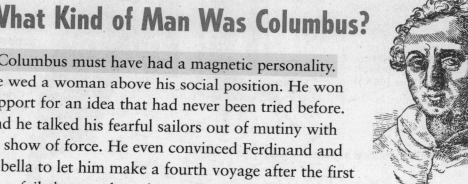

What Kind of Man Was Columbus?

Main idea — Columbus must have had a magnetic personality.

Details — He wed a woman above his social position. He won support for an idea that had never been tried before. And he talked his fearful sailors out of mutiny with no show of force. He even convinced Ferdinand and Isabella to let him make a fourth voyage after the first three failed to produce the wealth of the Indies.

—from *Kids Discover*

MARK IT UP > Read the following paragraph. Underline the main idea. Circle the details that support the main idea.

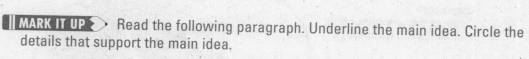

In Columbus's time, doctors did not know how to treat many illnesses. For example, when a terrible plague struck Europe, there was no medicine to fight the disease. So doctors struggled to find a cure. One doctor told his patients that inhaling the smell of a goat would combat the disease. Others treated patients by removing some of their blood. Of course, neither cure worked.

Problem and Solution

Does the proposed solution to a problem make sense? In order to decide, you need to look at each part of the text. Use the following strategies to read the text below.

- Look at the beginning or middle of a paragraph to find the **problem.**
- Look for the **details** that explain the problem.
- Look for the **proposed solution.**
- Identify the **details that support** the proposed solution.
- Think about whether the solution is a good one.

After-School Blues *by Emily Kling*

Statement of problem

For years, the neighbors of Maywood Middle School have complained about students standing around after school. Every day at three o'clock, they say, students hang around, blocking the sidewalks, horsing around in people's front yards, and leaving behind candy wrappers and soda cans.

Explanation of problem

The students, on the other hand, feel they have nowhere else to go. The local parks are used by after-school programs for younger kids. Also, nearby restaurants are too expensive for students.

These students are not bad kids. They just want to spend time with their friends before they go home for the evening. Why not open up the school gym and cafeteria for students after school? The school could provide some basic sports equipment and supervision. Then students would have time to play around and relax, and the neighbors would have nothing to complain about.

MARK IT UP After reading the text above, answer these questions.

1. In the third paragraph, underline the sentence that explains the proposed solution.

2. Circle a detail that supports the solution.

3. Do you think the solution is a good one? Explain your opinion. _____

_____

Sequence

It's important to understand the sequence, or order of events, in texts that you read. That way you know what happens and why. Read the tips below to make sure a sequence is clear to you. Then look at the example on the opposite page.

- Read through the passage and think about what the **main steps,** or stages, are.

- Look for words and phrases that **signal time:** *today, Monday, now, in an hour.*

- Look for words and phrases that **signal order:** *at first, during, then, once.*

MARK IT UP Read the passage on the next page, which describes how a butterfly grows and develops. Use the information from the passage and the tips above to answer the questions.

1. In the first paragraph, underline each of the four main stages of a butterfly's life.

2. Circle words or phrases that signal time or order. The first one is done for you.

3. Use the information from the passage to write captions for each of the steps illustrated below. Make sure to include signal words in your sentences.

The Life Cycle of a Butterfly

1. The egg

_____

_____

4. Butterfly

_____

_____

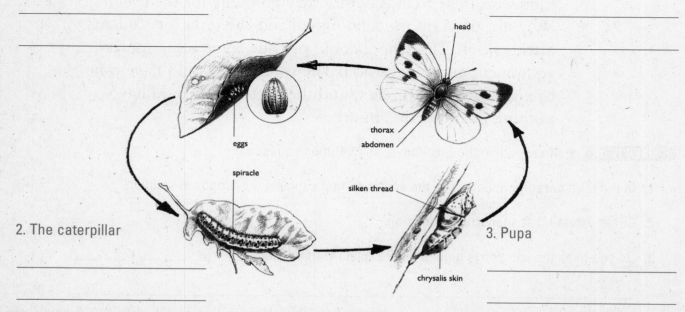

2. The caterpillar

_____

_____

3. Pupa

_____

_____

A Butterfly Gets Its Wings

How does a butterfly get its wings? During its life, the butterfly goes through different growth stages. There are four main stages altogether: 1) the egg, 2) the caterpillar, 3) the pupa, and 4) the adult. The ancient Greeks called this whole process *metamorphosis*, a word we still use today.

At first, the butterfly is a single slimy egg, no larger than a fingertip. (Imagine its baby pictures!) The baby insect grows within the egg until it is ready to hatch. For most types of butterflies, this first stage lasts about 10 days. When the egg cracks open, a caterpillar crawls out.

In the second stage, the caterpillar spends most of its time eating and growing (just like a teenager!). As the caterpillar becomes bigger, it sheds its spiky or fuzzy skin. This process is called *molting*. A caterpillar molts several times during its life. Once the caterpillar has shed its skin for the last time, it becomes a pupa.

In the third stage, the pupa immediately grows a hard shell called a *chrysalis*. Then, inside the chrysalis, the pupa goes through the changes that will make it a butterfly. The pupa's hormones turn its body into wings, antennas, and other butterfly parts. After all the changes are complete, the shell splits open. A butterfly is ready to make its entrance.

Finally, the adult butterfly breaks from the chrysalis. Its body, however, doesn't look quite right. It's all soft and wrinkly. As air and blood are pumped through the butterfly's body, it starts to look more like its usual self. In a short time, the butterfly is ready to try out its new wings. With a few flutters, it's off and away!

Cause and Effect

A cause is an event. An effect is something that happens as a result of that event. Identifying causes and effects helps you understand how events are related. The tips below can help you find causes and effects in any reading.

- Look for an action or event that answers the question "What happened?" This is the **effect**.

- Look for an action or event that answers the question "Why did it happen?" This is the **cause**.

- Identify words that **signal** causes and effects, such as *because, as a result, consequently, led to,* and *since*.

‖ MARK IT UP ▷ Read the cause-and-effect passage on the next page. Then answer the following questions. Notice that the first cause and effect in the passage are labeled.

1. Sometimes a cause has more than one effect. Double-underline the three effects that occurred because hunters wanted the biggest tusks they could find.

2. Circle words in the passage that signal causes and effects. The first one is done for you.

3. Use the causes and effects in the **second** paragraph to complete the following diagram.

Cause: *Numbers of African elephants were very low.* ┈┈▶ Effect:

Cause: ┈┈▶ Effect:

Cause: ┈┈▶ Effect:

African Elephants at Risk

For hundreds of years, African elephants have been killed for their ivory tusks. However, in the 1970s, the demand for ivory greatly increased. As a result, the number of African elephants greatly decreased. In addition, since hunters wanted the biggest tusks they could find, they killed the biggest elephants. Not surprisingly, many of the largest elephants have vanished. Today, tusks are only about half the size they were a hundred years ago.

Between 1979 and 1989, the African elephant population was nearly cut in half. Because the numbers were so low, the African elephant was placed on the endangered species list. Finally, in 1989, a law was passed that put an end to international ivory trade. Consequently, the number of African elephants began to increase. Some African countries, however, objected to the law. These countries depend on the ivory trade. Their objections led to a slight loosening of the law in 1997. Today, some people fear that great numbers of elephants will be killed again.

Comparison and Contrast

A comparison points out how two things are the same. A contrast points out how they are different. Comparisons and contrasts are important because they show how things or ideas are related. Use the following tips when you read any text that includes comparisons and contrasts, such as the example on the right.

- Watch for **direct statements of comparisons and contrasts:** "These are alike because . . . " or "There are some differences, such as. . . ."

- Look for **words and phrases that signal comparisons,** including *also, in the same way, both,* and *too.*

- Pay attention to **words and phrases that signal contrasts,** such as *on the other hand, yet, but,* and *unlike.*

MARK IT UP Read the article on the opposite page. Then answer the questions, using information from the article and the tips above.

1. Circle the words and phrases that signal comparisons. The first one is done for you.

2. Underline the words and phrases that signal contrasts. The first one is done for you.

3. In your own words, explain what a "mirror-image" twin is. Then draw a box around the part of the article that gives you that information.

_____

_____

4. A Venn diagram shows how two subjects are similar and how they are different. Complete this diagram, adding at least two similarities and two differences.

ANNIE
wore braces
has asthma

BOTH
right-handed

ELIZABETH
no braces

Face to Face with Twins

Identical but not the Same

Comparison

Contrast

Annie and Elizabeth say they're alike in many ways and different in others. That's common among identical twins. Annie and Elizabeth are both right-handed. They both wear contact lenses. Their hair looks the same. They lost their baby teeth at about the same time. And they both got their only cavity in the same tooth when they were 9.

"But Annie wore braces and I didn't," says Elizabeth, left. "Annie has asthma and I don't. Plus Annie has more freckles." The twins' mother often got confused when the girls were babies. How could she tell them apart? One of Elizabeth's toes was more crooked than Annie's.

About 10 percent of identical twins are "mirror-image" twins: For example, one is right-handed, and the other is left-handed. But all twins have different fingerprints.

Annie and Elizabeth say they're best friends, yet competitive. "We fight over everything, but we do have different tastes in guys," says Annie. Elizabeth adds, "Sometimes being a twin is so weird. It's also fun and kind of cool." Annie agrees.

—from *National Geographic World*

Argument

An argument is an opinion backed up with reasons and facts. Examining an opinion and the reasons that back it up will help you decide if the opinion makes sense. The following tips will help you read an argument.

- Look for words that **signal an opinion:** *I think, feel, argue,* or *claim.*

- Look for reasons, facts, or expert opinions that **support** the argument.

- Look for overgeneralizations or other **errors in reasoning** that may affect the argument.

|| MARK IT UP Read the argument on the next page and answer the following questions.

1. Circle the words that signal an opinion. The first one is done for you.

2. Underline the phrases that give the author's opinion.

3. Draw a box around the statement that is not supported by reasons or facts.

4. The author presents both sides of the issue. Fill in the chart below. The first one has been done for you.

Pros	Cons
Spirit Week is a way to show creativity.	

Daily Herald, Tuesday, April 2, 20

Save Spirit Week

by David Pinsky

(Signal word)   Teachers at Harrison Middle School (feel) that Spirit Week should be canceled. They argue that it interrupts classes in many ways. Students may forget to do their homework as they concentrate on the Spirit Week themes. A few students skip classes and some go to a different lunch period. Students spend extra time in the bathrooms combing their hair and adjusting their outfits. Some students goof around in class and find it hard to settle down. If Spirit Week isn't canceled, teachers warn that the school will no longer be a good place to learn.

We, the students, feel that Spirit Week encourages us to be better students. Spirit Week is a way for us to show our creativity. For example, last year we had a 70s theme. Students learned how a person dressed during this decade, and they tried to imitate those fashions. Such a theme teaches us about culture and history. Spirit Week also gives us a feeling of pride. At the end of the week, we wear our school colors and support our basketball team against our rivals, the Wildcats. Finally, we feel that Spirit Week teaches us how to work in groups and how to plan and organize an event. Everyone loves Spirit Week. We ask the Harrison School Board to consider our plea and save Spirit Week.

Social Studies

Social studies class becomes easier when you understand how your textbook's words, pictures, and maps work together to give you information. Following these tips can make you a better reader of social studies lessons. As you read the tips, look at the sample lesson on the right-hand page.

A Read the **title** to get the main idea of the lesson.

B The **subheads** tell you some of the major points the lesson covers.

C Carefully read the text, giving special attention to boldfaced or underlined **vocabulary terms.** These terms explain important ideas and are often on tests.

D Look closely at **maps** and **map titles.** Think about how the map and the text are related.

E Look at **pictures** and read the **captions.** These can help you learn and remember key points.

F Think about **ways that the information is organized.** Does the text compare and contrast two people or things? Does it describe causes and effects? Is there a clear sequence of events?

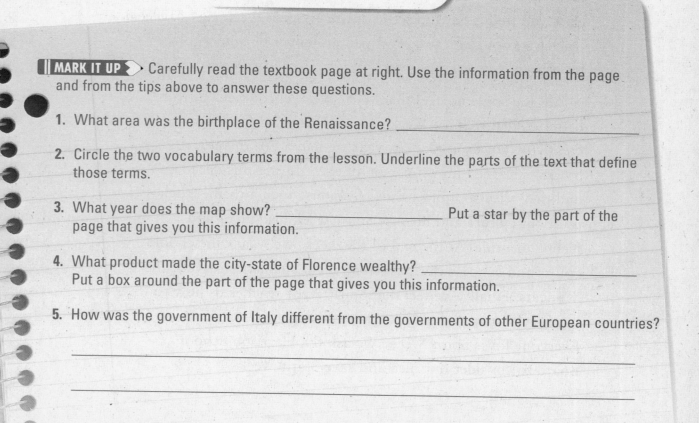

MARK IT UP > Carefully read the textbook page at right. Use the information from the page and from the tips above to answer these questions.

1. What area was the birthplace of the Renaissance? _____

2. Circle the two vocabulary terms from the lesson. Underline the parts of the text that define those terms.

3. What year does the map show? _____ Put a star by the part of the page that gives you this information.

4. What product made the city-state of Florence wealthy? _____
   Put a box around the part of the page that gives you this information.

5. How was the government of Italy different from the governments of other European countries?

   _____

   _____

The Birthplace of the Renaissance **A**

C The word **Renaissance** comes from a Latin word that means rebirth or revival. The term is used to describe a renewed attention to ideas from classical Greek and Roman culture. This renewal occurred first in northern Italy and then spread through Europe between the 1300s and mid-1600s.

Italian City-States **B**

F During the late Middle Ages, the government of Italy was different from those of other countries in Europe. In France and England, for example, strong central governments were forming. However, at the beginning of the Italian Renaissance, Italy was made up of about 250 small states. Most of these states were ruled by cities and were called city-states. Some of the cities were small, but others, like Venice and Milan, had as many as 100,000 people. Look at the map on this page to see how Italy was divided at this time.

Each Italian city-state was independent. All had formed when townspeople began to free themselves from the control of feudal landlords in the 1100s. Some Italian city-states had a republican **C** form of government. A **republic** is a government whose head of state is not a monarch. These cities were not republics like the U.S., as only a few people got to vote, and the cities were mostly run by a few rich families. Other city-states were ruled by a tyrant, or absolute ruler. These tyrants often passed on their jobs to their children, just like kings. Some even ruled so-called "republics," but controlled the elections.

The Ruling Class

Florence's ruling class was made up of about 800 of the city's wealthiest families. They were aristocrats or merchants and bankers who often led the major guilds. To maintain their control, members of the ruling families often excluded others from government and guilds.

These families lived in luxurious palaces that often took up an entire city block. They used their wealth to beautify their cities by hiring architects to design and build palaces. Inside these palaces, each family usually had an elaborate court of attendants. The court included family members and political advisers, as well as leading artists and scholars.

E

▲ The Italian city-states were often ruled by powerful families. This was especially true of Florence. This guild shield illustrates the trade that made Florence wealthy: wool.

Science

Reading in science will be easier when you understand how the explanations, drawings, and special terms work together. Use the strategies below to help you better understand your science textbook. Look at the examples on the opposite page as you read each strategy in this list.

A Preview the **title** and **subheadings** on the page to see what science concepts will be covered.

B Look for **boldface** and **italic** words that appear in the text. Look for **definitions** of those words.

C Many science pages also break information down into parts or categories. Look for **signal words,** such as *first, second,* and *third,* that show how the parts are broken down.

D Look for references to numbered **figures** in the text.

E Then look in the margin for these figures, which are **diagrams** or **pictures** with **captions.** See how they illustrate and explain the text.

**MARK IT UP** Use the sample science page to help you answer the following questions.

1. What science concept will be covered in this lesson? _____
   Put a star at the place where you found this information.

2. Circle the two subheads on the page.

3. Briefly explain the difference between the central nervous system and the peripheral nervous system.

   _____

   _____

4. In the third, fourth, and fifth paragraphs, underline the signal words that introduce the three different functions of the nervous system.

5. In the text, circle the reference to Figure 17-1.

6. Look at the diagram. Circle the part of the nervous system that is directly connected to the brain.

17.1 *The Nervous System*

Lesson Objectives

▸ **Describe** the parts and functions of the nervous system.

▸ **Explain** how neurons carry impulses throughout the body.

▸ **Compare** two main kinds of impulse pathways.

▸ **Activity** **State a conclusion** about the kind of impulse pathway that causes certain movements.

New Terms

central nervous system	impulse
spinal cord	sensory neurons
peripheral nervous system	motor neurons
receptors neurons	association neurons
	reflex

The nervous system is a group of organs that process information. In many ways, the nervous system is like a computer. It receives information from its surroundings, analyzes that information, and then responds in some way. Like a computer, the nervous system has a memory and can solve problems.

Parts and Functions of the Nervous System

As shown in Figure 17-1, the nervous system can be divided into two main parts. One part, called the **central nervous system**, includes the brain and spinal cord. Notice that the **spinal cord** is a cable of nerves extending from the base of the brain almost to the end of the spine. The spinal cord relays messages between the brain and all parts of the body. The other part, called the **peripheral** [pə rif′ ə rəl] **nervous system**, includes all the nerves that connect the brain and spinal cord with other parts of the body. For example, nerves that connect the brain with the eyes and ears are part of the peripheral nervous system. So are nerves that connect the spinal cord with muscles in the arms and legs.

The nervous system performs several important functions for your body. First, it receives information from the environment through special nerve endings called **receptors.** Receptors are often located in sense organs. Your eyes, ears, nose, tongue, and skin all contain receptors. Each type of receptor receives a different type of information. Suppose you eat an apple. Receptors in your nose receive information about the apple's odor, but receptors in your tongue receive information about the apple's taste.

Second, the nervous system directs your thought processes. Whenever you remember a telephone number, solve a math problem, or daydream about a special person, you are using your nervous system.

Third, the nervous system controls your movements. For example, in order for you to throw a ball, your brain must send messages along nerves to the muscles in your arm. The messages direct the muscles to move your bones so that you can throw the ball.

Neurons and Impulses

The brain, spinal cord, and nerves are made of nerve cells, or **neurons** [nyü ränz′]. Figure 17-2 shows the parts of a neuron. The cell body contains the nucleus and most of the cytoplasm. Dendrites are fibers that branch off the cell body

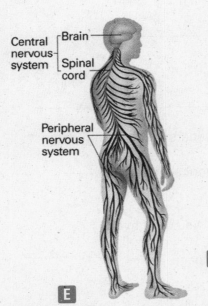

Central nervous system ┌ Brain
                       └ Spinal cord

Peripheral nervous system

Figure 17-1 Nerve length ranges from 1 cm to over 1 m.

Mathematics

Reading in mathematics is different from reading in all other subjects. Use the strategies below to help you better understand your mathematics textbook. Look at the examples on the opposite page as you read each strategy in this list.

A Preview the **title** and **headings** on the page to see what math concepts will be covered.

B Read **explanations** carefully.

C Find the **objectives** for the lesson.

D Pay special attention to any **boldface** or *italic* words. Look for **definitions** of those words.

E Look for **special features such as notes and tips** that provide more help or information.

F Study any **worked-out solutions** to example problems.

MARK IT UP Use the sample math page to help you answer the following questions.

1. What math concepts will be covered in this lesson? What part of the page gave you this information?

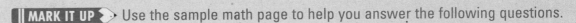

_____

2. Find a definition for the word *data* and write it here.

_____

3. On the page, draw a circle around a tip that helps you understand the word *data*.

4. Underline the part of the explanation that tells why numerical data should be organized.

5. Underline the two groups of words in Example 1 that tell you what to do.

6. Find and circle the solutions to the two problems on the page.

Tables and Graphs

A Goal **1** USING TABLES

C **In this lesson you'll:**
▶ Identify relationships within a data set.
▶ Know various forms of display for data sets.

Numbers or facts that describe something are called **data**. To be useful, numerical data should be organized so you can look for patterns and **D** relationships. One way to organize data is in a table. **B**

A EXAMPLE **1** **Making and Using a Table**

Data for the perimeters of six rectangles are shown below. Make a table to organize the data. Then describe a pattern for the data.

A. □
Perimeter = 4

B. □□
Perimeter = 6

C. □□□
Perimeter = 8

E **Student Help**
▶**VOCABULARY TIP**
The word *data* is plural for *datum*.

D. □□□□
Perimeter = 10

E. □□□□□
Perimeter = 12

F. □□□□□□
Perimeter = 14

Solution

Make a table with two rows. Compare the perimeters to find a pattern.

Rectangle	A	B	C	D	E	F
Perimeter	4	6	8	10	12	14

F

+2 +2 +2 +2 +2

ANSWER▶ From the table you can see that the perimeters increase by 2.

A EXAMPLE **2** **Comparing Data in a Table**

Below are winning and losing state high school football championship scores from 1993 to 2000. Look at the difference between the winning and losing scores. Which years have a difference *greater* than 20?

State High School Football Championship Scores								
Year	1993	1994	1995	1996	1997	1998	1999	2000
Winning score	55	20	37	52	30	49	27	35
Losing score	10	19	24	17	13	26	17	21

E **Student Help**
▶**STUDY TIP**
To record differences between the scores in Example 2, add a fourth row to the table.

Solution

Subtract the losing score from the winning score year by year. There are three years with differences greater than 20: 1993, 1996, and 1998. **F**

Reading an Application

Reading and understanding an application will help you fill it out correctly. Use the following strategies when reading the application on the next page.

A **Begin at the top.** Scan the application to see what the different sections are.

B Watch for **sections you don't have to fill in** or **questions you don't have to answer.**

C Look for **difficult words** or **abbreviations,** such as *NA* (not applicable), *ph.* (phone number), or *Y/N* (yes or no).

D Look for **instructions** about other materials to be included with the application.

|| MARK IT UP 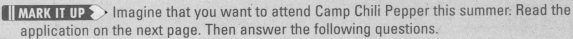 Imagine that you want to attend Camp Chili Pepper this summer. Read the application on the next page. Then answer the following questions.

1. On the application, number the three different sections.

2. Cross out the section you are *not* supposed to fill out.

3. Put an asterisk (*) next to all of the questions that have to do with your health or physical well-being.

4. Underline the materials you may have to submit along with the application.

5. Circle any questions, words, or abbreviations that you don't understand.

6. **ASSESSMENT PRACTICE** Which of the sections on the application should you leave blank?
   A. Emergency Contact
   B. Home Phone
   C. For Office Use Only
   D. Date of Birth

7. Fill out the application as best you can.

A CAMP CHILI PEPPER • DAY CAMP APPLICATION

CAMPER INFORMATION

Please print neatly.

Camper's Name _____ Today's Date _____

Address _____ City/State _____ Zip _____

Home Phone _____ Date of Birth _____ Male/Female (circle one)

YMCA Member? _____ **If so, enclose a copy of your membership card.** D

What school do you attend? _____ Grade _____

Mother's Name _____ Home Phone _____ Work Phone _____

Father's Name _____ Home Phone _____ Work Phone _____

Emergency Contact _____ Home Phone _____ Work Phone _____

Do you have a sibling attending camp? _____ If so, name _____

HEALTH INFORMATION: Check any of the following health problems that affect you:

____ asthma   ____ bee sting allergy   ____ food allergy   ____ diabetes

____ other (_____)   ____ NA C

Please enclose a doctor's note describing any special care or medications you need.

Can you swim? _____

Please write a brief paragraph explaining why you want to attend Camp Chili Pepper.

_____

_____

_____

SESSION INFORMATION

You may sign up for no more than two activities in each session. You may sign up for the same activity more than once (for example, you may sign up for Music & Art in both Session 1 and Session 2).

Session 1 (June 17–21)

____ Activity A: Music & Art

____ Activity B: Soccer

____ Activity C: Nature Hiking

Session 2 (June 25–30)

____ Activity A: Music & Art

____ Activity B: Soccer

____ Activity C: Nature Hiking

FOR OFFICE USE ONLY

B

Date _____   Session _____   Wait List _____   Siblings _____

Reading a Public Notice

If you don't read public notices, you might miss out on important events happening in your area. These tips can help you read all kinds of public notices. As you read each tip, look at the sample notice on the right.

A Read the notice's **title,** if it has one. The title will tell you what the notice is about.

B Ask yourself, **"Could the information in this notice affect me or someone I know?"** If your answer is yes, then you should pay attention to it.

C Read any **instructions**—actions the notice is asking or telling you to take.

D Look for a **logo, credit,** or other way of telling who created the notice.

E Watch for **details** that tell you how you can find out more on the topic.

F Look for **special features** designed to make the notice easier to understand, such as instructions in more than one language.

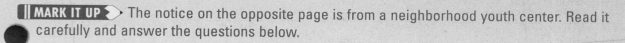

MARK IT UP The notice on the opposite page is from a neighborhood youth center. Read it carefully and answer the questions below.

1. What is this notice about?

   _____

2. Circle the part of the notice that tells you who is allowed to participate in activities at the youth center.

3. Which activity does not require parental permission? _____

4. Put a star next to the part of the notice that tells who created it.

5. Put a box around parts that tell where you can get more information.

6. **ASSESSMENT PRACTICE** It is especially important to sign up early for the swim class because
   A. parental permission is not required
   B. class will not be held on April 4
   C. there is room for only 15 students
   D. participants must bring cleats and shin pads

UPCOMING ACTIVITIES
at the Springfield Youth Center

All Springfield residents ages 7 to 18 are eligible to take part. Space is limited, so sign up now!

Youth Soccer

Having a good time is our goal! Teams are forming for ages 7 to 9, 10 to 12, and 13 to 18. Beginners are welcome. See page 14 for information on dates, times, locations, and fees. *Parental permission is required to participate. Bring cleats and shin pads if you own them.*

Learn to Swim

This class, taught by qualified instructors, will take you from treading water to dog paddling to the backstroke. It is held at the Richmond Aquatic Center at 1129 North Halsted. See page 14 for dates, times, and fees. *This class is limited to 15 students. Parental permission is required to participate.*

Jazz Band

Bring a musical instrument and your creative skills to the Youth Center at 4 P.M. on Tuesdays. Certified music teacher Chris Pizziferro will provide supervision and instruction. *Class will not be held on April 4.*

Youth Center

Springfield Youth Center
280 West Clark St.
Springfield, CA 90076-3304

For information: 555-4832

Para los hispanohablantes, llame por favor a 555-4844
Home page: http://www.springfield.ca.gov/youthctr.home.html

Reading a Web Page

You can use the World Wide Web to find information for reports, projects, or just for fun. The tips below will help you understand all kinds of Web pages. As you read the tips, look at the sample Web pages on the right.

A The page's **Web address**, sometimes called a URL, tells you where you are.

B Read the **title** of the page—it's usually near the top. It will give you a general idea of what topics the page covers.

C Look for **menu bars** along the top, bottom, or side of the page. These tell you about other parts of the site.

D Notice any **links** to related pages. Links are often underlined words.

E Some sites have **interactive areas** where you can ask a question or tell the site's creators what you think of their work.

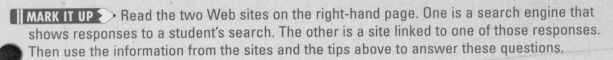 **MARK IT UP** Read the two Web sites on the right-hand page. One is a search engine that shows responses to a student's search. The other is a site linked to one of those responses. Then use the information from the sites and the tips above to answer these questions.

1. Put a star by the Web address of each page.

2. Circle the part of the "LookQuick" site that shows what question the student asked.

3. On the "All About Asteroids" site, which link would you click on if you wanted to learn about asteroids and dinosaurs?

_____

4. Which link would you click on to find a list of sources the "All About Asteroids" creators used?

_____

5. **ASSESSMENT PRACTICE** The "All About Asteroids" site gives information on
   A. how many asteroids hit Mars each year
   B. how people can make their own asteroids
   C. what an asteroid is
   D. all of the above

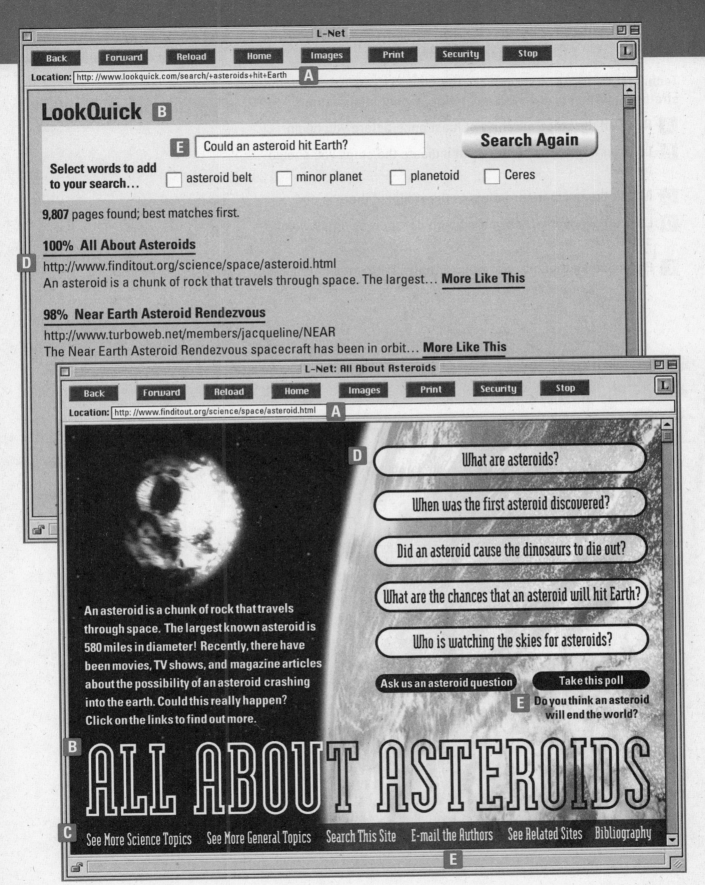

L–Net

Back | Forward | Reload | Home | Images | Print | Security | Stop

Location: http://www.lookquick.com/search/+asteroids+hit+Earth **A**

LookQuick **B**

E Could an asteroid hit Earth? **Search Again**

Select words to add to your search… ☐ asteroid belt ☐ minor planet ☐ planetoid ☐ Ceres

9,807 pages found; best matches first.

D

100% All About Asteroids

http://www.finditout.org/science/space/asteroid.html

An asteroid is a chunk of rock that travels through space. The largest… **More Like This**

98% Near Earth Asteroid Rendezvous

http://www.turboweb.net/members/jacqueline/NEAR

The Near Earth Asteroid Rendezvous spacecraft has been in orbit… **More Like This**

L–Net: All About Asteroids

Back | Forward | Reload | Home | Images | Print | Security | Stop

Location: http://www.finditout.org/science/space/asteroid.html **A**

D

What are asteroids?

When was the first asteroid discovered?

Did an asteroid cause the dinosaurs to die out?

What are the chances that an asteroid will hit Earth?

Who is watching the skies for asteroids?

Ask us an asteroid question | Take this poll

E Do you think an asteroid will end the world?

An asteroid is a chunk of rock that travels through space. The largest known asteroid is 580 miles in diameter! Recently, there have been movies, TV shows, and magazine articles about the possibility of an asteroid crashing into the earth. Could this really happen? Click on the links to find out more.

B

ALL ABOUT ASTEROIDS

C See More Science Topics | See More General Topics | Search This Site | E-mail the Authors | See Related Sites | Bibliography

E

Reading Technical Directions

Technical directions help you use the products you buy. The following strategies will help you read and follow technical directions.

A **Read all the steps** carefully at least once before you begin.

B Look for **numbers** or **letters** that indicate the steps you should follow.

C **Match the numbers or letters to the visual,** if there is one.

D Look for **words that tell you what to do,** such as *press, select, set,* or *turn.*

E Pay close attention to **warnings** or **notes** with more information.

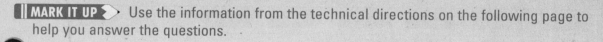 **MARK IT UP** Use the information from the technical directions on the following page to help you answer the questions.

1. Circle the words in each step that tell you what to do.

2. Look for the numbers that have multiple steps. Box the extra set of steps.

3. What happens when you press the ENTER button?

_____

4. Which step indicates that you will see a screen of the Timer Setup menu?

_____

5. What does the warning tell you?

_____

6. **ASSESSMENT PRACTICE** What key is used to make the Setup menu appear on screen?
   A. Enter
   B. Power
   C. Menu
   D. Timer

A Setting the Sleep Timer

1. Press the MENU key. The Setup menu will appear on your television.

2. Select the Timer Setup on your screen by using the UP/DOWN arrows on your remote control.

B 3. Now press the RIGHT/LEFT arrows. A menu of the Timer Setup will appear on the screen.

4. Sleep Timer: Use the RIGHT/LEFT arrows to program the length of time until the TV shuts down. You can select any time from ten minutes to four hours. Press ENTER or QUIT to return to TV viewing.

Setting On/Off Timer

5. Follow steps 1 and 2 above to get to the Timer Setup menu. Using the UP/DOWN arrows on the remote control, select On Time on your screen.

D 6. Press the RIGHT or LEFT arrow to adjust the time your television will turn on automatically.

7. Press the TIMER button to choose either A.M. or P.M.

8. Repeat steps 5 through 7 to set Off Time. Use the UP/DOWN arrows to select the On/Off Timer and activate the timer by pressing a RIGHT/LEFT arrow.

E WARNING: The On/Off timer will not work until the clock on your television has been set.

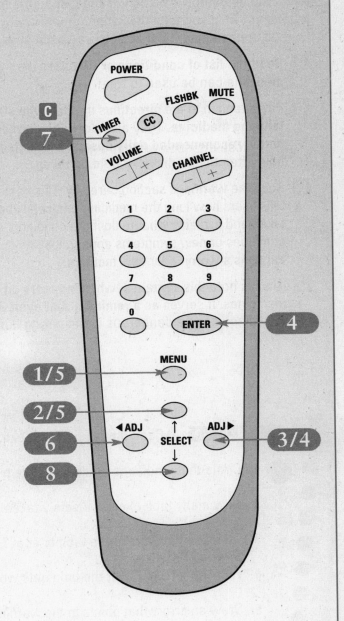

Product Information: Medicine Labels

The labels on such over-the-counter (OTC) medicines as pain relievers, cough syrups, and nasal sprays provide information about the medicines' use and dosage. Learning to read OTC labels will help you take these medicines safely and effectively. Look at the example label as you read each strategy below.

A Read the **list of conditions or illnesses** the medicine can be used to treat.

B Pay attention to the **directions** that tell **who should take the medicine.** They also provide information on the **recommended daily dose:** how much and how often the medicine should be taken.

C Read the **warnings** section carefully. This section tells users how long the medicine can safely be taken and explains what to do if the condition continues or new symptoms appear. It also contains a warning for new mothers.

D Always note this sentence, which appears on many medicines. It serves as a **reminder** that even OTC medicines can be dangerous in the wrong hands.

Extra-Strength Non-Aspirin

A **INDICATIONS:** For the temporary relief of minor aches and pains associated with the common cold, headache, toothache, muscular aches, backache, for the minor pain of arthritis, for the pain of cramps, and for the reduction of fever.

B **DIRECTIONS:** Adults and children 12 years of age and older: Take 2 tablets every 4 to 6 hours. No more than a total of 8 tablets in any 24-hour period, or as directed by a doctor. Not for use in children under 12 years of age.

C **WARNINGS:** Do not take for pain for more than 10 days or for fever for more than 3 days unless directed by a physician. If pain or fever persists or gets worse, if new symptoms occur, or if redness or swelling is present, consult a physician. If you are pregnant or nursing a baby, seek the advice of a health professional before using this product.

D **KEEP THIS AND ALL MEDICINES OUT OF CHILDREN'S REACH.** In case of accidental overdose, contact a physician or poison control center immediately.

 Mtd. for Aspirin Laboratories
Chicago, IL 60601

 0 18946 65238

‖ MARK IT UP Read the medicine label to help you answer these questions.

1. Circle the conditions or illnesses the medicine can be used to treat.

2. How many tablets can be safely taken in one day? _____

3. Who should not take the tablets at all? _____

4. What should you do if the pain gets worse after taking the tablets? _____

5. Draw an arrow that points to the warning about young children. What should be done if a child takes a handful of the tablets? _____

6. **ASSESSMENT PRACTICE** How often should the tablets be taken?
   A. every 4 to 6 hours
   B. every 8 hours
   C. every 12 hours
   D. every 24 hours

Reading a Bus Schedule

Knowing how to read a schedule accurately will help you get to places on time. Look at the example as you read each strategy in this list.

A Scan the **title** to learn what the schedule covers.

B Look at **labels of dates** or **days of the week** to learn when the schedule is in operation.

C Study **place labels**, such as stations, to understand specific stops on the schedule.

D Look at **expressions of time** to know what hours or minutes are listed on the schedule.

Bus Route 333: Grand Avenue **A**				Weekday Mornings—EASTBOUND **B**	
C Lawrence Station	Chestnut St. Mall	Grand & Lincoln	Memorial Hospital	Grand & Delaware	Three Rivers Station
D 4:57 A.M.	5:03 A.M.	5:06 A.M.	5:10 A.M.	5:16 A.M.	5:19 A.M.
5:38	5:44	5:48	5:53	5:59	6:02
5:55	6:02	6:06	6:11	6:18	6:22
6:15	6:22	6:26	6:31	6:38	6:42
6:35	6:42	6:46	6:51	6:58	7:02
7:00	7:08	7:13	7:19	7:28	7:33
7:15	7:23	7:28	7:34	7:43	7:48
7:30	7:38	7:43	7:49	7:58	8:03
7:55	8:03	8:08	8:14	8:23	8:28
8:25	8:33	8:38	8:44	8:52	8:57
8:50	8:58	9:03	9:09	9:17	9:22
9:20	9:28	9:33	9:39	9:47	9:52
9:50	9:58	10:03	10:09	10:17	10:22
10:20	10:28	10:33	10:39	10:47	10:52
10:50	10:58	11:03	11:09	11:17	11:22
11:20	11:28	11:33	11:39	11:47	11:52
11:50	11:58	12:03 P.M.	12:09 P.M.	12:17 P.M.	12:22 P.M.

MARK IT UP Use the schedule above to answer the following questions or statements.

1. What main street do the buses on this route take? _____
   Circle the part of the page that gave you this information.

2. Is this a weekday, weekend, or holiday schedule? _____
   Circle the part of the page that gave you this information.

3. Put an "X" by both the fourth and fifth stops on this route.

4. What time would you arrive at Three Rivers Station if you caught the 8:50 A.M. bus from Lawrence Station? Underline the part of the page that gave you this information.

5. **ASSESSMENT PRACTICE** In what direction do the buses on this route travel?
   A. west
   B. north
   C. south
   D. east

Test Preparation Strategies

In this section you'll find strategies and practice to help you with many different kinds of standardized tests. The strategies apply to questions based on long and short readings, as well as questions about charts, graphs, and product labels. You'll also find examples and practice for revising-and-editing tests and writing tests. Applying the strategies to the practice materials and thinking through the answers will help you succeed in many formal testing situations.

Test Preparation Strategies

You can prepare for tests in several ways. First, study and understand the content that will be on the test. Second, learn as many test-taking techniques as you can. These techniques will help you better understand the questions and how to answer them. Following are some general suggestions for preparing for and taking tests. Starting on page 382, you'll find more detailed suggestions and test-taking practice.

Successful Test Taking

 Study Content Throughout the Year

1. **Master the content of your language arts class.** The best way to study for tests is to read, understand, and review the content of your language arts class. Read your daily assignments carefully. Study the notes that you have taken in class. Participate in class discussions. Work with classmates in small groups to help one another learn. You might trade writing assignments and comment on your classmates' work.

2. **Use your textbook for practice.** Your textbook includes many different types of questions. Some may ask you to talk about a story you just read. Others may ask you to figure out what's wrong with a sentence or how to make a paragraph sound better. Try answering these questions out loud and in writing. This type of practice can make taking a test much easier.

3. **Learn how to understand the information in charts, maps, and graphic organizers.** One type of test question may ask you to look at a graphic organizer, such as a spider map, and explain something about the information you see there. Another type of question may ask you to look at a map to find a particular place, such as the Harlem setting of the story "Thank You M'am." You'll find charts, maps, and graphic organizers to study in your literature textbooks. You'll also find charts, maps and graphs in your science, mathematics, and social studies textbook. When you look at these, ask yourself, What information is being presented and why is it important?

4. **Practice taking tests.** Use copies of tests you have taken in the past or in other classes for practice. Every test has a time limit, so set a timer for 15 or 20 minutes and then begin your practice. Try to finish the test in the time you've given yourself.

✔ **Reading Check**
In what practical way can your textbook help you prepare for a test?

5. **Talk about test-taking experiences.** After you've taken a classroom test or quiz, talk about it with your teacher and classmates. Which types of questions were the hardest to understand? What made them difficult? Which questions seemed easiest, and why? When you share test-taking techniques with your classmates, everyone can become a successful test taker.

 Use Strategies During the Test

1. **Read the directions carefully.** You can't be a successful test taker unless you know exactly what you are expected to do. Look for key words and phrases, such as *circle the best answer, write a paragraph,* or *choose the word that best completes each sentence.*

2. **Learn how to read test questions.** Test questions can sometimes be difficult to figure out. They may include unfamiliar language or be written in an unfamiliar way. Try rephrasing the question in a simpler way using words you understand. Always ask yourself, What type of information does this question want me to provide?

3. **Pay special attention when using a separate answer sheet.** If you accidentally skip a line on an answer sheet, all the rest of your answers may be wrong! Try one or more of the following techniques:

   - Use a ruler on the answer sheet to make sure you are placing your answers on the correct line.

   - After every five answers, check to make sure you're on the right line.

   - Each time you turn a page of the test booklet, check to make sure the number of the question is the same as the number of the answer line on the answer sheet.

   - If the answer sheet has circles, fill them in neatly. A stray pencil mark might cause the scoring machine to count the answer as incorrect.

4. **If you're not sure of the answer, make your best guess.** Unless you've been told that there is a penalty for guessing, choose the answer that you think is likeliest to be correct.

5. **Keep track of the time.** Answering all the questions on a test usually results in a better score. That's why finishing the test is important. Keep track of the time you have left. At the beginning of the test, figure out how many questions you will have to answer by the halfway point in order to finish in the time given.

✔ Reading Check
What are at least two good ways to avoid skipping lines on an answer sheet?

Understand Types of Test Questions

Most tests include two types of questions: multiple choice and open-ended. Specific strategies will help you understand and correctly answer each type of question.

A **multiple-choice question** has two parts. The first part is the question itself, called the stem. The second part is a series of possible answers. Usually four possible answers are provided, and only one of them is correct. Your task is to choose the correct answer. Here are some strategies to help you do just that.

1. Read and think about each question carefully before looking at the possible answers.

2. Pay close attention to key words in the question. For example, look for the word *not,* as in "Which of the following is not a cause of the conflict in this story?"

3. Read and think about all of the possible answers before making your choice.

4. Reduce the number of choices by eliminating any answers you know are incorrect. Then, think about why some of the remaining choices might also be incorrect.

   • If two of the choices are pretty much the same, both are probably wrong.

   • Answers that contain any of the following words are usually incorrect: *always, never, none, all,* and *only.*

5. If you're still unsure about an answer, see if any of the following applies:

   • When one choice is longer and more detailed than the others, it is often the correct answer.

   • When a choice repeats a word that is in the question, it may be the correct answer.

   • When two choices are direct opposites, one of them is likely the correct answer.

   • When one choice includes one or more of the other choices, it is often the correct answer.

   • When a choice includes the word *some* or *often,* it may be the correct answer.

✔ **Reading Check**

What words in a multiple-choice question probably signal a wrong answer?

- If one of the choices is *All of the above,* make sure that at least two of the other choices seem correct.

- If one of the choices is *None of the above,* make sure that none of the other choices seems correct.

An **open-ended test item** can take many forms. It might ask you to write a word or phrase to complete a sentence. You might be asked to create a chart, draw a map, or fill in a graphic organizer. Sometimes, you will be asked to write one or more paragraphs in response to a writing prompt. Use the following strategies when reading and answering open-ended items:

1. If the item includes directions, read them carefully. Take note of any steps required.

2. Look for key words and phrases in the item as you plan how you will respond. Does the item ask you to identify a cause-and-effect relationship or to compare and contrast two or more things? Are you supposed to provide a sequence of events or make a generalization? Does the item ask you to write an essay in which you state your point of view and then try to persuade others that your view is correct?

3. If you're going to be writing a paragraph or more, plan your answer. Jot down notes and a brief outline of what you want to say before you begin writing.

4. Focus your answer. Don't include everything you can think of, but be sure to include everything the item asks for.

5. If you're creating a chart or drawing a map, make sure your work is as clear as possible.

✔ Reading Check
What are at least three key strategies for answering an open-ended question?

Reading Test Model
LONG SELECTIONS

DIRECTIONS Here are two selections, "Dinosaur Feathers!" by Martha Pickerill and "Meet a Bone-ified Explorer" by Ritu Upadhyay. Read each selection carefully. The notes in the side columns will help you prepare for the kinds of questions that are likely to follow readings like these. You might want to preview the questions on pages 385 and 386 before you begin reading.

Dinosaur Feathers!
The best proof yet of dinosaurs' link to birds
by Martha Pickerill

Farmers in northeastern China found the fossil of a duck-size dromaeosaur (DRO-me-uh-sawr) on their land last year. Little did they know that the fossil might settle a hot scientific debate: Are dinosaurs the closest relatives of birds?

The remains of the young dromaeosaur, revealed last week by the team of Chinese and American paleontologists who studied them, are the clearest link ever between birds and dinosaurs. The specimen boasts the best-preserved body covering of several birdlike dinosaur fossils found in recent years. It shows at least three different kinds of feathers, from head to tail.

"This fossil is the strongest evidence yet that dinosaurs were the ancestors of birds," said Richard Prum, an ornithologist (bird specialist) from the University of Kansas Natural History Museum. "It has things that are undeniably feathers, and it is clearly a small, vicious theropod similar to the velociraptors that chased the kids around the kitchen in *Jurassic Park*."

Did *T. Rex* Have Feathers?

The newfound fossil is between 124 million and 147 million years old. Dromaeosaurs didn't fly: they had no wings! So why did they have feathers? Scientists are still exploring that question. Some say dinosaurs developed primitive feathers for warmth, to attract mates or distract predators. Over millions

Find the main idea. What do you think the article will be about after reading the title and first paragraph? Write down your main idea statement.

Infer word meanings from context clues. What does a paleontologist do?

Evaluate conclusions. What do scientists believe the fossil proves? Why? Circle the evidence that led to their conclusion.

Look for cause-and-effect relationships. What *wasn't* a reason for dinosaur feathers? Circle the answer. Then underline some of the theories that scientists have proposed to explain the feathers.

of years feathers developed from tiny tufts of fluff to their modern structure, which helps birds fly.

Dromaeosaurs, velociraptors and Tyrannosaurus rex all belong to the group of birdlike meat-eating dinosaurs called theropods. Mark Norell of the American Museum of Natural History is the American leader of the scientific team in China. He believes we should now rethink the lizardlike way that theropods have been pictured in books and paintings. "When this thing was alive, it looked like a Persian cat with feathers instead of hair," he says. "There's a huge amount of evidence that all these things were feathered, at least when they were young. Even baby tyrannosaurs probably looked like this one."

Experts think the feathered dromaeosaur looked like this.

Analyze visual aids. Study this illustration and its caption. What ideas from the article does this sketch help you understand more clearly?

So Much in Common!
Besides feathers, theropod dinosaurs and birds both have . . .

a wishbone—The wishbone is where two clavicles meet. Clavicle bones connect the shoulders to the rib cage and breastbone.
long, thin shoulder blades
light, hollow bones—A bird's light bones enable it to fly. While dinosaurs that were not from the theropod group had heavy skeletons, quick-moving theropods had light bones.
swiveling wrists—Curved bones allow the hands to fold against the lower arm.
three-clawed feet—In both birds and dinosaurs, the middle claw is longest.
legs and feet built for two-legged walking—While theropods had arms instead of wings, they walked only on their hind legs.

Notice comparisons. What does the information in the chart tell you about the similarities between theropod dinosaurs and birds? Summarize what you learn from the chart.

Meet a Bone-ified Explorer
Her life is devoted to uncovering treasures.

by Ritu Upadhyay

Ever since she was a little girl in Munster, Indiana, Sue Hendrickson has been in a good position to find low-lying treasures. "I was really shy and always walked with my head down," she says, "but my curiosity was strong." Hendrickson developed that curiosity and her instinct for finding valuable things into an exciting job. Now she is a field paleontologist.

Hendrickson became famous after making a colossal discovery in August 1990. After a long day of digging in South Dakota, she stumbled upon one of the largest and most complete *T. rex* fossils ever found. Fellow fossil hunters named the great dino Sue in her honor. "It was as if she was just waiting to be discovered," Hendrickson says. "It took 67 million years, but we finally got to her."

When she's not digging for bones, Hendrickson dives in search of sunken treasure. She has been working with a team excavating the palace of Cleopatra off the coast of Alexandria, Egypt. The royal court sank underwater in a 5th century earthquake. "Sharing these finds with the world is the biggest thrill," she says.

Hendrickson, who lives in Honduras, has spent more than 30 years exploring in fossil fields and underwater. But it was the early years she spent buried in books that led her on her adventures. She hopes that other girls will follow her lead. "Spend some time volunteering out in the field with professionals," she recommends. "And focus on school. It will equip you to learn on your own."

Now answer questions 1 through 5. Base your answers on the articles "Dinosaur Feathers!" and "Meet a Bone-ified Explorer." Then check yourself by reading through the side-column notes.

1 What is the major importance of the dromaeosaur fossil?

   A. It proved that birds are really dinosaurs.
   B. It showed that dinosaurs are older than birds.
   C. It showed that dinosaurs couldn't fly.
   D. It provided a clear link between dinosaurs and birds.

2 Read the following quotation from "Dinosaur Feathers!"

   The remains of the young dromaeosaur, revealed last week by the team of Chinese and American paleontologists who studied them, are the clearest link ever between birds and dinosaurs.

   The meaning of the word *paleontologists* in this sentence is

   E. people who study fossils.
   F. people who speak several languages.
   G. people who make models of animals.
   H. people who are bird experts.

3 You can conclude from the chart and the illustration that

   A. theropod dinosaurs were birds.
   B. theropod dinosaurs and birds have the same bodies.
   C. theropod dinosaurs and birds share many characteristics.
   D. theropod dinosaurs could fly like birds.

4 What information from the article "Meet a Bone-ified Explorer" helps you better understand "Dinosaur Feathers!"?

   E. the details about the *T. rex* fossil Sue Hendrickson found
   F. the details about Hendrickson's work as a paleontologist
   G. the comparison of fossil hunting and treasure hunting
   H. the way the *T. rex* fossil Hendrickson found was named

Answer Strategies

Recall the main idea. The answer to this question is suggested by the title of the article. Review the conclusions scientists drew from the fossil to confirm this main idea.

Infer meanings. Use context clues to define *paleontologists*. Note that one of the answer choices uses the same verb as the quotation to describe paleontologists' activities. You can check your answer by locating the sentence in the article for more context.

Use visual aids. The chart and the illustration reveal that the bodies of dromaeosaurs and birds are not identical; nor could dromaeosaurs fly without wings. Therefore, C is the only valid conclusion.

Analyze details. Eliminate answers that appear in the second article but are not related to a main idea of the first. These include E, G, and H. Learning more about what paleontologists do helps clarify their role in the discovery of the dromaeosaur fossil.

Answers:
1.D, 2.E, 3.C, 4.F

Plan your response. First underline the information that is provided in the question. Then circle what you are being asked to do. Return to the passage and identify details to support your response.

5 You won't find the word *bone-ified*, which appears in the title "Meet a Bone-ified Explorer," in the dictionary. However, this made-up word is pronounced the same way as the Latin phrase *bona fide*, which means "genuine." Explain how this play on words helps the writer get across the main idea of the article. Use details and information from the article to support your answer.

Sample short response for question 5:

> The main idea of the article is that Sue Hendrickson looks for things under the surface of both land and sea. She's a bona fide, or genuine, explorer. She's most famous for digging for dinosaur bones, though. By calling her "bone-ified" in the title, the writer lets readers know that she has a lot to do with bones.

Study the response. This response covers everything the question asks for. The writer connects the article's main idea to the play on words and includes details from the passage.

Reading Test Practice
LONG SELECTIONS

DIRECTIONS Now it's time to practice what you've learned about reading test items and choosing the best answers. Read the following selection, "A Bouncing Baby Island" by Vijayalakshmi Chary. Use the side columns to make notes about the important parts of this selection: main ideas, cause and effect, comparisons and contrasts, difficult vocabulary, supporting details, and so on.

NOTES

A Bouncing Baby Island
by Vijayalakshmi Chary

RUMBLE, rumble. Kaboom! Loihi, an underwater volcano, spits out hot lava into the waters of the Pacific Ocean.

Scientists think Loihi is destined to become the newest Hawaiian island. But don't buy an airline ticket for Loihi yet.

Situated 19 miles south of Hawaii, it sits about half a mile underwater. From the sea floor, it rises 18,000 feet. It will take another 50,000 years for it to break the ocean's surface, says Alexander Malahoff, an oceanographer at the University of Hawaii. And when it does, "there will be a spectacular volcanism [eruption]," he says.

Why Is It There?

Below the ocean and land lies the earth's crust. The crust is made up of about a dozen huge, 50-mile-thick moving slabs or "tectonic plates." They fit together like a jigsaw puzzle.

The Hawaiian islands and Loihi sit on the Pacific tectonic plate. This plate moves slowly northwest—as slowly as your fingernail grows—a few inches a year.

Below the earth's crust is the mantle. Hiding in the mantle, underneath the Pacific plate, is a large well of magma called a hot spot. The hot magma or liquid rock melts the plate and erupts onto the ocean floor. The hot lava hardens and forms a seamount—in this case the Loihi seamount.

After countless eruptions, Loihi will emerge out of the waves and become an island volcano.

Like the Others

Loihi is forming as all the Hawaiian islands did 100 million years ago. The Pacific plate moves along over the hot spot like a conveyor belt while the hot spot leaves a line of island volcanoes.

When they are carried away by the plate, the volcanoes are cut off from their magma source and no longer erupt. Today, the active Hawaiian volcanoes Mauna Loa, Kilauea, and Loihi are still over the hot spot and erupting.

It's difficult to monitor an underwater volcano like Loihi. But scientists at the Hawaiian Volcano Observatory know that as the magma moves under Loihi, the earth shakes. They use seismographs to record these earthquakes and tremors.

Lotta Shakin' Goin' On

Before an eruption, the quakes get more frequent and powerful. In July 1996, more than 5,000 quakes rocked Loihi. Later, scientists confirmed that there were indeed eruptions.

Loihi is "essentially an island in the womb," says Dr. Malahoff. "This is the only time we have been able to see one forming in real life."

Scientists are discovering a lot from Loihi—from the chemical makeup of rocks to sea life around the volcano. When this exciting seamount will erupt again, no one can say for sure. But you can be sure geologists are keeping an eye on Loihi.

Now answer questions 1 through 5. Base your answers on the article
"A Bouncing Baby Island."

1 Hot lava from eruptions of Loihi is creating

   A. a tectonic plate.

   B. a new island.

   C. a layer of the earth's crust.

   D. a piece of mantle.

2 Read the following sentence from the article.

   They use seismographs to record these earthquakes and tremors.

The meaning of the word *seismographs* is

   E. submarines that map the depth of the ocean.

   F. computer programs that estimate the height of seamounts.

   G. equations that calculate the age of volcanoes.

   H. instruments that measure the strength of earthquakes.

3 When do Hawaiian volcanoes stop erupting?

   A. when they move away from a hot spot

   B. when they become a seamount

   C. when they reach the ocean's surface

   D. when they harden into a tectonic plate

4 What conclusion about earthquakes and volcanic eruptions can you draw from the article?

   E. Volcanic eruptions are the cause of earthquakes.

   F. Earthquakes are the cause of volcanic eruptions.

   G. Earthquakes and volcanic eruptions are not related.

   H. Earthquakes and volcanic eruptions are both caused by flowing magma.

5 Read the following passage from the article.

> Loihi is forming as all the Hawaiian islands did 100 million years ago. The Pacific plate moves along over the hot spot like a conveyor belt while the hot spot leaves a line of island volcanoes.

Using this information and details from the illustration—including the direction the Pacific tectonic plate is moving—tell which Hawaiian island was formed most recently and explain your answer.

THINKING IT THROUGH

The notes in the side columns will help you think through your answers. Check the key at the bottom of the page. How well did you do?

1 Hot lava from eruptions of Loihi is creating

   A. a tectonic plate.

   B. a new island.

   C. a layer of the earth's crust.

   D. a piece of mantle.

> This question asks you to identify a cause-and-effect relationship. Look back in the passage to determine which of the choices is the result of countless eruptions.

2 Read the following sentence from the article.

> **They use seismographs to record these earthquakes and tremors.**

The meaning of the word *seismographs* is

   E. submarines that map the depth of the ocean.

   F. computer programs that estimate the height of seamounts.

   G. equations that calculate the age of volcanoes.

   H. instruments that measure the strength of earthquakes.

> Narrow your choices. Which answer includes the same word or words as those used in the sentence from the passage?

3 When do Hawaiian volcanoes stop erupting?

   A. when they move away from a hot spot

   B. when they become a seamount

   C. when they reach the ocean's surface

   D. when they harden into a tectonic plate

> Skim the article to find the specific detail that answers this question.

4 What conclusion about earthquakes and volcanic eruptions can you draw from the article?

   E. Volcanic eruptions are the cause of earthquakes.

   F. Earthquakes are the cause of volcanic eruptions.

   G. Earthquakes and volcanic eruptions are not related.

   H. Earthquakes and volcanic eruptions are both caused by flowing magma.

> Reread the article to find the cause of eruptions and the cause of earthquakes so that you can determine the relationship between the two.

Answers:
1.B, 2.H, 3.A, 4.H

5 Read the following passage from the article.

> Loihi is forming as all the Hawaiian islands did 100 million years ago. The Pacific plate moves along over the hot spot like a conveyor belt while the hot spot leaves a line of island volcanoes.

Using this information and details from the illustration—including the direction the Pacific tectonic plate is moving—tell which Hawaiian island was formed most recently and explain your answer.

This response received a top score because it
- directly answers the question.
- includes details from both the illustration and the passage to develop the explanation.
- is clearly written.

Hawaii was formed most recently. The illustration shows that the tectonic plate is moving away from the hot spot under Loihi. That means that it was under the island closest to Loihi, or Hawaii, most recently. And that's when Hawaii was formed. The farther away from the hot spot on the tectonic "conveyor belt" an island is, the older it is.

Reading Test Model
SHORT SELECTIONS

DIRECTIONS This reading selection is a brief passage similar to one that might appear in a social studies textbook. The strategies you have just used can also help you with this shorter selection. As you read the selection, respond to the notes in the side column.

When you've finished reading, you'll find two multiple-choice questions. Again, use the side-column notes to help you understand what each question is asking and why each answer is correct.

Some Hazards of Early Exploration

Centuries ago, explorers did not have the benefits of technology that we take for granted today. No satellites sent photographs of Earth's surface. No precise, computer-generated maps existed. The maps that were available were crude and sometimes even inaccurate. Furthermore, weather balloons and radar, which now help scientists predict weather weeks in advance, did not exist.

Early explorers, such as Columbus and Magellan, sailed across the ocean not knowing what they would find. Would they encounter land or a never-ending ocean? They were not even sure if the world was round or flat. Many people believed that a boat might reach the edge of the earth and drop off.

What is the main idea of the passage?

1. A. Hundreds of years ago, many people believed that the earth was flat.
   B. Early explorers sailed without the benefits of today's technology.
   C. Columbus and Magellan were early explorers.
   D. It is hard to believe that early explorers found their way around the Earth.

According to the passage, how did the maps of the past differ from maps today?

E. They were crude and inaccurate.

Reading Strategies for Assessment

Find the main idea. Sometimes the main idea is stated in a sentence near the beginning of the passage. Underline the statement that you think expresses the main idea of this selection.

Notice supporting details. What did early explorers such as Columbus and Magellan rely upon to help them find their way? Circle the tool that was available to them. Then underline what they would be able to use if they were exploring today.

Answer Strategies

Recall the main idea. The key words in this question are *main idea*. Therefore, you can eliminate choices that just state facts, such as A and C. Then decide whether the central focus of the passage is on the advances in technology or the amazing achievements of early explorers.

Answer: 1. B

F. They were based on satellite photographs.
G. They were computer-generated.
H. They were used to predict weather.

Review details. Changing this question to a statement, such as "Maps of the past were _____," can help you identify the correct answer more easily. Clearly only one choice refers to maps of the past. Look for this detail in the passage to confirm your answer.

DIRECTIONS The following advertisement is another kind of passage that is written to give you information. Answer the questions that follow.

Reading Strategies for Assessment

Analyze purpose. What do you think is the goal of the advertisement? Write it here.

_____

_____

Evaluate persuasive techniques. What is the intended effect of including this quotation from Mick Slope? Note how he is described and what he says.

Distinguish between fact and opinion. Is the last statement a personal belief, or is it a fact that can be proven right or wrong?

Answer: 2. E

Champgloves: Serious Gloves for Serious Snowboarders

Serious about snowboarding? Then you can't afford to be without Champgloves.

State-of-the-art Champgloves keep your hands warm and your mind focused on the run.

Champion snowboarder Mick Slope wears them. Mick raves, "Champgloves are the only gloves for me. They're the greatest!"

Buy them at Snosport before Friday and get a **free** board sticker!

Champgloves—they're the best gloves for the serious snowboarder.

3 The quotation from Mick Slope is included to make you think that

   A. Mick is an excellent snowboarder.

   B. Champgloves are inexpensive.

   C. Mick started snowboarding as a child.

   D. wearing Champgloves will make you a champion snowboarder.

4 Which of the following states a fact?

   E. They're the greatest!

   F. Buy them at Snosport before Friday and get a **free** board sticker.

   G. You can't afford to be without Champgloves.

   H. They're the best gloves for the serious snowboarder.

5 Which of the following is closest in meaning to the word *raves* as it is used in the passage?

   A. complains

   B. argues

   C. enthuses

   D. whines

Answer Strategies

Recall the purpose. What is the purpose of the ad? Readers' belief in which of these choices will accomplish that purpose?

Identify facts and opinions. Eliminate the answers that express a personal belief or opinion. Keep in mind that superlative adjectives usually indicate opinions.

Analyze persuasive language. In this passage, *raves* is followed by words of praise uttered in an exclamatory or excited way. Therefore, the correct answer will be a word with a positive meaning. Eliminate choices that you know have negative associations.

Answers: 3.D, 4.F, 5.C

Test Preparation Strategies 395

Reading Test Practice
SHORT SELECTIONS

DIRECTIONS Use the following to practice your skills. Read the fairy tale entitled "Three Feathers" and circle the key ideas. Then answer the multiple-choice questions that follow.

Three Feathers: A Fairy Tale

Long ago, in a faraway land, there lived an old king who had one son and two daughters. It came time for the king to decide which of his children should succeed him to the throne.

The king decided on a plan. He called his three children to prepare for a journey. First came his oldest daughter Hildy, then his son Juan, and finally the youngest and most delicate, Grace. Hildy and Juan came with their knapsacks full of tools and food. Grace had only kindness in her heart. The king took three feathers and blew them up in the air. He told his children to choose a feather to follow—the first to return with the most beautiful rug on Earth would succeed him to the throne.

The first feather blew to the east. "That's MY feather—I deserve the best one!" cried Hildy, and she ran off after it. The second feather blew to the west. Juan pushed Grace aside, yelling "That one is for me!" as he ran after that feather. The third fell straight down to the ground, and Grace picked it up.

When Grace picked up her feather, she noticed a small, shiny silkworm squirming around on the ground. Grace offered her hand, and the worm crawled onto it. Suddenly a door opened and Grace followed steps that appeared, leading her down into a chamber below the castle where a giant mama silkworm was weaving silken cloths. Because of Grace's kindness to the baby silkworm, the mama worm gave Grace a beautiful rug woven of gold and silk threads and studded with crimson jewels.

The older two children were careless and returned with whatever old rugs they could find in the fields. When they saw Grace's beautiful rug, Hildy and Juan were outraged and pleaded with their father to let them have another chance to find a more beautiful rug. What do you think was the king's reply?

1 What is the main purpose of this passage?

   A. to tell a story with a message

   B. to inform readers about the ways of kings long ago

   C. to persuade people to watch out for worms

   D. to criticize Hildy's and Juan's behavior

2 Which is the closest in meaning to the words *succeed him to the throne*?

   E. walk before the king to the throne

   F. make the throne successful for the king

   G. become the new ruler after the old king retires

   H. replace the throne with a more beautiful one

3 What might the king have said to Hildy and Juan when they asked him for a second chance?

   A. Yes. You two deserve to try again.

   B. I will give you two a different task so that you can prove yourselves to me.

   C. In order to be fair, all three of you may complete a further task.

   D. Because your rugs showed me your hearts, there is no need for a second chance.

DIRECTIONS Use the graph to answer questions 4, 5, and 6.

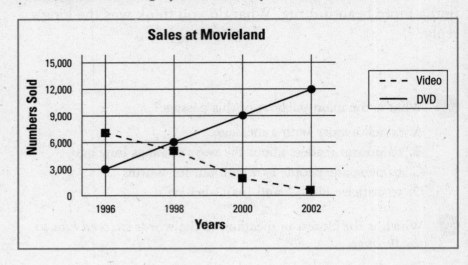

4 If DVD sales continue at the same rate, what can you predict about DVD sales in 2004?

    E. DVD sales will rise above 20,000.

    F. DVD sales will remain at 12,000.

    G. DVD sales will drop to about 1,000.

    H. DVD sales will rise to about 15,000.

5 Which of the following describes what the owner of Movieland will most likely do in 2003?

    A. Gradually stop offering DVDs for sale.

    B. Start offering only videos for sale.

    C. Decrease video offerings and increase DVD offerings.

    D. Increase video offerings.

6 Which of the following can be concluded from this graph?

    E. DVDs have become more popular than videos.

    F. Videos and DVDs have remained equally popular.

    G. Videos have become much more popular than DVDs.

    H. Videos and DVDs have both become less popular.

THINKING IT THROUGH

The notes in the side columns will help you think through your answers. Check the key at the bottom of each page. How well did you do?

1 What is the main purpose of this passage?

   A. to tell a story with a message
   B. to inform readers about the ways of kings long ago
   C. to persuade people to watch out for worms
   D. to criticize Hildy's and Juan's behavior

> Because the passage is a fairy tale, B can be eliminated. Of the remaining choices, only one refers to the reason behind the passage as a whole. The other two suggest a purpose for including specific elements.

2 Which is the closest in meaning to the words *succeed him to the throne*?

   E. walk before the king to the throne
   F. make the throne successful for the king
   G. become the new ruler after the old king retires
   H. replace the throne with a more beautiful one

> Find clues in the two paragraphs in which this phrase is located. If the king is old, he could die or become unable to rule. Think about the decision he must make before one of these events occurs and what the behavior of his children will reveal to him.

3 What might the king have said to Hildy and Juan when they asked him for a second chance?

   A. Yes. You two deserve to try again.
   B. I will give you two a different task so that you can prove yourselves to me.
   C. In order to be fair, all three of you may complete a further task.
   D. Because your rugs showed me your hearts, there is no need for a second chance.

> Read the choices carefully. If three of the answers express similar ideas, the fourth is often the correct one. Use evidence from the story to confirm your choice.

4 If DVD sales continue at the same rate, what can you predict about DVD sales in 2004?

   E. DVD sales will rise above 20,000.
   F. DVD sales will remain at 12,000.
   G. DVD sales will drop to about 1,000.
   H. DVD sales will rise to about 15,000.

> Analyze the information in the graph. How much did DVD sales increase in each two-year period up to 2002? Add that average increase to 12,000 to predict the total sales in 2004.

Answers: 1. A, 2. G, 3. D, 4. H

Often the longer, more detailed choice is the correct answer. Check the information in C to confirm that the data in the graph support it.

5 Which of the following describes what the owner of Movieland will most likely do in 2003?

    A. Gradually stop offering DVDs for sale.

    B. Start offering only videos for sale.

    C. Decrease video offerings and increase DVD offerings.

    D. Increase video offerings.

Return to the graph. Draw your own conclusions about the increase or decrease in DVD and video sales in recent years. Then look for the choice that expresses a similar idea.

6 Which of the following can be concluded from this graph?

    E. DVDs have become more popular than videos.

    F. Videos and DVDs have remained equally popular.

    G. Videos have become much more popular than DVDs.

    H. Videos and DVDs have both become less popular.

Answers:
5. C, 6. E

Functional Reading Test Model

DIRECTIONS Study the following directions for recording an answering machine announcement. Then answer the questions that follow.

Answering System Operation

Recording Your Announcement

Before using your new answering system, you should record an announcement message. This is the message callers will hear when you set the system to answer calls automatically.

1 Prepare your announcement. Your announcement message may be up to 2 minutes long.

   EXAMPLE: "Hello. I can't come to the phone right now. Please leave your name, telephone number, and a short message after you hear the beep. I will return your call as soon as I can. Thank you."

2 Check to make sure the *MESSAGES* light is on. If it is not, press *ON/OFF* (Figure 1) to turn the answering system on.

3 Press and **hold** *ANNC* (Figure 1).

4 When the system beeps, speak toward the microphone in a normal tone of voice. **Release** *ANNC* when finished.

5 To play back your announcement, wait for the tape to reset, then press and release *ANNC*.

To adjust volume, see "Message Volume Control" on page 11.

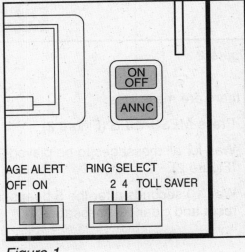

Figure 1

9

Reading Strategies for Assessment

Examine organization. Skim this set of directions to see how the information is organized before reading it carefully. Circle the two major headings under Answering System Operation.

Note sequence of steps. Circle or highlight the numbered steps that explain the actual process of recording the announcement.

Study diagrams. Look closely at the first diagram. Refer to it as you read through each step. Do the same with the second diagram.

Answering System Operation, continued

Changing Your Announcement

To change your announcement, repeat Steps 3, 4, and 5 under "Recording Your Announcement."

When you change your announcement, there must be no messages waiting—*MESSAGES* light (Figure 2) is on steady.

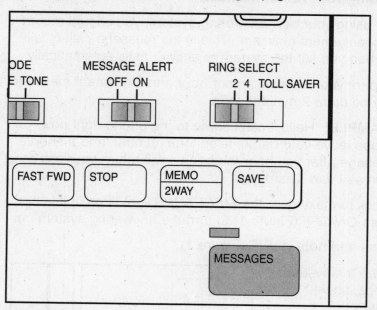

Figure 2

If there are messages:

1 Press *MESSAGES* (Figure 2).

2 Wait for all messages to be played—or press *FAST FWD* (Figure 2).

3 Wait 10 seconds after the 5 beeps, allowing the unit to reset and clear the messages.

10

Identify important instructions.
What must be done before the announcement can be changed?

1 What is the first step you should take after you have prepared your announcement?

A. Hold the button labeled *ANNC*.

B. Speak toward the microphone.

C. Make sure the *MESSAGES* light is on.

D. Press "Release."

Note the sequence of steps. Composing the announcement is step 1. What is step 2?

2 What must you do while recording your announcement?

E. Press *ON/OFF* to be sure the *MESSAGES* light is on.

F. Press and hold the *ANNC* button and speak toward the microphone after the beep.

G. Press and release the *ANNC* button.

H. Position yourself several inches away from the microphone.

Reread the steps that explain how to record the announcement. Which answer contains the same instructions?

3 What must you do if you want to change your announcement and the *MESSAGES* light is blinking?

A. Press and hold *ANNC* while speaking toward the microphone.

B. Play all messages and wait 10 seconds after the 5 beeps for the machine to reset.

C. Press the *ON/OFF* button and hold for 5 beeps; then record your message.

D. Do B, then A.

Recall that the directions are organized in two parts. Review the section entitled "Changing Your Announcement" to identify the correct answer.

Answer Strategies

Answers: 1.C, 2.F, 3.D

Functional Reading Test Practice

DIRECTIONS Study the following nutrition label from a package of provolone cheese. Notice the information it provides and how the information is organized. Then answer the multiple-choice questions that follow.

Nutrition Facts

Serv. Size 1 slice (19 g)
Servings Per Container 12

Amount Per Serving

Calories 70	Calories from Fat 45

Amount/Serving	**% Daily Value***
Total Fat 5g	8%
Sat. Fat 3.5g	17%
Cholesterol 15 mg	5%
Sodium 125 mg	5%
Total Carbohydrate 0g	0%
Dietary Fiber 0g	0%
Sugars 0g	
Protein 5g	

Vitamin A 4%	•	Vitamin C 0%
Calcium 15%	•	Iron 0%

*Percent Daily Values are based on a 2,000 calorie diet. Your daily values may be higher or lower depending on your calorie needs.

1 How many calories does one slice of this cheese contain?

A. 12
B. 19
C. 45
D. 70

2 What major nutrients and vitamins are NOT supplied by this cheese?

E. sodium, protein, fat
F. calcium, protein, vitamin A
G. dietary fiber, iron, vitamin C
H. sugars, saturated fat, vitamin A

3 If you are on a 2,000 calorie diet, what percentage of your daily supply of saturated fat is provided by one slice of this cheese?

    A. 3.5

    B. 5

    C. 8

    D. 17

4 If you need calcium but don't need saturated fat, is this cheese a good food choice for you?

    E. No. Although the % Daily Value of calcium per serving is high, the % Daily Value of saturated fat is higher.

    F. Yes. The % Daily Value of calcium is 15%.

    G. There is not enough information given to make a decision.

    H. Yes. There is no saturated fat in this product.

THINKING IT THROUGH

The notes in the side column will help you think through your answers. Check the key at the bottom of the page. How well did you do?

The serving size is one slice of cheese. Find the number of calories per serving (total calories, not calories from fat), and you'll know how many calories one slice contains.

1 How many calories does one slice of this cheese contain?

A. 12
B. 19
C. 45
D. 70

Look at the amounts and percentages of each of the nutrients listed. Which have a zero next to them?

2 What major nutrients and vitamins are NOT supplied by this cheese?

E. sodium, protein, fat
F. calcium, protein, vitamin A
G. dietary fiber, iron, vitamin C
H. sugars, saturated fat, vitamin A

All of the % Daily Value figures are for a 2,000 calorie diet. Be sure to look for the saturated fat (Sat. Fat) percentage, not total fat.

3 If you are on a 2,000 calorie diet, what percentage of your daily supply of saturated fat is provided by one slice of this cheese?

A. 3.5
B. 5
C. 8
D. 17

Examine all of the choices. Which one takes into account the daily values of both calcium and saturated fat?

4 If you need calcium but don't need saturated fat, is this cheese a good food choice for you?

E. No. Although the % Daily Value of calcium per serving is high, the % Daily Value of saturated fat is higher.
F. Yes. The % Daily Value of calcium is 15%.
G. There is not enough information given to make a decision.
H. Yes. There is no saturated fat in this product.

Revising-and-Editing Test Model

DIRECTIONS Read the following paragraph carefully. Then answer the multiple-choice questions that follow. After answering the questions, read the material in the side columns to check your answer strategies. An answer key appears at the bottom of page 408.

¹ Our principle, Mr. Dollinger, thinks that we don't need to have dances at our school. ² He says, you students already have too many activities." ³ It is true that some students are involved in sports others participate in the newspaper and the yearbook. ⁴ However, only 40 percent of the students take part in these activities. ⁵ Having dances on Valentine's Day, the first day of spring, and other special occasions would help to build school spirit. ⁶ Dances is one school activity that everyone can enjoy.

1 What is the correct spelling of *principle* as it is used in sentence 1?

A. *principul*
B. *principel*
C. *principle*
D. *principal*

2 What change, if any, should be made in sentence 2?

E. change *He says, you students* to *He says, "you students*
F. change *He says, you students* to *He says "You students*
G. change *He says, you students* to *He says, you, students*
H. change *He says, you students* to *He says, "You students*

3 What is the best way to rewrite sentence 3 in this paragraph?

A. It is true that some students are involved in sports, others participate in the newspaper and the yearbook.
B. It is true that some students are involved in sports, however others participate in the newspaper and the yearbook.
C. It is true that some students are involved in sports and others participate in the newspaper and the yearbook.
D. It is true that some students are involved in sports—others participate in the newspaper and the yearbook.

Reading Strategies for Assessment

Watch for common errors. Highlight or underline errors such as incorrect punctuation, spelling, or capitalization; incomplete or run-on sentences; and missing or misplaced information.

Answer Strategies

Commonly Confused Words
Principle means "code of conduct" or "basic truth." A *principal* is the head of a school.

Quotations Remember that a direct quotation is enclosed in quotation marks, and the first word is capitalized.
For help, see Pupil Edition, pp. R69, R93*
Grammar, Usage, and Mechanics Book, pp. 199–201

Run-on Sentences Three choices use incorrect punctuation to join the two thoughts and do not show the relationship between them. The correct answer shows that the two thoughts elaborate on the same idea by combining them with a conjunction.
For help, see Pupil Edition, pp. R71–R72
Grammar, Usage, and Mechanics Book, pp. 28–30

*Pages listed are for the Grammar Handbook in *The Language of Literature* Pupil Edition and the *Grammar, Usage, and Mechanics Book.*

Transitions The sentence *I don't agree* indicates a change in the direction of the paragraph. Where does the writer begin to present his or her argument disputing Mr. Dollinger's opinion?

Subject-Verb Agreement Identify the subject in each choice and determine whether the verb agrees with it in number. Choose the answer that is correct and most clearly phrased.
For help, see Pupil Edition, p. R72 Grammar, Usage, and Mechanics Book, pp. 163–165

Supporting Details Reread the paragraph to identify the main idea. Decide which detail would strengthen the argument that school dances would provide enjoyment for many students.

4 Where should the sentence *I don't agree* be added to the paragraph?

E. between sentences 1 and 2

F. between sentences 2 and 3

G. between sentences 3 and 4

H. between sentences 5 and 6

5 Which of the following is the best way to rewrite sentence 6?

A. Dances is one school activity enjoyed by everyone.

B. One school activity enjoyed by everyone are dances.

C. Everyone can be enjoying the school activity of dances.

D. Dances are one school activity that everyone can enjoy.

6 Which of the following details would best support the student's argument?

E. In a recent poll, 80 percent of the students said that they would attend school dances.

F. School dances were very popular 20 years ago.

G. On Valentine's Day, students only exchange cards and have a bake sale.

H. A dance could be held for the entire student body in the new gymnasium.

Answers:
1.D, 2.H, 3.C, 4.F, 5.D, 6.E

Revising-and-Editing Test Practice

DIRECTIONS Read the following paragraph carefully. As you read, circle each error that you find and identify the error in the side column—for example, *misspelled word* or *not a complete sentence*. When you have finished, circle the letter of the correct choice for each question that follows.

¹ A good sailor can determine their latitude by looking at the sun or stars. ² Calculating longitude depends on time, however. ³ The difference between the time on a ship and the time in its home port can be converted into longitude. ⁴ Nowadays that process seems simple years ago it was almost impossible. ⁵ Many ships became lost at sea, for instance, the *Eva Doran* sank in the Pacific Ocean when she hit land unexpectedly. ⁶ The problem in the late 18th century was not solved until John Harrison developed an accurate ship's clock. ⁷ Harrison's invention began a new era in navigation.

1 Which of the following is the correct way to rewrite sentence 1?

A. A good sailor can determine they're latitude by looking at the sun or stars.

B. Good sailors can determine their latitude by looking at the sun or stars.

C. A good sailor, can determine his latitude, by looking at the sun or stars.

D. Good sailors can determine their latitude. By looking at the sun or stars.

2 What type of sentence is sentence 2?

E. exclamatory

F. imperative

G. interrogative

H. declarative

3 Which sentence is a run-on sentence?

A. sentence 2

B. sentence 3

C. sentence 4

D. sentence 7

4 Which sentence in this paragraph is the topic sentence?

    E. sentence 1

    F. sentence 2

    G. sentence 4

    H. sentence 7

5 What change should be made to sentence 5?

    A. replace the comma after *sea* with a semicolon

    B. insert a comma after *Doran*

    C. insert a comma after *Ocean*

    D. delete the comma after *sea*

6 Which of the following is the best way to rewrite sentence 6?

    E. In the late 18th century, the problem was not solved until John Harrison developed an accurate ship's clock.

    F. Until John Harrison developed an accurate ship's clock, the problem was not solved in the late 18th century.

    G. The problem was not solved in the late 18th century until John Harrison developed an accurate ship's clock.

    H. The problem was not solved until John Harrison developed an accurate ship's clock in the late 18th century.

THINKING IT THROUGH

Use the notes in the side columns to help you understand why some answers are correct and others are not. Check the answer key at the bottom of each page. How well did you do?

1 Which of the following is the correct way to rewrite sentence 1?

A. A good sailor can determine they're latitude by looking at the sun or stars.

B. Good sailors can determine their latitude by looking at the sun or stars.

C. A good sailor, can determine his latitude, by looking at the sun or stars.

D. Good sailors can determine their latitude. By looking at the sun or stars.

2 What type of sentence is sentence 2?

E. exclamatory

F. imperative

G. interrogative

H. declarative

3 Which sentence is a run-on sentence?

A. sentence 2

B. sentence 3

C. sentence 4

D. sentence 7

4 Which sentence in this paragraph is the topic sentence?

E. sentence 1

F. sentence 2

G. sentence 4

H. sentence 7

In sentence 1, *their,* a plural pronoun, is incorrectly used with a singular antecedent. Which choice corrects that mistake?
For help, see Pupil Edition, p. R78* Grammar, Usage, and Mechanics Book, p. 64–66

First read the sentence to be sure that the period at the end is the correct punctuation. Then decide whether it is a command or a declarative statement.
For help, see Pupil Edition, p. R98 Grammar, Usage, and Mechanics Book, pp. 16–18

A run-on sentence is two or more complete thoughts written as one. Read each choice to see which lacks the correct punctuation.
For help, see Pupil Edition, pp. R71– R72 Grammar, Usage, and Mechanics Book, pp. 28–30

The topic sentence may come anywhere in the paragraph, although most often it is at the beginning or end. Look for the statement of the main idea that all the other sentences develop or support.

Answers:
1.B, 2.H, 3.C, 4.H

*Pages listed are for the Grammar Handbook in *The Language of Literature* Pupil Edition and the *Grammar, Usage, and Mechanics Book.*

This sentence is a run-on. Where should a semicolon or a comma and a conjunction be placed to fix it?
For help, see Pupil Edition, pp. R71–R72
Grammar, Usage, and Mechanics Book, pp. 28–30

Keep adverb phrases as close as possible to the words they modify. The phrase *in the 18th century* modifies *developed*. In which answer is that relationship clear?

5 What change should be made to sentence 5?

   A. replace the comma after *sea* with a semicolon
   B. insert a comma after *Doran*
   C. insert a comma after *Ocean*
   D. delete the comma after *sea*

6 Which of the following is the best way to rewrite sentence 6?

   E. In the late 18th century, the problem was not solved until John Harrison developed an accurate ship's clock.
   F. Until John Harrison developed an accurate ship's clock, the problem was not solved in the late 18th century.
   G. The problem was not solved in the late 18th century until John Harrison developed an accurate ship's clock.
   H. The problem was not solved until John Harrison developed an accurate ship's clock in the late 18th century.

Answers:
5. A, 6. H

Writing Test Model

DIRECTIONS Many tests ask you to write an essay in response to a writing prompt. A writing prompt is a brief statement that describes a writing situation. Some writing prompts ask you to explain what, why, or how. Others ask you to convince someone about something.

As you analyze the following writing prompts, read and respond to the notes in the side columns. Then look at the response to each prompt. The notes in the side columns will help you understand why each response is considered strong.

Prompt A

> Your class plans to raise money for charity. Think about which charity you would like your class to support. Now write to convince your classmates to adopt that charity as their project. Be sure to provide reasons that support your argument.

Strong Response

How would you feel if you couldn't read this sentence? What if you always ordered what everybody else was getting at a restaurant because you couldn't understand the words on the menu? None of us in this class will ever have this problem. But there are many adults in our town who struggle with it every day. I think our class should help these people by giving our money to Reading Right.

It's almost impossible to get along in the world today if you can't read. Everything from dialing a pay telephone to taking medication involves reading instructions. And then there's all the information about the world that is printed in newspapers and magazines. People who can't read miss out on so much that is going on around them. These people may be embarrassed to admit the problem and ashamed to ask for help.

Analyzing the Prompt

Determine your writing task. Circle what decision you must make before you begin to write. Underline what you must include in your essay.

Answer Strategies

Include a strong introduction. The writer's questions prompt her readers to begin thinking about the topic in a personal way.

State the position clearly. The writer leaves no doubt about the action she wants the class to take.

Choose a logical organization. This writer has chosen a problem-solution organization for her essay. By describing the problem first, she will convince her readers of the need to help solve it.

Incorporate specific examples. Specific instances instead of vague generalizations emphasize the seriousness and the extent of the problem.

Identify the solution. The writer connects the action she wants her readers to take with the solution to the problem she has described.

That's where Reading Right comes in. It is a program that is offered free to people in the community. I went with my mother when she volunteered there last year, and I saw people from many different countries working hard to improve their English skills. Like my mother, all of the teachers there are volunteers. The only reward they get is the smiles and thanks of the people they help.

Develop the argument with a variety of details. The writer includes a specific story that illustrates the success of the program.

Reading Right publishes a monthly newsletter that explains the program and describes two or three success stories. That's right, two or three success stories every month. This program really works! One story I especially liked was about a man who was living with relatives because he couldn't find a job. After working with a Reading Right volunteer for just two months, he found a job and got his own apartment.

Restate the opinion in the conclusion. The writer restates her view and reminds the readers of why they need to act on her proposal.

So I urge you to donate our class funds to Reading Right. Since it's an all-volunteer program, all the money we give would go to help the students. We were lucky enough to learn how to read in school. Reading Right can give adults in our community that chance they never had.

Prompt B

Everyone has memories of a day that was especially important. Think about a day that was important to you. Now explain why that day stands out in your memory.

Strong Response

It was March 26, 1999. The sky looked like a newly hatched robin's egg. The sun poured its warmth into my stiff winter muscles. It was the perfect day for our first neighborhood baseball game of the year. I had no way of knowing then that this would also become the most important day of my life. It was the day that would teach me how precious life really is.

I remember running after a fly ball. I was looking back over my shoulder to keep the ball in sight, and wasn't paying attention to where I was going. I leaped for the ball as it flew into the street. I heard screams and the sound of squealing tires. Then nothing until I woke up in the hospital three weeks later. I had been in a coma and had almost died.

When I came to, my legs were stretched out in front of me like monster stalagmites growing out of my body. My arms were strapped down and had tubes coming out of them. I didn't know where I was and I hurt everywhere. Eventually I learned that I had been hit by a car and that my skull, ribs, and legs were broken and that I had internal injuries, too.

I felt very sorry for myself as I lay totally helpless in my hospital bed. But then I began noticing the kids around me. Some had cancer. Some needed new hearts. Some would

Analyzing the Prompt

Identify your topic. Circle the focus of your essay as stated in the first sentence.

Prepare to write. Brainstorm details of the day you've chosen.

Answer Strategies

Set the scene. The writer's first sentences establish when and where the incident took place.

State the main idea. The writer explains the significance of the day he has chosen to write about.

Include vivid details. The writer uses words and phrases that appeal to the senses to re-create his experience for readers.

Signal the order of events. This essay is organized chronologically. Time order transitions (*when, eventually*) show the sequence of events.

Support the main idea. The writer shares with the readers the realizations that led to his change of heart.

never get well. Seeing them made me stop and think how lucky I was. My injuries would heal and I'd be able to walk and run and play baseball again. But I realized then that I'd never be quite the same person.

3/26/99. I'll never forget that day as long as I live. It's the day I almost lost my life, which taught me a lesson I'll never forget. Since then I feel so very lucky to be alive every single day. And if anyone ever wants to know my three lucky numbers, I bet you know what they are.

Develop a strong conclusion. The writer restates the focus and theme of his essay.

Writing Test Practice

DIRECTIONS Read the following writing prompt. Using the strategies you've learned in this section, analyze the prompt, plan your response, and then write an essay explaining your position.

Prompt C

Your school is trying to decide whether to end all sports, clubs, and other after-school activities.

Think about whether you believe after-school activities are important. Then write an essay to convince the school board to accept your point of view. Include support for your position.

Scoring Rubrics

DIRECTIONS Use the following checklist to see whether you have written a strong persuasive essay. You will have succeeded if you can check nearly all of the items.

The Prompt

☐ My response meets all the requirements stated in the prompt.

☐ I have stated my position clearly and supported it with details.

☐ I have addressed the audience appropriately.

☐ My essay fits the type of writing suggested in the prompt (letter to the editor, article for the school paper, and so on).

Reasons

☐ The reasons I offer really support my position.

☐ My audience will find the reasons convincing.

☐ I have stated my reasons clearly.

☐ I have given at least three reasons.

☐ I have supported my reasons with sufficient facts, examples, quotations, and other details.

☐ I have presented and responded to opposing arguments.

☐ My reasoning is sound. I have avoided faulty logic.

Order and Arrangement

☐ I have included a strong introduction.

☐ I have included a strong conclusion.

☐ The reasons are arranged in a logical order.

Word Choice

☐ The language of my essay is appropriate for my audience.

☐ I have used precise, vivid words and persuasive language.

Fluency

☐ I have used sentences of varying lengths and structures.

☐ I have connected ideas with transitions and other devices.

☐ I have used correct spelling, punctuation, and grammar.

Personal Word List

Use these pages to build your personal vocabulary. As you read the selections, take time to mark unfamiliar words. These should be words that seem interesting or important enough to add to your permanent vocabulary. After reading, look up the meanings of these words and record the information below. For each word, write a sentence that shows its correct use.

Review your list from time to time. Try to put these words into use in your writing and conversation.

Word: _____

Selection: _____

Page/Line: _____ / _____

Part of Speech: _____

Definition: _____

_____

_____

_____

Sentence: _____

_____

_____

_____

Word: _____

Selection: _____

Page/Line: _____ / _____

Part of Speech: _____

Definition: _____

_____

_____

Sentence: _____

_____

_____

_____

Word: _____

Selection: _____

Page/Line: _____ / _____

Part of Speech: _____

Definition: _____

_____

_____

Sentence: _____

_____

_____

_____

Word: _____

Selection: _____

Page/Line: _____ / _____

Part of Speech: _____

Definition: _____

_____

_____

Sentence: _____

_____

_____

_____

Word: _____

Selection: _____

Page/Line: _____ / _____

Part of Speech: _____

Definition: _____

_____

_____

Sentence: _____

_____

_____

Word: _____

Selection: _____

Page/Line: _____ / _____

Part of Speech: _____

Definition: _____

_____

_____

Sentence: _____

_____

_____

Word: _____

Selection: _____

Page/Line: _____ / _____

Part of Speech: _____

Definition: _____

_____

_____

Sentence: _____

_____

_____

Personal Word List

Word: _____

Selection: _____

Page/Line: _____ / _____

Part of Speech: _____

Definition: _____

_____

_____

Sentence: _____

_____

_____

_____

Word: _____

Selection: _____

Page/Line: _____ / _____

Part of Speech: _____

Definition: _____

_____

_____

Sentence: _____

_____

_____

_____

Word: _____

Selection: _____

Page/Line: _____ / _____

Part of Speech: _____

Definition: _____

_____

_____

Sentence: _____

_____

_____

_____

Word: _____

Selection: _____

Page/Line: _____ / _____

Part of Speech: _____

Definition: _____

_____

_____

Sentence: _____

_____

_____

_____

Word: _____

Selection: _____

Page/Line: _____ / _____

Part of Speech: _____

Definition: _____

_____

_____

Sentence: _____

_____

_____

_____

Word: _____

Selection: _____

Page/Line: _____ / _____

Part of Speech: _____

Definition: _____

_____

_____

Sentence: _____

_____

_____

_____

Word: _____

Selection: _____

Page/Line: _____ / _____

Part of Speech: _____

Definition: _____

_____

_____

Sentence: _____

_____

_____

_____

Word: _____

Selection: _____

Page/Line: _____ / _____

Part of Speech: _____

Definition: _____

_____

_____

Sentence: _____

_____

_____

Personal Word List

Word: _____

Selection: _____

Page/Line: _____ / _____

Part of Speech: _____

Definition: _____

_____

_____

Sentence: _____

_____

_____

_____

Word: _____

Selection: _____

Page/Line: _____ / _____

Part of Speech: _____

Definition: _____

_____

_____

Sentence: _____

_____

_____

_____

Word: _____

Selection: _____

Page/Line: _____ / _____

Part of Speech: _____

Definition: _____

_____

_____

Sentence: _____

_____

_____

_____

Word: _____

Selection: _____

Page/Line: _____ / _____

Part of Speech: _____

Definition: _____

_____

_____

Sentence: _____

_____

_____

_____

Word: _____

Selection: _____

Page/Line: _____ / _____

Part of Speech: _____

Definition: _____

_____

_____

Sentence: _____

_____

_____

_____

Word: _____

Selection: _____

Page/Line: _____ / _____

Part of Speech: _____

Definition: _____

_____

_____

Sentence: _____

_____

_____

Word: _____

Selection: _____

Page/Line: _____ / _____

Part of Speech: _____

Definition: _____

_____

_____

Sentence: _____

_____

_____

Word: _____

Selection: _____

Page/Line: _____ / _____

Part of Speech: _____

Definition: _____

_____

_____

Sentence: _____

_____

_____

Personal Word List

Word: _____

Selection: _____

Page/Line: _____ / _____

Part of Speech: _____

Definition: _____

_____

_____

Sentence: _____

_____

_____

_____

Word: _____

Selection: _____

Page/Line: _____ / _____

Part of Speech: _____

Definition: _____

_____

_____

Sentence: _____

_____

_____

_____

Word: _____

Selection: _____

Page/Line: _____ / _____

Part of Speech: _____

Definition: _____

_____

_____

Sentence: _____

_____

_____

_____

Word: _____

Selection: _____

Page/Line: _____ / _____

Part of Speech: _____

Definition: _____

_____

_____

Sentence: _____

_____

_____

_____

Word: _____

Selection: _____

Page/Line: _____ / _____

Part of Speech: _____

Definition: _____

_____

_____

Sentence: _____

_____

_____

_____

Word: _____

Selection: _____

Page/Line: _____ / _____

Part of Speech: _____

Definition: _____

_____

_____

Sentence: _____

_____

_____

_____

Word: _____

Selection: _____

Page/Line: _____ / _____

Part of Speech: _____

Definition: _____

_____

_____

Sentence: _____

_____

_____

_____

Word: _____

Selection: _____

Page/Line: _____ / _____

Part of Speech: _____

Definition: _____

_____

_____

Sentence: _____

_____

_____

_____

Personal Word List

Word: _____

Selection: _____

Page/Line: _____ / _____

Part of Speech: _____

Definition: _____

_____

_____

Sentence: _____

_____

_____

_____

Word: _____

Selection: _____

Page/Line: _____ / _____

Part of Speech: _____

Definition: _____

_____

_____

Sentence: _____

_____

_____

_____

Word: _____

Selection: _____

Page/Line: _____ / _____

Part of Speech: _____

Definition: _____

_____

_____

Sentence: _____

_____

_____

_____

Word: _____

Selection: _____

Page/Line: _____ / _____

Part of Speech: _____

Definition: _____

_____

_____

Sentence: _____

_____

_____

_____

Word: _____

Selection: _____

Page/Line: _____ / _____

Part of Speech: _____

Definition: _____

_____

_____

Sentence: _____

_____

_____

_____

Word: _____

Selection: _____

Page/Line: _____ / _____

Part of Speech: _____

Definition: _____

_____

_____

Sentence: _____

_____

_____

_____

Word: _____

Selection: _____

Page/Line: _____ / _____

Part of Speech: _____

Definition: _____

_____

_____

Sentence: _____

_____

_____

_____

Word: _____

Selection: _____

Page/Line: _____ / _____

Part of Speech: _____

Definition: _____

_____

_____

Sentence: _____

_____

_____

_____

Personal Word List

Word: _____

Selection: _____

Page/Line: _____ / _____

Part of Speech: _____

Definition: _____

_____

_____

Sentence: _____

_____

_____

_____

Word: _____

Selection: _____

Page/Line: _____ / _____

Part of Speech: _____

Definition: _____

_____

_____

Sentence: _____

_____

_____

_____

Word: _____

Selection: _____

Page/Line: _____ / _____

Part of Speech: _____

Definition: _____

_____

_____

Sentence: _____

_____

_____

_____

Word: _____

Selection: _____

Page/Line: _____ / _____

Part of Speech: _____

Definition: _____

_____

_____

Sentence: _____

_____

_____

_____

Word: _____

Selection: _____

Page/Line: _____ / _____

Part of Speech: _____

Definition: _____

_____

_____

Sentence: _____

_____

_____

_____

Word: _____

Selection: _____

Page/Line: _____ / _____

Part of Speech: _____

Definition: _____

_____

_____

Sentence: _____

_____

_____

_____

Word: _____

Selection: _____

Page/Line: _____ / _____

Part of Speech: _____

Definition: _____

_____

_____

Sentence: _____

_____

_____

_____

Word: _____

Selection: _____

Page/Line: _____ / _____

Part of Speech: _____

Definition: _____

_____

_____

Sentence: _____

_____

_____

_____

Personal Word List

Word: _____

Selection: _____

Page/Line: _____ / _____

Part of Speech: _____

Definition: _____

_____

_____

Sentence: _____

_____

_____

_____

Word: _____

Selection: _____

Page/Line: _____ / _____

Part of Speech: _____

Definition: _____

_____

_____

Sentence: _____

_____

_____

_____

Word: _____

Selection: _____

Page/Line: _____ / _____

Part of Speech: _____

Definition: _____

_____

_____

Sentence: _____

_____

_____

_____

Word: _____

Selection: _____

Page/Line: _____ / _____

Part of Speech: _____

Definition: _____

_____

_____

Sentence: _____

_____

_____

_____

Acknowledgments

(Continued from page ii)

Vijayalakshmi Chary: "A Bouncing Baby Island" by Vijayalakshmi Chary, from *Boys' Life Magazine,* April 2001, page 6. Copyright © 2001 by Vijayalakshmi Chary. Reprinted by permission of the author.

CMG Worldwide: Excerpt from *I Never Had It Made* by Jackie Robinson, as told to Alfred Duckett. Reprinted by permission of CMG Worldwide Inc. on behalf of Rachel Robinson. TM Jackie Robinson licensed by CMG Worldwide Inc., Indianapolis, Indiana, 46256 USA. www.cmgww.com.

Don Congdon Associates: "Dark They Were, and Golden-Eyed" by Ray Bradbury, from *Thrilling Wonder Stories,* August 1949. Copyright © 1949 by Standard Magazines, renewed 1976 by Ray Bradbury. Reprinted by permission of Don Congdon Associates, Inc.

Harcourt: "Seventh Grade," from *Baseball in April and Other Stories* by Gary Soto. Copyright © 1990 by Gary Soto. Reprinted by permission of Harcourt, Inc.

Hill and Wang: "Thank You, M'am," from *Short Stories* by Langston Hughes. Copyright © 1996 by Ramona Bass and Arnold Rampersad. Reprinted by permission of Hill and Wang, a division of Farrar, Straus and Giroux, LLC.

Henry Holt and Company: "The Pasture" by Robert Frost, from *The Poetry of Robert Frost,* edited by Edward Connery Lathem. Copyright 1944, © 1958 by Robert Frost. Copyright © 1967 by Lesley Frost Ballantine. Copyright 1930, 1939, © 1969 by Henry Holt and Company. Reprinted by permission of Henry Holt and Company, Inc.

"A Time to Talk" by Robert Frost, from *The Poetry of Robert Frost,* edited by Edward Connery Lathem. Copyright 1944, © 1958 by Robert Frost. Copyright © 1967 by Lesley Frost Ballantine. Copyright 1930, 1939, © 1969 by Henry Holt and Company. Reprinted by permission of Henry Holt and Company, Inc.

Alfred A. Knopf: "Zebra," from *Zebra and Other Stories* by Chaim Potok. Copyright © 1998 by Chaim Potok. Used by permission of Alfred A. Knopf, an imprint of Random House Children's Books, a division of Random House, Inc.

Excerpt from *Anthony Burns: The Defeat and Triumph of a Fugitive Slave* by Virginia Hamilton. Copyright © 1988 by Virginia Hamilton. Used by permission of Alfred A. Knopf, an imprint of Random House Children's Books, a division of Random House, Inc.

National Geographic Society: Excerpt from "Face-to-Face with Twins" by Judith Rinard, *National Geographic World,* April 1998. Copyright © 1998 by National Geographic Society. Reprinted by permission of the National Geographic Society.

Pantheon Books: "The War of the Wall," from *Deep Sightings and Rescue Missions* by Toni Cade Bambara. Copyright © 1996 by The Estate of Toni Cade Bambara. Used by permission of Pantheon Books, a division of Random House, Inc.

Scholastic: Excerpt from *Exploring the Titanic* by Robert D. Ballard. Copyright © 1988 by Madison Publishing Inc. Copyright © 1988 by Odyssey Corporation. Reprinted by permission of Scholastic Inc.

The Society of Authors: "The Highwayman" by Alfred Noyes. Reprinted by permission of the Society of Authors as the Literary Representative of the Estate of Alfred Noyes.

Piri Thomas: Excerpt from *Stories from El Barrio* by Piri Thomas. Copyright © 1978 by Piri Thomas. Reprinted by permission of the author.

Time for Kids: "Dinosaur Feathers!" by Martha Pickerill, *Time For Kids,* May 4, 2001, page 6. Copyright © 2001 by Time For Kids Magazine. Used with permission from Time For Kids Magazine.

Writers and Artists: "The Monsters Are Due on Maple Street" by Rod Serling. Copyright © 1960 by Rod Serling. Copyright © 1988 by Carolyn Serling, Jody Serling, and Anne Serling Sutton. Reprinted by permission of Writers and Artists on behalf of the Estate of Rod Serling.

Illustrations by Todd Graveline
2, 4, 7, 10, 12, 18, 20, 22, 28, 32, 34, 38, 40, 44, 45, 48, 52, 55, 58, 59, 61, 65, 74, 75, 77, 78, 82, 87, 88, 92, 94, 95, 98, 103, 104, 108, 110, 112, 122, 123, 125, 126, 130, 134, 136, 139, 142, 144, 146, 152, 153, 158, 159, 160, 161, 170, 174, 177, 181, 184, 186, 189, 200, 204, 206, 208, 209, 211, 217, 222, 223, 225, 228, 234, 235, 237, 239, 242, 244, 246, 247, 249, 251, 252, 254, 258, 261, 269, 273, 278, 286, 289, 295, 296, 300, 302, 305, 306, 312, 314, 327, 329, 333, 336.

Art Credits

vii Illustration copyright © 1999 Gary Overacre; **ix** Library of Congress; **2–15** Illustration by Pamela Daly; **26–37** Copyright © Artville L.L.C.; **38–39** *background* Detail of *Into My Night,* Nicholas Wilton; **40–69** *background* PhotoDisc; **71** Library of Congress; **72–107** PhotoDisc; **109** Copyright © Paolo Koch/Photo Researchers, Inc.; **134–135** *background* PhotoDisc; **135** Austin History Center, Austin Public Library; **136–155** PhotoDisc; **156** Used by permission of the Topps Company. Major League Baseball Properties, Inc. TM Rachel Robinson under license authorized by CMG Worldwide, www.JackieRobinson.com; **157** © Underwood & Underwood/Corbis; **174–203** PhotoDisc; **204–205** *background* Copyright © Archive/GettyImages; **232–257** Don Davis/NASA; **258–275** Photos by Sharon Hoogstraten; **276–299** *background* PhotoDisc; **277** *detail* Copyright © Ralph White/Corbis; **300–301** AP/Wide World Photos; **302–309** Photograph by Gordon Lewis; **310–339** Courtesy of The Bostonian Society; **343** Photo Disk; Copyright © 1991 D.C. Heath and Company; **352–353** Reproduced by Permission of Marshall Cavendish; **355** Photo courtesy of Gay Menges; **357** Copyright © Richard Nowitz/NGS Image Collection; **361** *bottom, Coat of Arms of the Arte della Lana* (Woolworker's guild). Luca della Robbia. Glazed terracotta roundel. Scala/Art Resource, NY.; Text and map from *Across the Centuries,* in *Houghton Mifflin Social Studies,* by Armento et al., Copyright © 1999 by Houghton Mifflin Company. All rights reserved; **363** Copyright © 1991 D.C. Heath and Company; **369** PhotoDisc; **371** Photos courtesy of NASA.

Cover

Illustration copyright © 1999 Gary Overacre.